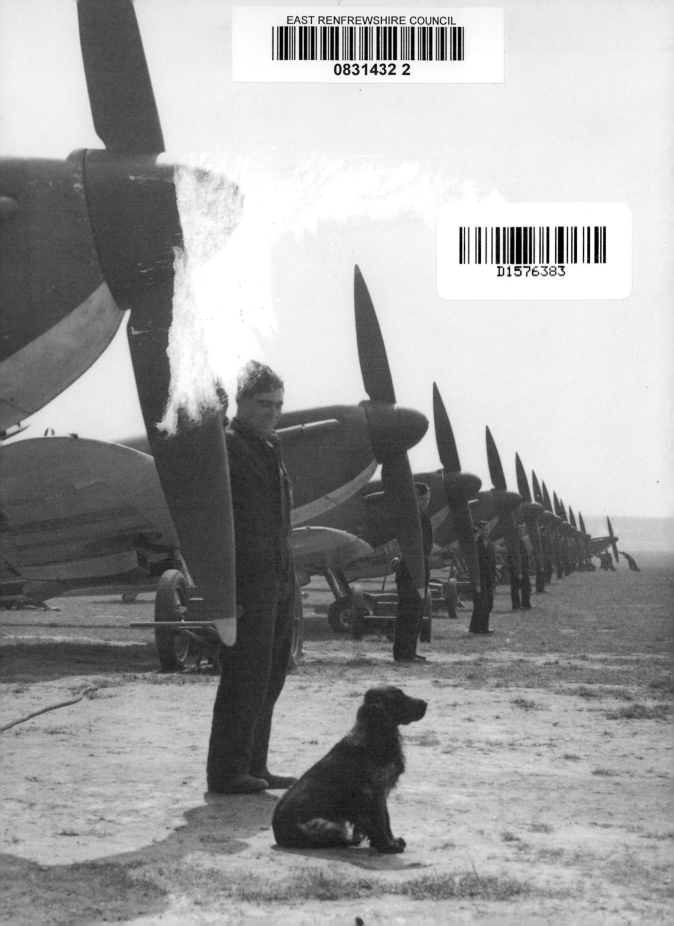

BATTLE OF BRITAIN

PATRICK BISHOP
BATTLE OF BRITAIN
A DAY-BY-DAY CHRONICLE
10 July 1940 to 31 October 1940

Quercus

CONTENTS

INTRODUCTION   **6**
A 'LIFE-AND-DEATH STRUGGLE' – HISTORY OR MYTH?

1 WATCHING, WAITING ... AND WITHDRAWING   **13**
SEPTEMBER 1939 TO JUNE 1940

2 BEGINNING THE DUEL   **55**
1 JULY TO 16 JULY 1940

3 PRODDING AND PROBING   **99**
17 JULY TO 31 JULY 1940

4 INTENSIFICATION   **143**
1 AUGUST TO 17 AUGUST 1940

5 HARDEST DAYS   **209**
18 August to 6 September 1940

6 CULMINATION   **297**
7 September to 15 October 1940

7 AFTERMATH   **370**

Aircraft of the Battle of Britain   376
Index   386
List of Tables, Maps and Sources   391
Acknowledgements   392

INTRODUCTION

A 'LIFE-AND-DEATH STRUGGLE'
– HISTORY OR MYTH?

The Battle of Britain was unique. Nothing like it had happened before. Nothing like it was to happen again. For the first time in history a great military encounter was fought in the air.

Appropriately for the Age of the Common Man it took place, spectacularly, in the full sight of ordinary people, above villages and fields, towns and cities. The visibility of the combat helped to give the battle its pre-eminent place in the British folk memory of the Second World War, becoming a towering legend of skill, determination and sacrifice that only seems to become more fascinating with the passing of time.

Since the end of the Second World War, the episode has been under constant reappraisal, however. The processes of historical revisionism have sought to shrink the legend to less epic proportions. But the point of a legend is that it has outgrown mere facts. No amount of academic reappraisal is likely to change the larger, more resonant, sense of the battle as a David-and-Goliath contest, in which virtue triumphed over the forces of evil.

In researching the history of the battle, one is struck by how remarkably sound the underpinnings of the myth actually are. Many of the scenes popularly associated with the event are, indeed, true, and the heroes of the tale closely match their propaganda images. Pilots really were, by and large, young, modest and surprisingly carefree, and would conclude a hard day's flying and fighting by climbing into jalopies and heading to the nearest pub.

The country was gripped by the feeling that, to use Churchill's phrase, 'a great climacteric' had been reached. However much historians might subsequently have questioned the seriousness of Hitler's invasion plans, a sense of impending onslaught felt frighteningly real to the people of Britain in the middle of 1940. Though later assessments might seek to downgrade the contribution the victory made to Germany's eventual defeat, that was not how it was seen at the time. In a BBC broadcast in September 1942, George Orwell described it as one of the greatest events in history. 'It is becoming clear,' he said, 'that the Battle of Britain ranks in importance with Trafalgar, Salamis, the defeat of the Spanish Armada and

other battles of the past in which the invading forces of a seemingly invincible monarch or dictator have been beaten back and which have formed a turning point in history.'

This judgement may have been rather premature; but it has turned out to be essentially true. The Battle of Britain did not make eventual victory certain, but it made it possible. It provided the answers to some crucial questions, and those answers were to shape the future direction of the war.

The first question was a basic one: would Britain fight? It is difficult now to imagine how dark the future seemed from Britain's perspective at the end of June 1940. The British Army was licking its wounds, having been beaten back across the Channel from Dunkirk. France had fallen with unimagined suddenness, its army and air force collapsing in a matter of a few weeks from the shock of a collision with an enemy that was bold, skilful and superbly equipped. Britain really did stand alone. It had friends, but no real allies. The United States was supportive, but remained prudent and watchful. It sensibly stood and awaited the evidence of Britain's fighting resolve before making any firm commitment.

The decision to stand and fight was by no means as inevitable as it has come to appear. Hitler seems to have genuinely hoped he could avoid a direct assault on Britain, and he believed that ultimately the country's rulers would see where their interests lay. It was for that reason that plans for invasion – codenamed *Seelöwe* (Sea Lion) – were drawn up only tardily. Even as late as 19 July, when the initial skirmishing in what has come to be seen as the battle period proper was well advanced, Hitler issued another appeal to British 'reason and common sense'.

It is not possible to gauge the seriousness of the offer. But Hitler had good grounds for thinking that his overture might be favourably received. Churchill had come to power only in May, and his appointment was not regarded with universal approval. To many, such as those for whom the memory of his responsibility regarding the inglorious Dardanelles campaign of the First World War was still fresh, he was a romantic and an adventurer who would make a disastrous war leader. He was flanked by ministers whose instinct was for a negotiated peace.

Two wartime cigarette cards depict the Spitfire, the aircraft that the Battle of Britain turned into a legend, and anti-aircraft personnel operating a searchlight.

It was piquant, then, that it was the man most associated with compromise with Nazi Germany, Foreign Secretary Lord Halifax, who was instructed to tell Hitler that his 'Appeal to Reason' had been rejected. The public quickly caught the mood of defiance. The isolation brought about by the French defeat in June even brought a sense of relief. 'Thank God we are on our own and not saddled with a craven ally' was the reaction of Peter Brothers, a No. 32 Squadron pilot at Biggin Hill, when he heard the news. It was a feeling shared by his monarch, George VI. But it was not until the Luftwaffe had been swept from Britain's daytime skies that Churchill's approach won general approval.

The 10 September 1940 issue of the Nazi propaganda magazine *Signal* (French-language edition) portrays the Luftwaffe inflicting crushing blows against Britain. The real story was somewhat different.

The second question was: having chosen to fight, could the British actually win? Did they have enough men and aircraft to do so? If they did, were they of the right sort? What about the assertion, made repeatedly in the interwar years by those who ought to know, that 'the bomber would always get through'?

The mythologizing that started within a few days of battle being joined has created a distorted picture of Britain's preparedness for the fight. The impression has been created of a grossly unequal struggle, in which the eventual victory of the RAF was little short of a miracle. It is easy to see how this distortion came about. The image of a handful of tiny fighter planes diving into a rolling phalanx of bombers is an indelible one. It also happened, on many occasions, to be accurate. But the notion of 'The Few' pitted against 'The Many' does not faithfully portray the strategic truth. In reality, the odds were much more finely balanced. The Luftwaffe might have had more aircraft than the RAF. But the RAF had enough of the right type needed to prevail in a defensive air battle. The outcome would depend, to a large extent, on the quality of the fighter planes and the availability and skill of men to fly them. The RAF had the Spitfire – which was at least as good as its German counterpart, the Messerschmitt Me109 – and the Hurricane, which was sturdy and fast enough to hold its own. At the beginning of the contest Fighter Command had just enough machines but a dearth of men to fly them. By the end, thanks to the (admittedly belated) efficiency of the pilot-training programme, it had a sufficiency of both.

The defenders had two other great assets as they faced up to the German attack. They had the wonderful advantage of radar, which allowed those controlling the fighting to get early warning of the German raids, as they formed up in the skies of northern France, and to make their dispositions to tackle them. In addition, the pilots were operating from their own soil, which brought obvious logistical benefits as well as the psychological boost of fighting in sight of the people and places they were chancing their lives to protect.

The fact that Britain's air defences were strong enough to meet the German challenge owed as much to luck as judgement. In keeping with a durable cliché about the British, the process of preparing for the battle was characterized by muddle as much as clear calculation. In the interwar years conventional thinking at the top of the air force had been firmly against the idea of large fleets of fighter aircraft. The bomber was the weapon that would win the war by landing a 'knock-out blow' on the enemy. To deter the Germans from striking first, the energy of the air marshals was poured into matching the Germans heavy plane for heavy plane. It was an obscure politician, Sir Thomas Inskip, who had the vision to realize that it was a waste of effort. His providential intervention made it possible for the Battle of Britain to be fought. Inskip was made Minister for Coordination of Defence in 1936. In December 1937, this unregarded lawyer came to the wise judgement that 'the role of our Air Force is not an early knock-out blow ... but to prevent the Germans from knocking us out'.

His conclusion was opposed fiercely by service experts, who claimed that this was a recipe for losing the next war. But Inskip stuck to his guns. He argued that this approach was not only better but cheaper. Fighters cost much less to produce than bombers. He succeeded in persuading the Cabinet, and henceforth the emphasis was on churning out fighters and the men to fly them.

It was the RAF's great good fortune that two superb fighter designs were already in existence – R.J. Mitchell's Spitfire and Sydney Camm's Hurricane. Britain's fortunes were further strengthened by the presence at the head of Fighter Command of Hugh Dowding. He was an awkward man, distant and unconvivial; but he possessed a strong understanding of how fighters should be used to the maximum effect as well as the strength of character to force his views through, over the objections of colleagues and politicians.

Dowding resisted Churchill's demand for Fighter Command to be thrown into the hopeless fight to save France and insisted that it be held back to build up its strength for the real battle ahead. While the opposing forces may not have been so unbalanced as the myth suggests, Fighter Command was to be stretched to snapping point at several times during the course of the Battle of Britain. Dowding and his lieutenants were operating on the tightest margins. They had to make constant, vital calculations as to how best to use their slender resources. They were helped by serious German miscalculations – like the decision in September to switch the weight of the attack away from Fighter Command's infrastructure and onto British cities. Nevertheless, the Battle of Britain was a remarkably close-run thing.

But a victory, no matter how narrow, is still a victory. It came at a time when Europe's fate had seemed sealed. The first significance of the Battle of Britain was that it proved that the Germans could be resisted. In the first year of war, Hitler had enjoyed a succession of swift, relatively easy victories. This was his first setback. The Battle of Britain did not destroy the Luftwaffe, which was to carry on bombing British cities by night until the spring of 1941, undeterred by the RAF. But it prevented the Luftwaffe from achieving its aim. Hitler had ordered the destruction of the British air force as a precondition for launching an invasion.

LEAVE HITLER TO ME SONNY — YOU OUGHT TO BE OUT OF LONDON

ISSUED BY THE MINISTRY OF HEALTH

A British propaganda poster by Dudley S. Clowes manages to combine sensible precautions for London's children with the reassurance that their dads will sort out the problem.

Frank Newbould's wartime depiction of the South Downs invokes a Britain of bucolic charm to embody the values threatened by Nazi tyranny.

When the Luftwaffe failed to achieve that goal, there was no chance that the conditions for an invasion could be established and Operation Sea Lion was postponed – indefinitely, as it turned out.

The outcome of what was essentially a small battle was to have great psychological implications, which were, in turn, to have even greater strategic consequences. The victory persuaded the British of the virtue of defiance. It encouraged the belief that Hitler could not only be resisted, but also beaten. No-one imagined that Britain could do that on its own. It needed the United States, and here the Battle of Britain played a crucial role. The RAF's success in driving back the Luftwaffe created the circumstances in which America could be steered towards the path of intervention, invasion and victory. This element of the battle was never far from Churchill's mind. The propaganda was managed with one eye trained on transatlantic public opinion. The British authorities gave US newspaper correspondents and newsreel teams preferential treatment over their home-grown colleagues. The approach was effective. A *March of Time* newsreel released in October 1940 carried a commentary declaring: 'Today as the world

your **BRITAI**

watches the Battle of Britain it sees England still mistress of the seas and, in over a year of solid war, the Royal Air Force still unconquered not only over Britain but in the Near East and Far East.'

The message sent to an undecided America, and received loud and clear, was that Britain was a reliable ally who was engaged in an open-ended fight. The fact of its survival would give America a launching pad into Europe, should it choose to join the struggle against Nazism. Had the battle been lost, and had Operation Sea Lion succeeded in spite of the Royal Navy, this option would no longer have been open and all Europe would indeed have sunk into the 'new Dark Age' predicted by Churchill.

Seen in purely military terms, the achievement of the pilots of Fighter Command was limited. It was to avoid defeat rather than to achieve a crushing victory. But it is, ultimately, in ideological terms that the Battle of Britain should be judged. The skill and fortitude of the 3000 men who flew in it ensured Britain's survival as a beacon of freedom and decency to inspire and rally the rest of the world. Seen in that light, the battle was a triumph, not just for Britain but for humanity.

FRANK NEWBOULD

fight for it now

DESIGNED BY P.R.2.B6.

1

WATCHING, WAITING ... AND WITHDRAWING

SEPTEMBER 1939 TO JUNE 1940

The events of the ten months before the Battle of Britain began left the country in the most perilous position of her modern history. On 3 September 1939, two days after Hitler's invasion of Poland, France and Britain reluctantly declared war in support of their ally, honouring their agreement of 1 April that year. By then, Poland was already reeling. Her army had been spread thinly over the long frontiers with Germany, Czechoslovakia and East Prussia (divided from the rest of Germany by the 'Polish Corridor'). Much of her air force was destroyed on the ground in the first few days of the war by a Luftwaffe that was ready, well trained, and combat-tested in the Spanish Civil War – and which outnumbered the Poles by at least four to one. It was a grossly unequal contest. German combat aircraft were five years more advanced in design and performance. German air superiority was immediate, and it was used to crushing effect as supply lines were ruptured, troops bombed and machine-gunned, and cities threatened with annihilation from above.

PREVIOUS PAGE
A group of Land Girls
working the fields watch
fighter planes fly over-
head. Many civilians in
Southeast England
would find themselves
transfixed by the skies
as the summer of
1940 unfolded.

The Polish pilots proved skilful, despite their poor machines, destroying nearly 300 German aircraft in the course of the fighting. But by 17 September the Polish capital, Warsaw, was surrounded, as Red Army troops invaded Poland from the east in support of their temporary German ally (under secret terms of the Nazi–Soviet Pact agreed in August). By 6 October the battle for Poland was over. But for many Polish soldiers and airmen it was only the beginning of their war. Some 100,000 managed to escape through Romania. They would go on to fight hard for the Allies, particularly during the Battle of Britain. Within a year Wladyslaw Gnys, who had been the first Polish fighter pilot of the war to shoot down a German aircraft, would be flying Hurricane fighters out of Northolt in Middlesex.

OPPOSITE
Ordinary life bustles
on during the evening
of 3 September 1939,
as the extraordinary
news of war steals
the headlines.

The rape of Poland produced no answering intervention from the French and British allies. They were in no position to do anything, and they busied themselves instead with preparing their own defences. Apart from sporadic skirmishing, nothing very much happened. In Britain this period, from September 1939 to May 1940, became known as the 'Phoney War'. In Germany it was called the *Sitzkrieg*, literally the 'sitting war'.

continued on page 18

YEAR 1939		AIRCRAFT		PILOT, OR 1ST PILOT	2ND PILOT, PUPIL OR PASSENGER	DUTY (INCLUDING RESULTS AND REMARKS)
MONTH	DATE	Type	No.			
—	—	—	—	—	—	— TOTALS BROUGHT FORWARD
AUGUST	11	Battle	K7586	Self	Sgt. Mather	Return to Wittering after striking camp.
	27	Hurricane	L1771	"	—	To West Raynham. Very boring day.
	27		L1771	"	—	Return to Wittering.
	29		L1789	"	—	West Raynham again.
	29		L1789	"	—	Return to Wittering.
	31		L1789	"	—	Once more W. Raynham.
	31		L1789	"	—	Back home again.
SEPT.	2		L1852	"	—	W.R. Had a false alarm at 1900 hrs. Most disappointing war!
	2		L1852	"	—	Return to Wittering. 52 surging badly.
	4		L1771	"	—	To West Raynham.
	4		L1771	"	—	Return to Wittering. Oxygen bottle leaking.
	4		L1819	"	—	Taking '89 back to W.R.
	4		L1819	"	—	Return Wittering. Bring on the war.
	5		L1784	"	—	Engine test.
	6		L1784	"	—	N/F. Black out V.G.
	7		L1852	"	—	Test a/c. Engine quite O.K.

GRAND TOTAL [Cols. (1) to (10)]

6 23 Hrs. 55 Mins.

TOTALS CARRIED FORWARD

The pilot's logbook of Flight Lieutenant Brian 'Sandy' Lane, of No. 19 Squadron, records the opening of what seemed to him then a 'Most disappointing war!'

SINGLE-ENGINE AIRCRAFT				MULTI-ENGINE AIRCRAFT						PASS-ENGER	INSTR/CLOUD FLYING [incl. in cols. (1) to (10)]	
DAY		NIGHT		DAY			NIGHT					
DUAL	PILOT	DUAL	PILOT	DUAL	1ST PILOT	2ND PILOT	DUAL	1ST PILOT	2ND PILOT		DUAL	PILOT
(1)	(2)	(3)	(4)	(5)	(6)	(7)	(8)	(9)	(10)	(11)	(12)	(13)
43:30	535:30	–	37:50									
	:10											
	:15											
	:15											
	:40											
	:25											
	:25											
	:30	←	←	WAR – 1939		←						
				1100 hrs.								
	:25											
	:25											
	:25											
	:20											
	:25											
	:25											
	:10											
	~~1:25~~		1:25									
	:25											
43:30	~~5~~	–	39:15									
(1)	541:10	(3)	(4)	(5)	(6)	(7)	(8)	(9)	(10)	(11)	(12)	(13)

September 1939 to October 1939

The start of the war saw the evacuation of millions, especially children, from the towns and built-up areas of Britain, particularly London. But as the expected waves of German bombers failed to materialize, many people drifted back to their homes as shelters filled with water and the miles of trenches dug in public parks crumbled and collapsed. War brought a host of rules and restrictions on movement, meetings and free expression. Strict blackout rules irked everyone.

The first days after the declaration of war were also characterized by false alarms and accidents. The most dramatic incident of the early days involved two friendly aircraft being shot up by their own side. One pilot was killed. The Battle of Barking Creek (see page 23) was hushed up, but harsh lessons were learned about the vital importance of positive identification of aircraft.

Despite the uneasy calm, everyone understood that the respite was only temporary. In anticipation of the inevitable German attack westwards, the RAF set up bases in France at the very outset of the war. The deployment had two elements. The Advanced Air Striking Force, consisting of eight squadrons of Battle and Blenheim bombers and two squadrons (Nos 1 and 73) of Hurricane fighters, was to reinforce the French army along the frontier with Germany. The other, the Air Component, with fighter-bombers and another two squadrons of Hurricanes (Nos 85 and 87), was to support the army's British Expeditionary Force (BEF), which started arriving in France as early as 10 September 1939. Britain's regular army of about five divisions, reinforced with Territorial Army units, was tiny compared with the French conscript army of eighty-eight divisions.

Peter 'Boy' Mould, the first RAF pilot to claim an enemy 'kill' (on 30 September 1939), photographed on 13 May 1940, now a pilot officer and with further victories to his name.

On the Franco-German border the fixed defences of the Maginot and Siegfried lines faced each other. The BEF, along with the First French Army, was positioned along the unprotected border between France and the neutral Low Countries, ready to move forward to the River Dyle (Dijle) in central Belgium should the Germans repeat their 1914 Schlieffen Plan and attack through Belgium.

The small RAF contingent, reinforced in the north by two squadrons (Nos 607 and 615), equipped with Gladiator biplanes, flew reconnaissance missions and patrols when the poor weather allowed and worked hard to improve the soggy French airfields, most of which were primitive and uncomfortable. The pilots had arrived in France full of excitement, only to find they had little to do. Bombing of Germany was forbidden for fear of reprisals. There were few enemy intruders. Those that appeared were often high-level reconnaissance planes, long gone by the time the Allied aircraft could climb high enough to meet them. Nevertheless, on 30 September, Flying Officer Peter 'Boy' Mould from No. 1 Squadron scored the first British success of the war, shooting down a Dornier Do17 reconnaissance plane that had appeared over his airfield. Attacking from behind, he seems to have taken the Germans by surprise 'as no evasive tactics were employed and no fire was encountered'. Raked from top to toe with bullets, the Dornier caught fire and crashed after a vertical dive. The squadron later found the wreckage, with the only

continued on page 22

SINGLE-ENGINE AIRCRAFT   MULTI-ENGINE AIRCRAFT

DAY   NIGHT   DAY   NIGHT   PASS-ENGER   INSTR/CLOUD FLYING [Incl. in cols. (1) to (10)]

DUAL   PILOT   DUAL   PILOT   DUAL   1ST PILOT   PILOT   DUAL   1ST PILOT   2ND PILOT   DUAL   PILOT

(1)   (2)   (9)   (10)   (11)   (12)   (13)

'THE BOMBER WILL ALWAYS GET THROUGH'

The first aerial bombs to hit London fell on 31 May 1915, when a German Zeppelin airship dropped a ton of explosives, killing seven people. By the end of the First World War, the British civilian death toll had risen to 670. The psychological effect was greater than the numbers suggest; in a grisly incident, a bomb fell on a school in Poplar, East London, killing 14 children. In a future war, it was felt, destruction would be much greater. A 1924 report by a defence committee chaired by Sir John Anderson predicted 28,000 deaths in a month of bombing. A later medical report warned of the likelihood of 'three to four million cases of acute panic, hysteria and other neurotic conditions during the first six months of air attack'. It was believed that armed forces would be needed to keep order.

London, predicted the philosopher (and pacifist) Bertrand Russell in 1936, would be 'one vast raving bedlam, the hospitals will be stormed, traffic will cease, the homeless will shriek for peace, the city will be a pandemonium'.

The commonly held opinion was that the city would be powerless to withstand these attacks. Prime Minister Stanley Baldwin told the House of Commons on 10 November 1932 that: 'The bomber will always get through.' The Japanese bombing of Shanghai in 1932 and the destruction of the Basque town of Guernica in 1937 at the hands of the German Condor Legion — aircraft at the service of General Franco's Spanish Nationalists — seemed to bear out theories of the bomber's destructive and irresistible force.

The skeletal remains of Guernica, in northern Spain, after the Luftwaffe's Condor Legion had finished with it on 26 April 1937. The age of the bomber had truly arrived.

PROTECTING AGAINST AIR RAIDS

After the Munich conference crisis of September 1938, when Neville Chamberlain and French Prime Minister Daladier acceded to Hitler's demands over Czechoslovakia, the British Air Raid Precaution (ARP) budget was tripled. By the end of the year, 90 per cent of Londoners had been issued with gas masks and over a million feet of trenches had been dug, zigzagging across parks and commons.

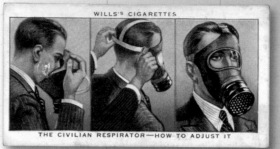

Gas mask procedures, as depicted in a 1940 cigarette card.

Plans for more substantial public shelters lagged behind, partly because of a fear of a direct hit killing a large concentration of people. It was thought preferable that people should build their own protection in the shape of the 'Anderson' shelter, named after the Lord Privy Seal (and soon Home Secretary) Sir John Anderson (1882–1958), who held responsibility for ARP measures. The shelter was cheap and easy to construct, made out of six curved sections of corrugated steel bolted together at the top and sunk into the ground over a shallow square-shaped hole about four feet deep and ten feet wide, lined with five other metal sheets. It was suggested that at least 18 inches of soil be loaded on top, which, it was hoped, would save the shelter's occupants from anything other than a direct hit.

The great flaw — apart from the need for a garden to place it in — was the lack of drainage, and many shelters quickly filled up with dirty water. The discomfort was compounded by the sacking, soaked in water, which was supposed to be hung over the entrance as a defence against poison gas. Nevertheless, by September 1939 nearly 1.5 million Anderson shelters had been distributed free to families with incomes of less than £250 per year. The more comfortably off were expected to pay for their own.

With the outbreak of war, people practised putting out fires and crawling through smoke-filled rooms, underwent first-aid training, and were told what to do if caught outside in a raid. They were instructed to lie face down, with hands over the ears, mouths half open and teeth parted. Works of art were removed from the National Gallery and the Tate Gallery to caves in Wales. Irreplaceable volumes and documents from the Public Records Office were shipped out of London or stored deep underground. London Zoo took the precaution of destroying its snakes in case they escaped during an air raid.

At the same time, the transformation of London, and Britain's other main cities, gathered pace. Famous Oxford Street stores boarded up their windows and converted their basements into air-raid shelters for their customers. Landmarks such as the Albert Memorial in Kensington were boxed up to minimize bomb damage. Sandbags, filled from pits dug in Hampstead Heath, appeared everywhere, stacked against windows and doors as blast-proofing. They soon turned mouldy. Windows were webbed with tape to prevent injuries from flying glass. Heavy dark curtains hung from every window, to keep the light in and make the blackout complete.

The blackout was one of the most unpopular of the new restrictions. London became as 'dark as a pocket'. It was frightening to be out at night. It was easy to get lost or hit by cars, which travelled with hoods over their headlamps. The dishonest thrived in the darkness, and petty crime soared. The local ARP wardens were ruthless in enforcing the blackout regulations, with a shout of 'Put that light out!' Estimates of what could be seen from an aircraft at altitude were ludicrously inaccurate. A German-Swiss resident of Kensington was accused of trying to provide guidance for the enemy by puffing too hard on his cigar.

EVACUATING THE CHILDREN

Evacuation lists for threatened cities had been drawn up before the start of war. Those on them included children, the handicapped, the ill and the blind. But registration was neither complete nor obligatory. Parents could decide for themselves whether or not their children should be sent away.

Three days before the war started, the government began moving 39,000 people from towns in Southeast England considered to be in the bombers' path. In London, about half the population of children departed. Around 1.5 million people travelled on the government scheme, with a further 2 million making their own arrangements.

For the rich, this meant moving to hotels in the north or the countryside. Ten thousand children from well-to-do families were sent abroad in the first year of the war, mainly to Canada or the United States. It did not necessarily make them safer: in September 1939, the liner *City of Benares* was torpedoed on the way to Canada, and only 13 of the 90 children on board survived.

Most evacuated children in Britain were taken in by rural families, with varying degrees of enthusiasm. Some children from London's East End found it difficult adjusting to their new surroundings. Used to a diet of bread, margarine, fish, chips and sweets, they viewed the fruit and vegetables now on offer with suspicion. Some of their middle-class hosts, cushioned from the reality of urban poverty, were appalled by their new charges. One Women's Institute reported that 'the children were filthy, and in this district we have never seen so many verminous children lacking any knowledge of clean and hygienic habits … it appeared they were unbathed for months.' [Quoted in Calder, p. 42]

EVACUATION

DETAILS OF FACILITIES ARRANGED FOR

(1) OFFICIAL PARTIES
(TO BILLETS PROVIDED BY THE GOVERNMENT)

Evacuation is available for

SCHOOL CHILDREN
MOTHERS with **CHILDREN** of School Age or under
EXPECTANT MOTHERS

(2) ASSISTED PRIVATE EVACUATION
A free travel voucher and billeting allowance are provided for

CHILDREN OF SCHOOL AGE or under
MOTHERS with **CHILDREN** OF SCHOOL AGE OR UNDER
EXPECTANT MOTHERS
AGED and **BLIND PEOPLE**
INFIRM and **INVALIDS**

who have made their own arrangements with relatives or friends for accommodation in a safer area

★ FOR INFORMATION ASK AT THE NEAREST SCHOOL

ISSUED BY THE MINISTRY OF HEALTH

A government poster advertises the evacuation criteria for the old and the young, the infirm and the pregnant.

Civilians in Islington, North London, take delivery of materials to build the novel Anderson shelters in their gardens.

discernible remains of the crew being five disembodied hands. Mould got very drunk that night, telling a friend: 'I'm bloody sorry I went and looked at the wreck. What gets me down is the thought that I did it.' [Richey, p. 24]

On the morning of 16 October, the first serious aerial raid on Britain's navy occurred, when 12 Junkers 88s attacked shipping at the Royal Navy base at Rosyth. A fault with the local radar station meant that the arrival of the bombers came as a surprise, and they were able to damage a destroyer, killing 16. Spitfires arrived only as the Junkers were leaving, chasing them out to sea and downing two.

November 1939 to February 1940

The winter was bitter. Snow and thick cloud prevented flying for weeks on end. Pilots became bored and frustrated. Nevertheless, the aerial skirmishes that did take place in northern France in the months prior to the Battle of Britain taught the British a number of useful lessons as well as familiarizing them with the ways of their opponents. The RAF began to copy Luftwaffe practices, painting the underside of its fighters duck-egg blue to make them less visible against the sky, and fitting steel plates behind the pilot's seat to increase protection. The Hurricane's propeller was altered to improve climbing speed. Tactics were adjusted too, including the adoption of a 'tail-end-Charlie', a single fighter weaving around behind the formation to guard against surprise attack from the rear.

The squadrons based in Britain were learning too. The German air force and army had been ordered to preserve their strength for the battles ahead. The Luftwaffe pilots on the Franco-German border were forbidden to seek combat, and activities were limited to reconnaissance, mine-laying in northern waters and some sporadic raiding of British naval bases. These operations meant that British-based squadrons, although hardly busy compared with the times to follow, probably had more to do than did their colleagues in France. Most of the German attacks that did take place were performed by high-level bombers – harassing attacks, designed to stretch British nerves. They provoked constant alarms, but offered little chance of a 'kill' for the British pilots.

The British pilots came to dislike the frequent patrols carried out to protect shipping around the coast, which were monotonous, tiring and nerve-wracking, with worries of mechanical failure, ditching and death never far away. There was little at that stage, though, to fear from the Luftwaffe. As in France, the lack of action was frustrating. The pilots in the outlying stations, where there were no towns to distract them, grew bored. In the satellite stations the harsh winter was made worse by the spartan conditions.

March 1940 to April 1940

In March 1940, the weather improved. There was more patrolling and a greater number of encounters between the Luftwaffe and RAF. On 2 March, the first Messerschmitt Me109 fighter (also known as the Bf109) was shot down; at the end of the month, the first Messerschmitt Me110 twin-engine fighter-bomber was

THE BATTLE OF BARKING CREEK

On 6 September, a searchlight battery in the Blackwater estuary in Essex reported a hostile aircraft crossing the coast. Hurricanes from No. 56 Squadron were ordered up from North Weald to intercept. As they climbed on the hunt for the intruder, they were picked up by a radar station in Essex, which mistook them for a large approaching enemy formation. Further fighters were scrambled, which, in turn, confused the radar picture even more. Among them were 12 Spitfires from 74 Squadron at Hornchurch. A three-man section led by Adolph 'Sailor' Malan took off first, followed by another section led by Flying Officer 'Paddy' Byrne. Behind Byrne was John Freeborn. 'I remember looking down and seeing we had cut a line through the haze where we had taken off,' he recalled. 'Malan was well in front ... We saw these aircraft and Malan gave the order: "Number One attack – go!" [Freeborn, in interview] Malan's section went in, then Byrne's. Byrne and Freeborn opened fire and saw two aircraft go down. Freeborn remembers feeling 'exhilarated'. But when he landed, he learned the truth: the aircraft they shot down – the first ever to fall to a Spitfire's guns – had been Hurricanes. One pilot was dead, another missing. Byrne and Freeborn were

put under arrest, and a general court martial was held on 7 October. According to Freeborn, Malan denied ever giving the order. Nevertheless, both men were acquitted.

On the same day that the tragedy occurred, film director Alexander Korda was at the Hornchurch airfield filming an RAF propaganda picture, *The Lion Has Wings*.

'Sailor' Malan quit a career as a merchant navy officer to join the RAF before the war. After the Barking Creek incident he went on to become one of Fighter Command's leading aces. He is shown here in 1944, now a group captain.

downed near Metz. These encounters were analysed closely for what they could reveal about the shape of things to come, and the shot-down aircraft were salvaged and studied.

By now, the military hibernation was drawing to an end. Germany was stirring again. Before launching his main attack in the west, Hitler wished to secure Germany's northern flank by occupying neutral Denmark and Norway. Control of the latter would also safeguard Germany's vital supplies of iron ore from Sweden via the northern Norwegian port of Narvik, as well as providing bases for an aerial attack on Britain from the east. The strategic importance of Norway was understood in London and, as the German High Command was well aware, Britain was simultaneously preparing a force to seize the port and looking at basing fighter and bomber aircraft in Norway.

The German invasion, ostensibly designed to protect Denmark and Norway

continued on page 27

ORIGINS OF THE RAF

The importance of aviation as a branch of warfare became increasingly obvious as the First World War progressed, and there were powerful voices who claimed that it would become the dominant means by which future wars were fought. This thinking led to the establishment of an independent air arm, the world's first. And thus the Royal Air Force was born in 1918 out of the Royal Flying Corps (the air arm of the British Army) and the Royal Naval Air Service.

It was not long though before the new service's existence was threatened. After the war, its commander-in-chief, Sir Hugh Trenchard (1873–1956), had to fight for its life, as the force was cut from 188 squadrons to 33 and its assets were eyed up greedily by the army and the navy. Trenchard, supported by the Minister of State for War and Air at the time, Winston Churchill, argued that an independent RAF could become 'a force that will profoundly alter the strategy of the future'. In the 1920s, Trenchard was a leading voice in the pro-bomber chorus. It seemed unlikely that a home-based fighter could make a successful interception on an incoming bomber force. If the attackers flew at 10,000 feet and at 200mph, they would be over London long before a defending fighter could climb to reach them. The answer to the problem was to create a deterrent bomber force that could match the enemy blow for blow.

The RAF survived, but the annual budget for the force remained under £20 million until 1935. Then, on 20 April 1935, the full might of the Luftwaffe was revealed at a huge air parade held in Berlin to mark Hitler's birthday. British observers were horrified at the show of strength. The realization grew that 'Britain was an island no more'. A scheme, known as Expansion Plan A, had been launched the year before in response to Hitler's accession to power, but now rearmament took on a greater urgency.

Forty-five new air stations were ordered in 1935, and plans were laid to increase the

Sir Hugh Trenchard,
'father of the RAF',
photographed in 1929.

Four RAF aircraft demonstrate the new art of aerial bombardment
by blasting a model village during a pageant at Hendon, 1921.

GRAND TOTAL [Cols. (I) to (10)]
.................Hrs.................Mins.

24

TOTALS CARRIED FORWARD

	SINGLE-ENGINE AIRCRAFT				MULTI-ENGINE AIRCRAFT						PASS-ENGER	INSTR/CLOUD FLYING (Incl. in cols. (1) to (10))	
	DAY		NIGHT		DAY			NIGHT					
DUAL	PILOT	DUAL	PILOT	DUAL	1ST PILOT	2ND PILOT	DUAL	1ST PILOT	2ND PILOT			DUAL	PILOT
(1)										(10)	(11)	(12)	(13)

Aviators and machines of RAF No. 1 Squadron at an aerodrome near Ypres, winter 1918 – the year the RAF was born.

number of home-based squadrons to one-hundred-and-twenty-three. RAF personnel increased fivefold between 1934 and the beginning of the Second World War, by which time the service had a strength of 118,000, with 45,000 reserves. The number of Auxiliary squadrons increased from eight to twenty, and another reserve force was established, the Royal Air Force Volunteer Reserve (RAFVR).

In 1936, the RAF was restructured into four Commands: Fighter, Bomber, Coastal and Training. Sir Hugh Dowding (1882–1970), then the head of research and development on the Air Council, was put in charge of Fighter Command, which would include responsibility for anti-aircraft assets such as guns and searchlights.

At the same time, the focus was changing: developments in radar and the emergence of faster fighters suggested that perhaps, after all, the bomber would not always get through. Now, the proportion of fighter to bomber squadrons started to near parity.

In December 1938, the long debate over investment in fighters or bombers was settled in favour, for the time being at least, of the fighters. This crucial change was led by Sir Thomas Inskip, the minister in charge of defence coordination. His argument was strengthened by the fact that fighters were a lot cheaper to produce than bombers. In 1937, for the first time, more money was spent on the Royal Air Force than on the British Army.

FIGHTER COMMAND'S SQUADRON STRUCTURE

The basic unit of Fighter Command was the squadron. At full strength, this consisted of about 20 pilots and 12–14 fighter aircraft. Within a squadron were two 'flights', each with two 'sections' of three aircraft each. Battle tactics as taught by Fighter Command were based on the faulty premise that the adversary in the skies over Britain would be fleets of unescorted bombers. The calculation was that the Messerschmitt Me109 fighter escorts did not have the range to reach Britain from bases in Germany.

Bombing had been in its infancy in the First World War, when aerial combat consisted of dogfights between aircraft whose main function was to act as spotter planes. The arrival of the bomber age appeared to call for an entirely different tactical approach. Fighter-to-fighter combat seemed to belong to the past. The purpose now was to bring the maximum amount of firepower to bear on heavily armoured bomber fleets.

From this aim emerged a series of complicated and difficult formation-attack patterns, which were practised endlessly by the Fighter Command pilots. The tactical unit was the 'vic' — three fighters flying in a close horizontal V-shape, with a leader and two wingmen. There were six different set-formation attacks, varying in terms of direction of approach and deployment of the squadron's different sections; it was up to the squadron commander to select and order which approach would be best.

'Flying in threes turned out to be crazy,' said George Unwin, a Spitfire pilot with No. 19 Squadron. 'If you're flying in threes and you want to turn quickly you can't without running into the other fellow. The Germans knew this and they flew in twos. We had to pick this up and reorganise our tactics accordingly.' [Parker, p. 40] It was found, too, that the formation attacks were time-consuming to set up, and because the wingmen of the 'vic' were concentrating on the target and on staying in position relative to the leader's plane, the attacking fighters were vulnerable to being 'bounced' from above.

The outmoded tactics had a surprisingly long life: even in late August and September 1940, inexperienced squadrons arriving in the south for the first time were still flying in 'vics'. Indeed, formation attacks were still being taught to fighter pilots in 1941.

A group of Spitfires fly in a three-plane 'vic' formation.

GRAND TOTAL [Cols. (1) to (10)]
..................Hrs..................Mins.

26

TOTALS CARRIED FORWARD

from Anglo-French aggression, was launched shortly after 5am in the morning of 9 April, with a simultaneous advance of land forces in Denmark and seaborne landings on the Danish islands and in Norwegian ports. Denmark fell in a day, as did key cities and airfields in Norway, the latter secured by history's first ever paratroop attacks. The valiant shore batteries on the Oslo fjord, equipped with Krupp guns installed in 1893, succeeded in sinking the German heavy cruiser *Blücher*, thereby giving the Norwegian government and royal family a chance to flee the country. But control of the air gave the invaders a vital advantage.

As the Germans crushed resistance in the south of Norway, British infantrymen landed on the west coast near Trondheim and at Narvik to the north. Later in the month they were reinforced by French and then Polish troops. But the poorly equipped Allied effort lacked both clear objectives and a unified command.

The RAF's contribution to the campaign was touched with the same chaotic, amateur feel that characterized the whole operation. The first squadron dispatched to Norway – No. 263 – was made up of Gloster Gladiators, biplanes that belonged to a bygone generation of fighter aircraft. Carried to within 50 miles of the Norwegian coast by the carrier HMS *Glorious*, the squadron landed on a makeshift airfield on the frozen ice of the Lesjaskogsvatnet (Lake Lesjaskog) on 24 April. In theory, the Gladiators were adapted to winter conditions, but vital supplies to keep the engines de-iced failed to turn up and the airfield lacked radar or adequate anti-aircraft guns. During the first night the wheels of many of the machines froze to the ice, leaving the squadron sitting ducks when an attack of Heinkel He111 bombers came in at just before eight in the morning.

Two Ju87 (Stuka) dive-bombers make a low-level attack during the battle for Norway (spring 1940).

Eight of the Gladiators were destroyed, and those that managed to take off found themselves heavily outnumbered. By the end of the day eleven had been lost and two had been destroyed and were beyond repair. Two days later there were no aircraft left.

The emerging débâcle in Norway fed dissatisfaction in the House of Commons, and in the country at large, with Neville Chamberlain's government. It seemed incompetent and irresolute, quite unfit to lead the country at the time of its greatest peril. On 30 April the well-connected Conservative MP Henry 'Chips' Channon wrote in his diary that there was a 'cabal against poor Neville. "They" are saying ... that Winston should be Prime Minister as he has more vigour and the country behind him.' During a long career Churchill had made many enemies in the country and in the House. Before the war he had established himself as the leading advocate of rearmament and Hitler's fiercest enemy. Now that his predictions had come true, he was being viewed with new respect.

May 1940

No. 263 Squadron returned to Norway in May, as Allied troops, driven out from the south, fought the Germans at Narvik. This time, they were accompanied by No. 43 Squadron of Hurricanes. The Hurricanes struggled to find a usable base.

For a time they operated from 'a strip by a fjord', remembered Flight Sergeant Richard Earp. 'The troops had been working very hard out there and they'd covered the place with coconut matting and wire netting.' There was no running water and only cramped tents to sleep in. 'All I had was a groundsheet and two blankets,' said Earp. 'You couldn't sleep. It was daylight all the time.' Above all, he remembered that it 'was terribly bloody cold.' [Earp, recording]

At home, the political intrigues and manoeuvrings reached a climax on 7 May, as the House of Commons met to debate the failures of the Norway campaign. Prime Minister Neville Chamberlain had lost the confidence of the House. The announcement of the result of a vote of censure brought shouts of 'Out! Out! Out!' from the Opposition benches. Chamberlain tried and failed to form a cross-party national government under his premiership. On 10 May, Chamberlain resigned his office, and the task fell to Winston Churchill, the fervent pre-war opponent of appeasement who had been summoned from the backbenches in September 1939 to become First Lord of the Admiralty.

Churchill immediately brought senior Opposition figures into a new Cabinet, and appointed his friend Lord Beaverbrook as head of a new ministry for aircraft production. Churchill felt touched by the hand of history. 'At last I had the authority to give directions over the whole scene,' he later wrote. 'I felt as if I were walking with destiny, and that all my past life had been but a preparation for this hour and for this trial.' [Churchill, Vol. 1, p. 257] There was to be no honeymoon period. His first crisis came the very same day, as the Germans launched *Blitzkrieg* in the west.

The opening blow came at first light, when more

ALL BEHIND YOU, WINSTON

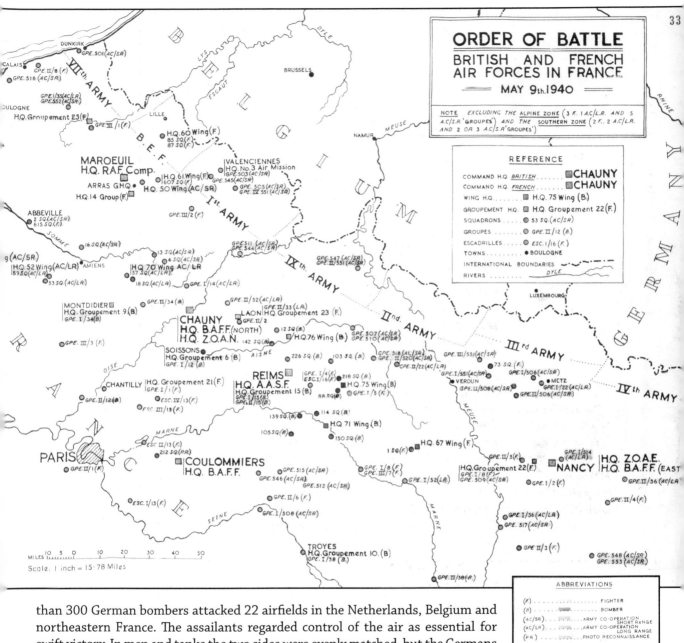

ORDER OF BATTLE
BRITISH AND FRENCH
AIR FORCES IN FRANCE
═══ MAY 9th.1940 ═══

NOTE EXCLUDING THE ALPINE ZONE (3 F. 1 AC/L.R. AND S
A.C./S.R. 'GROUPES') AND THE SOUTHERN ZONE (2 F. 2 AC/L.R.
AND 2 OR 3 A.C.S.R'GROUPES')

REFERENCE

COMMAND H.Q. *BRITISH*	■ CHAUNY
COMMAND H.Q. *FRENCH*	■ CHAUNY
WING H.Q.	■ H.Q. 75 Wing (B.)
GROUPEMENT H.Q.	⊙ H.Q. Groupement 22 (F.)
SQUADRONS	⊙ 53 SQ.(AC/SR)
GROUPES	⊙ GPE. II /12 (B.)
ESCADRILLES	⦾ ESC. 1/16 (F.)
TOWNS	● BOULOGNE
INTERNATIONAL BOUNDARIES	
RIVERS	DYLE

ABBREVIATIONS

(F.)	FIGHTER
(B.)	BOMBER
(AC/SR)	ARMY CO-OPERATION SHORT RANGE
(AC/LR)	ARMY CO-OPERATION LONG RANGE
(PR)	PHOTO RECONNAISSANCE

MILES 10 5 0   10   20   30   40   50
Scale. I inch = 15·78 Miles

than 300 German bombers attacked 22 airfields in the Netherlands, Belgium and northeastern France. The assailants regarded control of the air as essential for swift victory. In men and tanks the two sides were evenly matched, but the Germans had almost twice as many aircraft than all their opponents combined, amounting to some 4000 planes, of which over 1000 were Messerschmitt Me109s.

The German air force was divided into two commands: *Luftflotte* (Air Fleet) 2 was in the north, under Generaloberst Albert Kesselring, and *Luftflotte* 3, on the central front under Generaloberst Hugo Sperrle. Both reported to Generalfeldmarschall (Field Marshal) – and soon to be Reichsmarschall – Hermann Goering, the overall commander of the Luftwaffe.

As the fighting in western Europe erupted, in Britain acts of popular outrage replaced what had been a relatively tolerant atmosphere. On 12 May began the

ABOVE

A plan, from Air Ministry records at The National Archives, shows the Allied air forces' order of battle in the second week of May 1940.

rounding up of 'enemy aliens', to be placed in internment camps or sent abroad, despite the fact that many of them had been in Britain for decades and were vehemently opposed to Hitler and the fascist movements across the Continent.

At the front, the Belgian and Dutch air forces were soon destroyed. German reconnaissance planes roved ahead of the advancing forces, spotting targets and triggering devastating dive-bombing attacks. These raids were followed by airborne assaults on key bridges, airfields and fortresses. Meanwhile, tanks and motorized infantry units crossed the borders, swept aside resistance and raced to meet up with their advance units.

Positioned to support the British Expeditionary Force, No. 87 Hurricane Squadron had been put on alert the night before and told to expect *Blitzkrieg* the next morning. 'There was nothing unusual in that ... people had become a little sceptical,' reported the squadron's diary. But 'we were awakened at dawn by a tremendous anti-aircraft barrage, the drone of many aero engines and a deep thudding sound we had never previously heard. BOMBS!'

Most of the RAF contingent escaped being hit on the ground and was immediately in action. No. 1 Squadron took off at 5am and was active for almost the entire day, shooting down several Dorniers. As soon as the attack had started, four more Hurricane squadrons – Nos 3, 79, 501 and 504 – were rushed to France. Most were in action almost immediately. Their first day turned out to be their best. Much of the German bomber force had arrived without fighter escort. It was easy to find targets, as there were simply so many German aircraft in the skies. The RAF fighters flew 208 sorties and shot down at least 33 bombers, losing in the process only 7 Hurricanes, with 8 damaged and not a single pilot killed.

But each day thereafter was worse than the day before. Bombers now came escorted by swarms of Messerschmitts. Hurricane pilots were flying up to five sorties a day, taking off from underequipped airfields that were the target of regular attacks from dive-bombers. Perpetual exhaustion sapped the strength of the airmen, as the German aircraft roamed deeper and deeper into France. 'Our nerves were getting somewhat frayed,' wrote Paul Richey of No. 1 Squadron. 'We

German ground troops, probably from the 5th Panzer Division, race through a northern French village in late May 1940.

were jumpy and morose. Few of the boys smiled now – we were no longer the merry band of days gone by.' Richey had already baled out once, and the experience had shaken him greatly: 'I had a hell of a headache and was jumpy and snappy. Often I dared not speak for fear of bursting into tears.' [Richey, p. 80] But on the ground, the situation was soon even worse.

To the surprise of the Allies, the main German armoured thrust crashed through the supposedly 'untankable' Ardennes forest in southwestern Belgium (and bypassed the Maginot Line), aiming to establish a bridgehead across the Meuse, the most formidable river barrier protecting France. Here again, air superiority was decisive, with the key French fortress of Sedan, just to the east of the Meuse, pounded by 'airborne artillery': waves of dive-bombers that delivered the firepower of conventional big guns, but with much greater flexibility. Once successfully over the river, the German armoured columns headed northwest, hurrying towards the sea in order to split the Allied forces and pin the BEF and First French Army against the Channel.

The BEF had advanced, as planned, to the River Dyle (Dijle) in central Belgium. The British now threw their Blenheim and near obsolete Fairey Battle bombers against the advancing German columns, but with disastrous results. On 14 May, the Netherlands capitulated, her government and royal family already evacuated to England.

For the French leadership, the fall of Sedan had a huge psychological as well as strategic impact. What remained of the Allies' bomber force was now sent *en masse* against the Meuse bridgehead, but the only result was appalling losses from flak and German fighters. On 15 May, French Prime Minister Paul Reynaud telephoned Churchill and told him, in English, 'We have been defeated.' Nonetheless, he pleaded for further fighter squadrons to be sent from England.

Fighter Command's leader, Sir Hugh Dowding, was already dismayed at how precious assets were being sacrificed in actions that did little to change a hopeless situation. He insisted that the bleeding stop. He was allowed into the War Cabinet meeting of 15 May to make his case. If the same rate of attrition continued for the next ten days, he argued, there would not be a single Hurricane left in France or Britain. 'If the Home Defence Force is drained away in desperate attempts to remedy the situation in France,' he wrote in an official letter that night to the Under Secretary of State for Air, 'defeat in France will involve the final, complete and irremediable defeat of this country.'

Churchill, however, was still set on giving 'the last chance to the French army to rally its bravery and strength'. The next day, 16 May, he flew to Paris in an effort to reinforce the morale of the French leadership. All he found, though, was disillusion and despair. 'Utter dejection was written on every face,' Churchill later wrote. 'Where is the strategic reserve?' he asked the French Commander-in-Chief General Gamelin. 'Gamelin turned to me,' wrote Churchill, 'and with a shake of the head and a shrug, said "*Aucune*" [there is none]. There was another long pause. Outside in the garden of the Quai d'Orsay clouds of smoke arose from large bonfires, and I saw from the window venerable officials pushing wheelbarrows of archives on to them. Already, therefore, the evacuation of Paris was being prepared.' [Churchill, Vol. 2, p. 42]

In spite of the evidence of his eyes, and in the face of Dowding's dire warning,

✠ ENEMY ALIENS

Since 1933 there had been a continuous exodus from Germany to Britain of those who feared for their lives and security under the Nazis because of their politics or their Jewish blood. They were subsequently joined by those fleeing Austria, and then Czechoslovakia. They were met with sympathy on the whole, though the mounting alarm engendered by Hitler's voracious demands gave rise to some scare stories in the press. One such appeared in the London *Evening Standard* in February 1939, under the headline 'Hitler's Gestapo employing Jews for spying in England'.

At the start of the war there were about 80,000 Germans and Austrians in Britain. As citizens of an enemy power they were automatically suspect as potential spies, saboteurs or supporters of the Nazis in the event of an invasion. All those over the age of 16 were summoned to tribunals to be assessed. They were divided into three categories. Group A comprised high-risk Nazi sympathizers, of whom there were nearly 600, and they were immediately interned. Group B was made up of 6500 'doubtful cases', who were subject to restrictions on their movements and kept under supervision. Group C, by far the largest at 55,000, was designated 'no security risk' and left alone; the great majority of these people were Jewish.

The day after Hitler launched his *Blitzkrieg* in the west, the tolerant atmosphere changed. 'Enemy aliens', most of them refugees from fascism, were rounded up and imprisoned. The net was widened to include the 19,000 Italians resident in Britain, many of whom had lived there for decades. When Italy entered the war on 10 June 1940, Italian cafés and restaurants in Glasgow, Manchester and London's Soho district were attacked and wrecked. One long-assimilated restaurateur in London felt compelled to put up a notice in his window stating that all four of his sons were in the British Army. Spartan camps were set up on racecourses and half-finished housing estates. Most of the internees were sent to the Isle of Man, while another 7000 were deported, mainly to Canada and Australia, though not all of those ever made it into exile. The liner *Arandora Star*, which left for Canada on 1 July 1940, was torpedoed with the loss of 714 lives. The dead included the Italian ex-head chefs of the Savoy and the Ritz, as well as prominent German and Austrian anti-Nazi politicians and labour leaders.

In all, the British authorities interned 30,000 people, most of them fervent anti-Nazis. They included a high proportion of engineers, physicists, chemists and university professors, who had a potential contribution to make to the war effort. Opposition to the policy began to be voiced almost immediately in Parliament, and the first releases from the internment camps began in August 1940, as the Battle of Britain was reaching fever pitch. By February 1941, more than 10,000 had been freed, and by the summer of 1942 only 5000 internees were left.

British subjects, too, were interned – 1769 in total, of whom nearly half had been members of the British Union of Fascists. Its leader, Sir Oswald Mosley, and his wife were among them, held in Brixton prison, London.

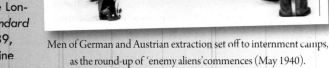

Men of German and Austrian extraction set off to internment camps, as the round-up of 'enemy aliens' commences (May 1940).

BELOW

Three Spitfire Mark 1s
of No. 611 Squadron
fly in a loose line astern
over two other aircraft
of the squadron at
Digby, Lincolnshire
(January 1940).

Churchill authorized the deployment of a further four Hurricane squadrons after his return to London. They were to fly each day from England, because there were now not enough airfields and facilities left in French hands to support them.

Nevertheless, by 17 May Churchill had succumbed to reality. He ordered a contingency plan for the complete withdrawal of the BEF and RAF from France. Churchill's private secretary, 'Jock' Colville, noted in his diary: 'Winston is depressed. He says the French are crumbling up as completely as did the Poles … There is a risk that the BEF may be cut off if the French do not rally in time.'

The BEF began retreating and the airmen fell back with them, hopping from one vulnerable airfield to another. The withdrawal was painful. Nos 1 and 73 squadrons lost 19 aircraft and 12 pilots in 7 days. In the 3 days from 16 May, Fighter Command lost 62 precious Hurricanes. The pilots of 32 Squadron were now flying in daily from Biggin Hill, Kent, an exhausting schedule that meant being woken up at 2.30am and sometimes not getting back until as late as 10.30pm. Across the English Channel they found chaos and despair. Pete Brothers remembered that 'We'd go to a French airfield, refuel and try to get some instructions but everything was chaotic and so we'd just go off and do a patrol around to see what we could find … it was pretty ghastly and the French, I'm afraid, were totally demoralized by this time.' [Brothers, in interview]

There was no effective control from the ground and few men were left to refuel and rearm the aircraft. Nor was there any effective early-warning system to get the Hurricanes airborne in time to intercept a raid. Above all, the British pilots were massively outnumbered in the air.

For the troops below, the situation was also desperate. Refugees clogged the roads, and overhead the terrifying Junkers Ju87 Stuka dive-bombers attacked seemingly at will. It was now clear that the French Ninth Army, originally positioned opposite the southern thrust from the Ardennes, had suffered a serious defeat. As the German Panzers raced for the Channel, they encountered virtually no resistance, covering on some days up to 40 miles. On 20 May, Amiens fell, cutting the Allied armies in two. The same day Gamelin was sacked, and his replacement, Weygand, immediately ordered a French counter-attack on the German armoured column. The British also counter-attacked near Arras, but the delay to the German advance was only brief. On 22 May, the Germans reached the outskirts of Boulogne and Calais, cutting off the BEF's supply route, and the army

continued on page 38

THE HOME GUARD

The Local Defence Volunteer force (LDV, renamed the 'Home Guard' by Churchill at the end of July 1940) was launched in a radio broadcast by the Secretary of State for War, Anthony Eden, on 14 May. He appealed to those between the ages of 17 and 65 to come forward to form an auxiliary force to counter any invasion, be it from the sea or the air. Within a day, a quarter of a million men had volunteered, and by the end of the month 400,000 were listed, about three times the expected number. Among them, and in spite of the supposed age ceiling, were some as old as 84 who had fought in Sudan for Queen Victoria. About a third were First World War veterans. To be back in uniform stirred many memories: 'I think none of us will forget our first LDV route march,' wrote one veteran. 'On it a quarter of a century slipped away in a flash. There came memories of the Menin Road ... of the smell of cordite and the scream of shrapnel, of the mud and stench and misery of Flanders, of hopes and fears in battles long ago.'

Some organizations formed their own units. Both Houses of Parliament had battalions, as did the BBC, the court at Buckingham Palace, London taxi drivers and dustmen, and the printers and typesetters of Fleet Street. To the dismay of the pro-Hitler US ambassador Joseph Kennedy, an American battalion was formed of

Men of the Home Guard hone their target skills at the War Office Training School, Osterley Park, west of London (21 September 1940).

expatriates living in London. In Sussex a group was assembled complete with horses, and soon a 50-strong unit known as the Lewes Cossacks was patrolling the South Downs.

All volunteers were unpaid and had to provide their own food, and they had to commit to ten hours' service a week. Uniforms and weapons were in very short supply. Pressed into service were rifles dating from the Indian Mutiny, pikes from theatre props rooms, golf clubs, hockey sticks and missiles made from potatoes studded with razor blades. Armbands were issued, and slowly the army released its unwanted uniforms to the LDV – the very large and very small sizes.

Sceptics, of whom there were plenty, said that LDV stood for 'Look, Duck and Vanish' or 'Last Desperate Venture'. 'We were prepared to lean out of a bedroom window, light a piece of rag in the neck of a bottle and throw it at a tank,' said Stanley Brand of the Middlesbrough Home Guard. 'How long would we have survived?' But Brand acknowledged that the force was not entirely useless: 'My unit would have achieved something but nothing permanent,' he said. 'We couldn't ever have defeated the Germans – only delayed them. The Home Guard was really a civilian morale builder. It made us feel we could do something useful.' [Brand, recording]

HERMANN GOERING

TOTALS BROUGHT FORWARD

Born in 1893 in Bavaria, Hermann Wilhelm Göring (usually Anglicized as 'Goering') served in the German infantry during the First World War, before transferring to the air force. He was an outstanding pilot, with a reported 22 kills and numerous decorations, including the 'Blue Max' award for valour. In July 1918 he took over as commander of the 'Flying Circus' unit made famous by the 'Red Baron' Manfred von Richthofen.

Disgusted with the postwar settlement, he joined the Nazi Party in 1922 and for a time was in charge of its paramilitary *Sturmabteilung* (SA, 'Storm Troop'). He played a part in the failed Munich Putsch of November 1923, when he was wounded in the groin and forced to flee to Austria. During painful treatment for his injury, he was given morphia, starting an addiction that he would battle for several years. He returned to Germany in 1927, where his distinguished war record and charm made him an effective promoter of the party among the wary upper classes. He was elected as a deputy to Germany's parliament, the Reichstag, in the following year, becoming its president in 1932.

With Hitler's assumption of power in 1933, Goering was in the first Cabinet and in charge of the powerful Prussian police force, which he soon turned into a political weapon for the Nazis. During the 1930s he played key roles in the Nazification of the country, in the suppression of internal opposition, and in international and economic affairs. He was also given the post of Special Commissioner for Aviation, then, shortly afterwards, Minister for Air, and he oversaw the secret expansion of the Luftwaffe. When the new air force became public in 1935, Goering was appointed its commander. In 1938, he became the first *Generalfeldmarschall* (Field Marshal) of the Luftwaffe, the promotion making him the highest ranking officer in Germany. Hitler named him his successor as leader of Germany and on 19 July 1940 made him the country's only *Reichsmarschall*.

Goering was an immensely powerful figure in the Third Reich, but he was also avaricious, vain, corrupt and decadent. Many years after the war, Me109 pilot Hans-Ekkehard Bob remembered meeting Goering on being presented with the Knight's Cross: 'He showed up wearing a raw silk shirt with puffed sleeves, a silk cravat with a great big emerald on the throat, light grey riding breeches and red boots. Even by today's standards, it was a pretty daring get-up.' [Bob, recording] Goering liked to be called 'The Iron Man', but at around 20 stone he was seriously overweight.

Goering's military reputation began to decline after the Luftwaffe's failure to stop the evacuation at Dunkirk. It fell further when the air force failed to make good his boast to smash the RAF in weeks, or to prevent Berlin from being bombed. His ignorant, impetuous approach added greatly to the Luftwaffe's difficulties during the Battle of Britain.

'At the beginning we had great respect for him,' said one Luftwaffe pilot, Gerhard Schöpfel. 'But later our feelings changed. He began to complain that we were not doing enough, but we needed far more machines and manpower to achieve what he wanted.' [Schöpfel, in interview] The failure to supply the German Sixth Army at Stalingrad was the final blow to the reputation of Goering and his Luftwaffe. In April 1945, he sent a message to Hitler in his Berlin bunker offering to take over the leadership of the Reich, an action which Hitler regarded as high treason: Goering was placed under arrest, before his surrender to US forces in early May 1945. He was convicted at Nuremberg of war crimes and crimes against humanity and sentenced to death. Poison was smuggled to his cell and he took his own life the night before his scheduled execution by hanging. The next morning his dead body was hanged anyway.

ABOVE Hitler greets Goering at the September 1938 Nuremberg Congress. As one of Hitler's longstanding fellow Nazis, Goering enjoyed a warm relationship with his Führer until war failures began to mount.

OPPOSITE A full-length photo portrait of Goering portrays the Luftwaffe supremo and *Reichsmarshall* in his full, ostentatious grandeur (1940).

was put on half rations. There was no option now but to retreat to the coast. As the scale of the disaster filtered down the ranks, there was disbelief and anger. For the British High Command, the army seemed doomed. Alan Brooke, commanding II Corps, wrote on 23 May: 'Nothing but a miracle can save the BEF now.'

From 24 May, British troops poured into Dunkirk (Dunkerque), on the coast east of Calais. The town and docks were already under attack from the air. The oil depot was soon on fire, gushing thick smoke that lay in a fat, black pall over the town and the shoreline. By 26 May, the port was wrecked beyond use. There was no salvation

there, and the men were ordered onto the beaches. Hermann Goering was confident that his Luftwaffe could prevent the escape of the trapped men. 'I hope the Tommies are good swimmers,' he declared delightedly on 26 May.

On the night of 26 May, a hastily organized evacuation plan – Operation Dynamo – was launched. Over the previous few days every available ship had been gathered to form a rescue armada, comprising nearly 850 vessels, from destroyers, to transports, down to ferries and pleasure boats. The great evacuation started that evening. It was a slow and laborious business ferrying the men in dinghies from

continued on page 42

In one of the many evocative images of the Dunkirk 'miracle', ships crammed with exhausted British and Allied soldiers attempt to make it back across the Channel.

SIR HUGH DOWDING

Sir Hugh Caswell Tremenheere Dowding (1882–1970) was 58 years old in the summer of 1940, and a remote figure to the pilots who flew under him in Fighter Command. His stiff manner, feathery moustache and pained demeanour made him appear a relict of the Edwardian era in which he had done his early soldiering as an artillery officer in imperial outposts. He seemed to suit his nickname, 'Stuffy'. But in other respects Dowding belonged firmly in the modern era. He had taken up the dangerous and dashing occupation of flying early on, gaining his pilot's certificate in December 1913, and he served with distinction in the Royal Flying Corps during the First World War, partly on active service in France and partly in logistics and training roles. In the interwar years that followed, he stood out against the pro-bomber theories that prevailed in the RAF and understood better than any other senior officer the vital importance of a strong, well-equipped fighter force. In July 1936, he became head of the new Fighter Command, based at Bentley Priory in northwest London, and the following year was promoted to Air Chief Marshal.

Many found it difficult to warm to Dowding personally. But behind his awkward manner there beat a warm heart, and he cared deeply for his men. (His son, Derek, was one of them, a Battle of Britain fighter pilot.) He made this clear at the close of the Dunkirk crisis, in a letter of 2 June directed to 'My Dear Fighter Boys' — the name by which the men who flew the Spitfires and Hurricanes were becoming known.

My Dear Fighter Boys

    I don't send out many congratulatory letters and signals but I feel that I must take this occasion, when the intensive fighting in northern France is for the time being over, to tell you how proud I am of you and the way in which you have fought since the "Blitzkrieg" started.

    I wish I could have visited you and spent my time visiting you and hearing your accounts of the fighting but I have occupied my self in working for you in other ways.

    I want you to know that my thoughts are always with you and that it is you and your fighting spirit which will crack the morale of the German Air Force and preserve our Country through the trials which yet lie ahead.

    Good luck to you.

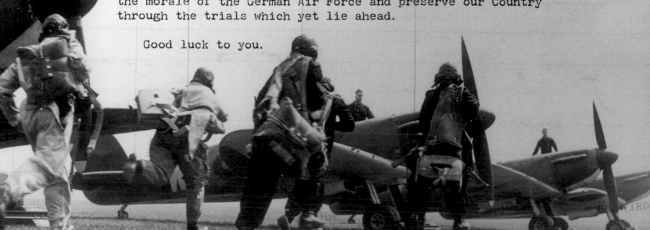

	SINGLE-ENGINE AIRCRAFT				MULTI-ENGINE AIRCRAFT					PASS-ENGER	INSTR/CLOUD FLYING [Incl. in cols. (1) to (10)]	
DAY		NIGHT		DAY			NIGHT					
DUAL	PILOT	DUAL	PILOT	DUAL	1ST PILOT	2ND PILOT	DUAL	1ST PILOT	2ND PILOT		DUAL	PILOT
(1)	(2)	(3)	(4)	(5)	(6)	(7)	(8)	(9)	(10)	(11)	(12)	(13)

His men felt their lives were in responsible hands. 'Even junior people like myself had enormous confidence in him,' said Christopher Foxley-Norris, then a young pilot with No. 3 Squadron. 'He was a father figure. You felt that as long as his hand was on the tiller, all was going to be well.' [Foxley-Norris, recording] The women who worked with him at Bentley Priory could sense the warmth behind the stiffness. 'We all admired our Stuffy enormously,' said Elizabeth Quayle, a WAAF (Women's Auxiliary Air Force) plotter in the operations room. 'We had great loyalty to him. I think you might call it affection. He built up a tremendous *esprit de corps* among us. He was very remote but if you met him he was always very considerate.' [Quayle, recording]

During the Battle of Britain, Dowding was the right man in the right job. Once it was done, Churchill unsentimentally moved him on. He was considered dour, stubborn and defensive-minded by jealous colleagues. But it was these very qualities that saved Fighter Command from destruction. In 1943, Dowding accepted a barony. He died in 1970, and his ashes were placed in Westminster Abbey, in the RAF chapel.

ABOVE With past differences over tactics behind them, Lord Dowding (*centre*) chats with Group Captain Douglas Bader and other Battle of Britain veterans before taking off from North Weald for a victory fly-past over London (15 September 1945). The other veterans identified here include (*left of Dowding*) John Ellis, Tim Vigors and Denis Crowley-Milling, and (*right of Bader*) Billy Drake (partially obscured) and Peter Brothers (facing out).

OPPOSITE, TOP Air Chief Marshal Dowding, as depicted in an official Ministry of Information photograph.

OPPOSITE, BOTTOM Some of Dowding's 'fighter boys' scramble to their waiting aircraft in 1940.

the beaches to the waiting boats, but luck was siding with the British. The next morning, 27 May, was grey and overcast, and the smoke in the air gave a measure of protection from the Luftwaffe. Then, when a breakwater in the harbour was adapted as a jetty, and piers were improvised on sunken lorries, the rate of evacuation improved dramatically. Some 47,000 were taken off on 29 May, and 68,000 on 31 May.

June 1940

The overall speed of the evacuation took the Germans by surprise. It was only with improving weather on 1 June, by which time about three-quarters of the BEF had escaped, that an all-out German air assault was ordered against the beaches and town of Dunkirk. The German armour also returned to the attack, but the delay had given the Allies a chance to throw a makeshift defensive perimeter around the pocket.

While Stuka dive-bombers attacked the beaches, the port and any shipping present, Messerschmitt Me109 fighters circled high above. The soldiers below

'Getting into some real hot places'

Sergeant Eric Bann of No. 238 Squadron wrote this letter home to his parents in Macclesfield, Lancashire, on 21 May 1940.

```
    Have been having a real rough time, lost nearly all my clothes and
have been sleeping in any old place, plus getting into some real hot
places. We have bagged about forty German planes in the last four days
but their numbers are terrific. Have been going in for about six of us
to forty or fifty of theirs, the air was thick. I think we lost the
Flight Commander yesterday, what a nice chap, they said he was engaged
by about ten fighters and went down fighting madly.
    Our Squadron had been flying every day and we are very tired …
Believe me to see the German dive-bombers in their hundred cutting
at our poor troops makes you only too glad to help - it's terrible.
```

-o-o-o-o-o-

would later bitterly complain that the 'Brylcreem Boys' of the RAF had left them to their fate, but in fact Fighter Command threw itself fully into the task of trying to shield the evacuation. Dowding at last deployed his precious Spitfires, and many squadrons based around London were ordered into the fight, some seeing action for the first time. Fighter Command flew 2739 sorties over the heads of the BEF, but much of this activity was hidden from the beaches by smoke or took place inland and out of sight, as fighters tried to get to the attacking bombers before they could discharge their loads. Many pilots were in the air for two, three or even four hours a day.

As always, 'green' pilots suffered against their more experienced enemies. The Intelligence Officer for 609 Spitfire Squadron later wrote: 'It was a bit like sending a football eleven, whose members had never played together before, against a crack team that had never tasted defeat.' Of the eighteen 609 pilots who fought over Dunkirk, five were killed and one was seriously injured.

The RAF was heavily outnumbered, partly because its fighters could not carry enough fuel to last over Dunkirk for more than half an hour, much less if in high-throttle combat. At first, small groups were sent out on rotation, but they found themselves so outnumbered as to be ineffective. Thereafter, the fighters were deployed in 'wings' of several squadrons combined, which inevitably left gaps in the air cover. But the evacuation continued below.

The British government had been keen to keep news of the BEF's retreat and evacuation from the people at home. On 28 May, the Director of Military Intelligence had called together the press at a London hotel. They should act, he told them, as 'shock absorbers' after the stunning defeat. That same day, Belgium's King Leopold had – in the face of Franco-British opposition and that of his own Cabinet – surrendered his country, thus giving German forces easier passage to the coast. In spite of the tens of thousands of British troops now being carried on trains away from the south coast of England, the press and radio declined to report the evacuation until 30 May. Then, at 6pm, the BBC announced that: 'All day men of the undefeated British Expeditionary Force have been coming home ... it is clear that if they have not come back in triumph they have come back in glory ... they are anxious only to be back again soon – as they put it – "to have another crack at Jerry".'

The manipulation worked. The troops returned, shattered after a nightmare of confused retreat in darkness, hunger, thirst and sleeplessnes, to an enthusiastic

A trio of Spitfires takes to the skies.

'We had no sense of order'

A 22-year-old insurance clerk, Peter Lambert joined a Territorial Artillery unit in April 1939, and was posted to France on 27 October. In an unpublished memoir he recounted his experiences of the chaotic retreat to Dunkirk.

```
    The very thought of the British army being in retreat to the
extent that we had to abandon everything was unbelievable. Despite
all the meandering around northern France one felt that, sooner or
later, things would stabilize and we could get into action.
    Then came that night when we were told by our sergeant that the
British army was to retreat to the coast around Dunkirk where we were
to be taken off by the Royal Navy. Not one of the gun positions we had
so diligently surveyed during the Phoney War was used. Instead we had
trundled these large things around the northern French countryside,
preparing for action only once, but not firing a single shot. We were
told to leave our vehicles having made them as useless as possible.
The guns were too damaged and dumped in the La Bassee canal and we
were to make our way on foot to Dunkirk.
    So began our trek to the coast. We moved at night to avoid the
bombing, accompanied everywhere by the barking of dogs whose owners
had fled, leaving them to fend for themselves. Everyone was afraid
of becoming detached from their comrades and lost. We had no sense of
order. Morale was low. We could hardly be described as a military unit
and on several occasions I remember hearing tanks all around us not
knowing whether whey were friend or foe.
```

-o-o-o-o-o-

welcome. 'We expected to slink back, a defeated army,' said Lance-Bombardier Peter Lambert, one of the last of those evacuated on 31 May. 'Instead there were cups of tea, food, waving flags. There were cheers, even.' [Unpublished memoir]

The handling of the Dunkirk evacuation for public consumption was a masterpiece of news management. The BEF had been smashed, leaving behind in France over 30,000 men and pretty much all its equipment; but the whole episode set a new tone of defiance. The press duly followed the government's line, reporting that the evacuation had been 'terrible, but glorious'. The BEF, wrote the *Daily Mail*, had survived despite the 'treachery' of the Belgian surrender. 'Bloody Marvellous' was the *Mirror*'s headline. The small, civilian sea vessels became a shining symbol of resourcefulness and resolve. J.B. Priestley, the novelist whose morale-lifting broadcasts were widely trusted, rhapsodized on the BBC about how 'the little holiday steamers made an excursion to Hell and came back glorious'. The implication was clear: this was a war of civilians as well as soldiers. Crucially, the new mood carried across the Atlantic. 'As long as the English tongue survives, the word Dunkirk will be spoken with reverence,' declared the *New York Times* on 1 June.

The resilience of public morale buoyed Churchill's argument that salvation lay in fighting on. He constantly stressed to his colleagues the necessity to persuade the United States that Britain was a solid ally, which could be relied on to continue the struggle. At a meeting at the end of May he had gathered together his junior ministers and declared: 'If this long island story of ours is to end at last, let it end only when each one of us lies choking in his blood upon the ground.' The rhetoric had its effect and he won their complete support amidst tears and backslapping.

Envigorated by their backing, Churchill headed for the House of Commons a few days later, on 4 June, having just that morning received the final, miraculous figures for the Dunkirk evacuation – where 338,000 Allied soldiers had embarked – heard encouraging reports from Fighter Command about aircraft production, and received news that the US Congress was to debate giving more extensive help for Britain.

Churchill's speech was a classic and immortal oration, delivered by one of the

BELOW
The waste of war. Abandoned vehicles and other matériel litter the Dunkirk beaches in June 1940.

'The beaches were a shambles'

Brian Kingcome was a pilot with No. 92 Squadron. He recorded his impressions of the beaches of Dunkirk as they appeared to him from the skies.

```
      The beaches were a shambles, littered with the smoking wreckage of
engines and equipment, destroyed either by enemy fire or else by our
own troops to stop them falling into German hands. The sands erupted
into huge geysers from exploding bombs and shells, while a backdrop to
the scene of the carnage and destruction was provided by the palls of
oily black smoke rising from the burning harbour and houses of Dunkirk
and hanging high in the still air. And yet there the orderly lines of
our troops stood, chaos and Armageddon at their backs, patiently waiting
their turn to wade into the sea towards the boats, or holding their
weapons above their heads as their turn finally came and they
waded in up to their waists. [A Willingness to Die, p. 137]
```

-0-0-0-0-0-

great artists of the English language. He started by emphasizing how the evacuation from Dunkirk had far exceeded planners' estimates. The architects of Operation Dynamo had hardly dared hope to rescue more than 30,000 troops. The real figure had exceeded that number tenfold. Thus, the 'root and core and brain' of the army had been saved, Churchill said, 'on which and around which ... great British armies' could be built. Britain had survived and Britain would fight on. For Berlin the words were a message of defiance, for Washington a plea for help.

Men of the British Expeditionary Force celebrate their unlikely deliverance after Dunkirk, as they arrive by train in London from the Channel ports.

It is now forgotten that much of the speech was devoted to the achievements of the Royal Navy in bringing about the 'miracle of Dunkirk' and highlighting its future role in defending the British Isles from invasion. Remembered rather better are the relatively short passages devoted to the RAF. The air force needed the balm of praise. Churchill was careful to laud its role in the rescue, countering the charges that it had failed to offer adequate protection from the Luftwaffe. At the same time he put the RAF and Fighter Command at the centre of the next phase of the crisis, laying the foundations of the myth before the Battle of Britain had properly begun. 'There has never been, I suppose in all the world, in all the history of war, such an opportunity for youth,' Churchill declared. The fighter pilots of the RAF, the prime minister went on, were like the Knights of the Round Table, but 'holding in their hands these instruments of colossal and shattering power'. Such paladins, he said, 'could outlive the menace of tyranny, if necessary for years, if necessary alone'.

As he spoke, Fighter Command was licking its wounds and scarcely in any condition to rise to the challenge. During the Dunkirk campaign it had lost 60 fighter pilots killed, 15 injured, and 2 more were missing, presumed dead. Those lost to Fighter Command included three squadron commanders killed and one taken prisoner, as well as about twelve section leaders.

Furthermore, while the public and politicians gave thanks for the relative deliverance that was Dunkirk, the RAF was still embroiled in the much less 'glorious' withdrawal from Norway. Nos 263 and 43 squadrons had been fighting hard during May, in bad weather, and were heavily outnumbered covering the evacuation of the Allied troops. By 7 June, 263 Squadron had flown 389 sorties over 12 days, been in combat 69 times and claimed 26 successes. Over the same time, 43 Squadron had taken part in 26 fights and claimed 11 kills. On 7 June, the remaining eight Gladiators flew out to the waiting HMS *Glorious*. Orders were given for the Hurricanes to be destroyed to prevent them falling into the enemy's hands. But, after a protest, their pilots were allowed to attempt to land their planes on the *Glorious*, in spite of the lack of 'arrester hooks' – the restraints to catch planes as they touched down – and the fact that none of the pilots had performed a deck landing before. In the event, all of the remaining ten Hurricanes landed safely, an amazing feat.

However, because of a lack of fuel, the *Glorious* was forced to steer a direct line home. It was unable to avoid the attentions of the German battlecruisers *Scharnhorst* and *Gneisenau*, patrolling off the coast. *Scharnhorst* opened fire

continued on page 50

Winston Churchill, House of Commons, 4 June 1940

'WE SHALL FIGHT THEM ON THE BEACHES'

When Winston Churchill addressed the House of Commons on 4 June 1940, he 'feared it would be my hard lot to announce the greatest military disaster in our long history'. Instead, he was able to describe a 'miracle of deliverance' at Dunkirk and stiffen the British resolve for the next onslaught.

'Even though large tracts of Europe and many old and famous States have fallen or may fall into the grip of the Gestapo and all the odious apparatus of Nazi rule, we shall not flag or fail. We shall go on to the end. We shall fight in France, we shall fight on the seas and oceans, we shall fight with growing confidence and growing strength in the air, we shall defend our island, whatever the cost may be. We shall fight on the beaches, we shall fight on the landing grounds, we shall fight in the fields and in the streets, we shall fight in the hills, we shall never surrender, and even if, which I do not for a moment believe, this island or a large part of it were subjugated and starving, then our Empire beyond the seas, armed and guarded by the British Fleet, would carry on the struggle, until, in God's good time, the New World, with all its power and might, steps forth to the rescue and liberation of the Old.'

THE HISTORY OF THE LUFTWAFFE

The German Luftwaffe ('Air Force') had been born in secret. Forbidden by the 1919 Treaty of Versailles to support a military air force, Germany had instead channelled energy, technical expertise and substantial state subsidy into the development of civil aviation. Hugo Junkers (1859–1935), the pioneer of metal aircraft, Claude Dornier (1884–1969), Ernst Heinkel (1888–1958) and Willy Messerschmitt (1898–1978), who all gave their names to Luftwaffe combat aircraft, started out designing and manufacturing civilian, or 'sporting', aircraft in the 1920s. A state carrier, Deutsche Lufthansa, was created in 1926 under the chairmanship of Erhard Milch, who had commanded a fighter *Geschwader* (wing) in the First World War. Within two years it was Europe's most efficient airline, and by 1930 it was bigger than the British and French civil airlines combined. At the same time, and long before the advent of the Nazi regime, 'air-mindedness' was encouraged, with state-sponsored gliding and flying clubs attracting tens of thousands of members. At a time when elsewhere flying was the preserve of the super-rich, in Germany it was a new and exciting sport for all.

But as early as 1923 a top-secret memorandum laid out plans for an independent military air force. Lufthansa openly and quite legally trained many hundreds of pilots, who in time would form a core for the future Luftwaffe. It would also deliberately develop designs for commercial aircraft that were easily convertible into bombers, such as the Junkers 52. More secret were the agreements with the Russians, who from the end of 1923 allowed the setting-up of a secluded base 200 miles southeast of Moscow. There, far from the eyes of the western Allies, many of the future Luftwaffe's senior personnel underwent thorough military training.

By the time the Luftwaffe was announced to the world in 1935, it had behind it the strongest aircraft industry in Europe. Generous subsidies and loans to Dornier, Heinkel and Junkers allowed a massive expansion of aircraft production, by more than 800 per cent in the two years after 1933.

Hermann Goering was the Luftwaffe's commander, but Erhard Milch (1892–1972), as Secretary of State for Air, exercised close control of a force that already numbered 20,000 men and nearly 2000 aircraft. Milch calculated that he needed ten years to build a Luftwaffe ready to fight a major war. Goering cemented his position by appointing First World War colleagues to senior positions. Meanwhile, Milch drove forward a vigorous expansion plan that by late 1935 was delivering 300 new aircraft a month, including many that would fight against Britain five years later.

All Lufthansa pilots now became Luftwaffe reservists, and training programmes for combat pilots were also massively expanded through the 1930s. At the outbreak of the war, Luftwaffe training units were producing pilots of a very high standard at the rate of 15,000 a year. Pilots had 250 hours' flying time behind them before being

Messerschmitt Me110 twin-engine fighters fly unchallenged over the landmarks of Paris in 1940, testifying to the German war machine's greatest victory thus far.

transferred to an operational flying school to receive specialist training in fighter, bombing or dive-bombing skills.

Many interwar German strategists endorsed the notion of the primacy of the bomber. The first Chief of the Air Staff of the new Luftwaffe, Walther Wever, supported by Milch, ordered the development of heavy four-engined bombers that would be able to deliver a significant bomb load from Germany as far away as Scotland or the Urals. But in June 1936 Wever was killed in an air crash and Goering, jealous of Milch's influence, sidelined him in favour of a First World War fighter ace crony, Ernst Udet. Udet had been a superb pilot but was inadequate to the tasks of aircraft procurement and production. Under his influence, supported by Goering and by Wever's successor, ex-army officer Albert Kesselring (1885–1960), the Luftwaffe abandoned the heavy bomber project in favour of shaping a force for infantry support, with lighter, faster bombers able to dive on ground targets.

The outbreak of the Spanish Civil War in July 1936 gave Goering a chance to measure the capabilities of his new force. Before the end of the year, the Condor Legion had come into being, made up of Luftwaffe 'volunteers' under the command first of General Hugo Sperrle (1885–1953), and then of General Wolfram von Richthofen, cousin of the famous First World War ace Baron von Richthofen. The war provided a test bed for the Luftwaffe's latest models and combat experience for its pilots. It was also the first time that a coordinated air and ground war had been fought, and the results were devastating. Von Richthofen returned to Berlin to press the case for continuing to develop air policy in the direction of ground support. Thus, the Luftwaffe that confronted Fighter Command in the summer of 1940 was designed to support the army, not to fight a strategic battle on its own.

Nevertheless, the Luftwaffe had proved itself a decisive weapon in the war so far. German confidence was high. In France and the Low Countries, the force had shot down or destroyed on the ground more than 3000 enemy aircraft. Losses from the earlier campaigns were quickly made good. As early as mid-June, the new airfields in the conquered northern European countries began launching exploratory raids on Britain on their own initiative. There were even training missions flown over British soil. The first large-scale raid came in on the night of 18 June, when 100 bombers attacked scattered and diverse targets between Yorkshire and Kent. Meanwhile, the full strength of the force was gathered for the battle ahead.

Hitler salutes veterans of the Condor Legion during a parade (6 June 1939) in their honour. They had pioneered the practice of aerial bombardment during the Spanish Civil War.

'The war has entered into a new and glorious phase'

The satirical novelist and journalist Evelyn Waugh took up characters he had used in earlier novels for his new creation, *Put Out More Flags*, in 1942. Chiefly concerning the Phoney War (Waugh's 'Bore War'), it makes fun of the way officialdom presented what had been a disaster — the BEF's failure — as a kind of triumph. The novel changes tone as the immensity of Britain's challenge becomes clear, a challenge clarified by Dunkirk and isolation.

> Finally when it was plain, even to Sir Joseph [Mainwaring], that in the space of a few days England had lost both the entire stores and equipment of her regular army and her only ally; that the enemy were less than twenty-five miles from her shores; that there were only a few battalions of fully armed, fully trained troops in the country; that she was committed to a war in the Mediterranean with a numerically superior enemy; that her cities lay open to air attack from fields closer to home than the extremities of her own islands; that her sea-routes were threatened from a dozen new bases, Sir Joseph said: 'Seen in the proper perspective I regard this as a great and tangible success ... The war has entered into a new and glorious phase.'

-0-0-0-0-0-

at long range, hitting the carrier and setting it on fire. Within an hour it had sunk, together with 1471 officers and men of the Royal Navy and 41 RAF personnel, including all but two of the pilots. It was the final tragedy in a disastrous campaign.

The last RAF squadrons based in France withdrew on 18 June. They took with them only 66 of the 452 fighters sent out to the Continent. The rest had been shot down, abandoned or in many cases destroyed to deny them to the Germans. On 22 June, the new French government, headed by the First World War veteran Marshal Philippe Pétain, formalized its surrender and signed the German terms of armistice.

Following the collapse of France, Britain was now alone, with a hostile and powerful enemy surveying it from Cap Gris Nez, within sight of the White Cliffs of Dover. On 30 June and 1 July the undefended Channel Islands were occupied, and German soldiers stood on British soil. Fighter bases were quickly established in the occupied area. From Europe came rumours of a huge fleet of invasion barges being prepared and paratroopers mustered.

The Luftwaffe now moved with great speed to redeploy for an attack on Britain. In Poland, Norway and France, the German air force had demonstrated its ability to push forward quickly, a key component of the success of *Blitzkrieg*. Soon, Luftwaffe bases were established in a huge threatening arc on the Continent, facing eastern and southern Britain, from Norway in the north, through

N

NORWAY
Stavanger
LUFTFLOTTE 5
(Generaloberst Hans-Jürgen Stumpff)

Aalborg

DENMARK

The German air fleets
threatening Britain in
summer 1940

Luftflotte boundaries
Fliegerkorps boundaries
Notable fighter and heavy fighter bases
(Me109s and Me110s)
Notable bomber and dive-bomber bases
(Ju87s, Ju88s, He111s, etc)
Luftflotte (HQ)
Fliegerkorps & Fliegerdivision HQ

0   100 km
0   100 miles

UNITED
KINGDOM

NETHERLANDS

Amsterdam
Soesterberg

LUFTFLOTTE 2
(Generalfeldmarschall Albert Kesselring)

Eindhoven
IX FLIEGERKORPS

II FLIEGERKORPS
Marck   Coquelles   Antwerp
Desvres   St Truiden
Audembert   Guînes   *GHENT*
Wissant   Brussels
Marquise   Lille-Nord   BELGIUM
Samer   St Omer
Grandvilliers   Cambrai-Epinoy   GERMANY
Tramecourt
Caffiers   Saint-Léger

I FLIEGERKORPS
Cherbourg   Le Havre   Rosières-en-Santerre
Crépon   *BEAUVAIS*   Montdidier   IV FLIEGERKORPS
Channel Islands   *DEAUVILLE*   Creil   *COMPIEGNE*
Caen   Evreux   Orly
Lannion   St André   Paris
DINARD   St-Malo   *VILLACOUBLAY*   **LUFTFLOTTE 3**
Brest   Dinan   Dreux   Etampes   (Generalfeldmarschall Hugo Sperrle)
Rennes   Chartres   Châteaudun
Laval   Orléans-Bricy   FRANCE
IV FLIEGERKORPS   Angers
Nantes   Tours
VIII FLIEGERKORPS   V FLIEGERKORPS

OPPOSITE

Churchill the statesman
and embodiment
of British defiance,
as captured in
Yousuf Karsh's
celebrated photo-
portrait of 1941

Denmark, Holland, Belgium and France as far west as the Atlantic coast of Brittany. Generaloberst Sperrle's *Luftflotte* 3, with its headquarters in Paris, was based in northwestern France, with Kesselring's *Luftflotte* 2, commanded from Brussels, operating from northeastern France and the Low Countries. A further *Luftflotte*, No. 5, was deployed to Denmark and Norway to threaten Britain's eastern coast all the way north to Scapa Flow in the Orkneys.

The reaction in Britain to its isolation was, in hindsight, extraordinary. The exit of France from the war was regarded by some as a relief, clearing the ground and simplifying matters. A newspaper headline after the French armistice was agreed on 18 June read: 'French sign peace treaty: we're in the finals.' The Labour Party leader, Clement Attlee, and his deputy, Arthur Greenwood, reassured Churchill that the working classes supported his defiant stand. Certainly, it was the end of the feeling of detachment that had characterized the Phoney War. It was now a war of national survival. George Orwell would write the following year: 'After eight months of vaguely wondering what the war was about, the people suddenly knew what they had to do ... it was like the awakening of a giant.'

Churchill was now anxious to create an atmosphere of action. Armaments factories churned out weapons and the training centres churned out troops. Almost half a million men were put in uniform between May and the end of July 1940. By mid-June a further 400,000 were enrolled in the Local Defence Volunteer force, later renamed the Home Guard. Small civilian vessels, fishing boats and other craft were diverted to watch Britain's long coastline for an invasion fleet.

Now everyone could feel part of the war effort. The numbers were, of course, misleading. The Home Guard (see page 35) was of minimal military value, while regular troops in key positions facing the likely landing sites in Kent and Sussex were barely equipped and only partly trained.

But, as Hitler appreciated, the invasion of Britain was not going to be like one of the river crossings his army had so successfully achieved in its operations to date. The most obvious obstacle facing the Germans was the Royal Navy, still majestically intact. Churchill's secretary, Sir John Colville, had used a vivid metaphor when describing the relative strengths of Germany and Britain. One was the elephant, a mighty terrestrial beast. The other was the whale, king of the seas. Neither was able to bring its strength to bear on the other. That left the third element in which modern wars were fought – the air. As Hitler considered how to tame the British, one thing seemed clear. In order for victory over Britain to be achieved, through invasion, blockade or demoralization, there was an essential precondition. Germany must have mastery of the skies. The scene was set for the Luftwaffe to launch itself into the greatest air battle in history.

'THEIR FINEST HOUR'

On 18 June, Winston Churchill broadcast to the nation the speech he had made earlier in the House of Commons, as it became clear that France was out of the fight and Britain stood alone against Germany and now Italy.

'What General Weygand called the Battle of France is over. I expect that the Battle of Britain is about to begin. Upon this battle depends the survival of Christian civilization ... the whole fury and might of the enemy must very soon be turned on us. Hitler knows that he will have to break us in this Island or lose the War. If we can stand up to him, all Europe may be free and the life of the world may move forward into broad sunlit uplands. But if we fail, then the whole world, including the United States, including all that we have known and cared for, will sink into the abyss of a new Dark Age made more sinister, and perhaps more protracted, by the lights of perverted science. Let us therefore brace ourselves to our duties, and so bear ourselves that, if the British Empire and its Commonwealth last for a thousand years, men will still say, "This was their finest hour."'

Winston Churchill

2

BEGINNING THE DUEL

1 JULY TO 16 JULY 1940

The decision to launch a full-scale aerial assault on Britain in 1940 was taken by the German Armed Forces Supreme Command (*Oberkommando der Wehrmacht*, or OKW) once it was confident that its assets were in place. By the beginning of July, the Luftwaffe had the use of the entire North Sea coastline from Norway to France.

From the start of the month the Luftwaffe probed the RAF's defences, looking for weak spots and aiming to wear down the defenders. A small raid could cause a disproportionate amount of wear and tear. On the night of 31 June/1 July, a force of only 20 bombers caused sirens to be sounded in 20 counties. The following day saw the first daylight raids, on Wick in Scotland and on Hull.

Thereafter *Luftflotte* 5 commenced fairly regular operations over northeastern Britain from its base at Stavanger, Norway, bringing home the reality of the huge front the British had to defend. Britain now felt vulnerable in the west, too, where it was exposed to attacks from the airfields near Brest and Cherbourg. In mid-1940, a new RAF group, 10 Group, was formed in the West Country and South Wales, under Air Vice-Marshal Sir Quintin Brand, with sector stations at Filton, near Bristol, and later Middle Wallop, Hampshire.

As the first days of July progressed, German operations picked up pace. But they were to be merely the overture to a symphony of violence that was to last the rest of the summer. By the end of 10 July, Fighter Command's resources were already being stretched and it seemed likely that there would be little chance of respite until the contest was settled. The scale of the attacks that day would signal the start of the Battle of Britain proper. The showdown had finally come.

2 July 1940 TUESDAY

Today, a Luftwaffe operational order set two objectives: to close the Channel to British shipping and to clear the air of British fighters. This was in keeping with a Hitler directive issued in November 1939, which had envisaged the Luftwaffe 'waging war against the English economy' once the Anglo-French armies had been

PREVIOUS PAGE
A Messerschmitt Me109 pursues a Spitfire, in a photograph dated to 1940.

OPPOSITE
The diabolical tourist. Hitler poses on the terrace of the Palais de Chaillot, with the Eiffel Tower behind, 28 June 1940. It would be the Führer's first and last trip to Paris.

July 1st. at Northolt.
Me and my Spitfire, the evening before
our patrol over France.

David Crook, of
No. 609 Squadron,
photographed in his
Spitfire at RAF Northolt,
with an annotation for
1 July 1940 taken from
his pilot's logbook.

disposed of. What happened next was largely dependent on how the British reacted to the assault on their economic existence. As will be seen, the approach taken by Hitler and his commanders to the problem of Britain was always clouded with vagueness.

The aircraft for the task of blockading the Channel from the air would be provided by *Fliegerkorps* (Air Corps) II based in the Pas de Calais and *Fliegerkorps* VII at Le Havre. The main bomber force would be augmented by two groups of Stuka dive-bombers and protected by two *Jagdgeschwader* (fighter wings), Nos 26 and 53.

The battle was to be called the *Kanalkampf* (Channel Battle) and the *Kanalkampf-führer* was to be Oberst (Colonel) Johannes Fink, a sombre, religious-minded 45-year-old, who had been one of the few men allowed to be trained each year as pilots under the draconian terms imposed on Germany at Versailles in 1919.

3 July 1940 WEDNESDAY

German operations began today, but tentatively. About 50 aeroplanes flew towards Britain, of which about a quarter were on reconnaissance missions, tasked with photographing airfields and ports in preparation for future attacks. The day was full of alarms as patrolling aircraft and civilians in the streets of southern England caught glimpses of the intruders. One event that day brought home an uncomfortable truth: henceforth, no-one under the skies in which battle would be fought could consider themselves entirely safe. In the village of Holmbury St Mary, near Dorking in Surrey, a policeman walking his beat caught sight of a low-flying bomber and alerted RAF Biggin Hill. Ten minutes later, two large bombs fell close by, on the market town of Guildford, killing 15 innocents.

Countering the Luftwaffe's probes that day cost a lot of effort. By evening, 28 fighter squadrons had flown more than 120 patrols, each involving three or six aircraft. The result of all this effort was only five German aircraft shot down. In the

continued on page 62

LUFTWAFFE FORMATIONS AND TACTICS

The Luftwaffe was organized into *Luftflotten* (air fleets). Within each of these were a number of *Fliegerkorps* (air corps), usually two or three, which in turn were divided into *Geschwader* (wings) of fighters, bombers, dive-bombers and so on. Bombers were in *Kampfgeschwader* (KG, battle wings), fighters in *Jagdgeschwader* (JG, fighter wings – literally 'hunter groups'), Messerschmitt Me110 heavy fighters in *Zerstörergeschwader* (ZG, destroyer wings), and Ju87 dive-bombers in *Sturzkampfgeschwader* (StG, dive-bomber wings). *Lehrgeschwader* (teaching wings) were mixed *Geschwader* of different types of aircraft, largely staffed by former instructors, and there were other types of *Geschwader* besides.

Each *Geschwader* contained, at full strength, some 90–120 aircraft, divided into 3 or 4 *Gruppen* (groups). The equivalent of the British squadron was the *Staffel* (echelon) of about 10–12 aircraft. Each *Gruppe* contained three or four *Staffeln*.

The Luftwaffe forgot the lessons of aerial combat learned in the First World War – as, indeed, did the RAF – and during its involvement in the Spanish Civil War it flew in very close wingtip-to-wingtip formation. But the German pilots soon realized the vulnerability of such tactics and adopted the formation, still in use today, of the two-aircraft *Rotte* (literally 'pack') and the four-aircraft *Schwarm* (swarm). As Hans-Ekkehard Bob, an Me109 pilot, explained: 'The Messerschmitt Me109s used the *Schwarm* four aircraft formation. Two aircraft [a *Rotte*] would fly together at the same altitude with a distance of 50 metres between them. Another two aircraft were flying alongside, further away, again with

a distance of 50 metres between them, so that we were flying in a broad row about 200 metres long. Each of the pilots was able to monitor to the rear and to the front and so see what was where.

'The wingman protected his leader from attack, or was in a position to fasten onto the tail of an enemy diving on the forward aircraft, while the leader navigated and was ready, in turn, to protect his wingman. Flying in this fashion meant that a Messerschmitt *Staffel* of 12 fighters stretched about a mile and a half across the sky, with each *Schwarm* at varying heights.' [Bob, recording]

Luftwaffe formations of Heinkel He111 bombers plough through the skies in the summer of 1940.

BRITISH RADAR

The rapid advance of science in the early years of the 20th century encouraged military planners to investigate possibilities that would previously have been thought fanciful and absurd. Most of them came to nothing. But one far-fetched idea would lead to a breakthrough crucial to Fighter Command's success in the Battle of Britain. At the end of 1934, the Director of Scientific Research at the Air Ministry, W.E. Wimperis, suggested that a committee be set up to explore any ideas, however unlikely, that might contribute to air defence. The Aeronautical Research Committee, under the leadership of Henry Tizard, first met in January 1935. Wimperis had already approached Robert Watson-Watt (1892–1973), a radio expert, and asked him about rumours concerning a German 'death ray', an electro-magnetic weapon that, it was suggested, could shut down the engine of a hostile plane in mid-air.

Watson-Watt, like aircraft designers Sydney Camm and Reginald Mitchell, would make a key behind-the-scenes technical contribution to the success of Fighter Command. A descendant of James Watt, the 18th-century inventor and pioneer of the steam engine, he had worked for the Meteorological Office, experimenting with equipment that could detect at long range the radio signal given off by thunderstorms. In late 1934 he was superintendent of the radio department at the National Physical Laboratory at Teddington, West London.

Watson-Watt brushed aside the idea of a 'death ray'. It would not be possible to generate a powerful enough signal to interfere with an engine and, anyway, the aircraft would have to be located first. But he did come up with another idea, which, though less dramatic, turned out to be of supreme importance. His work with weather detection had shown him that radio waves were bounced back to earth not only by certain atmospheric conditions but also by the metal fuselages of aircraft overhead.

On 12 February 1935, Watson-Watt and his assistant Arnold Wilkins produced a report entitled *The Detection and Location of Aircraft by Radio Methods*. Tizard's committee was impressed. So too was the head of research and development at the Air Ministry, Sir Hugh Dowding. Less than two weeks later Watson-Watt and Wilkins demonstrated a basic radar (RAdio Detection And Ranging) system to a member of Tizard's committee, A.P. Rowe. A Handley Page Heyford bomber was flown along the centre line of the 50-metre radio beam transmitted by the BBC's station at Daventry. In a field near Upper Stowe, Northamptonshire, receiving equipment had

Members of the Women's Auxiliary Air Force cluster around the plotting map in the receiver room at Bawdsey Chain Home radar station, Suffolk.

been set up linked to a cathode-ray oscilloscope to display the beam's signal. As the bomber passed within eight miles of the transmitter, the beam was measurably displaced.

Tizard's committee backed further development, establishing an experimental unit under Watson-Watt at Orford Ness on the Suffolk coast. Before the end of 1935, the range of the equipment had been expanded to 50 miles, and plans had been drawn up to create a chain of 20 coastal 'Chain Home' radar stations covering the approaches from Germany, and to make the new technology a cornerstone of air defence. When Sir Hugh Dowding took over Fighter Command in 1936, he brought with him both an understanding of radar and strong support for Watson-Watt's work.

Top-secret research continued on the project, which was now known, partly in the interests of vagueness, as 'Radio Direction Finding' or RDF. At Bawdsey Manor, near Orford Ness, an experimental station was opened in September 1936, with two more following the next year, at Dover and Canewdon, Essex. By now, the accuracy of the equipment had improved, and the range increased to 100 miles.

By February 1940, the 20 original Chain Home (CH) stations had been constructed as well as a further 12 covering the west and the north of England. Each consisted of a number of 350ft transmitter aerial masts, 250ft receiver aerial masts, a transmitter and a receiver block, and an office where the radar displays were situated.

The Chain Home stations, however, could not detect incoming aircraft at low altitude, and to fill this gap a second system of 'low-looking' Chain Home Low stations – and mobile units – was established from November 1939. These operated on a lower frequency and had a shorter range, but together with the CH stations they gave the RAF an excellent chance of detecting attacks in time to react effectively. (See map on page 149.)

Radar's development and deployment had been supported by many, from King George down, and certainly Dowding's enthusiasm had been enormously beneficial. But the greatest share of the credit belongs to Watson-Watt, who turned from the technical side of radar to building up a usable network of machines and the people to run them, as well as a layered organization that efficiently passed information along the chain of command. His contributions to the war effort earned him a knighthood in 1942. A decade later he was awarded £50,000 by the British government for his work on the development of radar.

Radar receiver towers loom over cliffs on the Isle of Wight.

months ahead, controllers from the top down would have to make constant fine judgements as to how to combat an ever-present but always altering threat while trying to preserve aircraft and men.

4 July 1940 THURSDAY

Thursday saw a bolder approach from the Germans. At first light, about 30 Stukas attacked the naval base at Portland. A merchant tanker suffered a direct hit from a 500-kilo bomb, and was set on fire. Next, the Stukas sank the largest vessel in the naval base, the 5500-ton HMS *Foyle Bank*. Further small ships were sunk or damaged, buildings battered and civilians killed. By the time fighters from 609 Squadron arrived from Middle Wallop, Hampshire, the Stukas were long gone.

At 2pm about 20 Dorniers, guarded by Messerschmitt Me109s, attacked a convoy of 9 ships as they passed through the Straits of Dover. High-flying German spotter planes had called in the attack when the convoy was without a fighter escort. The bombs struck several vessels, encouraging the Germans to linger over the area long enough for them to be caught by eight Hurricanes from 79 Squadron. But as the Hurricanes arrived, the escorting Me109 fighters dived to the rescue, shooting down a Hurricane over St Margaret's Bay, killing the pilot, and driving the rest of the squadron away.

Convoys delivering food, coal, raw materials and machinery were vital to the maintenance of Britain's very existence; but having to defend them around the country's coast was not a welcome prospect for Fighter Command. RAF planes frequently came under fire from overeager Royal Navy anti-aircraft gunners. In operations against shipping, the Germans had a crucial advantage. Before engaging offshore targets, attackers could form up out of range of radar and be over the vessels in ten minutes. It took British fighters at least 15 minutes to get sufficient altitude to make a successful attack possible. On several occasions during this first week of July, the intercepting British fighters arrived over a convoy only to find the bombers gone and the damage already done. Soon the Germans were timing Me109 fighter sweeps to coincide with the belated arrival of the British defenders, 'bouncing' the Spitfires or Hurricanes as they dived on stragglers.

Sometimes the relative inexperience of the RAF pilots showed too. Patrolling near Manston, Kent, on 4 July, a three-man section from 54 Squadron came across a formation of Messerschmitt Me110s crossing the coast near Dungeness. They were just about to attack 'when they were jumped from above by a formation of escorting Me109's'. According to 54 Squadron's Al Deere: 'This was a classic example of "beware the Hun in the sun".

Stukas – dark bringers of *Blitzkrieg*. Sirens screaming, Ju87 dive-bombers brought terror to troops and civilians alike as Hitler's armies overran western Europe in spring 1940.

Roland Pitchforth's painting *A Royal Observer Corps Post* (1944) depicts two observers, with binoculars and an aircraft range-finder, at the coastal post near Rottingdean, East Sussex.

'FOREWARNED IS FOREARMED' – THE OBSERVER CORPS

During the First World War, the reporting of enemy aircraft overhead had switched from the police to the army, then back to the police. A network of telephone communications had been established linking police stations with operations rooms. At the end of the war, the system was dismantled, but a pilot scheme with volunteer observers was launched in the 1920s. By the time of the 1925 Air Exercises, the Observer Corps had been formed with over 100 observation posts in Southeast England, manned by uniformed civilian volunteers.

In 1929 the Air Ministry took over control of the Observer Corps from the Home Office, and it now became linked to local sector airfields. The growing threat from Germany saw an expansion of the system during the late 1930s, and by the time of the Battle of Britain there were some 30,000 observers, of whom about 4000 were women, keeping watch at more than 1000 posts.

Observation posts were sited anywhere that provided a good field of vision: rooftops, clifftops or simply high ground. Many were in basic sandbagged enclosures, open to the elements and vulnerable to enemy attack, although a number of standard-design reporting posts were constructed of brick or concrete, usually two-storey with an open observation platform above a small lower-level room where the crew rested. Each post usually had a crew of two or three, all highly trained in aircraft recognition.

Once radar had picked up incoming aircraft over the sea, the Fighter Command Group HQ would alert the local Observer Corps Group HQ, which would in turn notify the relevant posts. Radar could not tell the types or number of aircraft coming over, nor their precise height. This information, vital for a successful interception, had to come from the Observer Corps. Once over land, radar lost the raiders altogether and only the Observer Corps could provide information.

Equipment was rudimentary – binoculars, earphones and a chest-mounted telephone, and a simple sextant device used to calculate the height of an incoming raid. The headquarters of each Fighter Command group controlled about 30–40 posts, each of which would be some 10–20 miles from its neighbour. At group headquarters were 12 plotters seated around a map, each receiving and noting information from two or three posts. From here, the plots were passed up the chain of command as well as direct to the nearest sector station.

In recognition of the contribution of the Observer Corps during the Battle of Britain, in 1941 the organization was granted the prefix 'Royal'. Its motto was: 'Forewarned is forearmed.'

The Spitfire pilots, to put it bluntly, were caught with their trousers down and two of our aircraft were shot down and a third damaged.' The pilots, luckily, all escaped with their lives. [Deere, p. 86]

7 July 1940 SUNDAY

Even with the benefit of radar, it was proving difficult to locate incoming German aircraft. The defenders had to fall back on the unsatisfactory precaution of constant patrolling, hoping that some of their aircraft would be in the air at the right time and place to intercept a raid. On 7 July a large convoy was making its way eastwards through the English Channel when it was spotted by a Dornier Do17 reconnaissance aircraft, one of a number scanning the coast. No. 145 Squadron happened to be patrolling over the Isle of Wight at the time. They managed to down the Do17, but then another appeared. Again it was chased away and shot down, this time by No. 43 Squadron from Tangmere, Sussex, which had taken over patrol duties as the convoy headed eastwards. Next on station was 601 Squadron, which also destroyed a Do17.

By now, however, Kesselring had all the reconnaissance information he needed. The main attack on the convoy was ready. At 7.30pm British time, 45 Dorniers took off from their base at Arras. Fifty-five minutes later they were over the convoy, sinking one ship and damaging three others. Fighters from Kenley, near Croydon, and Hornchurch, in outer East London, were too late to stop the attack, but they arrived in time to be caught by a 'free sweep' of Me109s timed to meet any Fighter Command response. As well as carrying out exhausting patrolling, the pilots of Fighter Command were having to rise to the challenges thrown down by German fighters engaged in such 'free sweeps', whereby small groups of Messerschmitt Me109s would range over the south coast looking for British patrols or trying to tempt aircraft up into combats in which the RAF tended to come off worse. On this occasion, the Messerschmitts caught No. 65 Squadron from above, and all three pilots of Green Section were shot down and killed.

Fighter Command was also carrying out sweeps of its own, reconnaissance patrols across the Channel to report back on activity in the Pas de Calais. Interception by hostile enemy fighters was almost inevitable, and pilots on constant lookout in the air found themselves struggling to provide sufficient information about military activity on the ground to make the missions worthwhile. Furthermore, they confused the vital radar picture over the Channel. Soon such operations were ended, although specially adapted Spitfires continued to fly on lone missions over northern Europe, photographing the preparations for the invasion of Britain.

MONDAY **8 July 1940**

With seven convoys at sea on 8 July, there was no respite. Heavy cloud failed to prevent German planes from shadowing, from the early morning, one convoy sailing up the Bristol Channel and another heading from the Thames Estuary to the Straits of Dover. By midday, Kent's radar stations were showing a build-up over the Pas de Calais. This time an interception was made, with a section of 610 Squadron encountering a *Staffel* (squadron) of unescorted Dorniers. The absence of German fighter protection did not mean that the bombers were easy targets. They were forced to scatter their bombs harmlessly, but then they moved into a defensive formation that maximized the crossfire from their guns, and enabled them to pump out an effective barrage. One of the British pilots was hit by several gunners at once and his aircraft burst into flames. Pilot Officer A.L.B. Raven baled out and was seen by one of his section swimming in the sea, but he drowned before he could be reached.

Nine Hurricanes from 79 Squadron were ordered off from Hawkinge, but they were bounced by a free chase of enemy fighters between Dover and the convoy. By the time the German planes were spotted, two Hurricanes were already spinning in flames towards the Channel. One pilot baled out and was rescued, but he died from his burns. The other died in his cockpit.

Today's events showed that even attacks on unescorted bombers were loaded with danger. On other occasions, fighters would be scrambled to intercept a bombing attack, only to discover that the intruders were in fact Me109 fighters. At this early stage, the heavily outnumbered British fighters were finding themselves capable of picking off stragglers or lone reconnaissance aircraft, and of breaking up bombing attacks – but little else.

A wartime convoy comes under German attack in the Straits of Dover.

continued on page 70

FORM 414

H3 (H) Squadron

ROYAL AIR FORCE

2ND. BOOK

PILOT'S FLYING

LOG BOOK

Name ___F/LT. B. J. LANE.___

The cover of Flight Lieutenant Brian 'Sandy' Lane's logbook, inscribed when he was serving with 213 Squadron, based at Northolt.
It is enlivened by his doodle of a Gloster Gauntlet, the biplane that 213 Squadron flew before it acquired its Hurricanes in 1938.

SINGLE-ENGINE AIRCRAFT				MULTI-ENGINE AIRCRAFT						PASS-ENGER	INSTR/CLOUD FLYING [Incl. in cols. (1) to (10)]	
DAY		NIGHT		DAY			NIGHT					
DUAL	PILOT	DUAL	PILOT	DUAL	1ST PILOT	2ND PILOT	DUAL	1ST PILOT	2ND PILOT		DUAL	PILOT
(1)	(2)	(3)	(4)	(5)	(6)	(7)	(8)	(9)	(10)	(11)	(12)	(13)
44.50	169.50	3.10	4.35							10.05	5.25	3.15
	.40											
	.20											
	.15											
	.30											
	.40											
	.25											
	.40											
	1.40											
			1.05									
	1.35											
	.40											
	.20											
	.55											
	.55											
	.20											
	.55											
	.30											
	1.50											
	1.35											
4.50	184.25	3.10	5.40							10.05	5.25	3.15
(1)	(2)	(3)	(4)	(5)	(6)	(7)	(8)	(9)	(10)	(11)	(12)	(13)

Re-arming my Spitfire after the fight on July 9th. A new oxygen bottle is being put in the cockpit.

⟵ ⟶ Frank Howell. in attacking a JU.88. got a bullet in his glycol. and had to bale out just off Bournemouth. He was picked up almost immediately but we did not know this and went out and did a long search for him. He was quite OK.

The record from David Crook's logbook carries a photograph of 609 Squadron groundcrew rearming his Spitfire 'after the fight on July 9th'.

RAF FIGHTER COMMAND – STRUCTURE AND OPERATIONS

Fighter Command had a simple but daunting task – to prove that the bomber would not always get through. For the purposes of organization, the territory of the British Isles was divided into geographical areas, each of which would be defended by a Fighter Command group, controlled from Air Chief Marshal Dowding's headquarters at Bentley Priory in Stanmore, on the outskirts of Northwest London. At the beginning of 1940 there were three groups: No. 11, covering southern England and London; No. 12, covering central England and Wales; and No. 13, covering the north and Scotland. A fourth group, No. 10, for the defence of the southwest, became operational in July 1940, so that 11 Group's remit became the southeast. Each group was subdivided into local sectors. (See detailed map of groups and sectors on page 73.)

In the lead-up to the war, potentially hostile bomber types became ever faster. To stop them, defenders had to have the earliest possible warning of their arrival. Dowding organized a system that, after much practice, reduced the time from detection to getting the intercepting fighters airborne to just six minutes. Radar and Observer Corps reports – with the estimated type, strength, height and position of aircraft – were telephoned through to the Filter Room at Bentley Priory, which would ascertain whether the planes were friendly or hostile and attempt to deal with inevitable inconsistencies in the reports. The processed information was then passed to the 'Operations (Ops) Room' next door, where the raid was plotted on a large map table, providing a striking visual representation of the situation. At the same time, the information was passed to the relevant groups and sectors, which had their own operations rooms and GSMs (general situation maps).

These maps were constantly updated by plotters wearing headphones, through which they received filtered information about sightings by radar, by members of the Observer Corps and by pilots themselves. Using what looked like a long-handled croupier's rake, the plotters pushed arrows across the map, each marked with an 'F' for friendly, 'H' for hostile, or 'X' for unknown and colour-coded to show the time of the report. Group and sector ops rooms would usually include in their personnel liaison officers from the Observer Corps and Royal Artillery. Both would relay information to their larger organizations, and the latter would attempt – sometimes unsuccessfully – to warn his anti-aircraft batteries when friendly aircraft were flying above them.

Bentley Priory was the brain of the Fighter Command system, while the radar and Observer stations were the eyes and ears, and the group and sector stations the arms and hands. Minute-by-minute tactical control was decentralized, while Bentley Priory took on the vital role of processing, analysing and then communicating incoming information. An American military attaché, Raymond Lee, visited the Priory in August 1940. In two great subterranean chambers he found one of 'the most intricate and modern organizations in the world'. He was greatly impressed with the calm atmosphere. It was 'almost silent – only a soft murmur of voices as messages come and go over headsets, and only a little movement as operators move counters and markers from point to point and others tend electric bulletins and switchboards … I had no idea the British could evolve and operate so intricate, so scientific and rapid an organization.' [Lee, p. 30]

Once a raid was confirmed, the controller of the sector or sectors affected would scramble his fighters and guide them to meet the attackers. The perfect interception was from above, when the German fighter escort was low on fuel (or, even better, already heading home), and

Map labels:
13 GROUP
12 GROUP
10 GROUP / 11 GROUP

before the bombers hit their target. Too early and the RAF aircraft might already be short of fuel, or back on the ground, by the time the raid came in. Too late and they would fail to disrupt the attack and expose themselves to being shot down by the escorts.

Once the aircraft were in place, the control passed to the pilots, as Squadron Leader Peter Devitt, sector controller at RAF Tangmere, explained. 'The controller controlled the aircraft once they got off the ground. I might be told by Group to get them up to a height of 18,000 feet over a certain place and to wait for further instructions. We used to get the further instructions and then we would tell the pilots where to go, what to expect and the number of German aircraft coming through. We were controlling them to get into the right position to attack the enemy. When I heard "Tally Ho!" from the pilots, I was finished with them and ready for anybody else going up.' [Devitt, recording]

Controllers also had to consider the limits of pilots and machines. Time was needed for men to recuperate and aircraft to be patched up. To manage this, commanders maintained their precious squadrons at various states of availability. 'Released' meant that, usually, they were free to leave the station for short periods. 'Available' required them to be ready to take

off at 10, 15, 30 or 60 minutes' notice. 'Readiness' demanded that they should be able to run to their aircraft to take off within five minutes. 'Readiness meant that you were sitting in the dispersal hut, togged up in your "Mae West" life vest, your aeroplane all ready for instant departure,' explained Flying Officer John Young of 249 Squadron. [Young, recording] 'The most stressful thing in the Battle of Britain was sitting at readiness waiting for the scramble telephone bell to ring,' said Sergeant Cyril 'Bam' Bamberger of 610 and 41 squadrons. 'I couldn't relax. You tried to read a book or you tried to play draughts or you pretended to doze. The phone would ring and immediately you jumped up but it was probably to say that the NAAFI van was coming with tea. Then you flopped back and tried to relax again.' [Bamberger, recording]

' "Standby" meant that you were sitting in the cockpit with your helmet on, your hood slid back, listening on the radio for start-up,' said Flying Officer John Young. From this state, the fighter should have been able to be airborne within two minutes.

On the wall of the sector and group ops rooms were slates with each squadron's ordered status marked, usually with coloured bulbs, as well as the number of aircraft each had operational.

LEFT
Members of the Women's Auxiliary Air Force and other staff at work in the operations room of Fighter Command HQ, Bentley Priory, Stanmore, overlooking London.

10 July 1940 WEDNESDAY ('THE FIRST DAY OF THE BATTLE')

Cloud and showers in the south.

As first light smudged the horizon on 10 July, the sky over the English Channel was cloaked in dense cloud. All along the clifftops, perched on sandbagged platforms, men and women of the Observer Corps peered into the swirling rain, searching for German aircraft. The likelihood was that, whatever the weather, sooner or later the Luftwaffe would appear. Events were settling into a routine. The previous ten days had seen more than a dozen raids, each of 50 or more aircraft. But history would judge this day to be special. It was the hour, historians would later decide, when the Battle of Britain proper began.

Above the heads of the Observer Corps, the fingers of Britain's radar stations probed the clouds, looking for enemy intruders. They were not long in finding one. It was the radar station at West Beckham on the Norfolk coast, part of the coastal Chain Home radar system, that picked up the first ominous blip on one of its small cathode-tube screens. The mechanisms of Britain's air defences clicked into action. At 7.30am, No. 66 Squadron based at Coltishall, Norfolk, received an order to 'scramble' and three of its Spitfires climbed into the wet skies. Led by Pilot Officer Charles Cooke, the section climbed fast through the rain and cloud, and then at about 10,000 feet broke through into brilliant sunshine. Cooke was given a vector bearing that led him to where the enemy aircraft was last spotted. At 8.15am the intruder came into view. It was a lone Dornier Do17 twin-engine bomber, probably on a reconnaissance mission to report back on the weather over the coast.

In one of the ineradicable images of the Battle of Britain, Hurricane pilots run to their aircraft after the call to scramble. It would be a scene repeated almost daily during the summer of 1940.

One by one, the Spitfires peeled off to attack. As they swooped down, the pilot of the Dornier threw his aircraft around the sky in a desperate effort to avoid the stream of incoming fire and to give his gunners a chance to shoot back. One bullet from the bomber's 7.9mm MG machine-guns hit Cooke's windscreen, flooding the cockpit with icy air. The Spitfires continued to harass the bomber until one fighter, attacking from underneath, raked the Dornier at close range with its eight Browning machine-guns. Smoke billowed from the bomber. It went into a banking turn, gliding steadily down until it struck the grey seas off Great Yarmouth and swiftly sank. None of the four-man crew survived, and the Spitfire section returned home to celebrate their success.

The German aeroplane had been one of several searching Britain's coastal waters for signs of convoys. That morning there were eight convoys at sea, slowly butting through the choppy waters, protected by naval escorts and the occasional fighter patrol.

The largest of the convoys, codenamed 'Bread', had set sail on the early morning tide from the Thames Estuary. At about 10am it rounded the North Foreland where it was spotted by another Dornier Do17 reconnaissance aircraft, this one guarded by about 30 Messerschmitt Me109 single-engine fighters.

continued on page 74

RAF Fighter Command Order of Battle *10 July 1940*

SECTOR	SQN	AIRCRAFT	BASED AT	COMMANDER
11 Group				
Biggin Hill	32	Hurricane	Biggin Hill	S/L John Worrall
	141	Defiant	Biggin Hill	S/L William Richardson
	610	Spitfire	Gravesend	S/L A.T. Smith
	600	Blenheim	Manston	S/L David Clark
North Weald	56	Hurricane	North Weald	S/L Minnie Manton
	151	Hurricane	North Weald	S/L Teddy Donaldson
	85	Hurricane	Martlesham	S/L Peter Townsend
	25	Blenheim	Martlesham	S/L K.A. McEwan
Kenley	64	Spitfire	Kenley	S/L N.C. Odbert
	615	Hurricane	Kenley	S/L Joseph Kayll
	111	Hurricane	Croydon	S/L John Thompson
	501	Hurricane	Croydon	S/L Harry Hogan
Hornchurch	65	Spitfire	Hornchurch	S/L Henry Sawyer
	74	Spitfire	Hornchurch	S/L Francis White
	54	Spitfire	Rochford	S/L James Leathart
Tangmere	43	Hurricane	Tangmere	S/L John Badger
	145	Hurricane	Tangmere	S/L John Peel
	601	Hurricane	Tangmere	S/L Max Aitken
Debden	17	Hurricane	Debden	S/L R.I.G. McDougal
Northolt	1	Hurricane	Northolt	S/L David Pemberton
	604	Blenheim	Northolt	S/L Michael Anderson
	257	Hurricane	Hendon	S/L H. Harkness
10 Group (Part of 11 Group until 21 July)				
Filton	92	Spitfire	Pembrey	S/L F.J. Saunders
	87	Hurricane	Exeter	S/L John Dewar
	213	Hurricane	Exeter	S/L H.D. McGregor
	234	Spitfire	St Eval	S/L R.E. Barnett
Middle Wallop	609	Spitfire	Middle Wallop	S/L Horace Darley
	238	Hurricane	Middle Wallop	S/L Harold Fenton
12 Group				
Duxford	264	Defiant	Duxford	S/L Philip Hunter
	19	Spitfire	Fowlmere	S/L Philip Pinkham
Coltishall	66	Spitfire	Coltishall	S/L Rupert Leigh
	242	Hurricane	Coltishall	S/L Douglas Bader
Kirton-in-Lindsey	222	Spitfire	Kirton	S/L H.W. Mermagen
Digby	46	Hurricane	Digby	F/L A.D. Murray
	611	Spitfire	Digby	S/L J. McComb
	29	Blenheim	Digby	F/L J.S. Adams
Wittering	229	Hurricane	Wittering	S/L H.J. McQuire
	266	Spitfire	Wittering	S/L R.L. Wilkinson
	23	Blenheim	Collyweston	S/L L.C. Bicknell
13 Group				
Church Fenton	73	Hurricane	Church Fenton	S/L J.W.C. More
	616	Spitfire	Church Fenton	S/L M. Robinson
	249	Hurricane	Leconfield	S/L John Grandy
Catterick	41	Spitfire	Catterick	S/L H. West
	219	Blenheim	Catterick	S/L J.H. Little
Usworth	607	Hurricane	Usworth	S/L J. Vick
	72	Spitfire	Acklington	S/L Ronald Lees
	152	Spitfire	Acklington	S/L Peter Devitt
Turnhouse	79	Hurricane	Turnhouse	S/L Hervey Heyworth
	253	Hurricane	Turnhouse	S/L Tom Gleave
	245	Hurricane	Turnhouse	S/L F.W. Whitley
	603	Spitfire	Turnhouse	S/L G. Denholm
	602	Spitfire	Drem	S/L Sandy Johnstone
	605	Hurricane	Drem	S/L W. Churchill
Dyce	263	Hurricane	Grangemouth	S/L H. Eeles
Wick	3	Hurricane	Wick	S/L S.F. Godden
	504	Hurricane	Castletown	S/L John Sample

Key S/L = Squadron Leader; F/L = Flight Lieutenant; W/C = Wing Commander

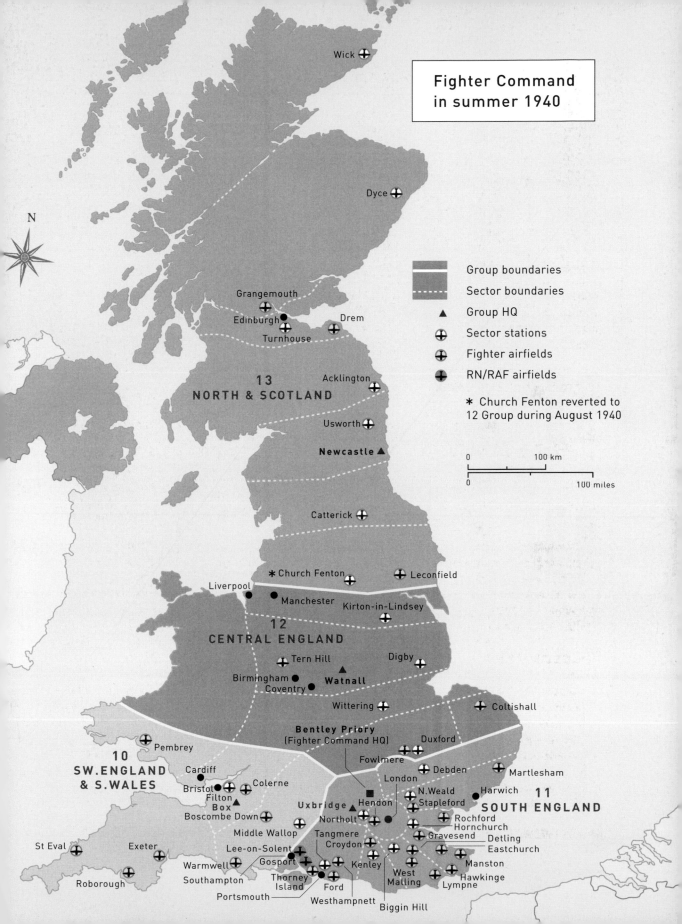

Fighter Command in summer 1940

N

Wick ✛

Dyce ✛

Grangemouth ✛
Edinburgh ● Drem ✛
Turnhouse ✛

Acklington ✛

13
NORTH & SCOTLAND

Usworth ✛

Newcastle ▲

Catterick ✛

✳ Church Fenton ✛   Leconfield ✛

Liverpool ● ● Manchester
Kirton-in-Lindsey ✛

12
CENTRAL ENGLAND

Tern Hill ✛   Digby ✛

Birmingham ● **Watnall** ▲
Coventry ●

Wittering ✛   Coltishall ✛

Bentley Priory
(Fighter Command HQ)   Duxford ✛

Pembrey ✛   Fowlmere ✛

10   Cardiff ●   Debden ✛   Martlesham ✛
SW.ENGLAND   Colerne ✛   London
& S.WALES   Bristol ●   N.Weald ✛   Harwich ●
Filton ✛   Stapleford ✛   **11**
Box ▲   **Uxbridge** ▲ Hendon ■   **SOUTH ENGLAND**
Boscombe Down ✛   Northolt ✛   Rochford ✛
Middle Wallop ✛   Hornchurch ✛
Tangmere ✛   Gravesend ✛   Detling ✛
St Eval ✛   Exeter ✛   Croydon ✛   Eastchurch ✛
Lee-on-Solent ✛   Kenley ✛   Manston ✛
Warmwell ✛   Gosport ●   West   Hawkinge ✛
Southampton   Thorney   Malling ✛   Lympne ✛
Roborough ✛   Island ● Ford ●
Portsmouth   Westhampnett ✛   Biggin Hill ✛

▬	Group boundaries
┈	Sector boundaries
▲	Group HQ
✛	Sector stations
✛	Fighter airfields
✛	RN/RAF airfields

✳ Church Fenton reverted to
12 Group during August 1940

0 ————— 100 km
0 ————— 100 miles

In Paul Nash's deceptively calm painting *The Raider on the Shore* (1940), a spirit of resistance is evoked in the contrast between the fragile remains of a Messerschmitt Me109 and the solidity of Dover's white cliffs.

As the Germans radioed back the position of a tempting target, six Spitfires, alerted by radar, were racing to the scene from Manston airfield, Kent, the nearest Fighter Command station. At just before 11am, battle was joined. The 74 Squadron Spitfires headed straight for the Dornier. The escorting fighters were waiting, however, and turned fast behind them, opening fire and damaging two of the attackers. The British pilots held their course, concentrating on the Dornier, scoring hits on the cockpit and setting it on fire. But soon the 109s were on top of them and the battle turned into a series of wheeling dogfights that drifted over the genteel Kent seaside town of Margate. The Dornier managed to limp away back across the Channel carrying one dead crewman and several injured, before crash-landing near Boulogne. One of the Me109s was hit but not badly damaged, and the rest escaped unscathed. The two Spitfires damaged during the first moments of the attack both managed to return to Manston. Their aircraft were just repairable, the pilots shaken but unhurt.

Meanwhile pressure was mounting elsewhere. At almost exactly the time that the Spitfires of 74 Squadron were clashing with the Dornier and its escorts, the order to scramble had been given at Biggin Hill. Radar plots and Observer Corps reports had shown a *Staffel* of Me109s – about a dozen aircraft, the equivalent of a British fighter squadron – roaring over Dover, searching for targets of opportunity. Nine Spitfires of 610 Squadron took off and raced to intercept. Combat was brief and inconclusive; one Spitfire was shot down and the raiders escaped unharmed.

The convoys were not the Germans' only targets that morning. Seventy German bombers, flying in from the west and taking the radar stations by surprise, attacked Swansea, killing thirty people and damaging ships, railways, a power station and a munitions factory. The shift of direction delayed Fighter Command's response, and when No. 92 Squadron, based in Pembrey in South Wales, was ordered to scramble, the planes arrived to find the raiders had gone. The appearance of the bombers provoked Wing Commander Ira Jones, a veteran of the First World War Flying Corps, to fly to the defence of his native Wales. He was in charge of the training airfield at Stormy Down, and he seized a Hawker Henley 'target tug' (a light bomber now used for towing targets for shooting practice) to take to the air and pursue a German Ju88 bomber. His sole weapon, however, was a Verey signal pistol, which failed to make any impression on the raider.

The main fighting of the day was focused on the Bread convoy. Although the Dornier reconnaissance aeroplane had been damaged, it had still been able to report the whereabouts of the ships. At 1.30pm, radar picked up an ominously heavy enemy build-up over the Pas de Calais. Twenty minutes later the sky above the convoy was crowded with hostile aircraft – a swarm of 26 Dornier Do17s, operating as bombers rather than reconnaissance aircraft, shielded by nearly 40 Me110 fighter-bombers and some 24 Me109s. The convoy's aerial protection amounted to a mere six Hurricanes from No. 32 Squadron. Mistaking the twin-engine Me110s for Do17s, the British pilots reported 'sixty Dorniers' and called for help. Among the first to arrive were the Hurricanes of 111 Squadron, who brought with them their own unique approach to tackling the bombers. With the entire formation flying abreast in a shallow V-shaped 'vic', the squadron headed at full speed head on into the German bomber pack. For those conducting the attack it was an extraordinarily risky tactic, but it delivered a devastating effect. 'You could see the front of the aircraft crumple,' said 111 Squadron pilot Ben Bowring. Pilots observed the panic-stricken bomber crews rearing up from their seats and stumbling backwards to try to avoid the blast of bullets. The aircraft were forced to break their tight self-defending formations and veer off course, missing their aim and making them easier prey for the British fighters. Inevitably there were collisions. Flying Officer Tom Higgs, aged 23, was still firing when he clipped his target Dornier. With one wing missing, the Hurricane span seawards, closely followed by the wrecked German bomber. Higgs seems to have baled out, but the launch that rescued the Dornier pilot and another member of his crew could find no sign of Higgs, nor of the two other Germans. Higgs's body eventually washed up on the Dutch coast at Noordwijk more than a month later.

By now the 'scramble' order had gone out to five Fighter Command airfields. German bombers had not been seen in such numbers before. At Fighter Command HQ, at Bentley Priory, the realization was growing that the Luftwaffe effort had moved to a higher and more dangerous tempo.

Soon, a huge dogfight developed over the Bread convoy, with more than 100 aircraft looping and circling, climbing and diving. High above, the Spitfires concentrated on their counterparts, the Messerschmitt Me109s, driving them away from their charges, letting the slower and less nimble Hurricanes in to harry the bomber formations and the sluggish Me110s. It was a Spitfire, though, flown by Flying Officer John Mungo-Park, which scored the first hit on a Dornier. Mungo-Park, slim

'Nothing between himself and the guns'

Flying Officer Brian Kingcome of No. 92 Squadron testified to the intimidatory effect of mounting a head-on fighter attack.

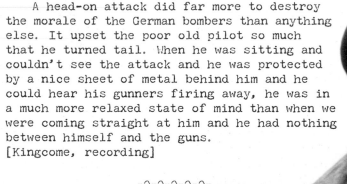

```
    A head-on attack did far more to destroy
the morale of the German bombers than anything
else. It upset the poor old pilot so much
that he turned tail. When he was sitting and
couldn't see the attack and he was protected
by a nice sheet of metal behind him and he
could hear his gunners firing away, he was in
a much more relaxed state of mind than when we
were coming straight at him and he had nothing
between himself and the guns.
[Kingcome, recording]


             -0-0-0-0-0-
```

and dark-haired, who was later regarded by his comrades as encapsulating the humour, courage and modesty of the Battle of Britain pilots, described watching the bomber 'turn lazily on its back and dive into the sea'.

Now that every fighter pilot was on his own, coordination became impossible, with the radio jammed by excited voices. Flying Officer Henry Ferriss, a little short of his 23rd birthday but already an experienced fighter pilot, arrived at the scene in his Hurricane as the second wave of German bombers prepared their attack on the convoy. 'It was a thrilling sight I must confess,' he told a BBC radio interviewer later. 'I looked down on the tiny ships below and saw two long lines of broken water where the first lot of bombs had fallen ... Just ahead were fountains of water leaping skywards from bombs newly dropped. In a second or two the sea down below spouted up to the height of about fifty feet or more in two lines alongside the convoy.' Ferris led his flight in an attack on the second wave of Dorniers. 'We went screaming down and pumped lead into our targets. We shook them up quite a bit.' Although neither side had gained the upper hand in the fighter dogfight, the bombing formation was starting to break up. After further damaging a stricken Dornier from the first wave, Ferriss chased a Messerschmitt Me109 far out to sea. 'He was going very fast, and I had to do 400 miles an hour to catch him up. Then, before I could fire, he flattened out to no more than fifty feet above the sea level, and went streaking for home.' But Ferriss stayed on his tail and got in five short bursts, 'all aimed very deliberately. Suddenly the Messerschmitt's port wing dropped down. The starboard wing went up, and then in a flash his nose went down

Brian Kingcome, wearing his 'Mae West' (lifejacket).

and he was gone. He simply vanished into the sea.' Just then Ferriss felt a sharp stinging sensation in his leg, and knew he had been hit. 'There were some Messerschmitt 109s right on my tail … I did a quick turn and made for home, but it wasn't quite so easy as that.' Ferriss's port aileron had been damaged, and his engine was running rough. There followed a 20-mile pursuit back to the English coast, with Ferriss throwing his Hurricane to the right each time the Me109s caught up with him and opened fire. As the beaches came into view, the pursuers turned back, and Ferriss managed to land his damaged plane. Almost immediately he 'got a fresh Hurricane, and rejoined my squadron before going on another patrol'. [Ferriss extracts, in *Winged Words*, pp. 50–2] Ferriss, who had been a medical student before joining the RAF in 1937, would be one of the victims of No. 111 Squadron's aggressive, front-on tactics. He was killed on 16 August in a collision with a Dornier Do17.

In happier times, Warmwell airbase was a place for public air shows, such as this 'Empire Air Day' on 20 May 1939. A little over a year later, it was at the frontline of Britain's air struggle.

One further Hurricane was hit that day, but also made it down safely. The Germans lost four aircraft, and several limped back with dead and dying on board. One hundred and fifty bombs had been dropped, but the attack had been successfully broken up. Only one ship in the convoy was struck.

Thus ended the first day of the Battle of Britain. It had been a good one for the RAF. The results seemed to endorse the soundness of the defensive preparations that had been made. The head of Fighter Command, Air Chief Marshal Dowding, judged that 'for this victory, we must thank the radar which placed us in readiness and allowed us to send our fighter squadrons out to meet them'. Looking back to the start of the summer, he comforted himself with the thought that the RAF had learned lessons from its bruising encounters with the Luftwaffe during the German surge westwards, achieving a kind of 'maturity'.

11 July 1940 THURSDAY

Overcast in the south; thunder with sunny spells elsewhere.

Early on Thursday morning, radar reported a formation approaching a convoy off the Dorset coast. No. 501 Squadron, patrolling above the vessels, was vectored to intercept, but before it reached the ten or so Ju87 Stuka dive-bombers, they were attacked by escorting Me109 fighters, with one Spitfire shot down. The pilot, 21-year-old Sergeant Frederick Dixon, baled out, only to drown before he could be rescued.

In the meantime, 609 Squadron had been scrambled to help. The unit was an Auxiliary squadron, drawn originally from the West Riding of Yorkshire, one of the 12 Auxiliary squadrons created in 1936 to boost the number of pilots available to the RAF. No. 609 Squadron had been blooded over Dunkirk, where it had lost six of its pilots, and with them much of its territorial identity. The vigorous leadership of a regular RAF officer, Squadron Leader H.S. 'George' Darley, had restored shattered morale, and on 9 July the squadron had moved from Middle Wallop,

ALBERT BALL, FIGHTER ACE

Albert Ball looked like a dreamer, but his lethal efficiency made him a legend in the skies over Flanders in 1916–17.

The culture of fighter 'aces' was born during the First World War in the skies over the trenches of Flanders. Many Battle of Britain pilots had been brought up on the exploits of such famous air warriors as Albert Ball (1896–1917) and Edward 'Mick' Mannock (1887–1918), whose spirit permeated the 0culture of Fighter Command. These characters were adventurous, dashing and independent-minded to the point of eccentricity, and their feats seemed to belong to the era of knightly combat rather than to the ghastly industrial warfare being waged in the trenches.

Albert Ball was brought up in a middle-class home in Nottingham. His father had started his life as a plumber but rose to be mayor of the city. Albert initially joined the infantry, but while waiting to be sent to France took private flying lessons, which propelled him into the Royal Flying Corps (RFC). He was posted to France as a lieutenant in the RFC at the time of the Somme offensive. A solitary figure, he had no interest in the cameraderie of the mess or the attractions of local women, preferring to spend hours playing the violin or chatting with his aeroplane's riggers and fixers, making endless adjustments to improve its efficiency. He would go up alone, and he soon adopted an effective, but highly dangerous, tactic of flying directly at packs of enemy aircraft, getting as near as he could before firing off his Lewis gun at close range. 'He had but one idea,' said a fellow pilot, Roderic Hill. 'That was to kill as many Huns as possible.' [Quoted in Bowyer, pp. 32ff.] But in a letter home he described his wish to 'leave all this beastly killing for a time'. His courage and aggression quickly made him a hero to the younger pilots, although, as one commented, 'one felt that it could only be a matter of time before he "bought it", as he was shot about so often'. By the end of 1916 he was the most famous pilot in the RFC and was taken off operations. He was invited to breakfast by the prime minister and showered with attention and honours, but, finding life away from the front difficult, he was soon agitating to return to action. Ball's aircraft crashed during combat in May 1917, killing him. He was awarded, posthumously, the Victoria Cross.

Hampshire, to a satellite station at Warmwell, Dorset, nearer the coast. The main role of the station was to help protect Portland naval base, which had been hit in the 4 July incident. So, by 11 July the airfield had only just become operational and conditions were spartan. It was described by one of its flight lieutenants, John Dundas, as 'possessing the two chief characteristics of a forward station – action and discomfort'. [Quoted in Ziegler, p. 116] There was no running water or sanitation, and the pilots were forced to sleep in the dispersal tent. It was very

THE AUXILIARY AIR FORCE
AND THE RAF VOLUNTEER RESERVE

The Auxiliary Air Force (AAF) was set up in 1924, with its first four squadrons formed the following year – No. 600 (City of London), No. 601 (County of London), No. 602 (City of Glasgow) and No. 603 (City of Edinburgh). Applicants were required to have learned to fly, which was expensive, and so the first Auxiliary squadrons were socially rather exclusive, in spite of Chief of the Air Staff Hugh Trenchard's wish that the ranks be open to all. Legend had it that 601, which became known as the 'Millionaires' Squadron', was founded at the ultra-exclusive White's club by the son of the Duke of Westminster. The scheme was enlarged as part of the expansion announced in 1934, and the Auxiliary pilots switched to fighter planes. By the time of the Battle of Britain, there were 21 Auxiliary squadrons, making up a quarter of Fighter Command's strength. The high number of casualties in the early period of the battle meant that they gradually lost their tight social cohesion.

In marked contrast, the Royal Air Force Volunteer Reserve (RAFVR), launched in 1936, had a reputation as a more egalitarian and democratic organization. This inspired creation gave adventurous, 'air-minded' young men, many of them doing dull jobs in offices and factories, the chance to learn to fly in their spare time, at no cost. Men aged between 18 and 25 joined as 'airmen under training', and they received commissions only on merit. The aim of the RAFVR was to train 800 airmen a year. Volunteers received £25 per year in pay and had to attend an annual 15-day flying course. By spring 1939, there were 2500 RAFVR pilots in training, and 310 in Fighter Command when war broke out. They would play an essential role in the Battle of Britain, as pilots from the regular pre-war RAF fell from the skies in the first months of the fighting.

A Hurricane of 601 'Millionaires' Squadron' is serviced at Exeter. The City of London Auxiliary squadron upgraded from Bristol Blenheims to Hurricanes in March 1940.

GRAND TOTAL [Cols. (1) to (10)]

.................Hrs.................Mins.

TOTALS CARRIED FORWAR

dry and the tent would become filled with dust and stones whenever an aircraft passed nearby.

Six 609 Spitfires from Warmwell arrived just as the Stukas were preparing to dive on the convoy. One section went for the bombers, while the other tried to hold off the escort. Although the convoy escaped serious damage, the encounter was otherwise a disaster for 609 Squadron. Facing odds of six-to-one, it failed to hit any of the German attackers, but lost two Spitfires and with them two pilots. Flight Lieutenant 'Pip' Barran was one of the squadron's founder members, a son of wealthy Yorkshire colliery owners and universally liked and respected. The other casualty was Pilot Officer Gordon Mitchell, another popular figure. The squadron was shaken and angry. David Crook, another 609 pilot officer, had been at school and university with Mitchell and felt his loss deeply. 'I just could not get used to the idea that we would not see him again,' he wrote later. 'He was a delightful person, a very amusing and charming companion and one of the most generous people. He was also a brilliant athlete, a Cambridge hockey blue and Scots international. He played any game with natural grace and ease.'

Others wondered whether the convoys they were laying down their lives to protect were actually necessary. 'They could have stopped at Plymouth or somewhere and put all their stuff on a train. But they went on and on with these convoys,' said 609 pilot John Bisdee. [Quoted in Parker, p. 140] David Crook summed up the emotions of the shattered squadron after the action. 'It is difficult to describe my feelings during the next few days. We had just lost three pilots in thirty-six hours, all of them in fights in which we had been hopelessly out-numbered, and I felt that there was now nothing left to care about, because obviously from the law of probability, one could not expect to survive many more encounters of a similar nature.' [Crook, p. 32]

Through the morning of 11 July, all three German *Luftflotten* sent reconnaissance aircraft, eighty in number, over British coastal waters, from the tip of Cornwall to the north of Scotland. Several were intercepted and shot down, including one by Squadron Leader Douglas Bader. Bader had lost both his legs in a flying accident in the 1930s and been invalided out of the RAF. Once equipped with artificial legs, he resumed flying, overcoming strong official opposition. He took part in the actions over Dunkirk, shooting down a Messerschmitt Me109 on 1 June. He was subsequently given command of 242 Squadron, made up mainly of Canadian pilots, and imposed forceful discipline. The Dornier Do17 he downed on 11 July was his first kill of the Battle of Britain.

Experience such as Bader possessed was undoubtedly a huge help in staying alive and scoring victories, but it was no guarantee of success. The highly skilled Squadron Leader Peter Townsend of 85 Squadron, who back in February had taken part in the downing of the first German bomber to be brought down on British soil since the First World War, was on a lone patrol near Harwich when he came across a Dornier Do17. As he went into the attack, his engine was hit by one of the bomber's gunners, and he was forced to bale out, to be picked up by a trawler 20 minutes later (see page 84).

The weather remained clearest in the west, and here the Germans struck again, with a force of two *Staffeln* of Ju87 Stukas, accompanied by about 40 Me110s, appearing over Portland at about 11am. It was fortunate timing for the attackers

continued on page 85

A vivid view from a tanker of a night-time convoy
under attack, painted by the official Ministry of Information
artist Roy Nockolds (1911–79), who served in the RAF during the war.

Roy Nockolds
1942

'DIVING VERTICALLY TOWARDS THE SEA'

T...... B.OUGHT FORWARD

Peter Townsend (*right, standing*), then a flight lieutenant with No. 43 Squadron, chats with groundcrew seated on his Hurricane, in spring 1940. He became No. 85's squadron leader in late May 1940.

Squadron Leader Peter Townsend of No. 85 Squadron (in later years to be the royal equerry and suitor of Princess Margaret) described his narrow escape from a watery tomb in the North Sea off Harwich on 11 July 1940: 'I was at 8000 feet and still climbing in and out of grey soggy rain clouds. Below yawned a dark, blue-grey void and somewhere at its bottom the sea. Suddenly an aircraft appeared out of the cloud above, going the other way. A Dornier 17!' Townsend wheeled his Hurricane round, craning his head backwards, his eyes riveted on the German bomber. But he felt 'enormously visible', and could only dimly see the Dornier through his rain-lashed windscreen. He opened the hood and slanted his head out into the battering slipstream to get a better view.

Then he was spotted. '*Achtung, Jäger!*' went the shout inside the bomber. The rear gunner, Werner Borner, spotted the Hurricane and opened fire. Townsend pressed closer and then hit the fire button. Suddenly 'pieces of metal and other fragments were flying everywhere', said Borner. Leutnant Berchein, on the starboard rear gun of the German plane, was hit in the head and slumped to the floor of the cabin.

Moments later, Feldwebel (Sergeant) Lohrer collapsed on top of him, hit in the head and throat. The bomber was now awash with blood. But Borner continued firing as the Hurricane came so close that he could see the pilot. 'I was still firing when suddenly there was a bright orange explosion in the cockpit in front of me,' says Townsend. 'The engine was hit.' As he glided down through the rain clouds, Townsend attempted to radio his position. There was no ship in sight. 'Now only two things mattered, life and death.' Townsend dived out head first and then pulled the rip cord. 'Far below I could see my Hurricane diving vertically towards the sea to disappear in an eruption of spume and spray.' He hit the water. 'When the big splash came I hit the harness release knob and sank, it seemed fathoms deep, into green obscurity … when at last I broke the surface I saw a little ship lying less than a mile away.' The ship, the trawler *Cap Finisterre*, lowered a boat that was soon alongside the downed pilot. One of the sailors was brandishing a boat hook. 'Blimey, if he ain't a fucking Hun!' he shouted. 'I'm not,' replied Townsend. 'I'm a fucking Englishman!' [All quotations in Townsend, *Duel of Eagles*, pp. 298–301]

as almost all the fighters in the Middle Wallop sector were on the ground refuelling. So six Hurricanes of 601 Squadron were sent from Tangmere, more than 50 miles away. They nonetheless arrived in time to disperse the raid and to down two of the Me110s. The squadron was in action again at 5.15pm, breaking up a smaller raid on the naval base at Portsmouth. Two Heinkel He111s were destroyed when they collided, and a third was badly damaged. One of the Hurricanes, however, was shot down by fire from anti-aircraft guns on the Isle of Wight.

By now the Spitfires of No. 54 Squadron had been allocated a gruelling routine, which meant leaving at first light from RAF Rochford, Essex, to the forward base at Manston, Kent. Late in the day on 11 July, two sections of 54 Squadron Spitfires, led by flight lieutenants Al Deere and Johnny Allen, were sent to investigate activity five miles east of Deal. It was Deere's fourth sortie of the day. 'We had just crossed the coast at a height of 1,500 feet when I spotted an aircraft flying at wave top height.' It was a Heinkel He59 seaplane, with Red Cross markings. The Luftwaffe had lost six aircraft into the waters of the Channel that day and was hoping to pick up survivors. Deere was wondering what to do when the voice of Flight Lieutenant Johnny Allen 'burst though on the R/T [radio telephone]. "Red Leader there are about a dozen 109s flying in loose formation, well behind and slightly above the seaplane." "Thanks, Johnny," Deere replied, "That makes the seaplane enemy as far as I am concerned."'

While Allen's 'Yellow' section went for the seaplane, Deere led his own section against the escort, banking around to get behind them. But as the section levelled out behind the Me109s, it was spotted, and at once the enemy formation split in two, each breaking upwards in a steep turn, one half to the left, one to the right. Although outnumbered six-to-one, the Spitfires attacked, breaking formation, each pilot choosing his target. Deere managed to fasten onto the tail of one of the yellow-nosed Messerschmitts and opened fire. 'There was an immediate response from my eight Brownings which, to the accompaniment of a slight bucketing from my aircraft, spat a stream of lethal lead targetwards,' he wrote. But just as he saw his bullets strike home, he spotted Me109s on his tail. 'I broke hard into the attack, pulling my Spitfire into a climbing, spiralling turn as I did so.' The action was gratifyingly effective. 'The Messerschmitts literally "fell out of the sky" as they stalled in an attempt to follow me.' [Deere, p. 90]

Deere was aware that at least one of the squadron's Spitfires had gone down in flames – he heard Allen's number two 'screaming for help over the R/T'; but Deere now fastened onto a new target, an Me109 turning to re-enter the fray. The German spotted him almost immediately 'and rolled out of his turn towards me so that a head-on attack became inevitable. Using both hands on the control column to steady the aircraft ... I peered through the reflector sight at the rapidly closing enemy aircraft. We opened fire

Hurricanes from No. 111 Squadron, based at the time at Northolt, almost touch wings as they fly in 1940. Great emphasis was placed on formation-flying in the years before the war, but it had little use in the battles to come.

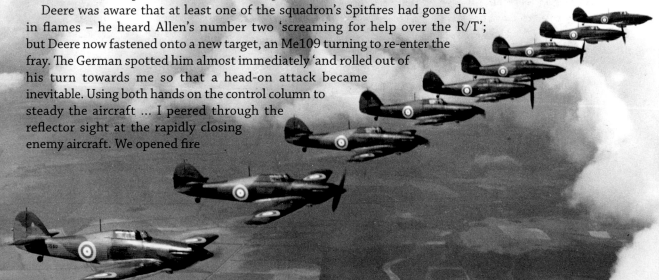

together, and immediately a hail of lead thudded into my Spitfire. One moment the Messerschmitt was a clearly defined shape, its wingspan nicely enclosed within the circle of my reflector sight, and the next it was on top of me, a terrifying blur which blotted out the sky ahead. Then we hit.'

The New Zealander Alan Deere (*right*) had an exhausting and danger-filled summer with No. 54 Squadron. He related his eventful war in his autobiography, *Nine Lives* (1959).

Deere was catapulted forwards. He realized immediately that his Spitfire was terminally damaged. He was amazed to be still alive. The engine, now on fire, vibrated wildly, throwing the control column around the cockpit. Then it abruptly stopped. He could see that the propeller blades had been 'bent almost double with the impact of the collision'. 'With smoke now pouring into the cockpit I reached blindly forward for the emergency hood release toggle and tugged at it violently.' But there was no welcoming rush of cold air into the cockpit, and the normal release catch did not work either. Gathering his strength, struggling to stay calm, Deere steered his now powerless aircraft into a glide towards the coast. With eyes streaming from the smoke, he peered forward, searching for open space in which to crash-land. 'Through a ... cloud of flame and smoke the ground suddenly appeared ahead of me. The next moment a post flashed by my wingtip and then the aircraft struck the ground and ricocheted into the air again finally returning to earth with a jarring impact.' The aircraft ploughed through a succession of wooden posts, driven into the open ground to deter German landings, before at last coming to a rest. 'With my bare hands wielding the strength of desperation, I battered at the Perspex hood which entombed me. With a splintering crash it finally cracked open.' Deere scrambled to a safe distance as his aircraft, enveloped by flames, started giving off a series of explosions. 'My hands were cut and bleeding,' he wrote, 'my eyebrows singed; both knees were badly bruised; and blood trickled into my mouth from a slightly cut lip. But I was alive!'

Others had been less lucky. The squadron had two Spitfires shot down during the fight with the seaplane escort. Neither pilot escaped his burning cockpit.

12 July 1940 FRIDAY

Foggy start over Channel; cloudy elsewhere.

Friday dawned grey and wet, but the pattern of attacks continued, with raids on convoys, this time concentrated off the east coast, together with small, scattered actions across the whole front. The heaviest fighting took place over a convoy codenamed 'Booty' as it steamed southwards off Harwich. A flight of six aircraft from No. 17 Squadron was patrolling overhead, and when the Germans arrived further fighters were scrambled from Nos 85, 242, 264 and 151 squadrons. The RAF lost two aircraft in the fighting, with both pilots – L. Jowitt and New Zealander J.H.L Allen – killed. Five Luftwaffe bombers were put out of action, either shot down or crash-landing on return to their bases. Deterioration in the weather kept further heavy German raids at bay.

SATURDAY **13 July 1940**

*Early fog in
southern parts,
clearing mid-morning.*

The weather was even worse on the Saturday, with fog over the Channel, which initially hampered both the rival air forces. But convoys were still shadowed by high-flying reconnaissance aircraft, and, as the sky cleared during the day, the Germans returned to the attack. Shortly before 3pm, elements of the two squadrons now roughing it at the forward base at Warmwell, Dorset, were scrambled to intercept

---

'At their own risk and peril'

A service was inaugurated by the Germans during the early part of the war to rescue airmen downed over the sea, using Heinkel He59 and Dornier Do18 seaplanes, which operated from bases in Norway, Denmark, Belgium and along the French coast. However, although these aircraft were painted white and adorned with numerous red crosses, they also often carried armaments and were observed carrying out reconnaissance tasks. The British government duly gave warning in a communiqué of 14 July that such planes would be considered legitimate targets.

```
    Enemy aircraft bearing civil markings and marked with the Red Cross
have recently flown over British ships at sea and in the vicinity of
the British coast, and they are being employed for purposes which
His Majesty's Government cannot regard as being consistent with the
privileges generally accorded to the Red Cross.
    His Majesty's Government desire to accord to ambulance aircraft
reasonable facilities for the transportation of the sick and wounded,
in accordance with the Red Cross Convention, and aircraft engaged in
the direct evacuation of the sick and wounded will be respected, provided
that they comply with the relevant provisions of the Convention.
    His Majesty's Government are unable, however, to grant immunity to
such aircraft flying over areas in which operations are in progress
on land or at sea, or approaching British or Allied territory, or
territory in British occupation, or British or Allied ships.
    Ambulance aircraft which do not comply with the above
requirements will do so at their own risk and peril.
```

-0-0-0-0-0-

The caption of this published German photograph, showing a Heinkel He59 seaplane wearing its Red Cross livery, complained that the aircraft were being 'shot at by English gentlemen …'.

an incoming raid on a convoy off Lyme Regis. Three Spitfires from 609 Squadron and twelve Hurricanes of 238 Squadron took off and roared into a steep climb. The latter squadron had been battered over France. It had been reinforced with a wave of new pilots, including Sergeant Eric Seabourne, who was setting off on his first combat. He had received little preparation for the test ahead. Before taking off he had only spent seven hours at the controls of a Hurricane.

The British fighters met the 50-strong attacking formation before either side reached the convoy. A flight of No. 238 Squadron, led by the Australian Flight Lieutenant John Kennedy, swooped on some straggling Dorniers, while the flight containing Seabourne squared up to the accompanying Me110s, which now formed themselves into a defensive ring. This manoeuvre, much practised by Me110 pilots, was known in the Luftwaffe as a 'death circle'. Each aircraft followed the one in front, rotating over a fixed point, thereby giving the rear gunners the best chance of providing defensive fire-power, while each fighter protected the tail of the one in front. This time, though, the attack by Seabourne's flight managed to break up the formation.

Moments later one of the German planes swooped down just above his cockpit. 'It was pale blue underneath,' Seabourne remembered, 'with black crosses on the wings, so I thought, it's not one of ours, and pressed the gun button and gave it a good blast. As I did so another appeared and I did the same again. They clearly took objection to this because then large holes started appearing in my port mainframe and I could feel bullets hitting the armour plating behind my seat.' Seabourne threw his Hurricane into a steep vertical dive. For a few seconds it did not seem that he could get out of it, as he tugged and heaved at the control column. Then, 'very slowly I started winding the tail trim back, something we had been told never to do. But it worked and I came out in a beautiful, gentle curve and I was again flying straight and level.' [Quoted in Parker, p. 154]

When Seabourne got back to Middle Wallop, his engineer expressed his amazement that the wing hadn't been pulled off in the dive, as two armour-piercing bullets had lodged in the main spar. He would not be the last pilot to be thankful for the Hurricane's rugged construction, which allowed it to sustain far more damage than the Spitfire or Me109 and still stay in the air. John Kennedy, who had shot down one of his target Dorniers over Chesil Beach, Dorset, and damaged another, must have sustained battle damage during the combat. Returning to the airfield, he crashed and was killed. Seabourne's reaction to the loss was less emotional than that expressed by David Crook over the loss of his friend Gordon Mitchell two days previously. It would be echoed many times in the months ahead, as the pilots learned to contain and suppress their responses to the violent deaths of comrades. 'It was just hard luck. You were all right and he wasn't. There simply wasn't the time to grieve. You registered – Oh God, that's awful – but then you had to get on.' [Quoted in Parker]

The haemorrhaging of experienced and aggressive pilots like Kennedy would now come to pose a serious threat to the effectiveness of Fighter Command. The aircraft factories were pumping out planes. But men were harder to replace. In the first two weeks of July, thirty-one of the country's 'fighter boys' had been killed. That was a significant figure given that there had been only 1104 trained pilots available at the start of the month and the fighting had clearly hardly begun. On 10 July the training

TRAINING THE PILOTS

Chief of the Air Staff Sir Hugh Trenchard had insisted that the RAF have its own independent training schools, and in 1920 a cadet college opened at Cranwell in Lincolnshire to provide a core of permanent officers. Selection criteria were stringent, and most recruits were from the public schools.

To provide a stream of skilled mechanics, riggers and fitters, Trenchard established a training school at Halton Park in Hertfordshire. Here, boys would serve a three-year apprenticeship before joining the ranks. The best three apprentices from each year were offered places at Cranwell.

In late 1921 it was announced that outstanding candidates from the ranks would also be offered the chance to learn to fly, serving for five years as sergeant pilots before returning to their trades. This created a new class of educated 'other ranks', for the first time in British military history.

Before the expansion plan of 1934, all pilots and crew were trained by the RAF, but as the numbers increased it became necessary to farm out the basic aviation training to civilian flying schools, 13 of which were operational by 1936. New pilots trained in two-seaters, Avro Tutors or De Havilland Tiger Moths, and during a course lasting between eight and twelve weeks pupils were taken through twenty-two different stages, from the first 'air experience' though to aerobatics, flying blind and recovering from a spin. Those without a natural feel for flying were 'washed out'. Those who were successful proceeded to the RAF Depot at Uxbridge, where for two weeks they drilled, trained and learned the customs of the air force.

This phase was followed by a six-week stint at an operation training unit (OTU), where the pilots would, in theory, fly the aircraft they would fight in and practise formation flying and combat tactics. Three new OTUs were set up after the losses of May and June 1940, which, from 10 July, rushed pilots through this last stage in just two weeks. But such was the pressure for new pilots that by the middle of the summer many were skipping the OTU stage altogether and posted to squadrons straight from flying school. Some novice fighter pilots fired their aircraft's guns for the first time when they were in actual combat.

BELOW An RAF recruiting poster. Volunteers often wanted to be glamorous fighter pilots, but after 1940 most vacancies were with Bomber Command.

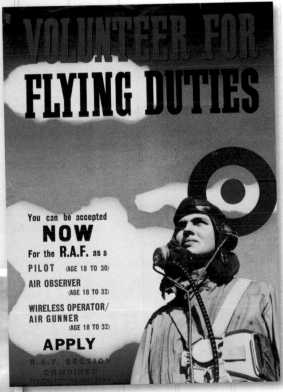

LEFT A Harvard aircraft of No. 2 Service Flying Training School, based at Brize Norton, in Oxfordshire, flies with its undercarriage down (17 July 1940).

Luftwaffe aircraft deployed *July 1940*

The following types and number of German aircraft were deployed during July 1940, and there were an additional 220 aircraft with *Luftflotte 5* in Norway and Denmark. Because of disruption caused by redeployment, still going on well into July, only about half the numbers below were combat ready.

Bombers (Heinkel He111s, Dornier Do17s, Junkers Ju88s)	1200
Ju87 Stuka dive-bombers	280
Messerschmitt Me109 single-engine fighters	760
Messerschmitt Me110 twin-engine fighters	220
Long-range reconnaissance aircraft	
(Dornier Do17s, Heinkel He111s, Messerschmitt Me110s, Junkers Ju88s)	50
Short-range reconnaissance aircraft (Henschel Hs126s)	90
Total aircraft	**2600**

–0–0–0–0–0–

period had been drastically truncated from six months to four weeks and there would be many novices like Eric Seabourne with only a handful of hours' experience in 'Spits' or 'Hurris' arriving fresh at squadrons throughout the rest of the battle.

On the afternoon of 13 July, the Luftwaffe's strength was again thrown against a Channel target. Just to the east of where 238 Squadron had fought off the morning attack, another convoy was risking the Dover Straits, within sight of German observation posts on the Pas de Calais coast. This time the attack was by a *Staffel* of Stuka dive-bombers, with at least three *Staffeln* of Me109s and Me110s circling high above. Eleven Hurricanes from No. 56 Squadron were on patrol between Calais and Dover, and they intercepted the raid at around 4pm. While some made for the dive-bombers, blasting them at short range before the escort could intervene, others peeled off to attack the German fighters, climbing as fast as they could. By the time the latter made contact, 'our three Hurricanes had managed to climb above the level of the twin-engine Me110s, but we were still below the single-seater Me109s,' wrote 56-Squadron fighter pilot Geoffrey Page. Then, led by Flight Lieutenant Edward 'Jumbo' Gracie, the section swooped into the attack, forcing the Me110s into a defensive circle. 'Being uncertain as to the best way to assail this orbiting group,' wrote Page, 'I decided to spray the area near two of the enemy before diving through the centre of the circle. The eight Browning machine-guns chattered away happily in the wings.' Page ducked his head as the return fire came in, which he described as 'orange glowing electric bulbs suspended in the air', before finding himself through the lethal zone. He climbed again and attacked from the other side, but to no visible effect except for a loosening of the formation. Then he found the Me109s on him.

'At that point the fight became a nightmare ... for the next few minutes I registered nothing but flashing wings bearing iron crosses and streaks of tracer searing the sunlit sky.' Then, as so often happened, suddenly the sky was clear, 'as if the hand of God has wiped the slate clean'. Moments later, Page spotted a lone Messerschmitt Me109 circling towards him. He turned his aircraft and the two sped towards each other in a frontal attack. 'Winking lights appeared on the leading edge of the enemy's wing.' Page returned fire. 'Both our aircraft roared by within inches of each other.' [Page, pp. 48ff.] Then, again, the sky was empty. At the time Page did not think he had hit his target. The Me109, though, was fatally damaged, its engine perforated by Page's bullets. The pilot somehow nursed his machine back over the Channel to make a belly landing near Boulogne. Page got back safely, but it had been a bad day for 56 Squadron. Sergeant James Cowsill, 20 years old, and Sergeant Joseph Whitfield, aged 21, were both shot down and killed by the Me109s.

SUNDAY 14 July 1940

Fighter Command continued to mount an exhausting watch over the Channel today, with 597 sorties flown on patrol or to intercept enemy reconnaissance flights or raids. The heaviest German attack was on a convoy plying the Channel between Eastbourne and Dover. It was led again by Stukas protected by about thirty Me109s. Twelve Spitfires from No. 610 Squadron, together with seven Hurricanes from No. 151 and nine from No. 615, made the interception. The action became one of the most famous in the Battle of Britain thanks to the presence on the ground of BBC reporter Charles Gardner, whose excited commentary caused an immediate controversy. Some listeners complained that the tone had reduced what was a life-and-death struggle to the level of a sporting contest. But Gardner's broadcast also touched a chord. His reactions were those of any of the hundreds of ordinary citizens who were watching the same event from the streets below. By the end of the summer many – perhaps most – of the inhabitants of southern England would have witnessed an aerial battle.

Fair all day.

MONDAY 15 July 1940

Poor flying conditions today turned out to be the beginning of several days of reduced activity due to the low cloud and heavy rain, which forced the Luftwaffe to scale down its operations. But the bad weather brought no advantages to the defenders. Training of replacement pilots had to be curtailed. And the hazards of foul-weather flying wore down pilots who were still flying convoy patrols, and so caused numerous accidents. Today there were more aircraft damaged through mishap than enemy attacks, which were limited to a light raid against an aircraft works at Yeovil in Somerset and half-hearted forays against convoys, driven off by the interceptions of Nos 56 and 151 squadrons.

Low cloud.

continued on page 95

'There's one going down in flames'

On 14 July, BBC radio journalist Charles Gardner reported live as British fighters battled with Ju87 dive-bombers attacking a convoy off Dover. He had donned a tin helmet and strapped a mattress to the roof of his car to watch the action high above the white cliffs.

```
     The Germans are dive-bombing a convoy out to sea; there are one,
two, three, four, five, six, seven German dive-bombers, Junkers 87s.
There's one going down on its target now - bomb! No, he missed the
ships … Now the British fighters are coming up. Here they come. The
Germans are coming in an absolute steep dive, and you can see their
bombs actually leave the machines and come into the water. You can
hear our guns going like anything now. I am looking round now. I can
hear machine gun fire, but I can't see our Spitfires. They must be
somewhere there. Oh! Here's one coming down.
     There's one going down in flames. Somebody's hit a German and he's
coming down with a long streak - coming down completely out of control
- a long streak of smoke - and now a man's baled out by parachute.
The pilot's baled out by parachute. He's a Junkers 87, and he's going
slap into the sea - and there he goes. Smash! A terrific column of
water and there was a Junkers 87. Only one man got out by parachute,
so presumably there was only a crew of one in it. Now then, ho,
there's a terrific mix-up over the Channel! It's impossible to tell
which are our machines and which are Germans … there are fighters
right over our heads … Oh boy! I've never seen anything as good
as this.[transcript adapted from www.bbc.co.uk]
```

The 'Junkers' Gardner described going down was in fact a Hurricane. The British pilot who baled out was rescued by the navy, but he died of his injuries the next day. After the broadcast, which had contrasted sharply with the style of the BBC's output thus far, there were numerous complaints about it being undignified and sensational, and the experiment was not repeated.

-0-0-0-0-0-

YEAR		AIRCRAFT		PILOT, OR	2ND PILOT, PUPIL	DUTY
MONTH	DATE	Type	No.	1ST PILOT	OR PASSENGER	(INCLUDING RESULTS AND REMARKS

TOTALS BROUGHT FORWARI

AIRCRAFT FACTORIES AND AEROPLANE FIXERS

By mid-July the quantity of aircraft emerging from British factories had significantly increased from what it had been a mere two months before. Behind much of this increase in output was the newspaper magnate Lord Beaverbrook, a crony of Winston Churchill, whom the prime minister appointed on 11 May to the task of galvanizing the aero factories. The new minister was abrasive but very effective. Churchill's secretary, Sir John Colville, described Beaverbrook as 'twenty-five per cent thug, fifteen per cent crook and the remainder a combination of genius and real goodness of heart'. From his appointment, he set about wresting control from the Air Ministry and injecting his energy and gusto into the fighter-aircraft factories. He recruited lieutenants from the commercial world, cut through red tape and defied labour regulations to keep factories busy. He caught the public's imagination in the struggle to produce, famously appealing for donations of pots and pans and garden railings to be turned into fighters and enabling citizens to contribute to the purchase of their 'own' Spitfire.

Two factory workers, Winnie and Dolly Bennett, do their bit to turn out Hurricanes at an unnamed Hawker plant.

The results were impressive. May's production figure of 325 fighters was nearly double that of the previous two months. In June, the figure jumped again by a further 120 aircraft. At the end of June, Beaverbrook informed Churchill with justifiable pride that there were now 1040 operational aircraft of all types available for service. 'I would remind you,' he continued, 'that there were 45 aircraft ready for service when your Administration began.' During July, just short of 500 fighters were produced – 200 more than Major Schmid was estimating, for German intelligence, that the British were capable of producing. Furthermore, technical improvements, such as the change from variable pitch to more efficient constant speed propellers, were carried out at impressive speed.

Aircraft were not only being produced, but also patched up. By now the Civilian Repair Organization (CRO) was in full swing. Aircraft too badly damaged for the airfield workshops were collected by civilian mechanics, who in mid-July were returning 160 fighters a week to the squadrons. In Oxford, No. 1 Civilian Repair Unit was working a 14-hour day, 7 days a week, and pilots could fly there directly for repairs. Some aircraft returned two or three times. Even seemingly total wrecks could be salvaged for spare parts, including German aircraft.

By the beginning of August, the RAF would have more serviceable aircraft than it had possessed at the beginning of July. By contrast, German factories produced only 164 Me109s in June and 220 in July. If the Luftwaffe's initial clear superiority was to have a decisive effect, it would have to move quickly.

GRAND TOTAL [Cols. (1) to (10)]
...................Hrs...................Mins.

94

TOTALS CARRIED FORWAF

TUESDAY **16 July 1940**

Tuesday saw a slight improvement in the weather late in the afternoon. At 5.05pm, Flying Officer William Rhodes-Moorhouse, leading six Hurricanes of 601 Squadron from the fighter station at Tangmere, on the Sussex coast, shot down a Ju88 bomber near the Isle of Wight. Rhodes-Moorhouse's father (also called William) had been a First World War pilot who had died of his wounds in April 1915, after a bombing raid that won him the first Victoria Cross awarded for valour in the air. His son, Willie, had gained his pilot's licence when only 17 years old, while still at school at Eton. He had flown Blenheim bombers at the start of the war, before No. 601 Squadron switched to Hurricanes, and took part in the Battle of France, where he had successfully downed a Heinkel and an Me109. He was not to survive the Battle of Britain; he was shot down and killed over Tunbridge Wells on 6 September.

Widespread fog over Dover Straits and the southeast.

It was clear by now that both sides were fighting a war of attrition. The question of how many aircraft your enemy had at his disposal was a vital one. Major Josef Schmid, chief of *Abteilung* (Department) V of the German intelligence service, had tried to answer it in a report entitled *A Comparative Appreciation of the Striking Power of the RAF and the Luftwaffe*, to be delivered to Hitler on 16 July. Schmid estimated that the RAF had 900 first-line fighters, of which 675 were fully operational. He was not far off. On a good day the true number was about 587 planes. Schmid had come to the optimistic conclusion that 'the Hurricane and Spitfire are both inferior to the Messerschmitt 109', although he conceded that the Spitfire could have the edge over the Me110 if the former were 'well piloted'. An intensification of the air war – 'decisive daylight operations' – would be to the advantage of the Luftwaffe, he concluded, 'so long as the large-scale operations are begun early enough to permit the exploitation of the relatively favourable meteorological conditions of July to early October'. Major Schmid also estimated British aircraft production at 180–300 first-line fighters per month, and predicted that the figure would fall once the German blockade and air attacks took their toll. Here, he was badly mistaken: his estimate was too low. By now, Lord Beaverbrook, Churchill's Minister for Aircraft Production, had spurred the aero factories to significantly better performance.

The Luftwaffe's attack had, in truth, been launched in a spirit of reckless optimism. Goering had boasted at the start of the *Kanalkampf* that 'my Luftwaffe is invincible'. The next victory, he predicted, would not be slow in coming. 'And so now we turn to England,' he mused. 'How long will this one last – two, three weeks?' [Quoted in Kennedy, p. 4] But by mid-July, the Luftwaffe had failed to achieve anything like the galloping success to which it had become accustomed. The start of the campaign had been cautious and the weather thus far had hampered its efforts. But it seemed obvious now that the goal of air superiority (the necessary prerequisite of the defeat of Britain, whether by capitulation or conquest) was still far away.

On 16 July, Hitler issued a directive which indicated that he no longer believed the subjugation of Britain was likely to be achieved by air battle and economic strangulation alone. In the preface to Directive No. 16 he ordered the preparation of an invasion plan to 'eliminate the English motherland as a base from which war against Germany can be continued': it was codenamed *Seelöwe* – Operation Sea Lion.

DIRECTIVE 16 –
'TO ELIMINATE THE ENGLISH MOTHERLAND'

Hitler's Directive No. 16, issued on 16 July 1940, authorized preparations for the invasion of Britain.

As England, despite her hopeless military situation, still shows no sign of willingness to come to terms, I have decided to prepare and if necessary to carry out a landing operation against her. The aim of this operation is to eliminate the English motherland as a base from which war against Germany can be continued, and, if this should become unavoidable, to occupy it to the full extent.

FOR THIS PURPOSE I ORDER THE FOLLOWING:

1. The landing must take the form of a surprise crossing on a broad front, approximately from Ramsgate to the region west of the Isle of Wight, whereby elements of the Luftwaffe will play the role of artillery and elements of the Kriegsmarine [navy] the role of engineers. Whether it is appropriate to conduct partial operations in advance of the main one, such as the occupation of the Isle of Wight or the county of Cornwall, is to be studied from the point of view of each branch of the Wehrmacht, and the results reported to me. I reserve the right to decide.

PREPARATIONS FOR THE TOTAL OPERATION MUST BE COMPLETED BY MID-AUGUST.

GRAND TOTAL [Cols. (1) to (10)]

TOTALS CARRIED FORWAR

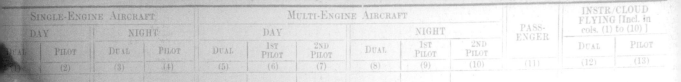

SINGLE-ENGINE AIRCRAFT				MULTI-ENGINE AIRCRAFT						PASS-ENGER	INSTR/CLOUD FLYING [Incl. in cols. (1) to (10)]	
DAY		NIGHT		DAY			NIGHT					
DUAL	PILOT	DUAL	PILOT	DUAL	1ST PILOT	2ND PILOT	DUAL	1ST PILOT	2ND PILOT		DUAL	PILOT
(1)	(2)	(3)	(4)	(5)	(6)	(7)	(8)	(9)	(10)	(11)	(12)	(13)

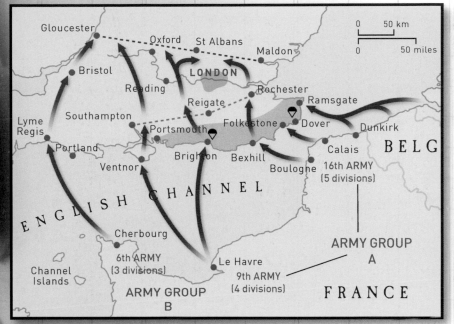

LEFT The plan for the landings of Operation Sea Lion.

FAR LEFT Hitler and his senior army men, (*left to right*) Jodl, Halder, Von Brauchitsch and Keitel, consider their invasion options, mid-July 1940.

2. Included in these preparations is the bringing about of those preconditions which make a landing in England possible:

a) The English air force must have been beaten down to such an extent morally and in actual fact that it can no longer muster any power of attack worth mentioning against the German crossing.

b) Mine-free routes must have been created.

c) The Straits of Dover on both flanks, as well as the western entrance to the Channel approximately on a line Alderney-Portland, must have been blocked by a dense mine barrier.

d) The coastal foreland must be dominated and secured artillery-wise by a strong coastal artillery.

e) Tying down of English naval forces shortly before the crossing both on the North Sea and in the Mediterranean (by the Italians) is desirable, in the course of which every effort must now be made to reduce English naval forces stationed in the home country through air and torpedo attacks.

... THE OPERATION WILL CARRY THE CODE NAME 'SEA LION'.
[Quoted by Kieser, pp. 274–7]

–O-O-O-O-O–

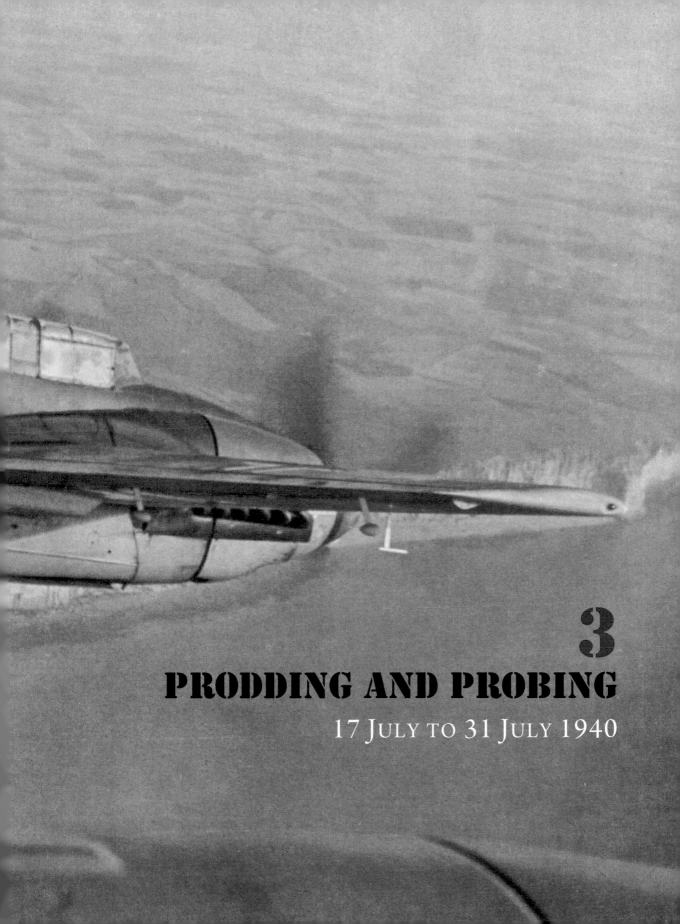

3

PRODDING AND PROBING

17 July to 31 July 1940

O peration Sea Lion looks now like something of an afterthought. Hitler's war preparations had taken little account of potential British intransigence. It was an inconvenient possibility that he appeared unwilling to think about. The swift and relatively painless seizure of France induced a holiday mood. Hitler had relaxed by heading off with a couple of old comrades to visit the battle-fields where he had fought bravely a quarter of a century before. On 28 June, he made a sightseeing trip to Paris, a city that had haunted his architectural fantasies. He was photographed, the diabolical tourist, in front of the Eiffel Tower. In northern France preparations had even been made to send up to 40 divisions home to Germany.

Hitler had all along hoped that Britain could be accommodated into his plans for continental Europe. This view was based partially on a logical appreciation of Britain's military position. The British Army had been smashed at Dunkirk, where its equipment lay rusting in the dunes. The air force and navy could still mount a daunting challenge to any attempted invasion. But they posed no substantial offensive threat to Germany, although the now almost nightly bombing raids by the RAF on Germany were certainly an embarrassment, even if they did little damage.

PREVIOUS PAGE
Messerschmitt Me110 twin-engine fighters fly over England's chalk cliffs.

OPPOSITE
The crew of a Heinkel He111 strap on their parachutes as they prepare for a bombing run.

Without France, and with the United States only a sympathetic onlooker, how long could Britain hold out? Hitler also had a strategic aversion to the idea of invading. His attitude was tinged with a certain sentimentality based on notions of shared racial identity. Crushing Britain would mean the destruction of its empire, an outcome that would not benefit Germany. The real winners, he told his generals, would be Japan, the United States and even the Soviet Union. There were good political reasons for thinking that an invasion would not be needed. The attitude of the British government, prior to the arrival of Churchill, had suggested that a deal was not only possible, but likely.

Thus, no invasion plan had been drawn up when Hitler and his commanders prepared for the great European expansion. The inevitable defeat of Poland and France would leave Britain in a hopeless situation. In the unlikely event of her

continued on page 104

THE VIEW FROM ACROSS THE POND

After the invasion of Poland, President Roosevelt sent an envoy, Sumner Welles, to Europe to attempt to broker a peace deal, but he had no success. With the fall of France, Britain's leaders were faced with the bleak choice of seeking terms with Germany or trying to hold out in the hope that America could be persuaded to come to the rescue. Throughout the fighting in the spring of 1940, Churchill kept Roosevelt vividly informed, writing to him on 15 May that: 'The small countries are simply smashed up, one by one, like matchwood.' In his speeches, Churchill frequently mentioned the United States, implying that it was a natural ally against Nazi barbarism.

The cause of inveigling America into the war was hampered, however, by the personality and attitudes of Roosevelt's envoy in London, Joseph Kennedy, who was an admirer of Hitler and whose Irish ancestry had nurtured in him a dislike of Britain and the British. He warned Washington against backing what he predicted could be the losing side. Churchill had asked Roosevelt for the loan of 50 obsolete US destroyers to help in home waters and on convoy patrols. But the president was wary. Although personally sympathetic to Churchill and Britain, he was reluctant to challenge the popular isolationist feeling before the presidential election in November 1940. Opinion in the United States was deeply divided. The traditionally more Europhile East Coast was in favour of helping Britain, but there was significant opposition to the idea of getting dragged into another European war.

Roosevelt's caution disappointed Churchill. On 27 May, the British prime minister commented bitterly that 'it would be very nice for him [Roosevelt] to pick up the bits of the British Empire if this country was overrun'. [Quoted in Gilbert, p. 428]. In Washington, worries were centred on the empire's credit-worthiness. Huge orders for US armaments were flowing in, with little solid capital to pay the bills. No-one wanted to give credit to a country about to fall. For Churchill, it became a prime aim of British diplomacy to convince the United States that Britain meant to fight on. The 'miracle of Dunkirk' impressed many in the United States and led to a relaxing of laws concerning the supply of arms to nations at war. Soon, half a million used American rifles were on their way

Joseph Kennedy, US Ambassador during the Battle of Britain, emerges from a heavily sandbagged Treasury building (28 September 1939). He was profoundly anti-British and his reports home painted a gloomy picture of the country's chances of surviving.

..............Hrs..............Mins.

across the Atlantic. Shortly afterwards, the British had another chance to demonstrate their resolve. Churchill had repeatedly urged the French to avoid letting their warships fall into enemy hands. But after the armistice with Germany in June 1940, trust had broken down. The French had freed 400 captive German pilots, in direct contravention of a promise made to Churchill. Now, confused and contradictory messages were coming back about the French fleet. On 3 July, those French ships that had slipped away to British ports were seized by force, and at Mers-el-Kébir in Algeria a concentration of French vessels was attacked by a Royal Navy task force after failing to conform to an ultimatum. Within a very short time, the French fleet was destroyed and 1297 of its officers and men died as a result.

It was a ruthless move, and it demonstrated, as a US military attaché in London, Raymond Lee, commented, that 'the British are not going to sit quietly and watch Hitler's plans mature'. [Lee, p. 12] Harry Hopkins, Roosevelt's Secretary of State in 1940, later told Churchill that the action at Mers-el-Kébir, more than anything else, had convinced the president that Britain meant to fight on whatever the cost.

The other major concern of the US leadership was the fate of the powerful British fleet, which in the hands of Germany would represent a considerable strategic threat to the United States. Churchill was aware of this and played on this fear, urging Canadian Prime Minister Mackenzie King to 'impress this danger upon the President'. To Lord Lothian, the British ambassador in Washington, he wrote on 9 June: 'If Great Britain broke under an invasion, a pro-German government might obtain far easier terms from Germany by surrendering the Fleet, thus making Germany and Japan masters of the New World.'

At the end of July, with the Battle of Britain under way, Joseph Kennedy was still reporting back from London that British surrender was 'inevitable'. Other Americans, such as Raymond Lee, took a more optimistic view. 'What a wonderful thing it will be if these blokes do win the war!' he wrote. 'They will be bankrupt but entitled to almost unlimited respect.' [Lee, p. 25]

It was not until February 1941, after the US presidential election was safely won, that Roosevelt was able to send his envoy Averell Harriman to London to 'recommend everything we can do, short of war, to keep the British Isles afloat'. [Quoted in Overy] Until then, the British were on their own.

The battleship *Provence* is destroyed, with other French ships, by the British task force at Mers-el-Kébir, Algeria (3 July 1940), a painful necessity to prevent the vessels falling into German hands. The French were slow to forgive or forget.

leaders choosing to hold out, a blockade was planned, using aircraft and U-boats, aimed at disrupting Britain's severe dependence on imported food and raw materials. This was the thinking that sustained the *Kanalkampf*.

This approach suited the German navy, the *Kriegsmarine*, and its commander Grossadmiral (Grand-Admiral) Erich Raeder. He was a complex figure. Raeder was 64, and he held strong opinions, which he was prepared to defend. He believed in a strategy that maximized the use of U-boats and small surface vessels to disrupt supply lines, rather than seeking a head-on confrontation with the Royal Navy. The British Home Fleet overmatched the German navy in northern waters. Raeder had little faith in the Luftwaffe's ability to win the mastery of the air over the Channel that he thought necessary to prevent his ships being smashed by the British navy.

Shortly after war began, Hitler had assured his *Grossadmiral* that the purpose of the navy was to act as a blockading force, as the German navy had done in the First World War. Since then, he had suffered the loss of the 'pocket battleship' *Graf Spee*, cornered by three British cruisers off the coast of Uruguay, and the destruction of a number of valuable ships during the fighting for Norway. Hitler tended to share his admiral's caution. 'On land I am a hero,' he told Raeder, 'at sea I am a coward.' [Quoted in Waite, p. 463]

Nonetheless, in November 1939 Raeder had felt it prudent to order that a study be made for an invasion across the Channel. The resulting report stressed the threat posed by the Royal Navy and the RAF, as well as the awkward tides, shallows and currents of the Channel. The army, too, carried out a study that envisaged airborne and infantry landings in East Anglia, with a diversionary action north of the Humber. The aim was to cut off London from the north. The plan was predicated on the other two services achieving daunting goals – the navy was to close the Straits of Dover to British ships from the south, and the Luftwaffe was to carry out the airborne landings as well as guarantee command of the air over the landing sites.

A Hurricane returns intact to a fighter base described vaguely, in the familiar parlance of wartime censorship, as being 'somewhere in England'.

The Luftwaffe responded that the plan demanded 'total air superiority' and 'total surprise'. It should only proceed, they said, as 'the final act in an already victorious war'. The navy, for its part, baulked at anything that looked like taking on the whole might of the Home Fleet and argued that the shipping required for transporting the 100,000 men the army envisaged necessary would take at least a year to

assemble. In fact, the only thing that all three branches of the armed forces could agree on was that overwhelming local air superiority was a prerequisite of any landing attempt.

In the euphoric atmosphere that followed the victories in the west, German caution tended to fade. Without any prompting from Hitler, the army began preparing invasion plans. Only 21 miles (34 kilometres) of water separated the victorious Germans from the obstinate British. A landing began to appear not only desirable, but comfortably achievable. The army plan proposed landings between Margate in Kent and the Isle of Wight. Divisions were to form up in northern France, thirteen in total, split into two waves. The first was to be made up of 90,000 men, the second of a further 170,000 troops, together with heavy weapons, 34,000 vehicles, 57,000 horses and 26,000 bicycles. Raeder's subordinates, anxious not to exclude the navy from a stake in future glory, gave positive cooperation. Raeder himself, though, continued to raise objections.

On 13 July, the generals Von Brauchitsch and Halder presented their proposals to the Führer at a meeting at his Alpine refuge at Berchtesgaden. As Egbert Kieser, the leading German historian of Sea Lion, recorded, to their surprise and 'completely at odds with his normal practice he [Hitler] asked no questions on specific operations, was not interested in details and recommended no improvements'. The plan, Hitler declared, was practicable and preparations were to begin immediately. His invasion directive followed three days later.

Taking the decision, though, did nothing to make the Luftwaffe's task easier. It was now faced with a number of objectives, each of which was daunting enough on its own. It had to continue its attacks on British shipping, wear down the RAF in the continuing battle of attrition and do what it could to reduce the Royal Navy's ability to menace a landing.

Grossadmiral Erich Raeder (1876–1960) became chief of the German navy, the *Kriegsmarine*, in 1928, and had few illusions about the practical difficulties of mounting an invasion of England in 1940.

WEDNESDAY 17 July 1940

Cloudy and wet.

Reichsmarschall Goering could report little progress today, the first day of operations following Hitler's invasion directive. The weather remained so bad that even many of the Luftwaffe's regular reconnaissance patrols were cancelled. Occasionally, though, the attackers could make clever use of the cloud. At around 2pm, a patrol of 12 Spitfires of No. 64 Squadron was over Beachy Head when suddenly Flying Officer Donald Taylor was hit and went plunging downwards. He crash-landed near Hailsham in Sussex and was taken to Eastbourne Hospital. No-one in the squadron caught a glimpse of their attackers, who had vanished back into the cloud. The heaviest raid was from Stavanger, with half a dozen He111s bombing the Imperial Chemical Industries' factory at Ardeer, Ayrshire. One of the raiders was caught on its way back and shot down by three 603 Squadron Spitfires.

18 July 1940 THURSDAY

Rain in southern England; cloudy over Straits of Dover.

The day saw an increase in activity in spite of continuing poor weather. In northern France, more Luftwaffe units had finished their preparations and were becoming operational. It was dawning on the Germans that their raids were being 'seen' by radar, and they started to take countermeasures. One method was to try to fool the watchers into reacting to spoof attacks. (The tactic was to be adopted by the British themselves in their bombing campaign against Germany.) Today saw the first 'dummy raid'. As a convoy passed through the Dover Straits shortly before nine in the morning, an enemy formation appeared on the radar moving towards it. No. 11 Group chief Sir Keith Park ordered up a dozen Spitfires from 610 Squadron at Biggin Hill, and they were duly vectored towards the raid. But it was a trap. Suddenly they were set on by a *Staffel* of Me109s, which shot down one of their number and then escaped unscathed into the low cloud. There were no bombers in attendance.

This was just the sort of combat that Dowding and Park were desperate to avoid. They had urged the pilots repeatedly to concentrate on bombers and avoid the temptation to tangle with the raiding Me109s. The instruction was usually heeded and fighter sweeps by Me109s would often go unchallenged as they roared over southern England and the Channel.

In the afternoon the bombers were back, though, with several raids on convoys along the south coast, and the squadrons at Tangmere and Middle Wallop were in constant action. It was another hard day for 609 Squadron, which had a further two Spitfires shot down while taking on a formation of Ju88s. Both pilots survived. At one point in the afternoon, a large dogfight developed over Beachy Head, when 28 Messerschmitt Me109s were engaged by 16 Spitfires from Nos 152 and 610 squadrons. One aircraft from the latter was shot down, but no enemy fighters were hit. It had been an ominous day. For the first time since the start of the battle on 10 July, the RAF lost more aircraft than the Germans.

With the increase in aircraft production, the loss of machines was less drastic than it would have been a month before. But if the trend continued, the potential impact on morale, civilian as well as military, would be considerable. The newspapers and the BBC were presenting the daily 'scores', and it was important that the home side was seen to be on a winning streak. Nerves were taut and the south of England was electrified by the prospect of imminent invasion.

19 July 1940 FRIDAY

Showers, with bright intervals.

The weather cleared today, and Fighter Command was expecting trouble because there were nine British convoys at sea. Squadrons flew to forward airfields to cut the time it would take to get into action. At around 8am, four Dorniers appeared over Glasgow, arriving from the west to confuse the radar operators. They made a pinpoint attack on the Rolls Royce works, causing heavy damage and casualties, before escaping unscathed. In the south, interceptions were made on Stuka attacks on Dover and Portland, but the British pilots, having driven away the bombers, soon found themselves embroiled in dogfights with the Me109 escorts.

	SINGLE-ENGINE AIRCRAFT				MULTI-ENGINE AIRCRAFT					PASS-ENGER	INSTR/CLOUD FLYING [Incl. in cols. (1) to (10)]	
DAY		NIGHT		DAY			NIGHT					
DUAL	PILOT	DUAL	PILOT	DUAL	1ST PILOT		DUAL	1ST PILOT	2ND PILOT		DUAL	PILOT
(1)	(2)	(3)	(4)	(5)				(9)	(10)	(11)	(12)	(13)

SIR KEITH PARK

A New Zealander by birth, Sir Keith Park (1892–1975) had been a distinguished aviator in the First World War, having transferred to the Royal Flying Corps after being wounded at Gallipoli in 1915 while serving with the New Zealand army. He was credited with downing 20 enemy aircraft and won an MC and Bar, DFC and Croix de Guerre for his exploits. In spring 1940, promoted to Air Vice-Marshal, he was given command of 11 Group. He was thus in charge of the most strategically sensitive area of Fighter Command's regional division, with responsibility for the section of the coastline most exposed to enemy attack as well as for the defence of London. In June 1940, he had come in for severe criticism over the perceived failure of his pilots to do more to protect the British Expeditionary Force on the Dunkirk beaches. But Park maintained that his duty was to preserve what was a largely untried force for the great battle ahead, and that 11 Group had done all it could within that crucial constraint.

Air Vice-Marshal Park had direct and exhausting responsibility for the Battle of Britain in crucial areas at crucial times. It was said that while Dowding controlled events from day to day, Park controlled them from hour to hour. He made a point of visiting his men, flying around the bases in his own Hurricane, taking a seat unannounced in the mess, listening rather than talking. Many pilots seem to have seen his long, lined face at some time during the summer of 1940.

His removal from command at the end of the battle was a source of bitterness to him for the rest of his life. However, his contribution to the victory was appreciated fully by those who understood it. Lord Tedder, then chief of the RAF, wrote in 1947: 'If any one man won the Battle of Britain he did. I do not believe it is realized how much that one man, with his leadership, his calm judgement and his skill, did to save not only this country, but the world.'

Sir Keith Park, pictured in flying kit in Malta (1942). As commander of 11 Group during the Battle of Britain, he held a pivotal position regarding the struggle's outcome.

STOP-LINES, DRAGON'S TEETH AND SILENT KILLERS

Feverish activity to combat an enemy landing was visible everywhere by mid-July 1940. Liquid fuel pipes were installed in the sea off likely landing beaches, with the purpose of setting the waves ablaze if necessary. The most vulnerable stretches of the coastline were strung with barbed wire and sown with mines. The main defence line, however, was inland, stretching from Somerset to Essex to protect London and the heart of England — the 'GHQ Line'. It was designed to be a continuous anti-tank obstacle, using natural features such as rivers and canals and, in between, huge anti-tank ditches and other obstructions. It was originally about 400 miles (640km) long, before being extended northwards via Newcastle to Edinburgh. In front of the GHQ Line in the south were other 'stop-lines' based as much as possible on natural features. Concrete 'dragon's teeth' were sown along roads and railway lines to impede the German armour. Ugly brick-

Defensive preparations created surreal scenes such as this one, at Cheriton, Kent (July 1940). Concrete barriers block the road, while the bus shelter behind has been transformed into a strongpoint.

and-concrete pill-boxes and strong-points were set up all over the countryside. By the end of July 1940, there were some 8000 of them, with a further 17,000 planned or under construction — so many that supplies of concrete and timber for construction were dwindling fast.

Should the main British force have to retreat to the GHQ Line, secret auxiliary units hiding out in well-stocked bases in caves and woods would strike the enemy behind their lines. 'We would have booby-trapped German stores and vehicles,' said Percy Clark, attached to a secret unit in Kent. 'We'd have tried to do something about any bridges that weren't blown up. We'd have stretched wires across the road to catch

necks. We were trained to be silent killers.' [Clark, recording] 'They told us our expected lifetime after the invasion would be seven days,' said George Pellet, another recruit to the underground organization. 'They reckoned that after seven days either Jerry would be back out of it or we'd all be finished.' [Pellet, recording]

General Sir Edmund Ironside had been appointed commander of Britain's defences on 27 May, but on 20 July General Sir Alan Brooke took over, and he considered the existing defences too static. British leaders from Churchill down were concerned about their soldiers becoming 'Maginot-minded', infected with the defensive mindset that, it was believed, had led to the defeat of France. So the huge number of men now in uniform were deliberately kept busy with marches and exercises as well as helping with the construction of defences. Weapons and ammunition were still in very short supply. To Bombardier Douglas Goddard, it was 'really rather comical. We had rifles with five rounds of ammunition, we had one 1914 Lewis gun and we had three London taxis. We patrolled the coast between Camber Sands and Dymchurch — where the invasion was due to land — in taxis.' [Goddard, recording] Captain Kenneth Johnstone of the 11th Battalion, Durham Light Infantry, remembered 'one officer being put on a charge by the brigadier because he didn't have a revolver, until it was explained to the brigadier that it wasn't his turn to wear the revolver, because we only had one between six of us'. [Johnstone, recording]

Among the units moved forward that morning was No. 141 Squadron. It had been formed only a month previously and was equipped with Boulton Paul Defiants. The Defiant was similar to the Hurricane, except that it had a large gun turret with four Browning machine-guns mounted to the rear of the cockpit and operated by a second crew-member. No. 141's sister squadron, No. 264, had enjoyed great success over Dunkirk, where its backward-firing guns had taken German attackers by surprise. However, 141 Squadron had flown only a few patrols and had yet to be tested in combat. Early in the afternoon, 12 Defiants of No. 141 were ordered to patrol at 5000 feet over Folkestone, Kent. Three of the pilots experienced engine trouble, but the remaining nine, led by Squadron Leader William Richardson, and including New Zealand Pilot Officer John Gard'ner, took off from Hawkinge and headed south.

Northeast of Dover an armed trawler was under attack from Me110s, escorted by 20 Messerschmitt Me109s of *Jagdgeschwader* 51, led by Hauptmann (Captain) Hannes Trautloft. Having shepherded the Me110s back to France, Trautloft decided to return to the English coast on a free hunt. He soon spotted the Defiants far below flying in a tight formation, seemingly unaware of his presence. This time, the British planes were correctly identified for what they were. Checking that there were no Spitfires or Hurricanes about, Trautloft led his Me109s in a dive out of the sun. 'I aimed at the right Defiant ... my guns fired ... pieces of the Defiant ... broke off and came hurtling towards me ... I saw a thin trail of smoke ... then suddenly just a fiery ball.' [Quoted in Townsend, *Duel of Eagles*, p. 276]

In this first attack, John Gard'ner's Defiant was also hit. 'The first that I knew,' he said, 'was suddenly I had white tracer bullets going through the cockpit and then I had a flash of airplanes right and left under fire. I thought, I'm going to get out of this. I dived down. The prop was dead in front of me. I was lucky I didn't catch fire. There was a dreadful smell of cordite and bluey smoke in the cockpit.' Meanwhile, the Me109s attacked again. Clearly, they had worked out the Defiant's debilitating weakness: an attack from the front and below met no resistance, as the Defiants had no forward-facing guns. In effect, as one pilot later complained, you had to fly past the enemy to fire at him. But as the Defiant was also slow – with a top speed of only 298mph – there was little chance of this happening when matched against Me109s. The Germans now attacked from head-on and below, and two more Defiants went down.

Meanwhile, John Gard'ner wrestled with the controls of his stricken aircraft: 'There was no engine and the rudder pedal was just loose under my foot. I don't know how I managed to keep it level. I saw this boat and I thought, I'm going to have to crash by that boat, but I was going so fast it was impossible. For some reason or other I stupidly undid my safety straps and I thought, I'm going to get into the water so I wanted to get out quickly, forgetting that I would hit at 100 m.p.h.' Gard'ner hurriedly pulled the hook back on the cockpit. 'At the moment of impact,' he says, 'I was thrown forward and hit my head. I blacked out and came to deep down in blackness. But the hood was open and I could get out. There was a big flap of skin that was hanging loose from my forehead and I had been hit on the back of the head as well.' [Quoted in Parker, p. 159]

Up above, the five surviving Defiants swerved into cloud to try to escape the Me109s. One, flown by Flight Lieutenant Ian Donald, was hit and set on fire.

continued on page 112

PARATROOPERS AND FIFTH COLUMNISTS

The prospect of invasion from the air — paratroopers followed by gliders or transport aircraft — was a major preoccupation in the summer of 1940. Such an attack could come almost anywhere.

The successes of the *Fallschirmjäger* — German parachutists — earlier in the year had made a strong impression on British civilians. They had struck first in Denmark, where they captured Aalborg airport at the start of the German invasion, and then in Norway. On 10 May, they scored their most dramatic victory, when a force of 78 men seized the supposedly impregnable Belgian fort of Eben-Emael, between Liège and Maastricht. The *Illustrated London News* that month carried a 'wonderful double page spread' showing the parachutists' methods.

Thus, it was widely expected that paratroopers would be used in an invasion of Britain, and they were not expected to confine themselves to conventional military activities or appearance. On 21 May, the Dutch foreign minister alleged, quite inaccurately, that German paratroopers had descended on his country disguised as nurses, tramcar conductors, nuns and monks. The military correspondent of the *Chichester and Southern Post* warned his readers on 28 June to be on the lookout for parachutists, 'mostly young men of the desperado type' whose task was to 'organize local fifth column members and arm them … [and] create panic and confusion and spread false news among the civil population'. Such advice made people panicky. A commercial traveller who failed to stop his car in time at a checkpoint near Wrexham, manned by Local Defence Volunteers, was shot dead. Enemy aliens were moved away from coastal areas, and innocents were arrested on suspicion of being spies, after tip-offs from neighbours.

What, with hindsight, looks like paranoia was by no means confined to the ignorant or overly nervous. Neither General Ironside, in charge of home defences at the time, nor Admiral Ramsay, the architect of Operation Dynamo, were immune to concerns about fifth columnist activity. On 30 May, Ironside wrote in his diary: 'Important telegraph poles marked, suspicious men moving at night all over the country.' [Quoted in Longmate, p. 476] Many Fighter Command pilots shared this fear. No. 85 Squadron was in battle on 1 September, and Sergeant Geoffrey

ENEMY UNIFORMS AT A GLANCE

THE object of this leaflet is to acquaint the Services and Civil Defence workers with the appearance of the standard types of German uniform, so that they can be recognised at a glance. The danger of invasion has by no means receded, and in the event of an emergency, every man and woman in authority must be able to detect a German soldier, sailor, or airman, even at a distance.
Study this leaflet carefully. If you are in the Services, the Police or any of the Civil Defence Services, pin this leaflet up on your notice board inside your post.

F488. Wt.25472.   8 41. Gp.961. Fosh & Cross Ltd.

"Spot at Sight" Chart

36

ENEMY UNIFORM AT A GLANCE

ISSUED BY THE MINISTRY OF INFORMATION

A Ministry of Information 'Spot at Sight' chart educates the public on how to recognize invaders who might fall from the skies.

Goodman found only his port guns firing. On returning to his base he discovered, according to a squadron report, that matchsticks had been forced into the airlines of his guns — clear evidence, it seemed, of sabotage 'by some German sympathiser at the depot', according to Squadron Leader Peter Townsend. Stories of parachutes being sabotaged by Irish Republican Army (IRA) sympathizers also did the rounds.

In order to make life difficult for the *Fallschirmjäger* once they had landed, road signs were uprooted and postal districts were blanked out on the nameplates on London streets. On 13 June, orders were given that church bells should only be rung to signal a parachute attack, and in mid-June a leaflet was distributed with instructions about what to do 'If the Invader Comes'. The population was told to disregard

GERMAN PARACHUTIST

LUFTWAFFE BADGE WORN ON RIGHT BREAST

STEEL HELMET (CRASH HELMET SHAPE) WITH 2 CHIN STRAPS (May be camouflaged)

THIS BADGE ON RIGHT SIDE OF HELMET (EAGLE BADGE ON LEFT SIDE)

GREY-GREEN OR CAMOUFLAGED GABERDINE OVERALLS ALWAYS WORN OVER TUNIC ZIP FASTENERS

BINOCULARS

ROLLED CAPE

2 HAVERSACKS

PISTOL

WATER BOTTLE

BOMB POCKETS

DETAIL OF TUNIC

TUNIC (Air Force Blue) PIPED SHOULDER STRAPS & COLLAR

UNIT NUMBER OF WHITE METAL

BOOTS AT SIDES RUBBER

chute troops, both officers and men, are easily nguished. Look for these features :—grey drill alls and steel helmet with double chin strap and small brim—like a motor cyclist's crash helmet. -up boots with rubber soles. Heavy belts and cross straps, large pockets over thighs. If you're close enough, you'll see on his helmet and right breast a curved-winged eagle carrying a swastika. Remember he'll be in overalls. There's no khaki in a German uniform.

rumours, only to take orders from a British officer — having first established that he was 'really British' and not 'pretending to be so' — and to immobilize transport, cars and bicycles. The basic order was to 'stay put' to avoid clogging the roads, as had happened in France, Belgium and the Netherlands.

As early as 12 May, Churchill's scientific adviser Professor Frederick Lindemann was recommending that holes be dug in all flat areas more than 400 yards (365 metres) long that were within 5 (later extended to 10) miles of any vulnerable and strategically important site. This was to defend against airborne landings. Fields, even those under crops, were planted with sharp obstructions — wooden stakes or old farm machinery — to prevent German gliders landing on them. They proved equally hazardous to stricken friendly aeroplanes when they tried to crash-land.

The Local Defence Volunteers, soon to be renamed the Home Guard, made up of men too old or too young for service, patrolled the streets and lanes or manned roadblocks, at first with just their improvised weapons. Their primary role was to be the first on the scene of any German invasion from the air. Such was their vigilance that it led to problems for Fighter Command, with RAF pilots descending on parachutes being shot at by overeager guards. On 5 September, the Air Ministry was forced to issue a notice reminding the public that not all parachutists were enemies

The fear of invasion that gripped the country did help to maintain energy and unity, essential in a 'people's war' when the civilians were now in the frontline. The 'great invasion scare', Churchill told his secretary Colville, 'is serving a very useful purpose ... it is keeping every man and woman tuned to a high pitch of readiness'. [Colville, p. 197] In many cases there was a real expectation of German occupation. People kept packed suitcases sitting in their halls for the seemingly inevitable flight. The writers Virginia and Leonard Woolf, the publisher Victor Gollancz and many others prepared the means for suicide. Even 19-year-olds were to be found writing their wills. Mollie Panter-Downes, writing for the *New Yorker* (24 May 1940), reported that: 'The Channel had now shrunk in men's minds to the size of the Thames.'

Unlike any of the other men on the downed Defiants, the gunner Pilot Officer Arthur Hamilton did manage to bale out but drowned. The pilot was killed and the aircraft hit the ground in Elmsvale Road, Dover. The carnage would have almost certainly been worse, had it not been for the arrival of Hurricanes from 111 Squadron, sent to the rescue from Hawkinge.

The remaining Defiants limped back to their airfield. One of them crashed on landing; another was so badly damaged as to be irreparable. The squadron was effectively a write-off. In just a quarter of an hour, six machines had been destroyed and ten men killed. John Gard'ner, quickly picked up by a coastguard launch, was the only survivor of any of the downed crews.

It was the worst part of another bad day for the RAF. Over 700 sorties were flown, but only 4 of the enemy had been shot down, and these had, for the most part, been stragglers or single aircraft on reconnaissance or mine-laying duties. For its part, Fighter Command lost a further five pilots killed, five wounded, and eleven fighter aircraft destroyed in combat. When dogfights had developed, the British had been all but overwhelmed.

Later that day, Reichsmarschall Goering held a meeting with senior Luftwaffe commanders in which he told his lieutenants Sperrle and Kesselring that: 'Fighting alone all these weeks on the Channel Front, *Jagdgeschwader* 51 has already shot

An Air Ministry poster describes the procedures by which the Air Sea Rescue (ASR) service could rescue pilots who have to ditch at sea. Many of Dowding's pilots had good reasons to value the service.

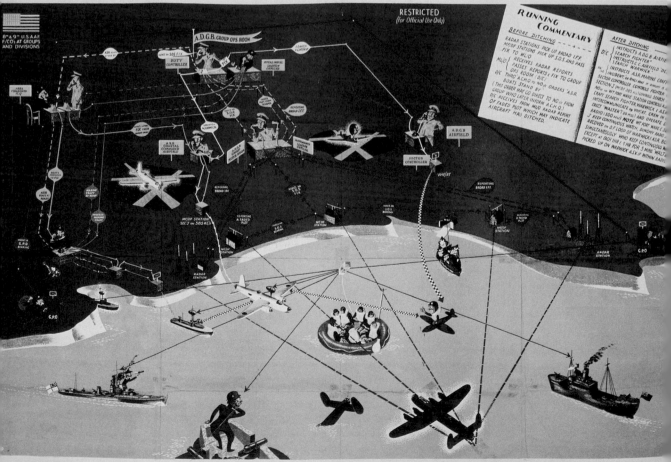

AIR SEA RESCUE SERVICES

'A few gallons of sea water in my stomach'

Sergeant Eric Bann, of 238 Squadron, described his fortunate escape in a letter to his parents, 19 July 1940.

I am very sorry for not having written sooner but things have been impossible just lately … Have been missing for three days. Poor May's heart was in her mouth but I got 24 hours leave upon arriving back at base just to go and prove to the dear girl that I was really OK.

The CO and two of us were out on early morning patrol when along came a shower of bombers to attack our convoy. In we went, roaring all over the sky with odds of seven to one, but this time I could not dodge quick enough and I was knocked for six right into the English Channel. Gosh it was cold so early in the morning. Well I broke all swimming records and was eventually picked up by a boat and landed at Portsmouth. There they detained me just to make sure that I was alright. However, apart from a few gallons of sea water in my stomach, I was otherwise OK and have been doing plenty of flying since.

-0-0-0-0-0-

down 150 of the enemy's aircraft: quite enough to have weakened him seriously. Think now of all the bombers we can parade in the English sky. The few RAF fighters will not be able to cope.' [Quoted in Bickers, p. 212]

Such assessments sustained Hitler's hopes that a British capitulation would avert the need for an invasion. On the evening of 19 July, Hitler made a speech that came to be known as 'The Last Appeal to Reason'. It was an appeal for a settlement with the British Empire, but it made no mention of negotiations and was, in effect, a surrender demand. Hitler delivered it in front of the Nazi elite and Reichstag deputies crammed into the Kroll Opera House, Berlin, for a ceremony to mark the elevation of eleven generals to the rank of *Generalfeldmarschall* (Field Marshal) in recognition of their contribution to the victories in western Europe. Goering was awarded the yet more exalted title of *Reichsmarschall* (Marshal of the Reich). He had ordered a special uniform, light blue and encrusted with gold braid, for the occasion.

Hitler told his audience that 'if this struggle continues, it can only end in the annihilation of one of us. Mr Churchill thinks it will be Germany. I know it will be Britain. I am not the vanquished, begging for mercy. I speak as a victor.' He warned his opponent: 'Mr Churchill ought perhaps, for once, to believe me when I prophesy that a great empire will be destroyed – an empire which it was never my intention to destroy or even harm.'

In the audience was the American correspondent William L. Shirer, who was reporting on events for CBS Radio. 'Under one roof I have never seen so many gold-braided generals before,' Shirer observed. 'Massed together, their chests heavy with

continued on page 117

HUGO SPERRLE

Born in February 1885, the son of a brewer, Hugo Sperrle joined the German army in 1903 and, like Goering, had served in the Luftwaffe's forerunner, the *Fliegertruppen des deutschen Kaiserreiches* (Imperial German Flying Service), during the First World War. At the end of the war, like many disaffected soldiers, he joined the right-wing paramilitary *Freikorps*, before returning to the army. In 1925, he was taken onto the staff of General Hans von Seeckt, the defence minister and effective army chief of staff, and was involved in the secret planning for a future independent Luftwaffe. During the 1920s Sperrle was one of the airmen sent for secret military training at Lipetsk, near Moscow. By the time of the Spanish Civil War he was a *Generalmajor* (major-general) and was given command of the Condor Legion operating in Spain, before handing over to his chief of staff, Wolfram Freiherr von Richthofen.

At the beginning of February 1939, Sperrle took over *Luftflotte* 3, with headquarters in Munich. The air fleet did not fight in Poland, but when unleashed in support of Von Rundstedt's Army Group 'A' during the *Blitzkrieg* in western Europe, his tactical forces — in particular the Ju87 'Stuka' dive-bombers — made a significant contribution to the rapid German victory. He received the rank of *Generalfeldmarschall* (field marshal) in July 1940. During the Battle of Britain, his air fleet would be deployed in northwestern France.

With his thick neck, huge frame and habitual monocle, Sperrle struck Hitler as one of his 'most brutal looking generals'. In reality, he was a highly experienced and intelligent officer, noted for his 'unusual vitality'. Unlike Goering and Kesselring, Sperrle did not underestimate Fighter Command's strength — in fact, he even overestimated the resources left to Dowding by the end of August. He argued unsuccessfully that daylight attacks should continue against Fighter Command rather than switch to London.

After capture by the Allies, Sperrle was tried by a US military tribunal for war crimes, along with other senior German officers, in 1947–8, but he was acquitted. He died in 1953.

A glum-looking Hugo Sperrle (*left,* with his customary monocle) and Albert Kesselring (*far right*) flank their Luftwaffe chief Goering and their Führer in October 1940.

ALBERT KESSELRING

Albert Kesselring (1885–1960) was a versatile commander and accomplished administrator, but he was arguably more effective in charge of ground troops than air forces. During the First World War, he served in the German artillery and in various staff positions. He remained in the army after the war, but in 1933 was transferred to the *Reichskommissariat für die Luftfahrt* (Air Transport Commission), a cover organization for planning the then clandestine Luftwaffe. In April 1936 he was made Luftwaffe Chief of the Air Staff and, as an ex-army man, was firmly on the side of those who wished to steer the new force to-wards concentrating on tactical ground support.

At the beginning of the Second World War, Kesselring held the rank of general and was in charge of *Luftflotte* 1, which, in support of Generalfeldmarschall (Field Marshal) von Bock's Army Group North, was instrumental in the rapid destruction of Polish forces. He had similar success in command of *Luftflotte* 2 during the battle in the west, and in both campaigns he worked very closely with army commanders on the ground.

During the Battle of Britain, the newly promoted Generalfeldmarschall Kesselring's *Luftflotte* 2 was based in eastern France and the Low Countries. Like Goering, Kesselring consistently underestimated the strength of Fighter Command. He was also a strong proponent of the terror bombing of London, a decision that, more than any other, lost Germany the battle.

In late 1941, after the dazzling success of his air forces in the opening months of Operation Barbarossa against the Soviet Union, Kesselring was appointed commander-in-chief of all German forces in the Mediterranean and North African theatres. His conduct of the Italian campaign, where superior Allied forces were successfully sucked into a battle of attrition in terrain that greatly favoured the defenders, earned him a reputation as one of Hitler's most able commanders.

At the end of the war Kessel-ring was charged with responsi-bility for atrocities committed in northern Italy by the SS and regular Wehrmacht soldiers after the surrender of Italy. He was sentenced to death, but this was commuted to life imprisonment. Freed because of ill health in 1952, he died eight years later.

E 65881

Dropped at North [illegible]
Somerset.
Sunday August 11. 1940.

A LAST APPEAL TO REASON

BY

ADOLF HITLER

Speech before the Reichstag, 19th July, 1940

I have summoned you to this meeting in the midst of our tremendous struggle for the freedom and the future of the German nation. I have done so, firstly, because I considered it imperative to give our own people an insight into the events, unique in history, that lie behind us, secondly, because I wished to express my gratitude to our magnificent soldiers, and thirdly, with the intention of appealing, once more and for the last time, to common sense in general.

If we compare the causes which prompted this historic struggle with the magnitude and the far-reaching effects of military events, we are forced to the conclusion that its general course and the sacrifices it has entailed are out of all proportion to the alleged reasons for its outbreak — unless they were nothing but a pretext for underlying intentions.

The programme of the National-Socialist Movement, in so far as it affected the future development of the Reich's relations with the rest of the world, was simply an attempt to bring about a definite revision of the Treaty of Versailles, though as far as at all possible, this was to be accomplished by peaceful means.

This revision was absolutely essential. The conditions imposed at Versailles were intolerable, not only because of their humiliating discrimination and because the disarmament which they ensured deprived the German nation of all its rights, but far more so because of the consequent destruction of the material existence of one of the great civilized nations in the world, and the proposed annihilation of its future, the utterly senseless accumulation of immense tracts of territory under the domination of a number of States, the theft of all the irreparable foundations of life and indispensable vital necessities from a conquered nation. While this dictate was being drawn up, men of insight even among our foes were uttering warnings about the terrible consequences which the ruthless application of its insane conditions would entail — a proof that even among them the conviction predominated that such a dictate could not possibly be upheld in days to come. Their objections and protests were silenced by the assurance that the statutes of the newly-created League of Nations provided for a revision of these conditions; in fact, the League was supposed to be the competent authority. The hope of revision was thus at no time regarded as presumptuous, but as something natural. Unfortunately, the Geneva institution, as those responsible for Versailles had intended, never looked upon itself as a body competent to undertake any sensible revision, but from the very outset as nothing more than the guarantor of the ruthless enforcement and maintenance of the conditions imposed at Versailles.

All attempts made by democratic Germany to obtain equality for the German people by a revision of the Treaty proved unavailing.

World War Enemies Unscrupulous Victors

It is always in the interests of a conqueror to represent stipulations that are to his advantage as sacrosanct, while the instinct of self-preservation in the vanquished leads him to reacquire the common human rights that he has lost. For him the dictate of an overbearing conqueror had all the less legal force, since he had never been honourably conquered. Owing to a rare misfortune, the German Empire, between 1914 and 1918, lacked good leadership. To this, and to the as yet unenlightened faith and trust placed by the German people in the words of democratic statesmen, our downfall was due.

Hence the Franco-British claim that the Dictate of Versailles was a sort of international, or even a supreme, code of laws, appeared to be nothing more than a piece of insolent arrogance to every honest German, the assumption, however, that British or French statesmen should actually claim to be the guardians of justice, and even of human culture, as mere stupid effrontery. A piece of effrontery that is thrown into a sufficiently glaring light by their own extremely negligible achievements in this direction. For seldom have any countries in the world been ruled with a lesser degree of wisdom, morality and culture than those which are at the moment exposed to the ragings of certain democratic statesmen.

The programme of the National-Socialist Movement, besides freeing the Reich from the innermost fetters of a small substratum of Jewish-capitalistic and pluto-democratic profiteers, proclaimed to the world our resolution to shake off the shackles of the Versailles Dictate.

Germany's demands for this revision were a vital necessity and essential to the existence and honour of every great nation. They will probably one day be regarded by posterity as extremely reasonable. In practice, all these demands had to be carried through contrary to the will of the Franco-British rulers. We all regarded it as a sure sign of successful leadership in the Third Reich that for years we were able to effect this revision without a war. Not that — as the British and French demagogues asserted — we were at that time incapable of fighting. When, thanks to growing common sense, it finally appeared as though international co-operation might lead to a peaceful solution of the remaining problems, the Agreement to this end signed in Munich on September 29, 1938, by the four leading interested States, was not only not welcomed in London and Paris, but was actually condemned as a sign of abominable weakness. Now that peaceful revision threatened to be crowned with success, the Jewish capitalist war-mongers, their hands stained with blood, saw their tangible pretexts for realizing their diabolical plans vanish into thin air. Once again we witnessed a conspiracy of wretched corruptible political creatures and money-grabbing financial magnates, for whom war was a welcome means of furthering their business ends. The poison scattered by the Jews throughout the nations began to exercise its disintegrating influence on sound common sense. Scribblers concentrated upon decrying honest men, who wanted peace, as weaklings and traitors, and upon denouncing the opposition parties as the Fifth Column, thus breaking all internal resistance to their criminal war policy. Jews and Freemasons, armaments manufacturers and war profiteers, international business-men and Stock Exchange jobbers seized upon political hirelings of the desperado and Herostrates type, who described war as something infinitely desirable.

It was the work of these criminal persons that spurred the Polish State on to adopt an attitude that was out of all proportion to Germany's demands and still less to the attendant consequences.

In its dealings with Poland, the German Reich has pre-eminently exercised genuine self-restraint since the National-Socialist régime came into power. One of the most despicable and foolish measures of the Versailles Dictate, namely, the severance of an old German province from the Reich, was crying out aloud for revision. Yet what were my requests?

I name myself in this connexion, because no other statesman might have dared to propose a solution such as mine to the German nation. It merely implied the return of Danzig — an ancient purely German city — to the Reich, and the creation of a means of communication between the Reich and its severed province. Even this was to be decided by a plebiscite subject to the control of an international body. If Mr Churchill and the rest of the war-mongers had felt a fraction of the responsibility towards Europe which inspired me, they could never have begun their infamous game.

It was only due to these and other European and non-European parties and their war interests, that Poland rejected my proposals, which in no way affected either her honour or her existence, and in their stead had recourse to terror and to the sword. In this case we once more showed unexampled and truly superhuman self-control, since for months, despite murderous attacks on minority Germans, and even despite the slaughter of tens of thousands of our German fellow-countrymen, we still sought an understanding by peaceful means.

What was the situation?

One of the most unnatural creations of the Dictate of Versailles, a popinjay puffed up with political and military pomp, insults another State for months on end and threatens to grind it to powder, to fight battles on the outskirts of Berlin, to hack the German armies to pieces, to extend its frontiers to the Oder or the Elbe, and so forth. Meanwhile, the other State, Germany, watches this tumult in patient silence, although a single movement of her arm would have sufficed to prick this bubble inflated with folly and hatred.

On September 2, the conflict might still have been averted — Mussolini proposed a plan for the immediate cessation of all hostilities and for peaceful negotiations. Though Germany saw her armies storming to victory, I nevertheless accepted his proposal. It was only the Franco-British war-mongers who desired war, not peace. More than that, as Mr Chamberlain said, they needed a long war, because they had now invested their capital in armaments shares, had purchased machinery and required time for the development of their business interests and the amortization of their investments. For, after all, what do these "citizens of the world" care about Poles, Czechs or such-like peoples?

On June 19, 1940, a German soldier found a curious document when searching some railway trucks standing in the station of La Charité. As the document bore a distinctive inscription, he immediately handed it over to his commanding officer. It was then passed on to other quarters where it was soon realized that we had lighted on an important discovery. The station was subjected to another, more thorough-going search.

Thus it was that the German High Command gained possession of a collection of documents of unique historical significance. They were the secret documents of the Allied Supreme War Council, and included the minutes of every meeting held by this illustrious body. This time Mr. Churchill will not succeed in contesting or lying about the veracity of these documents, as he tried to do when documents were discovered in Warsaw.

These documents bear marginal notes inscribed by Messieurs Gamelin, Daladier, Weygand, etc. They can thus at any time be confirmed or refuted by these very gentlemen. They further yield remarkable evidence of the machinations of the war-mongers and war-extenders. Above all, they show that those stony-hearted politicians regarded all the small nations as a means to their ends; that they had attempted to use Finland in their own interests; that they had determined to turn Norway and Sweden into a theatre of war; that they had planned to fan a conflagration in the Balkans in order to gain the assistance of a hundred divisions from those countries; that they had planned a bombardment of Batum and Baku by a ruthless and unscrupulous interpretation of Turkey's neutrality, who was not unfavourable to them; that they had inveigled Belgium and the Netherlands more and more completely, until they finally entrapped them into binding General Staff agreements, and so on, ad libitum.

The documents further give a picture of the dilettante methods by which these political war-mongers tried to quench the blaze which they had lighted, of their democratic militarism, which is in part to blame for the appalling fate that they have inflicted on hundreds of thousands, even millions of their own soldiers, of their barbarous unscrupulousness which caused them callously to force mass evacuation on their peoples, which brought them no military advantages, though the effects on the population were outrageously cruel.

These same criminals are responsible for having driven Poland into war.

Eighteen days later this campaign was, to all intents and purposes, at an end.

Britain and France Considered Understanding a Crime

On October 6, 1939, I addressed the German nation for the second time during this war at this very place. I was able to inform them of our glorious military victory over the Polish State. At the same time I appealed to the insight of the responsible men in the enemy States and to the nations themselves. I warned them not to continue this war, the consequences of which could only be devastating. I particularly warned the French of embarking on a war which would forcibly eat its way across the frontier and which, irrespective of its outcome, would have appalling consequences. At the same time, I addressed this appeal to the rest of the world, although I feared — as I expressly said — that my words would not be heard, but would more than ever arouse the fury of the interested war-mongers. Everything happened as I predicted. The responsible elements in Britain and France scented in my appeal a dangerous attack on their war profits. They therefore immediately began to declare that every thought of conciliation was out of the question, nay, even a crime; that the war had to be pursued in the name of civilization, of humanity, of happiness, of progress, and — to leave no stone unturned — in the name of religion itself. For this purpose, negroes and bushmen were to be mobilized. Victory, they then said, would come of its own accord, it was, in fact, within their easy reach, as I myself must know very well and have known for a long time since, or I should not have broadcast my appeal for peace throughout the world. For if I had had any justification for

crosses and other decorations, they filled a third of the first balcony.

'Hitler used his best oratorical techniques. His hands moved eloquently to emphasize his words; his body swayed in almost hypnotic fashion, and the crowd responded with cheers and outstretched saluting arms. But the generals, politicians and diplomats fell silent as Hitler came to the core of his speech. "In this hour I feel it to be my duty before my conscience to appeal once more to reason and common sense to Great Britain. I can see no reason why this war must go on ...."'

There was no applause, no cheering and no stamping of heavy boots. There was silence. And it was tense. For in their hearts, the Germans longed for peace now. Hitler waited a moment to allow tension to build up and then added with a subdued, almost sad voice: "I am grieved to think of the sacrifices which it [the war] will claim. I should like to avert them, also for my own people." [Quoted in Shirer, pp. 356–7]

SATURDAY 20 July 1940

All morning there were isolated enemy incursions, from Scotland to Dorset, but most action was centred again on the Channel, on a convoy codenamed 'Bosom'. In the Lyme Bay area, the patrolling duties fell to No. 238 Squadron, which lost a pilot and aircraft driving away a small number of Me109s. In mid-afternoon, 501 Squadron from Middle Wallop was scrambled to intercept an incoming force of Stukas escorted by Me109s. The enemy planes were encountered half way between Jersey and Portland Bill. The combat saw the first kill of the battle by Sergeant J.H. 'Ginger' Lacey; he would go on to become the top-scoring RAF Battle of Britain pilot (see page 118). He turned sharply on the inside of an Me109 that was heading for him and got three bursts off as he glued his Hurricane to the German's tail. 'I can clearly remember watching him slanting down the sky at a hell of a steep angle,' said Lacey. 'A beautiful little blue and grey mottled aircraft with white and black crosses standing out startlingly clear, getting smaller and smaller; and thinking what a terribly small splash he made when he went straight into the Channel.' Lacey then tailed another fighter heading north, knowing that he would have to turn for home at some point, 'and then I've got him'. The turn, when it came, was sharp enough to nearly cause a collision with the Hurricane, but Lacey opened fire and 'I suddenly saw the aeroplane almost stagger as I hit it. Its propeller started to slow down. We flashed past each other a few feet apart.' [Quoted in Bickers, p. 213] Another Hurricane finished off the second Me109 moments later.

Other squadrons took over as the convoy moved eastwards, watched by the shadowing German aircraft. As an attack seemed inevitable, Air Vice-Marshal Park was determined that this time his fighters would not be overwhelmed, and he increased the strength of patrols to as many as 24 aircraft. Convoy 'Bosom' was opposite Dover when, at around 6pm, the attacking force came into sight – Stukas protected by some 50 Me109s and Me110s. But in flying towards the convoy, the Germans were facing the sun, and they were 'bounced' by the Hurricanes of No. 32 Squadron, which flew straight through the Me109s and plunged onto the Stukas below, shooting down two and severely damaging four. Hurricanes of 615 Squadron and Spitfires of 610 Squadron then engaged the German fighters.

Occasional thunderstorms; cloudy in Straits of Dover, brightening later.

OPPOSITE

The translated text of Hitler's 19 July 'Last Appeal to Reason' appeared in this propaganda leaflet, which was dropped over parts of England in early August 1940. The invitation to surrender proved resistible.

A boyish-looking 'Ginger' Lacey sits in the cockpit of his Spitfire at Colerne airbase, Wiltshire, in May 1941.
By this time he had scored more than twenty successes in combat.

'GINGER' LACEY, FIGHTER ACE

Sergeant James Harry 'Ginger' Lacey (1917–89) was an exceptionally talented pilot and a supremely accurate marksman, who shot down at least 15 aircraft in the Battle of Britain. An exact total can never be known, because the confusion endemic to aerial combat means that even now, after close examination of records and excavation of crash sites, the scores of leading aces will never be accurately known.

Called 'Ginger' in reference to his hair colour, Lacey was born in Wetherby, Yorkshire, the son of a farmer. He attributed his later marksmanship to having shot rabbits when young. The grammar-school-educated boy did not, however, take up the farming life, and was instead working as a trainee pharmacist when, in 1937, he applied to join the RAF Volunteer Reserve. He was called up at the outbreak of war, joined No. 501 Squadron and went with it to France on 10 May 1940. By the time the squadron withdrew on 19 June, Lacey had accounted for one Me109, an Me110 and two Heinkel He111s.

Lacey narrowly escaped death on numerous occasions during the Battle of Britain, and was shot down or forced to land because of combat damage no less than nine times. On 23 August, he was awarded the Distinguished Flying Medal (DFM), and the following month came his celebrated shooting down of a Heinkel He111 that had earlier bombed Buckingham Palace.

A commission came in 1941, and from 1943 he was in action against the Japanese in Burma. After 1945, he remained in RAF service until his 1967 retirement as a squadron leader – with the reputation as the RAF pilot with the most kills to his name during the Battle of Britain.

The twin-engine Me110s retreated by forming a defensive orbiting circle, while the single-engine fighters clashed in a mass dogfight. The result was a clear victory for the pilots of Fighter Command. As well as the damage inflicted on the Stuka force, Fighter Command had shot down five Me109s while losing only two of its own fighters. After the previous few days, it was a very welcome boost.

The pilots were learning fast. There was no substitute for grim experience when it came to understanding how to survive and, if you were lucky, to kill. The pilots talked incessantly about their experiences, drawing from each other and sharing tips. The tempo of the fighting made untried pilots veterans in the space of a few days.

BELOW *Fight over Portland*, painted by Richard Eurich (1903–92) in 1940. He was commissioned to paint two works by the War Artists Advisory Committee, before becoming an official war artist for the Admiralty in 1941.

SUNDAY **21 July 1940**

On Sunday, a patrol from 238 Squadron started the day by shooting down a Dornier that was shadowing a convoy. Two more aircraft joined the patrol, and between them they shot down an Me110, which was also engaged in watching

Fine and fair early, clouding over during late morning.

the convoy as it headed westwards off the Dorset coast. When the flotilla was about ten miles south of the Needles, the chalky outcrops west of the Isle of Wight, it ran into an attacking force of a *Gruppe* of Dorniers together with about 50 Messerschmitt Me109s and Me110s. Hurricanes from No. 43 Squadron made an interception, successfully breaking up the bomber formation and shooting down one of the escorts. Yet more Hurricanes arrived from 238 Squadron, just as the Me110s, which had formed their usual defensive circle, started dive-bombing the convoy – the first time this tactic had been seen. One of the Me110s was severely damaged by a 238 pilot before the attackers made for home.

Pilots had mixed feelings about using forward bases such as Warmwell. In theory, they reduced the pilots' time to interception, but they also meant that the aircraft did not have time to climb as high as their operators would have liked. 'One of the great advantages of Middle Wallop,' said John Bisdee of 609 Squadron, 'was that it was about sixty miles from Portland and those sort of places, which gave you enough time when you scrambled to climb up and attack from the top.' Otherwise, you 'had to climb up underneath the Germans'. Eric Seabourne of 238 Squadron quickly learned that 'When the ground controller said, "Angels twelve", meaning at 12,000 feet, the squadron would go to 14,000. You always wanted maximum height. Once you'd got height you were in the driving seat.' [Quoted in Parker, p. 155]

Flight Lieutenant John Bisdee (1915–2001), of No. 609 (West Riding) Squadron, saw plenty of action during the Battle of Britain, racking up a number of 'kills'. He retired from the RAF in 1946 as a group captain.

It was from Warmwell that John Bisdee was scrambled in mid-July to protect the Portland naval base: 'the first time I'd ever seen a really large German formation. The controller on the R/T said, "One hundred-plus bandits" and then told us the direction. Moments later he said, "Two hundred-plus bandits" and then finally he said, "Very many bandits!" ... I remember the incredible sight of this great swarm of rotating German aircraft, each following their own tail, going round and round emitting condensation trails.' Indignation spurred Bisdee and his fellow pilots on. 'The feeling I had, and a lot of us had, was, What are these buggers doing here? How dare they? It was really quite a shock to see this vast number of back crosses and swastikas in the sky over our country. Then we all plunged in.' [Quoted in Parker, p. 142]

On Sunday 21 July, Hitler summoned his military commanders to discuss the invasion of Britain. They examined the logistics of occupation in detail. Already, organizations that were considered particularly hostile to Germany had been identified. These included trade unions, the Freemasons, the universities – and even the Boy Scouts, described as 'a disguised instrument of power for British cultural propaganda'. A list of nearly 3000 names for immediate arrest had been drawn up for use by the *Einsatzgruppen*, the Gestapo-led units formed to follow in the wake of the army to crush possible dissent. At today's meeting, planning was carried out for detailed civil regulations and a currency conversion rate – at £1 sterling to 9.6 Deutschmarks, designed to ensure that much of Britain's wealth flowed to Berlin, following the pattern imposed in France and other occupied lands. There was also a scheme to deport all males between the ages of 17 and 45.

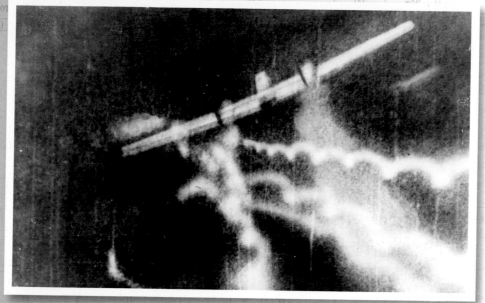

A grainy still from the gun camera of a Spitfire (of No. 74 Squadron) shows tracer hitting the port engine of a Messerschmitt Me110. Pilots on both sides had to accustom their nerves to the dangerous skies.

'I HAD NEVER KNOWN ANY FEAR LIKE THAT'

Tim Vigors, a pilot officer with 222 Squadron, got his first experience of battle on 29 May 1940. He was woken at Duxford at 4am by his batman with a cup of tea. He gave his beloved dog, a lurcher named Snipe, a farewell hug, telling him he would see him that evening, and was driven out to dispersal.

'I walked over to my aircraft to make sure everything was in order. My mouth was dry and for the first time I understood the meaning of the expression "taste of fear". I suddenly realized that the moment had arrived ... within an hour I would be battling for my life, being shot at with real bullets by a man whose one desire in life was to kill me. Up until now it had all somehow been a game, like a Biggles book where the heroes always survived the battles and it was generally only the baddies who got the chop. I was dead scared and knew I had somehow to control this fear and not show it to my fellow pilots.'

Near Dunkirk, his flight — led by Douglas Bader — climbed to attack some Me109s. In the dogfight that followed Vigors found himself being chased by a Messerschmitt, which fired white tracer past his port wingtip. In that moment his first reaction was 'extreme fear which temporarily froze my ability to think. This was quickly replaced by an overwhelming desire for self-preservation.' He escaped unharmed and later managed to get some shots into another Me109. As he returned home after one-and-a-half exhausting hours, he examined his feelings. His biggest concern was 'how deadly scared I'd been when I first saw those enemy bullets streaming past my wingtip. I had never known any fear like that before in my life ... I just fervently hoped I could keep it under control.' Vigors succeeded and went on to shoot down five German aircraft and gather a further four probable kills. [Manuscript for Vigors, 2006]

AIRBORNE RADAR

The invention of radar opened up the possibility that defending aircraft operating at night-time would be able to 'see in the dark'. But to make a night-time interception, the defending fighter plane had to be able to make visual contact with the raider, and this required it to be only some 325 yards (300 metres) away. The Chain Home High and Chain Home Low radar stations (the latter created to try to track low-flying aircraft) were simply not accurate enough to be able to guide the fighter this close. This meant that the night-fighter had to have its own on-board radar system, which presented enormous difficulties. Second World War radar was based on low-frequency signals and needed large antennae, making it impractical for mounting on a ship or aircraft.

As early as 1936 it was realized that the Luftwaffe might turn to night bombing if a daylight campaign faltered. Robert Watson-Watt, the principal figure behind British radar (see page 60), had put another of the staff from the Radio Research Station, Edward Bowen, in charge of developing a radar that could be carried by a fighter. Bowen decided that an airborne radar should not exceed 90kg (200 lbs) in weight, and require no more than 500 watts of power. To reduce the drag of the antennae, the operating wavelength could not be much greater than one metre, difficult for the electronics of that time. Nevertheless, such a system, known as 'AI' (Airborne Interception), was developed by 1940. It would prove instrumental in ending the Blitz of 1941. Bowen also fitted airborne radar to maritime patrol aircraft to reduce the threat from submarines.

A Hurricane Mark 1 night-fighter, of No. 85 Squadron, taxis along the runway at Debden sector station as it prepares to take off.

But Hitler's enthusiasm for an amphibious attack was waning again. His attention was turning towards the Soviet Union, and Operation Sea Lion was now appearing a wasteful and risky diversion. 'The invasion of Britain is an exceptionally dangerous undertaking,' he told Grossadmiral Raeder. 'Even if the way is short this is not just a river crossing, but the crossing of sea which is dominated by the enemy ... Operational surprise cannot be expected; a defensively prepared and utterly determined enemy face us and dominate the sea area we must use ... The prerequisites,' he concluded, 'are complete mastery of the air, the operational use of powerful artillery in the Straits of Dover and protection by minefields. The time of year is an important factor, too ... if it is not certain that preparations can be completed by the beginning of September, other plans must be considered.' [Quoted in Longmate, p. 491]

With a lack of firm and enthusiastic leadership of the operation at the top, the various service chiefs argued among themselves. The German navy pleaded for more attacks on Britain's naval assets in the Channel, including the bombing and mining of the ports of Dover, Plymouth, Portland and Portsmouth. Other ports on the south coast were to be left undamaged for the use of the Wehrmacht invasion forces. The army said that it would not guarantee success unless the navy transported 40 divisions; but the navy accepted responsibility for only 10. Generalfeldmarschall Halder, chief of the army general staff, considered this smaller number suicidal. Goering, with his habitual blind optimism, then declared that, given five days of good weather, he could so reduce the British defences that ten divisions would be more than enough. He then summoned Kesselring and Sperrle and ordered them to make plans for the successful conclusion of the *Kanalkampf*. There was, however, general agreement about one thing: the first priority was the destruction of Fighter Command.

A Dornier Do18 seaplane prepares for take-off in the North Sea (1940). The aircraft was used for reconnaissance by the Luftwaffe prior to big attacks during the Battle of Britain.

MONDAY 22 July 1940

This morning Britain gave its defiant response to Hitler's speech of 19 July. On behalf of the British government, Lord Halifax, who had hitherto been an advocate of a negotiated peace, delivered the reply to Hitler's 'Last Appeal to Reason', and his words were broadcast to the nation today:

Straits of Dover fair, but Channel generally cloudy.

'Many of you will have read two days ago the speech in which Herr Hitler summoned Great Britain to capitulate to his will. I will not waste your time by dealing with his distortion of almost every main event since the war began. He says he has no desire to destroy the British Empire. But there was in his speech no suggestion that peace must be based on justice, no word of recognition that the other nations of Europe had any right to self determination, the principle that he has so often invoked for Germans. His only appeal was to the base instincts of fear, and his only arguments were threats ...

Hitler has now made it plain that he is preparing to direct the whole weight of German might against this country. That is why in every part of Britain there is only one spirit, a spirit of indomitable resolution. Nor has anyone any doubt that if Hitler were to succeed it would be the end, for many besides ourselves, of all those things which make life worth living. We realize that the struggle may cost us everything, but just because the things we are defending are worth any sacrifice, it is a noble privilege to be the defenders of things so precious ...

We never wanted the war. Certainly no one here wants the war to go on for a day longer than is necessary. But we shall not stop fighting till freedom, for ourselves and others, is secure.'

Up in the skies, there was little activity during the hours of daylight, with only sporadic reconnaissance and occasional ineffective attacks on shipping. But that night, from bases of all three *Luftflotten*, German aircraft flew over 100 mine-laying sorties. The mines sown were about 1100 pounds in weight, and the bombers usually carried two each. It was a difficult task technically, requiring accurate navigation and low-altitude, low-speed flying.

One of these sorties would provide the RAF with a considerable breakthrough. For the first time, a night raider was intercepted using airborne radar. The victim was a Dornier picked up by the Chain Home Low radar station at Poling, Kent. The position of the Dornier was tracked and passed to the operations room at Tangmere, where the Fighter Interception Unit, made up of Blenheims equipped with onboard radar, was based. The controller guided one of the Blenheims towards the inbound aircraft, and soon one of the first AI Mark III sets had located the intruder south of Brighton. Then the observer, Pilot Officer Geoffrey Morris, glimpsed the Dornier crossing ahead and above and shouted to the pilot, Flying Officer Glynn Ashfield, to turn. He swung the aircraft around so that the bomber lay dead ahead, silhouetted by the moon. Ashfield fired a ten-second burst, which set the Dornier's fuel tanks on fire, and the German plane went flaming down into the sea.

Even with the new airborne radar, the problem of intercepting night raids was a formidable one, and the vast majority of sorties in darkness failed to find enemy aircraft. On the same busy night of 22/23 July, however, 'Ginger' Lacey had a piece of luck. 'After being vectored all over the sky by the controller, I unexpectedly saw a Heinkel 111 caught in the searchlights some two miles ahead and slightly above, so I started to climb after it.' [Quoted in Bickers, p. 214] But then some of the searchlights switched to his Hurricane. The procedure to identify oneself as a friend was for a bomber to fire the Verey-light colours of the day, and for a fighter to flash the 'letters of the day' on its downward light. This Lacey duly did, but then the Heinkel fired a red light followed by a green, which through luck or excellent intelligence was the correct signal of the day. Thereupon, all the searchlights switched to Lacey; ten seconds later the anti-aircraft guns opened up at him. Blinded by the lights, and in danger of being shot down, he lost the Heinkel.

23 July 1940 TUESDAY

Slight haze in the Straits of Dover.

The threat posed by barrage balloons to low-flying German aircraft was brought home to Hauptmann Hans-Joachim ('Hajo') Herrmann on the night of 22/23 July, when, with three other Ju88 dive-bombers, he was attempting to lay mines in Plymouth Sound. He planned to descend to about 300 feet to drop his cargo along the harbour breakwater. As he lost height he saw the great outline of a balloon wallowing ahead, and his aircraft became entangled in the balloon's upper surface. Then, barrage balloon and bomber began sinking earthwards. 'It only lasted a few seconds, though it felt like an hour,' he remembered. 'Then I notice[d] the British searchlights were shining from above – we had fallen off the balloon, and now we were upside down, with virtually no forward speed, and I was going down out of control.' It felt 'as if I was playing a piano which was falling from a fifth storey'. [Quoted in Mason, p. 146] He ordered his crew to bale out. But then the bomber regained flying speed and with every gun in the sound bearing on him he completed his mine-laying mission, before heading thankfully for home.

The day itself, though, was a quiet one for the defenders. Two German bombers were shot down while following convoys, but Fighter Command suffered no combat losses.

WEDNESDAY 24 July 1940

The day would see the return of heavy formation attacks by the Luftwaffe. At about 8am, two *Staffeln* of Dorniers attacked a convoy in the Straits of Dover. Six Spitfires of No. 54 Squadron succeeded in disrupting their bombing runs but did not bring any of the enemy aircraft down. The squadron was scrambled again at 11.20am, after radar picked up a large force approaching a convoy leaving the mouth of the River Medway, Kent. When the fighters made visual contact over Margate, they reported 18 Dorniers flying in tight formation, with about 40 Messerschmitt Me109s protecting them above. No. 65 Squadron was also scrambled to help, while nine Spitfires from No. 610 Squadron at Biggin Hill were vectored to patrol the Dover Straits area to cut off the German retreat.

Cloudy, rainy, and fog in the west spreading east.

Adolf Galland, newly promoted to major, was leading the Me109s, which now joined battle with the six Spitfires of 54 Squadron. Two of the German aircraft were hit first, in both cases killing the pilots. Then, one of the victors, Sergeant G.R. Collett, was himself hit and compelled to land. Almost immediately afterwards, Pilot Officer Johnny Allen, an accredited 'ace' with eight victories to his credit, was also hit. According to his number two, Al Deere, who stuck with him as he went down, he 'glided towards the coast. Just as he crossed his engine appeared to pick up again and turned towards Manston hoping, no doubt, to get it down safely there. The next moment fire broke out in the engine and at once the aircraft flicked on to its back and dived into the ground on the outskirts of Foreness.' Allen did not survive.

In the meantime, the arriving No. 65 Squadron had gone after the Dorniers, but through accurate crossfire the British fighters were kept out of effective range by the tight formation. They did, however, manage to down a further Me109, before the Germans, low on fuel, dived for home. As they did so, a fresh *Jagdgeschwader* roared in to protect their withdrawal. But they were surprised by the lurking 610 Squadron, which shot down two aircraft straightaway and drove the rest back. One of the squadron's number was killed crash-landing back at Biggin Hill.

It had been a comparatively quiet day in the Channel, but nonetheless 17,000 tons of shipping from three convoys had been sunk, and other vessels were badly damaged. By now, the Germans had established radar installations on the cliffs at Wissant, on the Channel coast opposite Folkestone. They could now track convoys easily, and their grip on the Channel – as demanded by the *Kriegsmarine* – seemed ever tighter.

25 July 1940 THURSDAY

Fine day; hazy in Straits of Dover.

Early on Thursday, the new German radar installations picked up a convoy of 21 merchant ships, codenamed CW8, with escorts off Southend, heading westwards. At first the Germans sent over only fighter sweeps. Shortly after midday, one of these was met by Spitfires from No. 65 Squadron. One of the Me109s crashed into the sea during a low-level pursuit. Both sides threw more fighters into the combat. By 12.45pm, 20 Hurricanes from Nos 32 and 615 squadrons were engaged in a furious dogfight with 40 Me109s, which only came to an end when fuel ran low for both sides. At this moment, with the skies above the convoy empty, a mass attack of more than 60 Stukas swept in. Five vessels were sunk and a further five damaged. Nine Spitfires from No. 54 Squadron rushed to help, but they arrived just as German fighters appeared in huge numbers. Two of the British aircraft were shot down, with one pilot killed.

Thirty Ju88s, together with more than fifty Me109s, launched a further attack on the beleaguered convoy at 2.30 in the afternoon. On guard over the vessels was a paltry force of just eight Spitfires from No. 64 Squadron. As the rest of the squadron was scrambled, along with 12 Hurricanes from 111 Squadron, the small force went in on the attack, outnumbered five to one. With the arrival of the reinforcements, the Junkers and their escort broke for home. But the convoy did not stay unmolested for long. As it passed Folkestone, it was strafed by Me109s, then pounded again by Ju88 dive-bombers, which managed to time their attack between fighter patrols. Two escorting destroyers, sent out from Dover, were badly damaged. No. 56 Squadron arrived as the bombing was under way, and soon Spitfires from Nos 64 and 54 squadrons were also involved, taking on a huge swarm of Me109s. Both 54 and 64 squadrons lost three aircraft each. The Germans also deployed their fast surface E-boats against the vessels, and by the time the convoy reached its destination at Portland – itself under attack this day from *Luftflotte* 3 – only two of the original twenty-one coal transporters and coasters were undamaged.

26 July 1940 FRIDAY

Low cloud and heavy rain.

No. 54 Squadron had lost five pilots killed and three wounded in the previous three weeks, including, says Al Deere, 'two of our most experienced leaders'. The squadron had, in the same time, flown 504 combat sorties and was exhausted. 'The strain of long hours at readiness and repeated combats against overwhelming numbers was having a depressing effect on the more inexperienced squadron pilots,' said Deere. Of the original seventeen pilots serving when the Dunkirk fighting opened, only five remained. These five, though rich in experience, 'had reached the point of physical and mental tiredness beyond which lies the realm of fear', which, Deere said, could spread like a disease down through the squadron and even affect the groundcrews. [Deere, p. 99] Today, the squadron was withdrawn from the frontline. As No. 54 Squadron moved north to Catterick, No. 41 took its place at Hornchurch.

In spite of atrocious flying weather today – low dark cloud and heavy rain all over Britain – the Luftwaffe still came, albeit in small numbers. In the early morning,

SINGLE-ENGINE AIRCRAFT				MULTI-ENGINE AIRCRAFT						PASS-ENGER	INSTR/CLOUD FLYING [Incl. in cols. (1) to (10)]	
DAY		NIGHT		DAY			NIGHT					
DUAL	PILOT	DUAL	PILOT	DUAL	1ST PILOT	2ND PILOT	DUAL	1ST PILOT	2ND PILOT		DUAL	PILOT
(1)	(2)	(3)	(4)					(9)	(10)	(11)	(12)	(13)

GERMAN RADAR

It was a German physicist, Heinrich Hertz, who in 1887 began experimenting with radio waves in his laboratory. He found that they could be transmitted through different types of materials, but were reflected by others. In 1904, another German, Christian Hülsmeyer (1881–1957), gave public demonstrations in Germany and the Netherlands of his patented *Telemobiloskop*, which used radio echoes to detect ships so that collisions could be avoided. This was the moment when, in essence, radar was invented. But while French and American physicists set to work developing the new technology, in Germany the invention was all but ignored for 30 years.

Eventually, in 1934, two German scientists, Hans Hollmann and Hans-Karl von Willisen, built the first commercial radar system for detecting ships. It could detect ships up to ten kilometres away, although it was unable to show range. It was the German navy, rather than the Luftwaffe, that took an interest. In the summer of 1935 a pulse radar was developed, which, in tests, was shown to be able to spot a large vessel eight kilometres away, accurately enough for guns to be laid. The same system could also detect an aircraft at 500-metre altitude at a distance of 28 kilo-metres, and somewhat belatedly the Luftwaffe became interested in the technology, ordering a dozen sets of what became known as *Freya*. (The seaborne version was known as *Seetakt*.)

The German radar had nothing in common with the huge masts that rose along the English coast. *Freya* operated in the 1.2-metre wavelength (a tenth of that of the Chain Home system), and it was much smaller, with a better resolution. Yet by the start of the war only eight of these units were in operation, on Germany's border. While the Telefunken company developed a superior system, named *Würzburg*, for home defence, radar was of limited use to the Germans while the Luftwaffe was on the offensive in the Battle of Britain, except for finding targets in the waters of the Channel.

A *Freya* radar installation at Auderville, on the Normandy coast, as seen by a low-level RAF reconnaissance flight in 1941.

Fighter pilots mingle in the summer of 1940. In between actions, pilots traded experiences, anxious to glean any information that might help them improve their performance and their chances of survival. Some tried to rest. But the constant buzz of anxiety meant it was usually a vain hope.

Hurricanes from 601 Squadron at Tangmere were called to the assistance of a convoy south of the Isle of Wight under attack from *Fliegerkorps* VIII dive-bombers. The convoy was undamaged, but the squadron lost an aircraft and pilot to accompanying Me109s. Just before midday another convoy was raided, this time in Middle Wallop's part of the Channel. No. 238 Squadron intercepted and succeeded in shooting down one of the fighter escort, and for once all their aircraft and pilots returned unharmed. The Luftwaffe lost a further two reconnaissance bombers that afternoon, but isolated German raids dropped bombs on Hastings, Weymouth, Bristol and Aberdeen.

27 July 1940 SATURDAY

Cloudy, later clearing.

Heavy thunderstorms threatened this morning, but as the clouds cleared, the Luftwaffe again joined battle for control of the Channel. At dawn the Germans spotted a large eastbound convoy, codenamed 'Bacon', off Portland, and at 8am 30 Stukas took off from their base near Caen on the Normandy coast. Collecting a fighter escort of a *Jagdgeschwader* of Me109s, they met the convoy over Weymouth Bay. Three Hurricanes of 238 Squadron scrambled from Middle Wallop and intercepted the Stukas just as they were preparing to dive on the ships below. Flying Officer Charles Davis shot down one dive-bomber, but the rest were too well protected by their escort and they escaped unscathed. In the meantime, a second wave of 20 more Stukas had taken off from Caen to attack the convoy near Swanage, Dorset. Although Hurricanes from 238 Squadron and six Spitfires from 609 Squadron were on patrol over the ships, they failed to get through the Me109s to the Stukas, and the Spitfire of James 'Buck' Buchanan, John Bisdee's great friend in 609 Squadron, simply vanished. No-one saw him shot down and, once the attackers had departed, two of his fellow pilots searched out to sea for some sign of him, but without success. John Bisdee remembers his car, a small sports model: 'It sat forlornly outside the dispersal hut for several days until someone could be found to take it away. The empty motor car definitely had an effect on me. I'd been in it on many occasions. I was quite pleased to see that little car go.' [Quoted in Parker, p. 147] In the nine weeks since the start of Dunkirk, 609 Squadron, which prided itself on its dash and insouciance, had lost nine pilots, including seven of the twelve Auxiliary officers who had made up the squadron at the start of the war.

The Royal Navy was also having a bad day. Off the Suffolk coast, where convoys had come under sporadic attacks, He111s sank the destroyer HMS *Wren*. Then Dover was attacked twice, with Messerschmitt Me109s used as fighter-bombers for the first time. This tactic made them slow and vulnerable, and less able to carry sufficient fuel. It was a move understandably unpopular with their pilots. But it did mean, in theory, that Me109s could no longer be ignored by Fighter Command if flying on their own.

The second raid, by Junkers Ju88s and 87s as well as Dorniers, heavily escorted, succeeded in landing a bomb alongside the destroyer HMS *Codrington*. The explosion broke the back of the ship, which sank in two pieces, with the stern beached on the seafront by Dover's White Cliff Hotel, where it would lie for the remainder of the war. Two other vessels were severely damaged, and burning oil spread over the harbour. It was clear that Dover's anti-aircraft defences, crippled by pre-war austerity, were inadequate.

RAF reconnaissance had reported during the day that preparations were underway at Cap Gris Nez for a giant artillery position, of a size more than capable of landing shells on Dover. This, together with the success of the day's enemy attack, led to the abandonment by the Royal Navy of Dover as a destroyer base. The remaining warships there withdrew to the North Sea ports of Harwich and Sheerness. From there, destroyers could still be effective against an invasion force in the Dover Straits. But a frontline position had effectively been lost and the Royal Navy denied freedom of the English Channel. It was a significant victory for the Luftwaffe.

Ships in a convoy narrowly escape the exploding bombs of a German air raid in the Straits of Dover.

'SAILOR' MALAN, FIGHTER ACE

In July 1940, Adolph Gysbert Malan (1910–63) was a flight lieutenant with No. 74 Squadron, which he would soon take command of. Thirty years old, he had endured a tough upbringing in South Africa, where he had been a sea cadet (1924–6) under the brutal discipline of the training ship *General Botha* and endured a flogging that left him scarred for life. He served as an officer in the merchant navy, with the Union Castle line, and in 1932 joined Britain's Royal Naval Volunteer Reserve. It was the years of maritime experience that gave him his subsequent nickname, 'Sailor'.

Then, in 1935–6, he learned to fly and applied for an RAF short-service commission, rising to flight lieutenant by 1939. Seeing his first action – and his first kills – in late May 1940, Malan was to prove an exceptional pilot and an inspiration to others. He was brilliant, accurate and deadly: it was said of him that he could 'spot a fly on the Great Wall of China at five miles'. [Quoted in Allen, p. 77] By August 1940 he was leading No. 74 Squadron, at which point he compiled his influential *aide-mémoire* 'Ten of My Rules of Air Fighting'; by March 1941 he was wing commander at Biggin Hill.

Older than most of the other Battle of Britain pilots, Malan was married, with a son (Jonathan) who had Winston Churchill as a godfather. Malan survived the war, leaving RAF service in 1946 for civilian life in a changing South Africa, where he remained an opponent of the developing apartheid policies until his death, from Parkinson's disease, in 1963. But by then his reputation had long been secure, as the RAF fighter pilot with the most 'kills' to his name – 32 – over the course of the war.

'Sailor' Malan in the cockpit of his Spitfire, January 1943.

TEN OF MY RULES FOR AIR FIGHTING

1. Wait until you see the whites of his eyes. Fire short bursts of one to two seconds only when your sights are definitely "ON".
2. Whilst shooting think of nothing else, brace the whole of your body: have both hands on the stick: concentrate on your ring sight.
3. Always keep a sharp lookout. "Keep your finger out".
4. Height gives you the initiative.
5. Always turn and face the attack.
6. Make your decisions promptly. It is better to act quickly even though your tactics are not the best.
7. Never fly straight and level for more than 30 seconds in the combat area.
8. When diving to attack always leave a proportion of your formation above to act as a top guard.
9. INITIATIVE, AGGRESSION, AIR DISCIPLINE, and TEAM WORK are words that MEAN something in Air Fighting.
10. Go in quickly - Punch hard - Get out!

SUNDAY 28 July 1940

Fine and fair; cloudy in evening.

In accordance with the preparations ordered for Operation Sea Lion, attacks on Dover now rose in frequency and strength. At noon on Sunday, radar stations at Dover, Rye and Pevensey picked up a large formation to the west of Calais, and then, soon after, another to the east of the city. Their progress was tracked to the mid-Channel, when, inexplicably, the bombers turned back. At 1.30pm though, the radar screens were again busy, with a formation heading for Dover. Eight squadrons from No. 11 Group had been moved to the forward airfields of Hawkinge, Manston and Martlesham. As the attacking formation neared the English coast, Observer Corps reported more than 60 Heinkel He111s along with 40-odd Messerschmitt Me109s. Spitfires from 74 and 41 squadrons and Hurricanes from Nos 111 and 257 were ordered up to intercept, with instructions that the former handle the escort while the latter take on the bombers. First to arrive was No. 74 Squadron from nearby Manston, led by South African 'Sailor' Malan.

The squadron made a determined attack on the Me109s of *Jagdgeschwader* 51 led by German ace Major Werner Mölders, who had 25 kills to his name (see page 132). Three Messerschmitts were shot down and two more damaged, for the loss of two Spitfires, with one pilot killed. No. 41 Squadron then arrived and had the biggest success of the day. Flight Lieutenant John Webster managed to hit Mölders' Me109. The German ace made it back to his base at Wissant, but he was severely wounded and would play no part in the battle for the following month.

MONDAY 29 July 1940

Clear and fine; slight mist in Straits of Dover.

The Monday saw perfect flying weather, and Fighter Command braced itself for heavy attacks. At 7am the first enemy formations were detected crossing the Channel, heading for Dover. The Air Ministry had been pleading with Air Vice-Marshal Park to provide more protection for the port, and the 11 Group commander now obliged, sending 11 Spitfires of 41 Squadron from Manston to attack the formation's right flank and 12 Hurricanes of 501 Squadron from Hawkinge against its left. The Spitfires arrived first, to find that they were still massively outnumbered, facing 48 Stuka dive-bombers and, high and to the right, about 80 Messerschmitt Me109s. No. 41 Squadron split into two, with one flight attacking the bombers, and the other engaging the fighters. But the Me109s had the advantage of height; straightaway Flying Officer D.R. Gamblen was shot down and killed. Four more of the squadron's Spitfires were hit and forced to crash-land, though the pilots survived unhurt. Those attacking the bombers had more success, shooting down two of them. As No. 501 Squadron arrived, followed by re-inforcements in the shape of No. 56 Squadron Hurricanes, the sky above Dover became a mass of vapour trails, as a huge dogfight developed involving about 200 aircraft. As bombs fell in Dover harbour, so too did the bombers, with two further Stukas crashing into the sea along with a Hurricane from 56 Squadron.

Soon after, two convoys in the Channel were attacked, the first by Ju88s, which had flown in low enough to avoid radar detection. One bomber was downed by a barrage balloon and another by anti-aircraft fire from the ships, but the fighter

continued on page 135

WERNER MÖLDERS, GERMAN ACE

Serious and introverted, a devout Catholic with little apparent enthusiasm for the Nazis, Werner Mölders (1913–41) was Germany's best fighter pilot of the early years of the war, and arguably one of the greatest fighter pilots of all time. Although only 27 years old in 1940, he was known as *Vati* – 'Daddy' – and was mentor to aces such as Adolf Galland and Helmut Wick. He was commanding a *Staffel* (squadron) before the age of 22, a good teacher and an inspirational figure to other fighter pilots. Perhaps most importantly, he was the main architect of the tactics employed by the German *Geschwader* (fighter wings) during the Battle of Britain.

Mölders' father had been killed in the First World War, but in 1931, aged 18, Mölders joined the German army before requesting transfer to the new Luftwaffe three years later. Initially rejected as an unsuitable fighter pilot, he overcame problems with nausea and vomiting to become a squadron leader and instructor. Like Galland and Wick, Mölders was inspired by the example of First World War aces such as Baron von Richthofen and Oswald Boelcke. Flying an Me109, he shot down 14 aircraft during the Condor Legion's intervention in the Spanish Civil War, where he was instrumental in developing the *Rotte/Schwärme* type of fighter formation that became the German standard procedure (see page 59).

During the Battle of France Mölders claimed 25 kills, and he was rapidly promoted. He was shot down in early June 1940 and taken prisoner, but he was released less than three weeks later after the armistice between Germany and France. At the end of July he was put in charge of *Jagdgeschwader* 51. He was out of action for a month, after having been wounded on 28 July 1940, but by the end of the Battle of Britain he had 30 claimed kills to add to his tally, which continued to rise during 1941 as the RAF followed its controversial policy of engaging the Luftwaffe over France and the Channel.

Action on the Eastern Front made Mölders the highest-scoring fighter pilot in history, with more than 100 kills. In August 1941 he was made the Luftwaffe's *General der Jagdflieger* (Fighter General), giving him responsibility for tactical planning. It all came to an end when he was killed on 22 November 1941, after the He111 carrying him from the Crimea to Berlin crash-landed during a thunderstorm. Afterwards, his fighter wing, *Jagdgeschwader* 51, carried his name.

After the war, Mölders continued to be honoured by the Federal German military, with a destroyer, a battalion of signallers and a fighter *Geschwader* named after him. The last was, however, removed by the German parliament, the Bundestag, in 1998, a gesture for the 61st anniversary of the bombing of Guernica. Petitions of protest poured in, but the decision remained unchanged. The Bundestag decided that the Condor Legion 'should not be honoured any more', and doubts were cast on Mölders' anti-Nazi credentials.

RIGHT Goering poses with his two star fighter aces, Major Werner Mölders (*left*) and Major Adolf Galland (*right*), in a staged conversation. (The *Reichsmarschall* was not a good listener.) As with some of their British counterparts, the two pilots became national celebrities.

ADOLF GALLAND, GERMAN ACE

Adolf Galland (1912–96) was, with Werner Mölders, one of the two most famous German pilots of 1940. As with many German airmen, Galland first took to the air in a glider, at one of the schools set up in the interwar years to get around the Versailles restrictions on the development of a German air force. As a boy he read stories of the First World War aces Oswald Boelcke and 'Red' Baron von Richthofen. In 1932, aged 20, he was accepted for pilot training at a commercial school. His talents were noticed and he was selected for secret military training, before joining the civil airline Lufthansa as a pilot, flying airliners to Barcelona. In 1933, with Hitler in power, he switched to the air force, and in April 1937 went to Spain to fly biplane fighters in the Luftwaffe-directed Condor Legion in support of General Franco's nationalist rebels.

By the middle of 1940, Galland was in what he felt was his element, emulating his childhood heroes in combat against the British. Galland was a complex and deceptive personality. He seemed, at first glance, to fit one established image of the dashing aviator, with his love of wine, women and good times. He appeared good-humoured, unimpressed by authority and relaxed about discipline. But Galland was also, like Richthofen before him, a calculating warrior who took a scientific approach to killing.

Although indeed 'one of the boys', Galland was also intimate with the top brass. Initially at least, he admired Goering, another First World War ace, and admitted to his biographer that, after leaving his first private meeting with Hitler, 'he felt a mutual respect had been forged'. In 1941, Galland succeeded Mölders as *General der Jagdflieger*, responsible for tactical fighter planning, until he was relieved of the role in early 1945 and sent back to the frontline, having fallen out with Goering and other leading Nazis. A prisoner of war from 1945 to 1947, he spent his subsequent career in aviation, working in Argentina and Germany.

Galland's powerful, gregarious personality enabled him to play the part of the 'Good German' in the forgiving atmosphere that prevailed among the rival airmen after the war. He and Douglas Bader were photographed together, and he met the British ace Bob Stanford-Tuck on a number of occasions. Some of those he fought were never persuaded, however. In the blunt opinion of Christopher Foxley-Norris, 'Galland was a shit.' [Foxley-Norris, interview]

BACK THEM UP!

PRINTED FOR H.M. STATIONERY OFFICE BY FOSH & CROSS LTD., LONDON. (51/9020)

cover from 610 Squadron arrived too late to help. An attack on the second convoy by Me110s was intercepted and driven away, but not without substantial damage to two Hurricanes from 151 Squadron.

In the east, a heavy raid on Harwich by He111s and Do17s was driven away by three squadrons of fighters (Nos 66, 17 and 85). Three Heinkels were shot down. Further west, the raiders were more successful. Again using the low-level approach to avoid radar detection, a lightning raid on shipping off Portland saw another precious British destroyer, HMS *Delight*, hit by a bomb and sunk.

TUESDAY 30 July 1940

Poor weather on Tuesday led to a much-reduced level of enemy activity, but the RAF still flew nearly 700 sorties today, many in response to nuisance raids launched against Northeast Britain by bombers based in Norway. Two German raiders were shot down, and the RAF suffered no casualties.

Drizzle and low cloud.

In fact, the British had initiated a respite in the Channel Battle by sending through no convoys for a few days, which meant no patrolling Fighter Command aircraft were drawn unwillingly into battle over the Channel. Fighter sweeps went unchallenged, much to the frustration of Major Galland, who relished the pure combat that they entailed, redolent of the pioneering days of aerial warfare over the Western Front 25 years before. The Germans did all they could to tempt the British fighters into combat, sending weak bomber forces as decoys while strong fighter formations waited at high altitude, but Air Chief Marshal Dowding held back.

The month of July had cost Fighter Command dearly in pilots and the Luftwaffe had yet to unleash its full force. By now, Dowding had lost 80 flight commanders and squadron leaders. Of the pilots left, only about half had any experience of combat. Those who had been involved in the fighting were approaching physical and mental exhaustion. On 27 July Dowding had ordered that each should have a minimum of eight hours off duty in every twenty-four, and a continuous twenty-four hours off every week. To preserve their men, Dowding and Park limited the numbers they sent up, even if it meant they were hopelessly outnumbered at the point of interception.

Thus, German fighter sweeps were either ignored or intercepted late. Dowding knew that the Messerschmitt Me109 could usually carry enough fuel for only 80 minutes' flying time, which meant, having crossed the Channel, a mere 20 minutes over England – less if involved in a high-speed combat. So, sector controllers would attempt to intercept just as the Messerschmitts were heading home. Any delay to their journey home could be fatal for the Germans. The Me109 pilot Gunther Busgen remembers how much his colleagues feared the choppy waters of the Channel: 'On one occasion the English drove the whole unit off course to the Isle of Wight. Six planes went down in the Channel because they had simply run out of fuel. They just fell into the sea and the pilots drowned. It's something you never forget.' [Quoted in Parker, p. 166] Many German pilots developed a gastric complaint they came to call 'Channel Sickness'. Some theorized that it was caused by looking at the waves. Others put it down to fear of ditching and an almost inevitable watery death.

OPPOSITE
A dramatic Ministry of Information poster carries a straightforward exhortation to support the efforts of the 'fighter boys', whose feats made for such striking imagery.

31 July 1940 WEDNESDAY

Fine and fair; haze over the Channel.

A thick haze blanketed the Channel on the morning of the last day of July. Nevertheless, German bombers probed the south coast from dawn. No. 111 Squadron, operating in dangerously bad visibility, found a Ju88 bomber over the Channel and sent it back heavily shot up and carrying a dead crew-member. 'Sailor' Malan believed that the return of damaged aircraft could have a greater impact on the morale of the Luftwaffe than the non-appearance of a bomber that had been destroyed. Later in the battle, he told a doctor acquaintance how he had changed his tactics to cripple bombers rather than shoot them down outright. 'If you shoot them down they don't get back and no-one in Germany is a whit the wiser,' he said. 'So I figure the right thing to do is to let them get back. With a dead rear gunner, a dead navigator and the pilot coughing his guts up as he lands … if you do that it has a better effect on their morale.' [Quoted in Walker, p. 99]

The day saw an improvement in the defences over Dover, perched at the tip of Britain's frontline. Twenty-three balloons rose over the cliffs and town, attached to motor winches cemented in the ground. Beleaguered residents of the frontline town cheered their arrival. Barrage balloons were simple but very effective, as the Luftwaffe knew well. Their deployment produced a swift response. At about 3.30pm, a large enemy formation was spotted approaching Dover, and 11 Group reacted vigorously, scrambling 30 Spitfires and 24 Hurricanes. But only No. 74 Squadron's 12 Spitfires, taking off from Manston, Kent, were over Dover in time to intercept the two *Staffeln* of Me109s, which had arrived, it appeared, to shoot up the port's new balloon barrage in preparation for a bombing raid.

As before, proximity to the attackers meant that the defenders intercepted quickly but lacked the time to gain height. 'B' Flight of 74 Squadron was still climbing when it reached the German fighters, and it would suffer accordingly.

continued on page 141

'Channel sickness'

Ulrich Steinhilper, the pilot of a Messerschmitt Me109, testified to the effects of 'Channel Sickness' on German airmen in the summer of 1940 as they prepared for flight or overflew the Channel.

```
    I believe we were exhausted too much which is why we had the so-called
Kanalkrankheit - Channel sickness. In the beginning, Channel sickness
was just a funny expression, more or less a nickname, nobody ever thought
it would occur. But after a while, some pilots really were vomiting
before flight or in flight, some of them got ulcers and had real
problems with the stomach. I too had a high temperature.[Steinhilper,
recording]


                        -0-0-0-0-0-
```

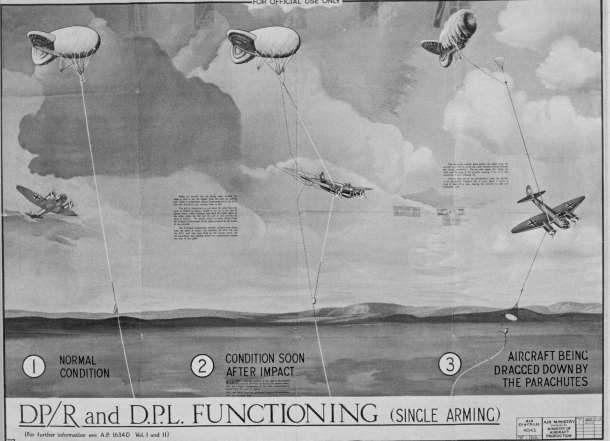

FOR OFFICIAL USE ONLY

① NORMAL CONDITION

② CONDITION SOON AFTER IMPACT

③ AIRCRAFT BEING DRAGGED DOWN BY THE PARACHUTES

DP/R and D.P.L. FUNCTIONING (SINGLE ARMING)

(For further information see A.P. 1634 D Vol. I and II)

AIR DIAGRAM 4043	AIR MINISTRY PRODUCED BY MINISTRY OF AIRCRAFT PRODUCTION	DATE

An Air Ministry graphic portrays one means by which barrage balloons could prove deadly. In this scenario, part of the cable would detach itself on contact, small parachutes on the cable would open, and, with luck, the weight and drag would cause the plane to crash.

DEATH BY BALLOON

In 1938 British Balloon Command was established under the leadership of Air Marshal Sir E. Leslie Gossage (1891–1949) to protect cities and other key targets. By the middle of 1940 there were 1400 balloons, a third of them over the London area.

Barrage balloons were designed to deter low-level bombing attacks – at 5000 feet or under – thus forcing raiders to go higher, from where accuracy was more difficult. This also assisted the efforts of anti-aircraft units, who could not traverse fast enough to attack aircraft flying at low altitude and high speed. Most balloons were a little over 29 feet (8.9 metres) long and 25 feet (7.6 metres) in diameter, and were connected to a ground site or a lorry by either a single steel cable or a series of cables. The balloons could float in the sky at up to about 4925 feet (1500 metres), the maximum height that the weight of their cables allowed.

The steel wire between the balloon and the ground could, like a cheese-wire, slice straight through the wing of an aircraft, dealing it a knockout blow. The barrage balloons presented a surreal but comforting sight wallowing in the skies above Britain's towns. They loom large in many childhood memories of Britain during the Second World War.

Paul Nash's *Battle of Britain* (1941) is perhaps the most famous work of art to be inspired by the aerial struggle of summer 1940. Rather than a depiction of a single dogfight, on a particular day, it was an attempt to encapsulate and characterize the entire battle in a single image. It embraces the vapour trails and black smoke of combat, balloons and parachutes, and the fierce summer heat. It also expresses a compressed geography, in which the English foreground gives way to a narrow strip of Channel, which separates the landscape of the homeland from the threatening Continent beyond, from which the ranks of German aircraft emanate. The painting was exhibited at the National Gallery in 1942.

FIGHTER COMMAND LOSSES *IN JULY 1940*

Aircraft type	Numbers destroyed	Numbers damaged	Pilots killed	Pilots missing	Pilots wounded
Hurricane	33	17	23	0	11
Spitfire	34	24	25	0	9
Blenheim	4	1	9	0	1
Defiant	6	1	10	0	2
All types (total)	**77**	**43**	**67**	**0**	**23**

LUFTWAFFE LOSSES *IN JULY 1940*

Aircraft type	Numbers destroyed	Numbers damaged	Pilots killed	Pilots missing	Pilots wounded
Dornier Do17	39	13	30	74	19
Heinkel He111	32	3	52	85	6
Junkers Ju88	39	11	52	67	11
Junkers Ju87	13	11	10	12	3
Messerschmitt Me109	48	14	17	14	13
Messerschmitt Me110	18	4	13	17	2
Other types	27	1	19	33	15
All types (total)	**216**	**57**	**193**	**302**	**69**

The smoking wreckage of a German aircraft is testament to one ill-advised incursion over England.

Three of the six Spitfires were hit in the two minutes from 3.48pm to 3.50pm. Two of the pilots were killed, but the third managed to steer his stricken aircraft back to Manston. The squadron succeeded in damaging one of the attackers, but the rest escaped before the other British fighters arrived.

As July drew to a close, both air forces could reflect on their material and human losses during the month. The numbers of German air force dead and missing, nearing 500, were much higher than those of the British of course, for each time a bomber went down it took with it several men in contrast to a single-piloted fighter plane. But those bombers were inflicting death and destruction on the ground and on the convoys. Now Hitler was considering his next move. The Battle of Britain was about to enter a new and more intense phase.

ABOVE

Troops and locals glee-fully display their booty from the remains of a marauding Messerschmitt Me109 that had crashed in Southeast England. In this particular case, the Luftwaffe pilot escaped the fate of his aircraft by baling out.

4

INTENSIFICATION

1 August to 17 August 1940

As the month of August 1940 opened, Adolf Hitler issued Directive 17, announcing his intention 'to intensify air and sea warfare against the English homeland'. The next day, Goering laid out orders for an all-out assault. His aim was to overwhelm the RAF in the air and crush it on the ground in a concentrated series of massive raids. The operation was to be called *Adlerangriff* – Attack of the Eagle – and it would commence on *Adlertag* (Eagle Day), whose date would be decided by meteorological forecasts of a spell of fair weather.

Goering intended to throw all the resources of *Luftflotten* 2, 3 and 5 into the effort, bombing Fighter Command in its bases or luring its aircraft up to be destroyed in aerial combat. The attack would also be directed at the infrastructure that sustained Britain's air defence, including radar installations. With his customary optimism, Goering expected the RAF to survive only a few days under such an assault. All that was needed was a final period of preparation and then three consecutive days of good weather. Initially, *Adlertag* was set for 10 August, eight days after the orders had been given.

PREVIOUS PAGE
Free French pilots scramble to their Spitfires. Airmen from the defeated nations of Europe flocked to join the RAF.

OPPOSITE
Goering and Hitler consider their options in 1940. Hitler habitually interfered with his subordinates' plans, but, surprisingly, made few attempts to micro-manage Operation Sea Lion.

The decisiveness of the orders and the confidence with which they were issued suggests a unanimity of view among the Nazi hierarchy as to the wisdom and necessity of the invasion plan. But uncertainties still persisted, not least in the mind of Hitler himself. His attention was increasingly being drawn eastwards. On 31 July, he had scheduled the invasion of Britain for 15 September. But two days previously, he had announced to his military staff that he wanted to attack the Soviet Union as soon as possible – his real enemy and the focus of his ideological hatred. The question of when to invade was taking on a new urgency. At the beginning of July, Sir Stafford Cripps, the British ambassador in Moscow, had handed Stalin a memorandum from Churchill urging him to break his pact with Hitler and turn against Germany. The communication soon found its way into the hands of the German Embassy in Moscow, and it supported the view that, by striking at Russia, Germany would also be effectively defusing the threat from Britain. Hitler now believed that 'Russia is the factor by which England sets the greatest store. If Russia is beaten,' he announced, 'England's last hope is gone.'

These reflections did nothing, however, to slow down the preparations for the

DIRECTIVE 17 –
'THE FINAL CONQUEST OF ENGLAND'

From his headquarters on 1 August, Adolf Hitler signalled to his armed forces an intensification of German air and sea warfare against England in Directive 17.

In order to establish the necessary conditions for the final conquest of England I intend to intensify air and sea warfare against the English homeland. I therefore order as follows:

1. The German Air Force is to overpower the English Air Force with all the forces at its command, in the shortest time possible. The attacks are to be directed primarily against flying units, their ground installations, and their supply organizations, but also against the aircraft industry, including that manufacturing anti-aircraft equipment.

2. After achieving temporary or local air superiority the air war is to be continued against ports, in particular against stores of food, and also against stores of provisions in the interior of the country. Attacks on the south coast ports will be made on the smallest possible scale, in view of our own forthcoming operations.

3. On the other hand, air attacks on enemy warships and merchant ships may be reduced except where some particularly favourable target happens to present itself, where such attacks would lend additional effectiveness to those mentioned in Paragraph 2, or where such attacks are necessary for the training of air crews for further operations.

4. The intensified air warfare will be carried out in such a way that the Air Force can at any time be called upon to give adequate support to naval operations against suitable targets. It must also be ready to take part in full force in Operation Sea Lion.

5. I reserve to myself the right to decide on terror attacks as measures of reprisal.

6. The intensification of the air war may begin on or after 5 August. The exact time is to be decided by the Air Force after completion of preparations and in the light of the weather.
   The Navy is authorized to begin the proposed intensified naval war at the same time.

-o-o-o-o-o-

Adlerangriff, which meant a lull in the fighting. The first few days of the month saw skirmishing but few major combats. The Luftwaffe's energies were spent, instead, in moving units to forward bases nearer the coast. Both sides intensified crew training. The flying conditions were often poor, with rain, cloud and fog, and for the first week of August more men and machines on both sides were lost through accident than enemy action.

In Britain, the relative quiet only encouraged a feeling that a great storm was about to break. On 31 July, Churchill's secretary, Jock Colville, had heard that the head of the Secret Service had 'now received news of imminent invasion from over 260 sources. The main attack would be in the south, with diversions against Hull, Scotland and Ireland.' [Colville, p. 205] By early August, the English landscape itself had altered, reflecting the sense of drama and dread. Seaside towns that would, in normal times, be thronged with holidaymakers were full of men and women in uniform, and the beaches were forlorn and empty. The question of maintaining morale was now of even greater significance to the government. The authorities regarded the strength of public resolve – the population's ability to absorb the physical and psychological pain of a protracted bombing campaign – as of equal importance to Britain's capacity to resist the Germans militarily. For many ordinary people, though, the prevailing feelings were of fear and doubt.

THURSDAY **1 August 1940**

On the first day of August, British fighters intercepted enemy raids off the east and south coasts, but 30 He111s managed to break through the defences unmolested and drop bombs on Norwich. The Boulton Paul aircraft factory was hit, as were some railway goods yards and a timber yard. Six people were killed and some forty injured.

Fair inland, but Channel overcast.

That night, bombers ranged all over the country, carrying hundreds of thousands of leaflets with the translated text of Hitler's 'Appeal to Reason' of the previous month, urging British surrender (see page 116). Most of the leaflets fell among the sheep and cattle of East Anglia. The newspapers later carried jocular pictures of citizens cutting up the leaflets and fastening them to their privy doors, for use as lavatory paper. The prospect of a settlement had disappeared long before the paper fluttered to the ground, as Hitler himself recognized. And today, the Führer issued his Directive 17, revealing his intention to turn up the pressure for the next stage of the *Kanalkampf*.

FRIDAY **2 August 1940**

Following Hitler's Directive 17, Goering drew up plans for an overwhelming, knockout assault to gain air superiority over Britain, including the comprehensive destruction of RAF Fighter Command, its bases and the radar installations. Consequently – and with poor weather hindering normal operations in the air and at sea – German efforts were put largely into continental preparations for *Adlerangriff*. Hampshire was the recipient of a couple of minor bombing raids.

Cloudy in eastern areas, and Channel overcast.

continued on page 150

ABBEY 5411.

TELEPHONE :

Extn. ....

Any communications on the
subject of this letter should
be addressed to :—

THE
UNDER SECRETARY
OF STATE,

and the following number
quoted :—

S.5723/D.C.A.S.

AIR MINISTRY,

LONDON, S.W.1.

1st August, 1940.

SECRET.

Sir,

<u>ANTI-INVASION PLANS - STANDARDISATION OF
STATES OF READINESS.</u>

I am directed to inform you that the question of
standardising some system - preferably common to the three
Services - for ensuring a similar degree of readiness in which
the armed forces are required to be held against any impending
invasion threat, has been under consideration.

2.   Before carrying this project to the stage of inter-
departmental discussion it is desired to obtain the opinion of
Air Officers Commanding-in-Chief upon the utility and application of this proposal.

3.   It is proposed that there should be three states of
readiness imposed by higher authority:-

<u>Readiness No. 1</u> - When attack is regarded as improbable
within the following three days, although an invasion
threat is believed to exist.

<u>Readiness No. 2</u> - When attack is regarded as probable
within the following three days.

<u>Readiness No. 3</u> - When attack is regarded as imminent and
likely to occur within the next 12 hours.

4.   I am to say that under this scheme it would be
required that instructions should be issued throughout operational commands and Flying Training Command, defining the fore-
going states of readiness, laying down the outline of any
action to be taken at the Formation Headquarters issuing the
instructions, and requiring subordinate Formation Headquarters
and units to maintain corresponding tabulations for each state
of readiness.   It is thought that such a tabulation of the
preparatory duties to be performed by various branches of
Command Staffs and at subordinate formations would ensure that
detail matters of preparation would not, in the stress of
circumstances, be overlooked.

5.   It is appreciated that the nature of the preparations
to be undertaken must depend largely upon the geographical
location of the expected attack, and whether by air-borne or
sea-borne forces.   Certain precautionary measures which would

/be

The Air Officer Commanding-in-Chief,
      Headquarters, Fighter Command,
            Royal Air Force,
                  Stanmore,
                        Middlesex.

ABOVE An Air Ministry memo of 1 August 1940 sounds out air chiefs about how to define degrees of readiness with regard to possible invasion.
OPPOSITE A map showing British radar coverage during the Battle of Britain.

The Chain Home radar
network in summer 1940

◎ Chain Home (High) radar stations
◎ Chain Home (Low) radar stations
Range of high level radar
Range of low level radar

0   100 km
0   100 miles

N

Caitnip
Nether Button

Thrumster

SCOTLAND

Rosehearty   Hillhead

Doonies Hill
School Hill

St Cyrus
Douglas Wood

Anstruther
Cockburnspath
Drone Hill

Bamburgh

Cresswell

Ottercops Moss

N. IRELAND

Shotton

Danby Beacon

EIRE
(neutral)

Staxton Wold
Flamborough Head

Easington

Stenigot
Ingoldmels

West Beckham
Happisburgh

Strumble Head

WALES

Stoke Holy Cross   Hopton
Dunwich
High Street
Bawdsey

Haycastle   St Twynells
Warren

ENGLAND

Walton
Bromley
Canewdon

NETHERLANDS

arnanton

Rame
Head

Whitstable   Foreness
Dunkirk
Truleigh   Dover
Poling   Rye

Dry Tree

West
Prawle

Worth
Matravers   Ventnor   Beachy Head   Fairlight

Hawks
Tor

Pevensey

BELGIUM

FRANCE

Today, the American ambassador in London, Joseph Kennedy, reported to Washington that if German air power was as formidable as believed, it would shortly put the RAF 'out of commission', after which British surrender would be 'inevitable'. A few days later came worrying news from Britain's head of armament purchasing in the United States. There was a growing doubt about 'the capability of Britain to survive', he said. America was becoming 'shy of starting production of weapons for a country which might "go under" at any moment'.

During these first low-key days of August, the Luftwaffe did fly a number of minelaying and reconnaissance missions, and attacked the few vessels that were now plying the Channel. But the relative lull allowed Fighter Command to replenish its squadrons: 720 aircraft now became available compared with 587 on 30 July, and the numbers of aircrew grew to 1465, compared with 1200 at the end of July. New units came into existence too: today another Polish fighter squadron, No. 303, was created to join 302, which had been formed in mid-July.

3 August 1940 SATURDAY

Fog and cloud in the south; occasional bright intervals.

A thick fog in the south of England gave way to cloud. Today saw the Channel empty of shipping, and there were only a few scattered bombing raids in the west.

4 August 1940 SUNDAY

Cloud and fog, clearing by evening.

Sunday was cloudy and foggy, and, except for Luftwaffe reconnaissance over the Bristol Channel and the English south coast, today was even quieter than the previous day. During the night, however, there were bombing raids in the north and west – on Bradford, Crewe, Liverpool, South Wales and the Firth of Forth.

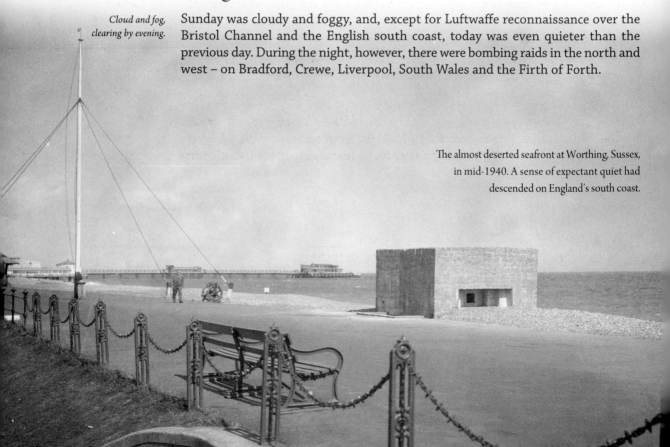

The almost deserted seafront at Worthing, Sussex, in mid-1940. A sense of expectant quiet had descended on England's south coast.

'Not even an echo'

As the Battle of Britain got under way, most of Britain's holiday beaches were now out of bounds to civilians and strewn with anti-invasion defences. On 14 July, the novelist J.B. Priestley, who played an important role in maintaining British spirits, related in one of his regular BBC broadcasts a visit to the Kent resort of Margate.

```
    Everything was there: bathing pools, bandstands, gardens blazing
with flowers, lido, theatres, and the like; and miles of firm golden
sands all spread out beneath the July sun. But no people - not a soul.
Of all those hundreds of thousands of holidaymakers, of entertainers
and hawkers and boatmen - not one. And no sound - not the very ghost
of an echo of all that cheerful hullabaloo - children shouting and
laughing, bands playing, concert parties singing, men selling ice-cream,
whelks and peppermint rock, which I'd remembered hearing along this
shore. No, not even an echo. Silence. It was as if an evil magician
had whisked everybody away.
```

-o-o-o-o-o-

MONDAY 5 August 1940

With improving weather today, German aircraft patrolled the Channel in strength, looking for shipping. At 8.30 in the morning, a patrol of six Spitfires from No. 64 Squadron was 'bounced' – attacked from above in the glare of the sun – by a *Staffel* of Messerschmitt Me109s from *Jagdgeschwader* 54. Lacking height, two of the British planes were downed, and one pilot, Sergeant Lewis Isaac, was killed; he had joined the squadron only a few days previously. Below the fight, a convoy chugged eastwards, left alone by the Luftwaffe, which was clearly saving its efforts for the big effort ahead. Only when the ships reached the Straits of Dover were the vessels attacked – this time by Ju88s, escorted by Me109s. Hurricanes from 151 Squadron successfully intervened, shooting down a fighter and damaging one of the bombers.

Fine and fair; hazy over Channel.

TUESDAY 6 August 1940

Today was, again, quiet. At Carinhall, the Prussian estate Goering had named in memory of his sickly aristocratic wife, the *Reichsmarschall* outlined his plans to his *Luftflotte* commanders. To destroy the RAF, he said, 'all fighter escorts will be doubled in number and will fly at staggering levels of height'.

Cloudy with strong winds.

WEDNESDAY 7 August 1940

The Times today reported that: 'To celebrate the run of *Black Velvet*, now approaching its 550th performance at the London Hippodrome, George Black and Moss'

Mainly fair; some cloud, and thunderstorms in east.

continued on page 154

RAF Fighter Command Order of Battle *1 August 1940*

SECTOR	SQN	AIRCRAFT	BASED AT	COMMANDER
11 Group				
Biggin Hill	32	Hurricane	Biggin Hill	S/L John Worrall
	501	Hurricane	Gravesend	S/L Harry Hogan
	600	Blenheim	Manston	S/L David Clark
	610	Spitfire	Biggin Hill	S/L J. Ellis
North Weald	56	Hurricane	North Weald	S/L Minnie Manton
	151	Hurricane	North Weald	S/L Teddy Donaldson
	85	Hurricane	Martlesham	S/L Peter Townsend
	25	Blenheim	Martlesham	S/L K.A. McEwan
Kenley	64	Spitfire	Kenley	S/L A.R.D. MacDonald
	615	Hurricane	Kenley	S/L Joseph Kayll
	111	Hurricane	Croydon	S/L John Thompson
Hornchurch	41	Spitfire	Hornchurch	S/L H. West
	65	Spitfire	Hornchurch	S/L Henry Sawyer
	74	Spitfire	Hornchurch	S/L Francis White
Tangmere	1	Hurricane	Tangmere	S/L David Pemberton
	145	Hurricane	Westhampnett	S/L John Peel
	266	Spitfire	Tangmere	S/L R.L. Wilkinson
	601	Hurricane	Tangmere	S/L W.F.C. Hobson
	FIU	Blenheim	Tangmere	W/C G.P. Chamberlain
Debden	17	Hurricane	Debden	S/L C.W. Williams
Northolt	43	Hurricane	Northolt	S/L John Badger
	257	Hurricane	Hendon	S/L H. Harkness
10 Group				
Filton	87	Hurricane	Exeter	S/L T.G. Lovell-Gregg
	93	Spitfire	Pembrey	S/L P.J. Sanders
	213	Hurricane	Exeter	S/L H.D. McGregor
	234	Spitfire	St Eval	S/L R.E. Barnett
Middle Wallop	152	Spitfire	Warmwell	S/L Peter Devitt
	238	Hurricane	Middle Wallop	S/L Harold Fenton
	604	Blenheim	Middle Wallop	S/L Michael Anderson
	609	Spitfire	Middle Wallop	S/L Horace Darley
12 Group				
Duxford	19	Spitfire	Fowlmere	S/L Philip Pinkham
Coltishall	66	Spitfire	Coltishall	S/L Rupert Leigh
	242	Hurricane	Coltishall	S/L Douglas Bader
Kirton-in-Lindsey	222	Spitfire	Kirton	S/L J.H. Hill
	264	Defiant	Kirton	S/L Philip Hunter
Digby	46	Hurricane	Digby	F/L A.D. Murray
	611	Spitfire	Digby	S/L J. McComb
	29	Blenheim	Digby	F/L S.C. Widdows
Wittering	229	Hurricane	Wittering	S/L H.J. McQuire
	23	Blenheim	Collyweston	S/L L.C. Bicknell
13 Group (Church Fenton sector reverted to 12 Group control during August)				
Church Fenton	73	Hurricane	Church Fenton	S/L J.W.C. More
	616	Spitfire	Leconfield	S/L M. Robinson
	249	Hurricane	Church Fenton	S/L John Grandy
Catterick	54	Spitfire	Catterick	S/L James Leathart
	219	Blenheim	Leeming	S/L J.H. Little
Usworth	607	Hurricane	Usworth	S/L J. Vick
	72	Spitfire	Acklington	S/L A.R. Collins
	79	Hurricane	Acklington	S/L Hervey Heyworth
Turnhouse	253	Hurricane	Turnhouse	S/L Tom Gleave
	602	Spitfire	Drem	S/L Sandy Johnstone
	603	Spitfire	Turnhouse	No officer commanding
	605	Hurricane	Drem	S/L W. Churchill
Dyce	263	Hurricane	Grangemouth	S/L H. Eeles
Wick	3	Hurricane	Wick	S/L S.F. Godden
	232	Hurricane	Sumburgh	F/L M.M. Stephens
	504	Hurricane	Castletown	S/L John Sample
Prestwick	141	Defiant	Prestwick	S/L William Richardson
Aldergrove	245	Hurricane	Aldergrove	S/L F.W. Whitley

Key S/L = Squadron Leader; F/L = Flight Lieutenant; W/C = Wing Commander; FIU = Fighter Interception Unit (i.e. night-fighters)

THE POLISH SQUADRONS

Polish airmen who had escaped from their homeland to Britain to carry on the fight against the Nazis were initially distributed around Fighter Command units. On 13 July 1940, however, they got a squadron of their own. It was named No. 302 (City of Poznań), equipped with Hurricanes, and it became operational in late August, arriving on the frontline in October to take part in the last phase of the Battle of Britain. It was overshadowed, though, by its younger sister, No. 303 (Kosciuśzko), which came into being on 2 August 1940. This unit was the descendant of the squadron that had fought against the Soviet armies in Poland's war with her Russian and Ukrainian neighbours in 1920. It took its name from the Polish military hero Tadeusz Kosciuśzko, who had led an uprising against Russia in 1794. The squadron claimed its first kill before it was officially operational, when Flying Officer Ludwik Paszkiewicz, a 33-year-old veteran of the air battles over Poland and France, broke away from a training flight to shoot down a marauding Me110. He returned to Northolt to be reprimanded, then congratulated. His action was typical of the dash and determination exhibited by the Polish airmen.

The experiences of seeing their homelands at the mercy of the Germans had hardened the Poles and Czechs, and they were regarded by their fellow pilots as more than usually concentrated and aggressive. They had shown extraordinary determination in escaping after the fall of Poland, making their way via Romania and, by a variety of routes, to France. There, many of them took part in the air battles of the *Blitzkrieg*. After that defeat, they escaped once again to continue their fight.

Despite arriving late to the Battle of Britain, No. 303 Squadron went on to destroy more German aircraft than any other Hurricane squadron and was the fourth-highest scorer of all the fighter units. In all, 145 Polish pilots would serve as fighter pilots in the battle, with 30 losing their lives. The squadron also included the Czech pilot Josef František, who is credited in some lists as the highest scoring pilot of the Battle of Britain. Overall, the Poles accounted for nearly 20 per cent of enemy kills in the battle.

Stories circulated of Polish pilots shooting baled-out German aircrew as they dangled on their parachutes. There is little evidence that this was a regular practice. However, the historian Adam Zamoyski records that 'it is true that some pilots ... finished off parachuting Germans by flying directly over them; the slipstream would cause the parachute to cannon and the man would fall to the ground like a stone'.

The Czech ace Josef František, as drawn by Cuthbert Orde in September 1940.

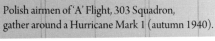

Polish airmen of 'A' Flight, 303 Squadron, gather around a Hurricane Mark 1 (autumn 1940).

Empires will give all the admission receipts from all performances for the next four weeks for the purchase of Spitfire fighters. George Black hopes to provide at least two Spitfires, to be named "Black Velvet" and "Black Vanities", the latter being the title of the new show which will succeed *Black Velvet*.' It was an example of the continuing and highly successful campaign for communities to 'buy' their own Spitfire, a practice that symbolized the way in which the British people were finding themselves bound more closely to this war than any other in their history.

In the skies, the day began as quietly as the previous day. The reduced enemy activity prompted the British to restart shipping activity in the Channel. In the evening, 20 ships lying in the mouths of the Medway and the Thames prepared for a dash through the Channel to deliver a cargo of coal to Dorset. The convoy was codenamed 'Peewit', and great care was taken to avoid a repeat of the devastation wrought on Convoy CW8 on 25 July. Peewit would have nine naval escorts, improved anti-aircraft cover and its own balloon barrage. Furthermore, it would be timed so that it passed through the Straits of Dover in darkness. The plan, however, took no account of the German *Freya* radar system newly installed on the heights of Cap Blanc Nez near Calais, which soon picked up the convoy and gave the Luftwaffe time to prepare their attack.

The ships that made up Peewit totalled about 70,000 tons. They moved out of the river mouths on the evening tide and met up with their escort. The convoy formed into two columns, each led by a balloon ship. Twenty-six-year-old Arthur Hague was captain of the *Borealis*, to which one of the balloons was tethered, and he recorded how 'night fell as we passed Dover and in a calm sea under a moonless sky we crept past Beachy Head ... Some time in the middle watch I became aware of the powerful throb of engines and assumed this to come from enemy bombers crossing the Channel on a night raid. Suddenly a loud explosion lit the sky and I saw that the coaster immediately astern of *Borealis* had fallen out of line and was listing. In a flash, it occurred to me that the throbbing I had heard was not aircraft but German E-boats, and they were on the shoreward side of us, attacking from under the cliffs.' [Quoted in Parker, pp. 189–92]

The E-boats were fast, designed for the rough conditions of the North Sea and armed with four torpedoes each. They launched their weapons into the mass of shipping, and panic ensued. Tracer fire from the anti-aircraft ships lit up the sky, as every gun on the convoy opened fire. Two ships smashed into each other while taking evasive action, and the convoy scattered. The E-boats continued to harry the ships along the south coast, sinking two vessels and damaging a third.

8 August 1940 THURSDAY

Showers, with bright intervals and high winds.

Daylight on 8 August saw the surviving ships of convoy Peewit steaming close under the south coast cliffs for safety, as the Royal Naval vessels tried to shepherd them back into two columns. By 10.30am, they were on their way again, with a fighter escort from 145 Squadron overhead. The planes, together with the convoy's balloons, kept at bay sporadic raids by enemy dive-bombers.

Shortly after midday, when Peewit was about five miles south of St Catherine's Point, on the most southerly tip of the Isle of Wight, Me109s suddenly appeared

and headed straight for the barrage balloons. The gasbags, wallowing in the wind, made easy targets. 'Under a hail of incendiary bullets,' recorded Arthur Hague, 'the *Borealis*' balloon disintegrated in flames. Then, out of the sun, roared a flight of Ju87 dive-bombers.'

Luftflotte 3 had sent 57 Stukas against the convoy, escorted by 20 Me110s and 30 Me109s. Arthur Hague was on the bridge of the *Borealis*. 'I saw this W-shaped silhouette of the dive-bomber coming zooming down towards us. I saw the bomb leave the plane before it zoomed off upwards and a fraction of a second later there was a violent explosion on the foredeck. The foremast jack-knifed and everything movable on the bridge crashed around us. Then, within minutes, RAF Hurricanes fortuitously appeared overhead.'

The radar at Ventnor, on the Isle of Wight, had picked up the large German formation, and Air Chief Marshal Dowding was ready with 18 Hurricanes from three squadrons, as well as the Spitfires of 609 Squadron at Warmwell. No. 145 Squadron from Tangmere was among the Hurricane interceptors. 'Our first view of the convoy near St Catherine's Point was of Ju87s in their bombing dives,' said 145 pilot Peter Parrot. 'Above the Ju87s were the escorting Me109s and farther to the southeast were two more large formations of enemy aircraft approaching the convoy – a formidable sight. I had already taken part in the Battle for France, and patrolled over Dunkirk during the evacuation, but I had never before seen so many aircraft in the sky at once.' [Quoted in *145 Squadron Newsletter*, Autumn/Winter 1995] Parrot's squadron dived out of the sun at the flank of the formation, sliding through the fighter screen to shoot down two of the Stukas. But, despite the weight of numbers on the British side, many found themselves caught up in dogfights with the Messerschmitt escorts and were unable to prevent the Stukas plunging on the vessels below. Within minutes, four ships had been sunk and a further seven badly damaged.

The dogfight, involving about 150 aircraft, lasted for 20 minutes, before dwindling fuel forced the raiders to turn home. Two Hurricanes from 238 Squadron had been shot down, and the Germans had lost three Ju87s, one Me110 and

A Ju87 (Stuka) turns sharply into its characteristic steep dive. Despite its fearsome reputation, the Ju87 was relatively easy prey for Fighter Command, proving especially vulnerable as it came out of its dive.

continued on page 158

TOTALS BROUGHT FORWARD

William Joyce (*far left*), the future 'Lord Haw-Haw', appears with Oswald Mosley
(*centre*) and other members of the British Union of Fascists in 1935.

CARELESS TALK, LORD HAW-HAW
AND THE 'MINISTRY OF AGGRAVATION'

The maintenance of a positive attitude among the public towards the war effort was one of the main strategic concerns of the government. Churchill told the nation in July that 'this is not a war of chieftains or of princes, of dynasties or national ambition. It is a war of people and of causes.' Bureaucrats pumped out a stream of publicity material about security consciousness and the need for selflessness. Posters warned citizens that 'Careless Talk Costs Lives' and that it was their duty to remain 'cheerful' and 'resolute'. Exhortation was reinforced with threats. On 11 June, it was made a criminal offence 'to make or report any statement likely to cause alarm and despondency'. Prosecutions soon followed. One man was imprisoned for three months for telling two New Zealanders: 'You don't want to fight in this bloody war'; another who supported Indian independence received a two-month sentence.

In spite of this, dark rumours flourished. At the end of May, the *New York Times* reported a story, emanating from Britain, that the Germans had reared a voracious strain of grasshopper, which was to be released in Britain to devastate crops and the food supply. There was talk of poisoned chocolate or cigarettes being distributed, and of frightening new weapons the Germans were set to unleash. Above all, fifth columnists were believed to be everywhere, directing enemy aircraft or preparing the way for parachutists.

The rumours filled the vacuum caused by official censorship of the news. At the beginning of the war, television broadcasts, which were in their infancy and reached only a handful of people, were shut down 'for the duration'. The radio, or 'wireless', ruled the airwaves, and there were six news bulletins a day on the BBC Home Service. The reports of the fighting, as with the content of *The Times* and other newspapers, consisted largely of communiqués from the Air Ministry and the Ministry of Home Security. The tone was usually upbeat. 'The superiority of our airmen and machines was most convincing,' reported *The Times*, quoting an eyewitness to fighting over the Channel on 10 July. 'All day long the pilots' combat reports came in. Always they told the same story – victory against the odds,' wrote the paper the following day.

The unvaried diet of good news created an appetite for something different. The broadcasts of the American-born Irishman and Mosleyite William Joyce, better known by his pejorative nickname 'Lord Haw-Haw', filled that gap.

GRAND TOTAL [Cols. (1) to (10)]

..................Hrs..................Mins.

TOTALS CARRIED FORWARD

Joyce, a fervent anti-Semite and anti-communist, had slipped out of Britain in August 1939 when fascist sympathizers were starting to be rounded up. He was then installed in Berlin to broadcast to Britain. Sounding like an 'old-fashioned schoolmaster, loaded with sarcasm' [Gillies, p. xx], he warned the British of their impending defeat and derided their military efforts. It passed into legend that his bulletins were packed with details suggesting that German eyes were eveywhere, such as the mention of a stopped clock on a village church. But there are no records of such details, and the stories of his alleged omniscience appear to have been spread by his British supporters.

YOUR COURAGE
YOUR CHEERFULNESS
YOUR RESOLUTION
WILL BRING
US VICTORY

A Ministry of Information poster designed to keep up spirits (1939).

Joyce's nasal, jeering broadcasts amused more than they demoralized Britons in 1940. Nonetheless, he was hanged for treason after the war.

The job of sustaining morale was given to the Ministry of Information. At the outset it was amateurish, condescending and unpopular with press and Parliament alike. Facile suggestions emanated from the ministry, such as telling actors that they were 'counted upon to keep people cheerful, lead singing etc.'. 'Your Courage, Your Cheerfulness, Your Resolution Will Bring Us Victory,' proclaimed one poster: the sentiments were denounced by *The Times* as 'insipid and patronizing invocations', which caused nothing but 'exasperation'. A comedian, Tommy Handley, renamed the Ministry of Information the 'Ministry of Aggravation and Mysteries'.

CARELESS TALK MAY COST HIS LIFE
DON'T TALK ABOUT AERODROMES or AIRCRAFT FACTORIES

A handout from the wartime 'Careless Talk Costs Lives' campaign focuses on the dangers to airmen. It also shows how much more of a modern 'look' airmen had, compared with the other branches of the armed forces.

'Our Air Force is sublime'

The American-born Conservative MP for Southend West, Henry 'Chips' Channon, put a positive spin on the aerial duels of 8 August 1940 in his published diary.

... a great air battle over the Channel, and a vast number of German aeroplanes have been brought down over the coast! Our Air Force is sublime. 53 raiders, the newspapers announce, were brought down today.

-0-0-0-0-0-

three Me109s, with similar numbers damaged. The scattered remnants of the convoy now reassembled. The *Borealis* had lost its steering and had to be taken under tow. But *Luftflotte* 3 commander Sperrle was not finished with Peewit yet. At about 4pm, over 80 Stukas attacked, escorted by 68 fighters. Two squadrons of Hurricanes, Nos 145 (in its third major combat of the day) and 43, dived out of the sun to hit the raiders. Three Stukas were shot down and five damaged by 145, while No. 43 engaged the Me109s, shooting down two. Each of the Hurricane squadrons lost three of their number in the Channel.

Of the 21 vessels that had left Southend, only 4 arrived undamaged at their destination of Swanage. The destruction of Peewit was to be the worst marine disaster in British waters during the entire war. But the significance of the fighting lay in the way the respective air forces had performed.

The scale of the combat today overshadowed anything that had come before. Thirteen Hurricanes had been lost, with four more damaged, as well as one Spitfire; twelve pilots had been killed and three wounded. The Luftwaffe had lost eight Me109s, one Me110, and seven Ju87s. Eighteen more German aircraft had been damaged, some past repair. For the Luftwaffe, Peewit had been a target of opportunity, not part of Goering's *Adlerangriff* plans. But the huge size of the attacking formations led Fighter Command to the conclusion that the all-out assault had started. The RAF order of the day, issued that night, read: 'The Battle of Britain is about to begin. Members of the Royal Air Force, the fate of generations lies in your hands.'

Fighter Command had learned an encouraging lesson. The day's actions had shown Dowding and his commanders that mass attacks by the Germans could be picked up by the radar stations in enough time to scramble fighters so they were in the best position to confront the raid.

9 August 1940 FRIDAY

Cloudy with some showers; Channel overcast.

Today saw a relative drop in the tempo of fighting, as the Luftwaffe prepared for *Adlerangriff*, in theory due to commence the following day. Nonetheless, they still flew several hundred sorties. Off the east coast, half a dozen He111s searched unsuccessfully for a convoy, and then dropped their bombs on coastal towns in

SINGLE-ENGINE AIRCRAFT				MULTI-ENGINE AIRCRAFT						PASS-ENGER	INSTR/CLOUD FLYING [Incl. in cols. (1) to (10)]	
DAY		NIGHT		DAY				NIGHT			DUAL	PILOT
DUAL	PILOT	DUAL	PILOT	DUAL	1ST PILOT	2ND PILOT	DUAL	1ST PILOT	2ND PILOT			
(1)	(2)	(3)	(4)	(5)	(6)		(8)	(9)	(10)	(11)	(12)	(13)

SPITFIRE FUNDS

The *Times* from the summer of 1940 is full of reports of donations, big and small, to 'Spitfire funds' to finance new aircraft. On 10 August, the paper reports, the Canadian biscuit baron and MP for Macclesfield, Garfield Weston, presented £100,000 to the fund. All over the country fundraisers were finding novel ways of attracting donations. A 'Dorothy fund' was established, whereby the nation's Dorothys could make a contribution and see a fighter plane named after them. In Brighton, the paper wrote, a special dog-race meeting had raised £400. Lloyds Bank presented enough money for a Spitfire, which was to be called 'Black Horse' after its trademark. Supporting the funds was good publicity.

The fundraising effort also spread to the dominions. Under the heading 'Empire Gifts', *The Times* of 3 August 1940 reported that the contribution from the Gold Coast (modern-day Ghana) had reached £25,000 and that Trinidad had also contributed more than £10,000. These were very large sums for small, impoverished colonies. Based on average earnings, £10,000 in 1940 would be nearly £1.5 million today. On 6 August 1940, *The Times* reported that an appeal in the *Madras Mail* had raised £22,500. This would pay for four Spitfires, which were to be named *Kerala*, *Andhradesa*, *Tamilnad* and *Karnataka*. In Jamaica, *The Gleaner* newspaper was also busy raising money, sending in £5000.

ABOVE A shopper does her bit for her local Spitfire fund, at Lambeth Walk market, South London (August 1940).

RIGHT London Transport was one of the many organizations to run its own Spitfire fund, as this 1940 poster by 'Beath' (John M. Fleming) shows.

LONDON TRANSPORT

SPITFIRE FUND

SUBSCRIPTION FORMS ARE NOW OBTAINABLE FROM THE PAYMASTER

GET YOURS, GIVE WHAT YOU CAN AND KEEP GIVING

One Spitfire = £5,000
Nine Spitfires = 40 Messerschmitts
Give as many penny units as you can afford

Yorkshire and elsewhere in the north. Hurricanes from 79 Squadron at Acklington intercepted, shooting down a bomber that had just successfully hit Sunderland's shipyard. On the south coast there was a further attack by fighters on the Dover balloon barrage, and a Ju88 was found circling the remnants of convoy Peewit. Hurricanes from Nos 234 and 601 squadrons brought it down at about 2.30 in the afternoon.

As the afternoon progressed, there was no sign of the clear weather predicted by the Luftwaffe's meteorologists. If anything, conditions seemed to be worsening. Goering decided to postpone his great assault for 24 hours.

10 August 1940 SATURDAY

Thundery, with rain and winds; some bright intervals; Channel cloudy.

Today brought cloud, rain and thunderstorms over northern France, the Channel and southern England. A handful of scattered raids and reconnaissance sorties by the Luftwaffe either foundered in the poor weather or were driven away. For the last time for many weeks to come, there were no combat casualties on either side.

11 August 1940 SUNDAY

Fair in morning, turning cloudy.

This morning started promisingly for the Germans with fair weather, but then deteriorated. The meteorology reports said it might be two days before there was a sustained improvement. Luftwaffe weather-reconnaissance aircraft reported an area of high pressure approaching from the mid-Atlantic, which would deliver a few days of fine weather over southern England and the Channel. Zero hour for *Adlertag* was now set for 05.30hrs on 13 August.

A higher number of attacks occurred today, however, in what seemed like a dress rehearsal for Eagle Day. Early in the morning, No. 74 Squadron was patrolling the south coast when two formations of Me109s and Me110s swept across the Channel to target, once more, the Dover barrage balloons. The 109s shot up three of the balloons, and then the Me110s, carrying small bombs, managed to hit the port, although they caused little serious damage. No. 74 Squadron arrived as the enemy planes were departing, but before the squadron could engage them properly it was intercepted by a *Staffel* of Me109s. The German forces shot down one British pilot, Pilot Officer Peter Stevenson, but he survived.

At the same time, German fighters were roaming along the southeast coastline in an attempt to lure their British counterparts to challenge them. A sweep over Sussex was intercepted by Spitfires from No. 64 Squadron, which shot down two Me109s. On the whole, though, Air Vice-Marshal Park avoided rising to the provocation, preserving his resources for the bomber fleets that would surely soon be on their way again. Just before 10am, the radar station at Ventnor, Isle of Wight, reported what looked like a heavy raid assembling over the Cherbourg peninsula in Normandy. Park and the commander of 10 Group, Air Vice-Marshal Sir Quintin Brand, decided that this was probably the enemy's main effort of the day, and they began to organize a response. Spitfires from 609 Squadron at Warmwell were ordered up to patrol, while No. 1 Squadron was scrambled from Tangmere. Six other squadrons in the west were put at 'readiness' level.

Within a few minutes of the initial warning, it was clear that the formation was huge and that the raid was advancing rapidly. It appeared to be heading for the Royal Navy base at Portland in Dorset. Elements of six further squadrons – Nos 152, 145, 87, 213 and 238 – were scrambled. Although forewarned of the size of the force, the pilots were still taken aback at what they saw approaching. Rank after rank of small dark shapes were coming out of the west, a swarm of 54 Ju88s, 20 He111s, 61 Me110s and 30 Me109s – a total of 165 aircraft. It was the largest single raid launched against England so far. In the vanguard were the fighters, a mixture of Me109s and 110s, at various heights, circling and clearly aiming to distract intercepting fighters to give the bombers a clear run. The two sides clashed, just before 11am, in the skies above Dorset between Weymouth and Swanage.

The German tactics had some success, and the British fighters found themselves caught up in an enormous dogfight south of Portland, as planes swooped and turned, shooting and trying to avoid being shot. The bombers unloaded their cargoes, setting two oil tanks on fire. One of the Heinkels was pursued and shot down by Eric Bann and Sergeant Henry Marsh of 238 Squadron. It was a successful moment in an otherwise terrible day for the squadron. Five of their Hurricanes went down, with four of their pilots killed. The dead included Flight Lieutenant Stuart Walch, a 23-year-old Australian who had transferred to the RAF in 1937 and was one of the most experienced pilots in the squadron. Another was Flying

With parachutes bumping against the backs of their legs, fighter pilots rush to get airborne following the warning of a big raid (1940).

'I saw my machine crash into the sea'

On 11 August 1940, Pilot Officer Peter Stevenson of No. 74 Squadron was lucky to survive an onslaught of Messerschmitt Me109s and a bale-out into the treacherous waters of the Channel.

I climbed up to him. He must have thought I was an Me 109 but when he suddenly dived away I followed him and gave him a two-second deflection burst. The enemy aircraft lurched slightly and went into a vertical dive. I kept my height at 15,000 feet and watched. I saw the enemy aircraft dive straight into the sea fifteen miles south-east of Dover and disappear in a big splash of water. I then climbed to 23,000 feet up-sun and saw a formation of twelve Me 109s 2,000 feet beneath me, proceeding north of Dover. It was my intention to attach myself to the back of this formation from out of the sun, and spray the whole formation. As I was diving for them, a really large volume of cannon and machine-gun fire came from behind. There were about twelve Me 109s diving at me from the sun and at least half of them must have been firing deflection shots at me. There was a popping noise and my control column became useless. I found myself doing a vertical dive, getting faster and faster. I pulled the hood back. I got my head out of the cockpit, and the slipstream tore the rest of me clean out of the machine. My trouser leg and both shoes were torn off. I saw my machine crash into the sea a mile off Deal. It took me twenty minutes to come down. I had been drifting eleven miles out to sea.

One string of my parachute did not come undone, and I was dragged along by my left leg at ten miles an hour with my head underneath the water. After three minutes I was almost unconscious; then the string came undone. I got my breath back and started swimming. There was a heavy sea running … After one-and-a-half hours, an MTB [motor torpedo boat] came to look for me. I fired my revolver at it. It went out of sight, but came back. I changed magazines and fired all my shots over it. It heard my shots and I kicked up a foam in the water, and it saw me. It then picked me up and took me to Dover. [Quoted by Turner, pp. 32-4]

-0-0-0-0-0-

Officer Michal Steborowski, a 31-year-old veteran and one of the Polish airmen who had escaped to England to continue the fight against the Nazis. He had joined the squadron only six days before and had already shot down an Me110. The youngest of the victims was Flight Sergeant Geoffrey Gledhill, who had arrived at 238 Squadron a week before his death. He was 19 years old. No. 111 Squadron also lost four of its pilots that day, as did 601 Squadron, all shot down by Messerschmitts over Portland. The mess at the squadron's Tangmere base was a chilly place that evening.

After such a day it was hard not to come to the conclusion that survival was as much about luck as skill. The dead included highly experienced pre-war service officers, like Flight Officer James Gillan of 601 Squadron, as well as gifted amateurs and greenhorns. The same rule of luck applied to squadrons as well as individuals. No. 609, in the same skies against the same enemy, had had a successful day and escaped virtually unscathed. After being scrambled from Warmwell, Squadron Leader George Darley led 'B' Flight in an attack on a formation of Me110s. Flying straight across the top of the circle of twin-engine fighters, Darley almost collided with one of the Me110s as he shot it down, killing the pilot and wounding the gunner. Four more Me110s fell to the squadron in their first attack. One of the men who had not flown that day watched the fighters of 609 return, noting 'to my surprise nobody was missing. After such a fierce scrap it seemed too good to be true.' [Quoted in Ziegler, p. 114]

In the afternoon, a group of Dorniers and Me110s launched an unsuccessful attack on a convoy off Harwich. No. 74 Squadron, some of whose pilots had already flown three sorties before lunch, intercepted, together with sections from Nos 17 and 85 squadrons. Two fighters from 74 Squadron and one from 17 Squadron were shot down by the Me110s, and their pilots killed. As this German force retreated, another appeared, heading for the Thames Estuary. Again, 74 Squadron was in action, along with 111 Squadron. They drove the raid back, but by now the weather was deteriorating fast, with huge clouds forming over southeast England. The rest of the afternoon was mercifully quiet.

It had been a day of terrible attrition. The Luftwaffe had lost just over 30 aircraft, but the RAF's losses were just as heavy. Twenty-seven fighters had gone down to the Luftwaffe's guns. More alarmingly, 25 British pilots had died. Fighter Command could not sustain such losses for long without suffering a serious decline in efficiency and morale.

MONDAY 12 August 1940

By now, the Luftwaffe was ready to start executing the orders laid out by Goering in his *Adlerangriff* plan. On the urging of General Wolfgang Martini, head of the *Luftnachrichtentruppe* (the Luftwaffe signals branch), it was decided to turn the Luftwaffe's destructive power against one of the defenders' crucial resources. Coordinated attacks were ordered on every known radar installation on the south coast ahead of the great attack. Subsequent raids on RAF coastal stations would test out whether a 'black-out' had been achieved.

At just after 7am, nine Me109s of *Jagdgeschwader* 52 sped across the coast at Dover and moved rapidly eastwards over Kent. Despite the strictures from HQ against being drawn into these provocations, 12 Spitfires from 610 Squadron, based at Biggin Hill, took up the chase. One Spitfire was shot down and four more damaged, though two of the Me109s also fell in the skies over New Romney.

Now that one squadron of defenders was successfully preoccupied with the diversion, the Luftwaffe launched its attack on the south coast radar stations. Sixteen Me110s from Experimental Group 210, led by Stuka ace Hauptmann Walter Rubensdörffer, attacked in four groups in a skilful manoeuvre, flying low and changing direction to fool the defences. First, the Home Chain Low station at Dover, for detecting low-flying aircraft, was hit by four of the Me110s, followed two minutes later by a strike on the station at Rye. Pevensey was next, where a bomb

Fine with some mist patches.

continued on page 166

SINGLE-ENGINE AIRCRAFT				MULTI-ENGINE AIRCRAFT						PASS-ENGER	INSTR/CLOUD FLYING [Incl. in cols. (1) to (10)]	
DAY		NIGHT		DAY			NIGHT					
DUAL	PILOT	DUAL	PILOT	DUAL	1ST PILOT	2ND PILOT	DUAL	1ST PILOT	2ND PILOT		DUAL	PILOT
(1)	(2)	(3)	(4)	(5)	(6)	(7)	(8)	(9)	(10)	(11)	(12)	(13)
44.50	208.20	3.10	6.55							10.05	5.25	3.15

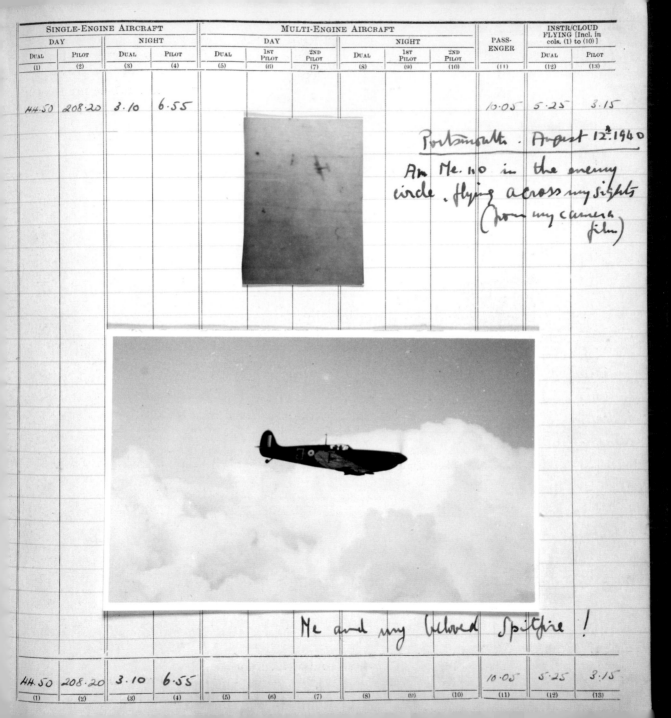

Portsmouth . August 12th 1940

An Me. 110 in the enemy circle . flying across my sights (from my camera film)

Me and my beloved Spitfire !

| 44.50 | 208.20 | 3.10 | 6.55 | | | | | | | 10.05 | 5.25 | 3.15 |
| (1) | (2) | (3) | (4) | (5) | (6) | (7) | (8) | (9) | (10) | (11) | (12) | (13) |

4·50	208·20	3·10	6·55							10·05	5·25 to	3·15
	·30											
	1·05											
	1·15											

Re-arming my Spitfire after the fight above Portland. August 13. 1940.

← → Actual score was.   13 destroyed Confirmed.

This was the record "bag" for   3 destroyed probably.

·40 one Squadron in one fight during the whole Battle of Britain   4 damaged.

N.B. 13 is our lucky number   August 13th — 13 of us in the fight. and 13 Huns down.

50	211·50	3·10	6·55							10·05	5·25	3·15
	(2)	(3)	(4)	(5)	(6)	(7)	(8)	(9)	(10)	(11)	(12)	(13)

'A pile of burning wreckage'

John Bisdee, of 609 Squadron, reported his successful dispatch of a Messerschmitt Me110 on 11 August 1940, in the skies over Dorset.

```
    I hit one of the Messerschmitt 110s and one of its engines started
pouring smoke. It turned over on its back to try to evade but I was
determined not to let the bugger go. I turned over as well and shot
down after him. I lost him for an instant and the next thing I saw
was a pile of burning wreckage down below just near the long man,
the Cerne Abbas giant, who had a very rude male organ sticking up.
I remember seeing a whole lot of farm labourers dancing around it
waving pitchforks and that kind of thing. So I beat the thing up
and did a victory roll and at that moment I looked up in the clouds
and two parachutes appeared. The crew of this thing had got out.
They landed safely a long way away from the farm labourers with their
pitchforks, who might have given them a rather unpleasant reception.
[Quoted in Parker, p. 152]
```

-0-0-0-0-0-

OPPOSITE
Luftwaffe aircrew huddle together for a briefing before a mission. Behind them is a Ju87 dive-bomber.

cut off the electricity supply. All three stations were now out of action. A fourth attack on the Chain Home High Station at Dunkirk, near Canterbury, caused no vital damage.

As emergency measures swung into place to restore radar coverage, a substantial German bomber force streamed through the gap to attack the RAF's forward stations. Lympne, near Folkestone, was the first to suffer, struck by 141 bombs from Ju88 dive-bombers. Fortunately for 11 Group, this was only an emergency satellite station, and the damage caused had little effect on the sectors' operations. The fact that this airfield was chosen gave an early hint that the Luftwaffe's intelligence about the workings of Fighter Command was far from complete. There was a more damaging attack on Hawkinge, a few miles away to the east, which blew up two hangars, destroyed four fighters on the ground and also damaged maintenance workshops. Work started immediately to fill the 28 craters on the airfield.

Meanwhile, over the French coast a substantial force of some 100 Ju88s (of *Kampfgeschwader* – Battle Wing – 51), 120 Me110s (of *Zerstörergeschwader* – 'Destroyer Wing' – 2) and 25 Me109s (of *Zerstörergeschwader* 53) had taken advantage of the holes torn in the radar curtain to form up undetected. They were well on their way to their target before being spotted by Poling radar station, Kent, at 11.45am. But even then, no-one was sure where the aircraft were heading. For a time, it looked like they were aiming to cross the coast near Brighton, but then Observer Corps personnel reported the huge fleet veering westwards towards the Isle of Wight. Faced with such numbers, Park and Dowding once again committed relatively large forces, throwing 48 Hurricanes and 10 Spitfires against them. While the Me110s adopted their orbiting 'circle of death' formation, trying to provoke the British

'Our great Luftwaffe would be at last attacking England'

Feldwebel (Technical Sergeant) Karl Hoffmann of *Gruppe 1*, *Kampfgeschwader* 30, found himself awestruck at the size of the aerial armada being gathered for the *Adlertag* onslaught on Britain.

```
    We had been briefed the day previous to Adler Tag that we would
be going across the Channel in strong formations to attack England.
At last, we would be concentrating in large bomber formations with
a fighter escort. For so long, we had been flying our individual
missions on simple operations like photographic reconnaissance or
minelaying duties. Some, like us, had not even seen a British fighter
or even fired a shot in anger and it hardly seemed as if a war was
on at all. Now, our airfields had many bombers at the ready, many
had been flown in from inland airfields, and I could see that now
our great Luftwaffe would be at last attacking England. [Quoted on
www.battleofbritain1940.net.]


                       -0-0-0-0-0-
```

'A scene of devastation'

Eric Clayton, an RAF fitter with No. 56 Squadron, described the scenes that greeted him during a mid-August 1940 visit to the vulnerable RAF airbase at Manston, Kent.

Chiefy Spreadborough detailed me, and a colleague called Grimshaw, to get ready to proceed to RAF Manston to fit a new radiator to Sutton's Hurricane so that it could be flown back to North Weald. We set out in a Humber shooting brake, carrying the necessary spares, on the morning of the 15th August. After slow progress through the bomb damaged East End of London, we approached Manston in the afternoon. As we neared the airfield we encountered a great cloud of chalk dust; at the station barrier the MP [Military Policeman] informed us that we had just missed a heavy bombing attack. As we entered the station (incredibly, a public road ran right through it), there was a scene of devastation; wrecked hangars, several damaged Blenheims and the airfield pitted with craters, including recently filled ones.

During this raid, two Bf 110s [Me110s] had been shot down by ground-fire, one of which had crashed on to the tarmac apron in front of the hangars. Because of the haze we did not see these at the time. This was an appropriate baptism, for during our stay the airfield was subjected to almost daily attacks, mainly low level dive-bombing by Bf 110s and strafing by Bf 109s [Me109s]. A nerve wracking feature was the existence of a permanent yellow status, because Manston was on the coast and enemy aircraft could rapidly change from attacking coastal shipping to appear over the airfield.

A Luftwaffe bomb detonates at RAF Helmswell, Lincolnshire (August 1940), in this case a controlled explosion after the bomb failed to explode on impact.

This was reflected by a warning voice over the Tannoy urgently announcing a change in status to red (which meant attack imminent) and almost immediately to purple coinciding with the crump of exploding bombs. There was little time for us to dive for cover into a nearby shelter. It was considerably worse for the unfortunate airmen and soldiers who were detailed to fill in bomb craters immediately after a raid, in order to try and keep the base operational.

It was a lethal activity, for when a red was announced, they had to jump into a lorry and, from the middle of the airfield, hurtle to some distant cover. Inevitably there were casualties. The Hurricane we had come to repair had been pushed into a small Bellman hangar near the main road and on the opposite side of the airfield from the defending fighter squadrons, 32, 65 and 610. We set to work but found we had neglected to bring a particular spare part; we hoped the station stores would have it. Reluctantly, we set out next morning along the main road to reach the stores on the other side of the airfield. We passed an unoccupied gun emplacement from which, we were told, one of the Bf 110s had been shot down.

Shortly, we came upon the crashed aircraft and gingerly approached it. The body of the dead pilot could just be seen through a hole in the fuselage and from the point of impact there was a trail of wreckage and shreds of flesh - a grisly indicator of the air-gunner's dreadful end. Under the wing of the Me110, I noticed the magneto from one of its Daimler-Benz engines; it was quite different from that of the Merlin engine. Out of curiosity, I quite improperly kept it as a souvenir.

-o-o-o-o-o-

fighters into a risky attack, about 70 Ju88s found a gap in the thicket of barrage balloons protecting Portsmouth and struck the town hard. The Royal Dockyards, the railway station and ships in the harbour all suffered, as well as shops and homes. Twenty-three people were killed and a hundred injured. The British fighters were kept back by the heavy flak being pumped into the air over the harbour. They waited for the bombers to leave before pouncing. The formation's lead bomber fell as it headed for home and plunged into the sea off Bognor Regis.

While the main German force had been attacking Portsmouth, a smaller group of Ju88s swung in on the Isle of Wight and dived on the radar station at Ventnor, whose commanding position on the high ground behind the town made it of particular interest to the Luftwaffe. The attack was accurate and devastating. Fifteen 500-kilo bombs demolished almost every structure in the compound. The aerial lattice between the transmitter towers was also severely damaged. The British moved a mobile unit to the area and broadcast dummy signals to try to fool the Germans into thinking that the station was still operational. It was not until 15 August that Ventnor was really functioning again, and then only partially so.

Spitfires of No. 609 Squadron arrived over the Isle of Wight to find about 200

German aircraft circling. Again, the German fighters waited on high, but as at Portsmouth they were ignored by 609 and its accompanying squadron, No. 152. The British fighters concentrated on the bombers, shooting down two of them. But the bombers' gunners were able to inflict equal damage, shooting down two of 152 Squadron's Spitfires and killing their pilots. The German fighter escort descended to join the mêlée but were unable to chase away the British fighters, suffering the loss of four Me110s and two Me109s in the process within the space of a few minutes.

Just before 1pm, the Luftwaffe launched another airfield raid, the third of the day. Spitfires from No. 65 Squadron were about to take off on patrol from Manston, Kent, when a group of Me110s swooped in to bomb and strafe. At the same time, 18 Dorniers made a pass over the airfield, dropping 250-kilo and fragmentation bombs. The airfield erupted into smoke, chalk dust and chaos. Jeffrey Quill, the legendary test pilot who was the second man to fly the Supermarine Spitfire and was now serving with 65 Squadron, described how 'we were just formed up on the ground and waiting Sam's signal to start rolling. I was therefore looking out to my left towards the leading section when I became aware of, rather than actually hearing, a sort of reverberating "crump" behind and to my right. I looked quickly over my right shoulder to see one of the hangar roofs close behind us ascending heavenwards ... I caught a glimpse through smoke of what looked like a Bf110 [Me110] pulling sharply out of a dive and immediately concluded that it was high time for Quill to be airborne.' [Quill, recording] Manston was the most forward and exposed point in the Fighter Command network, stuck on the bare promontory of the North Foreland. Not only did its position make it particularly liable to attack, but its pilots also had little time to gain height before the raiders' arrival.

The pressure on the radar stations was maintained until the early evening, when Kesselring sent three small raids against Dover and Hastings. But the attacks were intercepted in good time. The defenders had learned another tactical lesson and were now ignoring the fighter escorts forming an umbrella overhead in favour of tearing into the ranks of the bombers. That night, Luftwaffe signals chief Martini assessed the damage done to the British radar. The reports were disappointing. From monitoring radio signals from the target stations it seemed that all of them were back in action by the afternoon. Assuming that their workings must be deep underground, Martini came to the conclusion that it was possible to shut down British radar cover for short periods only.

The gun camera of a 609 Squadron Spitfire targets a formation of Heinkel He111 bombers on its way back from a raid (summer 1940).

13 August 1940 TUESDAY (THE LUFTWAFFE'S 'EAGLE DAY')

Cloud and drizzle, turning fair later.

As the German pilots went to bed on the eve of what was to be their Eagle Day, the weather worsened. As dawn broke on 13 August it was no better. Fog clung to many of the bases of northern France, and a thick blanket of cloud pressed down on the Channel. The plan of attack, as set out by Goering, envisaged great fleets of bombers, protected by a swarm of escorts flying at maximum height so as to be able to swoop like raptors on the British fighters as they attacked. But in these weather conditions the Messerschmitts would be unable to see through the mattress of cloud, leaving Fighter Command to savage their charges.

Goering looked at the unrelieved grey overhead and hesitated. There was some hope that another humiliating postponement could be avoided, for the meteorology men claimed things would improve in the afternoon. So the *Reichsmarschall* ordered operations to be held back until 2pm. The message, though, was slow to filter down the line.

Oberst Johannes Fink, the *Kanalkampfführer* himself, had already taken off in command of 74 Dorniers of *Kampfgeschwader* 2. He led the formation towards the French coast, where he was due, at 5.30am, to meet a fighter escort of 60 Me110s from *Zerstörergeschwader* 26. Then he was to proceed to targets on the Isle of Sheppey. News of the delay was signalled to him, but it never got through. Fink's radio was out of action and he pressed on, blithely unaware of the change of plan. The Messerschmitts were in place, but, as Fink said, 'they kept coming up and diving down in the most peculiar way. I thought this was their way of saying they were ready. So I went on and found to my surprise that the fighters didn't follow.' Clearly the fighters had, unlike Fink, received the postponement order, but with no radio link between the fighters and the bombers, the message could not be relayed.

The heavy cloud protected the bombers, and, as they crossed the North Foreland, their direction could not be accurately divined by the Observer Corps personnel straining to scan the murky skies. The radar cover was makeshift, provided by the emergency set installed after the preceding day's attacks. The result was that, of the five squadrons scrambled to intercept, only No. 74, led by 'Sailor' Malan, succeeded in engaging the bombers before they reached the Isle of Sheppey.

Fink's formation now split in two, with one *Gruppe* heading for the naval base at Sheerness and the other for Eastchurch air base. Like Lympne, which was attacked the day before, Eastchurch was not an important part of No. 11 Group's set-up. It was primarily a Coastal Command station, focused on German naval raiders rather than the vital air-to-air struggle. By chance, however, there was a squadron of Spitfires at the base, No. 266, which had just been moved south from the Midlands.

The first bomb landed soon after seven in the morning. No. 266 Squadron pilot Dennis Armitage remembered waking 'to find my bed waltzing around the room, which seemed most unpleasant but was caused by what in reality was a blessing ... the bogginess of the land. The whole place shook as if we were having a major earthquake, but the bombs ... buried themselves deeply before exploding, leaving nothing but a little pile of earth.' Nonetheless, the raid caused considerable damage. Five Coastal Command Blenheims were destroyed on the ground, as well as a hangar containing 266's ammunition and other important equipment. One of the groundcrew's huts was also hit, killing 16 men and injuring more. But none of the fighter pilots was killed, and only one Spitfire was destroyed on the ground, the rest having been carefully dispersed around the airfield.

As Fink's bombers wheeled away from their target to race for the protection of the clouds, they were set upon by fighters from 111 and 151 squadrons. Flight Lieutenant Roddick Smith of No. 151 Squadron was flying the only Hurricane in the RAF that currently had cannon: 'I ordered the attack, telling my pilots to dive through the enemy formation and on into the clouds, as I assumed the rear formation were Messerschmitt 110s and three quarters of my pilots were new.

continued on page 174

MACHINE-GUNS VERSUS CANNON

The challenge in terms of armament for the single-engine fighters was to maximize firepower while minimizing the weight of guns and ammunition. A special Air Ministry meeting on armaments in July 1934 decided that the high speeds of the new generation of monoplane fighters would mean that they would only be able to hold an enemy bomber in their sights for two seconds. For such a brief attack to be decisive, argued ballistics expert Captain F.W. Hill, the fighter would need at least eight guns firing 1000 rounds per minute.

This suggestion encountered stiff resistance from older officers used to only two – or a maximum of four – guns on a fighter; but in 1935 specification F.5/34 was issued, which included instructions to the designers of the Spitfire and Hurricane that both should carry eight Browning machine-guns with 300 rounds each, enough for about 14 seconds' firing.

The nose of a captured Messerschmitt Me110 is opened to reveal the four 7.9mm machine-guns contained within.

The American-manufactured Browning, which dated from the First World War, was an excellent weapon, reliable and fast-firing, capable of up to 1260 rounds per minute. At first the guns were imported, but soon manufacturing rights were acquired by the Vickers Company to make them in Britain. For the sturdy Hurricane, these instructions presented no difficulties, and the guns were mounted in the wings in four-gun batteries. But the Spitfire had much thinner wings, and it proved impossible to group the guns in a single gun bay. Instead, two two-gun batteries were installed, which made for slower rearming. For both fighters, Dunlop developed and supplied electrically controlled pneumatic cocking and firing systems. It was also necessary to provide hot-air ducts to prevent the gun

lubricant from freezing at the unprecedented heights at which these new fighters could operate.

The bullets they fired were 0.303 inches in calibre, the same as standard-issue rifles.

It became clear in the early stages of the Battle of Britain that these were not always able to penetrate the armour installed in German bombers and fighters. Fighter Command armourers started introducing De Wilde incendiaries and armour-piercing bullets, which increased effectiveness, but they still required a 'lucky hit' – on an engine, a vital control, or the pilot – to bring an enemy aircraft down.

Luftwaffe Me109s were armed with two wing-mounted Oerlikon 20mm cannon and two 7.9mm calibre machine-guns in the nose. In the small-framed Messerschmitt there was room for only 60 cannon rounds per gun, and the rate of fire at 520 rounds per minute was under half that of the British fighters' machine-guns. But the Me109 still carried a heavier punch – a three-second burst from an RAF fighter weighed about 13 pounds (almost 6kg); the same from an Me109 delivered 18 pounds (over 8kg). Also, the cannon had a much higher muzzle velocity and its shells exploded on impact, which meant that one or two hits could bring down a metal-skinned Spitfire.

Me109 pilot Hans-Ekkehard Bob explained the difference. 'Our cannons used special ammunition so we only needed to score a few hits to bring an English plane down. In a fraction of a second, I could bring down a Spitfire. If I could hit it twice, I could destroy it. The English had to score a great many hits with their machine-guns to bring a plane down but they didn't need to shoot as accurately.' [Bob, recording]

The Minister for Aircraft Production, Lord Beaverbrook, was an advocate of the cannon and pushed for conversion. A suitable weapon seemed to be available – the 20mm cannon that Hispano-Suiza had been manufacturing in Britain since 1937. Beaverbrook argued successfully for Fighter Command's most experienced Spitfire Squadron – No. 19 – to try out cannon-firing fighters in battle, even though tests were far from being completed. So, at the beginning of July, the first of the Mark 1B Spitfires were delivered to Fowlmere, armed with a Hispano-Suiza 20mm cannon in each wing. The squadron soon discovered that the

guns provided great accuracy, destructive power and range. But the feed mechanism was unreliable and the ejector caused repeated jamming of spent cases and stoppages. If one gun stopped, the asymmetric recoil made it impossible to fire the other one accurately. It was also prone to icing up at heights above 20,000 feet, and the small amount of ammunition – 6 seconds' worth – was deemed insufficient. But Beaverbrook was not deterred and the squadron, with its new armament, was sent into battle. The gremlins were eventually shaken out, and in 1941 Hurricanes were armed with four Hispano Mark II guns. Continuing difficulties with the Spitfires meant that most carried only two cannon, alongside six machine-guns.

An Air Ministry diagram reveals the inner workings of the Browning 0.303 machine-gun, as carried by Spitfires and Hurricanes.

'I THOUGHT IT WAS TIME TO ABANDON SHIP'

Eric Seabourne had experienced his first combat on 13 July and his first kill – an Me109 – on 8 August. But on 13 August his luck ran out. 'I didn't see who it was but I got a cannon shell in the radiator. I watched the oil temperature just going up and up and up until all of sudden there's a bang and the engine just stopped dead.' But he was still under attack, and now bullets struck the gravity tank just in front of his cockpit, which started 'burning quite happily. It got hotter and hotter, so I thought it was time to abandon ship.' He unstrapped himself, but the cockpit hood was jammed. This was the nightmare that every pilot dreaded – slow death by burning. Already Seabourne's clothes were scorched, and his wrists and face burnt. His non-issue rubber goggles had melted onto his face. 'All the time the three Me109s on my tail kept firing at me and then suddenly my port wing broke off. The aircraft turned over on its back.' Loose in the cockpit, Seabourne's body crashed against the hood and it fell away at last. He was out: 'The cold air revived me, I can tell you.' Fearful of being strafed by the enemy fighters, he waited until he was in the cloud at 2000 feet before pulling the ripcord on his parachute. 'The only snag was that when the thing opened up two of the straps were crossed about my neck, so with my burnt hands I had to hold them to one side to ease the pressure on my neck. The next minute there was an almighty splash and I was in the water.'

He had been told that it was imperative for pilots landed in water to free themselves from their parachutes: 'Well, I ignored that completely. I don't know why but I still kept my parachute, which billowed out all around me.' He did, though, blow up his Mae West lifejacket and floated around in the Channel for about an hour, which 'after the burning cockpit even seemed quite pleasant'. As Seabourne drifted in and out of consciousness, he was suddenly alerted by a large bow wave that his rescue was imminent. It was a destroyer, the *Bulldog*, which was still in action, firing its anti-aircraft guns and keen to keep on the move. A scrambling net holding two seamen appeared over the side and Seabourne was firmly grabbed. 'But I still had the parachute tied around my right leg so as he got under way of course there was a nasty crack and the leg snapped.' Seabourne hardly felt it; the experience of being burned in his aircraft seemed to have extinguished his ability to feel pain. Once on board the vessel, he was pumped full of morphine and eventually delivered to the naval hospital in Portsmouth. There he lay next but one to an injured German pilot: 'He was an English speaker and he was creating because he had been shot down by a Hurricane, which he thought was much below his dignity. If it had been a Spitfire it would have been OK, but not a Hurricane.' [Quotations from Parker, p. 206]

I opened fire at about 300 yards with my cannon, firing into the general mass as the enemy were in exceptionally close formation. One immediately burst into flames and another started smoking when my windscreen front panel was completely shattered by enemy fire, and I broke away downwards and returned to North Weald.' [Quoted in Mason, p. 189, footnote]

The Hurricanes of No. 111 Squadron launched another frontal attack, causing havoc. Five Dorniers were shot down and several more of them were damaged. On his return, a furious Fink telephoned Generalfeldmarschall Kesselring 'and shouted down the line exactly what I thought about it. I asked what …

the people at HQ thought they were doing to send us out unprotected.'

Another German group had also failed to receive the delay message. At about 6.30am, radar picked up an enemy formation approaching the coast between Hastings and Bognor. Fighter Command sent up four squadrons, and No. 43 made contact first, with what turned out to be a fighter formation of Me109s and Me110s of *Jagdgeschwader* 2. As they raced westwards, a German fighter was shot down between Petworth and Shoreham. But more Me109s arrived to bolster the force. As 11 Group's fighters peeled off to return to base, ammunition exhausted, No. 238 Squadron from 10 Group rose up to meet the raiders, though the British pilots were heavily outnumbered. 'We had rather a shock,' said pilot Gordon Batt. 'We were instantly in a mass of aircraft.' As always, with closing speeds of up to 600 miles an hour, everything happened in fractions of a second. 'We were attacked first by Me109s from above, which chopped me off from the other five of the flight.' Finding himself suddenly alone, Batt peered around the empty sky before spotting some eight or nine Me109s below him. 'I started to dive to attack, when it suddenly felt as if a steam-roller had hit me. The aircraft bucked and jumped out of my control.' Batt opened the hood to jump, but then changed his mind. Although his propeller had stopped and his machine was streaming engine coolant, he turned his stricken Hurricane north, breaking cloud at 2000 feet. To his great relief, he was over land. 'There was not a field bigger than a postage stamp, so I elected to force-land with the wheels up in a field near to a farmhouse, so that if I did get into difficulties the farmer would come to my aid.' Pulling his straps tight, he prepared for a rough landing. 'As I hit the field, the big air scoop under the Hurricane dug in and rocked me forward ... eventually, having made a nasty groove in the farmer's crop, I came to a standstill. I rapidly released my safety straps and parachute harness, heaved myself out of the cockpit and ran along the wing, falling over backwards into the dusty barley and dry earth.' High above, the raiders had turned for home, their fuel exhausted, but not before consigning another Hurricane to destruction. [Batt, pp. 39–40]

An Me110 plummets to its destruction in the skies above Sussex.

The westward-headed free chases had been designed to draw defending fighters away from a raid by Ju88s from *Kampfgeschwader* 54 against an airfield at Odiham in Hampshire (again, one with little defensive importance) and the Royal Aircraft establishment at Farnborough. But the formation was spotted by 'A' Flight of 601 Squadron, which was climbing towards the German fighter sweep. Harassed by the fighters, and struggling to fly and navigate in the poor weather, the Ju88s turned back when only ten miles inland.

Shortly before midday, a force from *Zerstörergeschwader* 2 had also jumped the gun. A group of 28 Me110s had been due to escort Ju88s of *Kampfgeschwader* 54 on a diversion raid on Portland. This time the bombers received the postponement order but not the fighters, which set course for the naval base nonetheless. Two squadrons of British fighters – Nos 238, again, and 601 – were waiting for them, and before they could escape, one of the Me110s was shot down and two more badly damaged by 238 Squadron Hurricanes. But the beleaguered squadron, which had lost five aircraft and four pilots two days previously, saw two more of its fighters shot down, with one pilot, Sergeant Marsh, who had shared a victory with his number two Eric Bann a few days previously, missing and presumed dead. Bann blamed himself, as he described in a letter home shortly afterwards (15 August): 'Tony Marsh, my section leader, and I were the last two in action and I think I must have done too much flying for I fainted and I, poor Tony's guard, left him to the mercy of all. Oh dear, I did feel bad, when I learned he never came back.'

As the confusion that muddled the opening of Eagle Day cleared, so did the skies. At 1pm the word went out that *Adlertag* was now definitely 'on'. The first attack of the afternoon formed up over Cherbourg and the Channel Islands. At 3.30pm it appeared on the radar screens across a 40-mile front. As Sir Hugh Dowding at Fighter Command HQ watched the WAAF operators push the enemy markers across the board with their croupiers' rakes, he concluded that the Germans were heading for 10 Group in the west.

There was no doubting now that this was an all-out assault. It was the largest formation yet launched against England. On the eastern flank were 120 Ju88s of *Kampfgeschwader* 54 and the mixed-aircraft *Lehrgeschwader* (Teaching Wing) 1, escorted by 30 Me110s of the latter. On the western flank were 27 Ju87s of *Sturzkampfgeschwader* (dive-bomber wing) 2. In the vanguard flew 30 Me109s of *Jagdgeschwader* 53, and behind them 52 Ju87s of *Sturzkampfgeschwader* 77, escorted by Me109s of *Jagdgeschwader* 27.

Before the main thrust crossed the Channel, a free sweep by Me109s of *Jagdgeschwader* 5 raced along the coast near Portland, attempting to draw defending fighters to the west. No. 152 Squadron's Spitfires took up the chase, but all the early attack had achieved was to bring more British fighters to readiness. Soon just under 80 Hurricanes and Spitfires were airborne to take on the main formation.

Ploughing through by sheer weight of numbers, one German bomber group hit Southampton at about 4.05pm, causing heavy damage to the port and to residential areas. Meanwhile, 40 Ju88s of *Kampfgeschwader* 54 were now carrying out the raid on Portland from which they had been recalled in the morning. But an interception by fighters from Nos 152, 213 and 601 squadrons drove them back, with 601 downing three of their Me110 escorts. At the same time, a force of Ju87s had managed to cross the coast undetected, and wheeled northeast intent on bombing the important sector station at Middle Wallop. But the formation had taken a long

BELOW

A newspaper cutting, pasted in his pilot's log-book by David Crook, summarizes 609 Squadron's success on 13 August.

HIGH SPOTS

Here are some high spots from the records of their achievements in the sunny days of last August:—

August 13.—County of London Squadron carried out three patrols in which they destroyed 13 enemy machines, probably destroyed 14; damaged 15 others.

August 13.—Within a few minutes, near Portland, the West Riding Squadron shot down nine Junkers 87 dive-bombers and four Messerschmitt 109's. Damaged another seven. The squadron had no casualties.

August 15.—The County of Gloucester Squadron destroyed 12 enemy machines. Ten were Junkers 87's shot down out of a formation of 20 off the Kent coast.

August 25.—In their first big battle near Dorchester, City of Glasgow Squadron shot down 12 without losing a pilot.

August 31.—In three patrols, City of Edinburgh Squadron destroyed 14 of the enemy and probably three more.

'I hear the buzzing of planes on high'

The Conservative MP and diarist Henry 'Chips' Channon noted his sense of crescendo in the aerial drama on 13 August, after frenetic activity in the skies that day.

Another big day along the Channel, with many planes down: shall we be invaded tomorrow? As I write, I hear the buzzing of planes on high, and think that London will certainly be raided soon. I feel that at long last we are entering upon a decisive phase of the war. [Channon, p. 263]

-0-0-0-0-0-

SINGLE-ENGINE AIRCRAFT				MULTI-ENGINE AIRCRAFT						PASS-ENGER	INSTR/CLOUD FLYING [Incl. in cols. (1) to (10)]	
DAY		NIGHT		DAY			NIGHT					
UAL	PILOT	DUAL	PILOT	DUAL	1ST PILOT	2ND PILOT	DUAL	1ST PILOT	2ND PILOT		DUAL	PILOT
(1)	(2)										(12)	(13)

Building Spitfires, painted by Norman Wilkinson (1878–1971). In the First World War Wilkinson had designed the Royal Navy's 'dazzle' camouflage.

SHADOW FACTORIES

The Shadow Factory Scheme was an example of British far-sightedness that contrasted sharply with the surprisingly short-term approach taken by Germany towards waging aerial war. Long before the conflict began, British planners had understood the inevitability of aviation-industry factories becoming prime targets for enemy bombers. In April 1936, the government established a scheme to set up 'shadow factories', which would provide alternative production capability for the military aircraft industry by using the enormous capacity of the motor-car industry. Arrangements were made for Austin, Rover, Humber, Standard and Daimler plants to produce parts for aircraft engines. Other factories started producing propellers and ammunition. The Rootes group factory at Speke, Liverpool, was equipped to produce Blenheims, and the Austin Motor Company in Oxford was adapted for manufacturing Fairey Battles. Rolls-Royce set up shadow factories in Crewe and Glasgow to manufacture Merlin engines, and by 1938 a wide network of subcontractors had come into existence at hundreds of sites around the country.

Production of the Spitfire was ensured by Supermarine's shadow factories at Cosford in Shropshire and Desford in Leicestershire, should its Southampton works be knocked out. The Nuffield Group, which owned Morris Motors, also built a large new factory at Castle Bromwich near Birmingham for Spitfire production.

Should – despite such precautions – Hurricane and Spitfire production be obliterated, there was a contingency plan for the rapid mass production of a basic, nimble eight-gun fighter, the Miles M20, which could be thrown into a last-ditch battle, should all else fail.

route over the Channel, and by now the Stukas' fighter escort's dwindling fuel reserves had forced it to turn back. No. 609 Squadron was scrambled in time to gain the height to make a devastating attack on a *Staffel* from *Sturzkampfgeschwader* 2. Weighed down by their bombs, the Stukas were even slower than usual and six of them were shot down. John Dundas, who was one of those claiming kills, wrote in the squadron's diary: 'Thirteen Spitfires left Warmwell for a memorable tea-party over Lyme Bay, and an unlucky day for the species Ju87.' [Quoted in Ziegler, pp. 120–1] Returning back to base, one of the Ju87 crew survivors reported: 'They ripped our backs open right up to the collar.' [Quoted in Collier, p. 72]

Other Stuka formations crossed the coast unopposed, but, searching for the forward base at Warmwell, they got lost and ditched their bombs at random, before heading home. Yet more Ju87s had been ordered to target Middle Wallop, but they bombed the grass airstrip at Andover in error. Only one found Middle Wallop, but dropped its bombs on the village rather than the base.

As the attack in the west faded, Kesselring's *Luftflotte* 2 began to launch raids in Southeast England. Two Stuka groups crossed the coast, one over Dover, the other near Dungeness. No. 56 Squadron intercepted, but was soon involved in battles with escorting Me109s as the formation moved northwards. The Stukas never found whatever targets they were seeking, and ended up jettisoning their bombs over Canterbury, Ashford and Ramsgate in Kent.

The other group of 40 Stukas of *Lehrgeschwader* 1, led by Hauptmann Berndt von Brauchitsch, son of the German army's commander-in-chief, had greater impact. Throughout the day the German tactic had been to use fighter sweeps in an attempt to divert the Fighter Command forces, while bombers arrived shortly afterwards to exploit the defensive gap. Often the bomber force had arrived too late, giving the British fighters time to engage the raiding fighters, return to base, refuel, rearm and get airborne again in time to meet the bombers. But this time, over Kent, the plan worked, and as a fighter sweep by Me109s of *Jagdgeschwader* 26 drew Nos 56 and 65 squadrons away, shooting down four of 56's Hurricanes, von Brauchitsch's Stukas proceeded to Detling airfield, near Rochester.

The attack came as a complete surprise. No air-raid sirens were sounded, and the airfield defences were slow to react. The first many of the staff knew of the raid was the sight of Me109s racing in low with their cannons blazing. The dive-bombers followed. It was just after 5pm, and the mess halls were full. All the hangars were hit, as well as the operations block where the commanding officer, Group Captain Edward Davis, was killed by falling concrete. The fuel dump was set ablaze, and the runways and hard standings were cratered. The raid killed 67 people and destroyed 22 aircraft. But the operation had no effect on the efficiency of Dowding's defences, for Detling was a Coastal Command airfield.

During the night of 13/14 August, the Luftwaffe was busy again, hitting targets as disparate as Aberdeen, Norwich, Swansea, Liverpool and Belfast. In the latter city, the Short's factory was hit, destroying five of the RAF's new groundbreaking four-engine Sterling bombers. The heaviest raid was on the new 'shadow' Spitfire factory (to provide additional and contingency capacity) – at Castle Bromwich, near Birmingham, which was badly damaged.

That evening, as both sides assessed the day's damage, it seemed to the Germans that they had destroyed 84 British fighters. The British reckoned they had knocked down 64 German aircraft. The true figures were closer to 47 German losses against 13 British fighters in the air, 3 of whose pilots were killed. The importance of the day lay in the fact that Goering's Luftwaffe had failed to land anything like the sort of heavy blow on which his plan's success depended.

WEDNESDAY **14 August 1940**

To Goering's frustration, the weather today was similar to that of the morning before, with thick clouds at 2000 feet making large-scale operations impossible. Fighter Command had a morning's respite to rotate exhausted squadrons and repair damaged aircraft.

Heavy cloud over Channel, brighter inland.

At around noon, however, radar at Dover showed a substantial enemy force building up over Calais. Air Vice-Marshal Park ordered up 42 fighters from Nos 32, 65, 610 and 65 squadrons. Over Dover they met three *Gruppen* (about 90 aircraft) of Me109s from *Jagdgeschwader* 26 along with 80 Stuka dive-bombers. One *Gruppe* of the Messerschmitts stayed with the Stukas, while the others successfully drew the intercepting British fighters into battle. Because they were operating close to their bases, the Me109s were able to remain in combat for longer than usual, and a huge 200-aircraft dogfight developed. A formation of the Me109s shot down eight of Dover's barrage balloons and Stukas sunk the *Goodwin* lightship. Two Me109s were shot down, as well as three Stukas, and the RAF defenders lost seven fighters and two of its pilots.

While Park's forces were occupied, Manston airfield came under attack again

---

'We are all down with nerve trouble'

No. 238 Squadron was one of the hardest-hit squadrons during the Battle of Britain, and was withdrawn from the frontline on 14 August 1940 to rest and absorb replacement pilots. Most of its original pilots had been killed or injured. 'We'd lost pilots and, of course, aircraft, in a devastating way,' said Sergeant Gordon Batt. 'I do wonder why I was spared.' The next day, together with his commanding officer, he went to visit his friend Eric Seabourne at the naval hospital in Portsmouth. Seabourne had been shot down the previous morning (see page 174) and was very badly burned. Batt remembered sitting on Seabourne's bed and asking him how he slept without eyelids. [Batt, p. 45] From their new temporary home at St Eval airfield in Cornwall, Eric Bann wrote to his parents:

I am afraid that our duty at the front line has told its tale upon our systems. Our engagements have been really hectic … we are all down with nerve trouble and have been sent to this rest camp … just Gordon Batt and I remain among the sergeants and many of our officers have gone. [Private letter, 15 August 1940]

-o-o-o-o-o-

from Me110s of the elite Experimental Group 210. They destroyed three Blenheims on the ground, and four hangars took direct hits. One raider was brought down by fire from a Bofors gun manned by aircrew from the Blenheim squadron. Manston's exposed position and proximity to the Luftwaffe bases made it particularly open to attack, and returning German aircraft with bombs still on board were now in the habit of dropping them on this convenient target of opportunity. The extreme vulnerability of the aerodrome created an atmosphere of danger in which death could come without warning, at any time of day.

In the west, the weather brightened during the afternoon, and Generalfeldmarschall Sperrle's *Luftflotte* 3 began sending out small raiding formations, spread over a front of about 100 miles. Inevitably, some of the bombers got through 10 Group's stretched defences. Shortly before 6pm, a lone Junkers Ju88 appeared suddenly out of the clouds above Middle Wallop, Dorset. Groundcrew rushed to close the heavy hangar doors to protect the Spitfires inside. But now the Ju88 had gone into its steep bombing dive. At 1500 feet it released its 500-kilo bombs, scoring a direct hit on Hangar No. 5. Three men struggling to close the door were crushed to

Flight Lieutenant John Dundas was one of the 609 Squadron pilots to take part in what he called the 13 August 'tea party', at which a group of hapless Stukas were unwilling guests.

death as the roof, walls and doors collapsed. A No. 609 Squadron pilot, 'Red' Tobin – one of ten Americans who fought in the Battle of Britain – was nearby: 'My head was spinning, it felt as though I had a permanent ringing in my ears, I felt the blast go over me as I lay there flattened on the ground. I got up and my instinct was to run towards the hangar. It was carnage, I saw one overalled person with his foot and half a leg blown off, another had a great red patch on his chest with a load of mess hanging from it, another was rolling in agony with one of his arms missing.' [Quoted in Kershaw, p. 117]

As the bombs fell, a flight from 609 Squadron struggled to get airborne, dodging explosions and craters on the runway. A Spitfire on patrol above the airfield had shot down the Ju88 as the bomber came out of its dive, but now the squadron encountered a small group of He111s from *Kampfgeschwader* 55. David Crook and John Dundas singled out the leader, and together they destroyed it. When the wreckage was examined later, it was found to contain the bodies of three senior Luftwaffe officers. 'They had probably come over to see how the operations against England were progressing,' wrote Crook. 'I hope they were suitably impressed!' [Crook, p. 51]

Another Heinkel group penetrated 10 Group's defences and bombed an airfield at Colerne in Wiltshire. The Luftwaffe had clearly spotted Hurricanes there (which were in fact inoperational while undergoing maintenance) and added Colerne to its target list. Little serious destruction resulted. A further group got as far as Sealand in Cheshire, home of No. 30 Maintenance Unit. The damage was more substantial but it was quickly repaired. On the coast, most of the small German raids were driven back, but Southampton was bombed, and its main railway line was blocked for a while. Bombs also fell on residential areas.

At the end of the day, assured that Middle Wallop was again operational and that Manston would be back in action in 12 hours, Park and Dowding were confident that when the weather improved enough to allow another all-out attack, Fighter Command would be ready.

(THE LUFTWAFFE'S 'BLACK THURSDAY') 15 August 1940

Early in the day, the poor weather continued. Goering took the opportunity to summon his *Luftflotte* commanders and senior officers to his mansion, Carinhall, to discuss the failures of the 13 August attack and to reassess tactics. Those present included Kesselring, Sperrle, General Bruno Lörzer of *Fliegerkorps* II, who had flown with Goering in the previous war, and Generalmajor Joachim Coler of *Fliegerdivision* XI. At the end of the meeting, Goering issued a directive that suggested growing disquiet at the top of the Luftwaffe. It identified Stukas and Messerschmitt Me110s as vulnerable. Goering now ordered that three fighter *Gruppen* should accompany every Stuka *Gruppe*, one to go ahead and draw away intercepting fighters, the second to dive alongside the bombers, the third to give cover high above.

This was a highly impractical suggestion. It was not possible for the fighters to maintain the slower pace of the bombers without flying with their flaps down and weaving, which would waste fuel and severely limit their time over the target. Furthermore, the Me109 did not have the Stuka's air brakes, which extended below the wings outboard of the fixed undercarriage and enabled the bomber's

Some cloud over Channel, but fine elsewhere.

Keith Henderson's *A North-east Coast Aerodrome* (1940) has a calm and orderly ambience – appropriately, given the relatively quiet summer that 13 Group was having in contrast to its southerly neighbours.

THE AMERICANS OF FIGHTER COMMAND

Although the United States was officially neutral at the time, ten American citizens, impelled by ideology, chance or adventure, served in Fighter Command during the Battle of Britain. The best-known was Pilot Officer William 'Billy' Fiske, a Cambridge graduate and US Olympic bobsleigh team member, who joined 601 Squadron at Tangmere in July 1940. He crash-landed there on 16 August, following a fight with a Ju87 over Bognor, and died of his wounds the next day. A memorial to him was unveiled in St Paul's Cathedral the following year, engraved with the words 'An American Citizen who died that England might live.' Three young aviators – Vernon Keogh, Andrew Mamedoff and Eugene Tobin – travelled from the United States together to fight the Germans. They started off in Finland, then moved on to France during the *Blitzkrieg* before ending up in 609 Squadron. They later became the first members of No. 71 Squadron, the first 'Eagle Squadron' made up of American volunteers. All were subsequently killed in action. The other US Battle of Britain pilots were pilot officers Phillip Leckrone (616 Squadron), Arthur Donahue (64 Squadron), John Haviland (151 Squadron) Hugh Reilley (64 and 66 squadrons), De Peyster Brown (1 RCAF Squadron) and Flying Officer Carl Davis (601 Squadron).

Eugene Tobin observes Andrew Mamedoff placing their new 71 Squadron badge on the shoulder of Vernon 'Shorty' Keogh at Church Fenton sector station (October 1940). The three US volunteers fought – and died – serving with Fighter Command.

steep but slow dive. The twin-engine Me110s, Goering declared, must be used more economically, 'only where the range of other fighters is inadequate, or where it is for the purpose of assisting our single-engine aircraft to break off combat'. He also ordered that there must be only one officer in any crew flying over Britain – a reflection of the losses of experienced personnel.

Goering judged the attack on radar stations to have been a waste of time, as the stations had been restored to service so swiftly. In other respects, the directive sought to focus the efforts of the Luftwaffe more closely on what Hitler had ordered as the prime goal – the destruction of the RAF. Secondary targets should be chosen more carefully and shipping ignored unless circumstances were exceptionally favourable.

While the discussions continued, the weather in northern France and southern England improved significantly. By 11am there was only a light wind and a clear blue sky – ideal weather for a large attack. The chief of staff of *Fliegerkorps* II, whose massive force of 800 bombers and 1000 fighters had been scheduled to lead the day's attack, was Oberst (Colonel) Paul Deichmann. Unable to contact his superiors – Goering had ordered that his meeting with senior officers not be disturbed for any reason – Deichmann launched the attack on his own authority. And so, the largest German aerial force mustered so far readied for take-off.

A few minutes after 11am, radar on the Kent coast picked up the first of the formations over Calais. There were two *Staffeln* of Stukas from *Lehrgeschwader* 1,

BELOW
Pilots from 234 Squadron take an *al fresco* rest, at the 10 Group airfield of St Eval, Cornwall (1940).

'I did not intend to sit on the ground and be bombed'

Pilot Officer David Crook of 609 Squadron was just waiting to get airborne as a Ju88 bomber visited his Middle Wallop airfield with lethal consequences on 14 August 1940.

We sat in our aircraft and waited. A few minutes later we heard the unmistakable 'ooma-ooma' of a German bomber above the clouds. I immediately signalled to my ground crew to stand by, as I did not intend to sit on the ground and be bombed. I kept my finger on the engine starter button and waited expectantly. Almost immediately the enemy bomber, a Junkers 88, broke out of the cloud to the north of the aerodrome, turned slightly to get on his course and then dived at very high speed towards the hangars. At about 1,500 feet he let go four bombs - we could see them very distinctly as they plunged down, and seconds later there was an earth-shaking 'whoom' and four great clouds of dust arose. All this happened in a matter of seconds only, but by this time, everybody had got their engines started and we all roared helter-skelter across the aerodrome. Why there were no collisions I don't know, but we got safely into the air and turned round to chase the enemy. [Crook, p. 50]

-o-o-o-o-o-

Hurricanes take off from
11 Group's Gravesend
aerodrome after
refuelling and rearming
(summer 1940).

which were soon joined by another 26 Ju87s from *Sturzkampfgeschwader* 1 and dozens of Me109s. As the first wave advanced, a second appeared behind it. Soon there were too many plots on the radar to distinguish between formations as hundreds of German planes took to the air.

At Hawkinge forward airfield, near Folkestone, two squadrons were at readiness. At 11.10am, eleven Hurricanes of 501 Squadron were scrambled; eight minutes later, twelve Spitfires of 54 Squadron were sent up. It was good timing for Fighter Command. Fifteen minutes later, the first wave of Ju87s – lavishly protected by Me109s – was overhead. But, thanks to the radar warning, the British fighters were in the air, and with plenty of height to manoeuvre. By this stage of the battle, the division of labour was well established. The Hurricanes pursued the bombers, while the Spitfires took on their high-flying escorts. Two Spitfires were shot down engaging the top cover. Then, to protect the now dive-bombing Stukas, the Me109s swooped on the Hurricanes. Pilot John Gibson of 501 Squadron had shot down a Stuka and damaged another before he felt the sickening jolt of Me109 cannon-fire hitting his aircraft. As he went through the now familiar preparations to bale out – he had been shot down twice before – he realized that his Hurricane was heading directly for a built-up area of Folkestone. Steering his stricken fighter towards the sea, he baled out at just 1000 feet. Still over land, he had the presence of mind to take off his new shoes as he descended, dropping them in a field before his parachute followed his aircraft into the Channel. 'I had a brand-new pair of shoes handmade at Duke Street in London. We used to fly in a jacket, collar and tie, because we were gentlemen,' he later laughed. 'I thought I was going to get these shoes wet in the Channel so I took them off while I was still in the parachute.' [Quoted in Parker, p. 215] On his return to Hawkinge, Gibson was awarded the Distinguished Flying Cross (DFC), but he was also reunited with his precious shoes, sent in by a farmer on the off-chance that they belonged to one of the local pilots.

While the British fighters struggled with hugely superior numbers of Me109s, Stukas had succeeded in diving on Hawkinge to drop fifteen 250-kilo and 50-kilo fragmentation bombs on the airfield. Direct hits destroyed a hangar and pulverized one end of a barrack block. But the intention had been to destroy fighters on the ground, and the early warning meant that the targets were already airborne.

Meanwhile, other parts of the giant formation had wheeled away to pound nearby Lympne once more. Unopposed by British fighters, Ju87s battered the base's infrastructure. Both Hawkinge and Lympne would be out of action for several crucial days.

As the decisions reached at Carinhall had yet to be communicated to the Luftwaffe squadrons, radar targets had been included in their orders. A group of Stukas from the Hawkinge raid peeled away, still carrying their bombs, to strike at the Chain Home Low station at Foreness and the Chain Home High stations at Dover and Rye. This time, the Germans had more luck: bombs falling outside the compounds cut power to all three, putting them out of action for the rest of the day. The destruction increased the already heavy burden on the shoulders of the Observer Corps.

continued on page 188

'We cheered them on in every dogfight'

For the first time in British history, non-combatants witnessed a battle on which national survival depended. Mrs Joanna Thompson, a housewife, watched the drama from the garden of her home in Kent.

The sound was unthinkable, you never heard anything like it, and there, out of the sky planes were falling blazing to the ground, parachutes with little men hanging helplessly underneath drifted towards earth, even flying boots and pieces of aircraft came down hitting the tin shelter with a terrific thud. I think it was now that this war was so close to home, that we suddenly became proud of these pilots, men and young men, who we didn't even know, yet we cheered them on in every dogfight that we saw.

-0-0-0-0-0-

RIGGERS, FITTERS AND ARMOURERS

Fighter aircraft relied on a team of skilled mechanics, whose efficiency and speed were of vital importance. Each fighter had a dedicated team of armourer, fitter and rigger. There were also specialist technicians for the radio, the instruments and the electrics. Fred Roberts was an armourer for No. 19 Squadron Spitfires at Fowlmere. He explained how two-man teams would work on each wing to reload fighters after combat. 'First we'd drop the empty tanks out, and while I was pushing the full tanks back up in and pulling the belt through, my assistant would be running the cleaning rod down the barrel. This had to be done before the plane was re-armed, otherwise the first round in the belt would already be in the breech. So you had to push the cleaning rod down, clean it out quick, a bit of oily four-by-two, and as soon as the assistant pushed that through, we pulled the belt through and let the breech rod go forward. Once we'd done that with each of the four guns on each side, the plane was fully loaded.' [Roberts, recording] The whole process took about three and a half minutes.

The rigger had responsibility for wheels, tyres, airframe and the hood. Often he could be identified by his ever-present polish and cloth – pilots insisted that the glass be totally free of specks, which might be mistaken for German aircraft. The fitter looked after the engine. Leading Aircraftman Joe Roddis was a fitter with No. 234 Squadron. 'When the aircraft returned, I'd refuel the engine and put oil in it,' he explained. 'If there was a snag and it was within my capability to fix it, I would, and then I'd run it up to see that I'd resolved the problem. I would always do an "afterflight". That meant giving the engine a real good going-over. You might look at it and think that nothing's happened but a bullet could have gone through the cowling or the propeller. It would take about half an hour and they'd bring us back on readiness when all the other trades had finished their jobs.' [Roddis, recording]

'Of course the pilot, he became part of the team of armourer, rigger and fitter,' said Fred Roberts. 'We three and the pilot were a team of four. The radio operator, the electrician and the instrument mechanic, they probably had

RIGHT
Armourer Fred Roberts rearms a Spitfire Mark 1 of No. 19 Squadron at Fowlmere, Cambridgeshire (September 1940), while Pilot Sergeant Jennings chats with a mechanic.

OPPOSITE ABOVE
Raymond McGrath's *Fitters Working on a Spitfire*, painted in 1940.

GRAND TOTAL [Cols. (1) to (10)]

..................Hrs..................Mins.

three or four aircraft to look after, so they weren't part of our team. But we three were always together and usually when we had a scramble, you were there, the fitter was in the cockpit starting the engine up, the armourer was there, sometimes he would be on the starter trolley pressing the accumulator to start the engine. The airframe wallah, he was there with us ready to pull the chocks away. As soon as the engine was warmed up, the pilot came, he got into the cockpit, the rigger was on one side, the fitter was the other side, I'd be there strapping him into his harness. When that was done, the other two would come back to the tail with me and all three of us lay across the tail, to hold it down while the pilot revved. As soon as he had revved the engine up, then the rigger, the fitter and the armourer went to each wing tip to guide him out onto the airfield. We worked as a team and we became close to the pilot like that.' [Roberts, recording]

Some pilots were friendly with their ground-crew, taking care to learn their first names and nicknames. Peter Brothers, while his squadron was 'commuting' to France, made a habit of

bringing his crew a crate of beer at the end of the day and spending some time discussing the day's action. 'We wouldn't have got off the ground but for them,' he said. 'They were all super. And of course, their aircraft had to be the best in the squadron, naturally.' [Brothers, recording] Other pilots were 'a bit stand-offish.' Most of them, particularly at the start of the war, said fitter Joe Roddis, 'were university graduates, clever lads from well-to-do families, and they'd not been brought up to mix with mechanics'. Fred Roberts said that, on the whole, the crew looked up to the pilots, 'and we looked up more to the NCO pilots because they understood us better, they had been through the ranks with us'. Generally, there was a feeling of mutual respect and admiration between pilot and crew, but there remained a distinct social divide. 'I would never ever call an officer by his first name,' said Roddis. 'But we got on with them because they realized our worth as much as we realized theirs ... We didn't go out drinking with them. It was pilots and groundcrews and that's the way we liked it.'

RICHARD SAUL

TOTALS BROUGHT FORWAR

Air Vice-Marshal Richard Saul (1891–1965) commanded 13 Group during the Battle of Britain, where he was responsible for 200-odd aircraft and the sector stations defending the north of England, Scotland and the strategically important base at Scapa Flow.

During the First World War Saul had served in the Royal Flying Corps as an observer and was awarded the Distinguished Flying Cross (DFC). He spent part of the 1920s and 1930s stationed in Iraq, and by 1933 he was commanding 203 Squadron. He was an exceptional sportsman, and during the 1920s he represented the RAF at rugby and hockey; he also won the RAF tennis championship twice (1928 and 1932). Saul was a fine organizer, and during the 1930s he helped devise the structure of Fighter Command. He was Senior Air Staff Officer at Fighter Command HQ before eventually becoming the commander of No. 13 Group in July 1939, with his headquarters at Newcastle.

Saul moved on to command 12 Group in December 1940; two years later he was in charge of air defences in the eastern Mediterranean. His RAF retirement came in 1944. But later his organizational abilities were put at the service of the United Nations Relief and Rehabilitation Administration (UNRRA), attempting to ensure effective relief supplies in the former Axis-occupied Balkans.

After the war, he served for a time as Vice-Chairman of the International Transport Commission, based in Rome, before moving to Canada in the 1950s, where he took up a rather different occupation — managing the bookshop of the University of Toronto.

The consequent radar blind spot meant that a midday raid by Me110s of *Zerstörergeschwader* 76 arrived over hard-pressed Manston unopposed. Fortunately, No. 54 Squadron had just taken off again, after refuelling; but two Spitfires from 66 Squadron were destroyed on the ground and sixteen groundcrew were killed as the twin-engine fighters strafed the base with cannon and machine-gun fire.

Meanwhile, at the opposite end of the country, the Luftwaffe made its boldest move of the day. After the fall of Norway, Dowding knew his northern flank was vulnerable. The Germans were convinced that northern Britain had been stripped of fighter defences to feed the heavy combat in the south. Fighter Command forces were spread thinly, and many of the squadrons were unblooded, but Dowding also had a couple of battle-tested fighter squadrons 'resting' in Air Vice-Marshal Richard Saul's 13 Group.

The attack on what the Luftwaffe imagined was a vulnerable point got under way at 9.30am, when a *Staffel* of Heinkel He115 seaplanes took off from their base in Norway and set course across the North Sea towards Dundee. The move was designed to lure defending fighters away to the north, while the main attack hit airfields at Usworth, near Newcastle, and Dishforth, north of Leeds. Half an hour later, 72 He111s of *Kampfgeschwader* 26, each loaded with 3000 lbs of bombs, left their bases at Stavanger and Sola. They were joined 20 minutes later by 21 Me110 heavy fighters of *Zerstörergeschwader* 76 as their escort. The long distances involved meant the mission was beyond the range of the single-engine Me109s of *Luftflotte* 5. The Messerschmitt Me110s carried long-range fuel tanks, and some were stripped of their rear gunners to lessen the load and reduce fuel consumption.

The 'decoy' He115 seaplanes did their job well, appearing on the Anstruther Chain Home High radar shortly after midday, heading for the Firth of Forth before turning back some 40 miles from the Scottish coast. But from then on, the plan started to unravel with disastrous consequences for the Germans. Because of a navigational error, the He111 and Me110 formation – minus nine Heinkels that had turned back with mechanical trouble – found itself also heading for the Firth of Forth only a few miles south of the diversionary thrust. The ruse had backfired.

Realizing their mistake, the bombers turned south, but this took them directly into the path of eleven Spitfires from No. 72 Squadron, scrambled from Acklington, Northumberland, and now heading north. The squadron, veterans of France and Dunkirk, made contact off the Farne Islands to find they were facing not thirty raiders, as had been reported, but over a hundred. 'None of us had ever seen so many aircraft in the sky at one time,' said Pilot Officer Robert Elliott. But the Spitfires had been given plenty of time to gain height, and now found themselves 3000 feet above the enemy formation. Wheeling to the seaward side of the Germans, they dived down out of the sun. 'There was a gap between the lines of bombers and the Me 110s coming up in the rear, so in there we went,' wrote Elliott. 'I do not think they saw us to begin with. When they did, the number of bombs rapidly jettisoned was fantastic. You could see them falling

---

'I attacked the section of Me110s'

Pilot Officer E.A. Shipman, of No. 41 Squadron based in Catterick, was in action against Messerschmitt Me110s on 15 August 1940.

```
    We were ordered to attack Me110 fighters escorting He111s at
18,000ft in the Durham area. Leading Green Section, I attacked the
section of Me110s on the left of the formation, but before getting
into range my target turned about and offered a brief opportunity to
fire a two-second burst, without result. I then picked another target
and managed to get in a series of deflection shots while the enemy
aircraft was evading quite violently. Finally at 200 yards range I put
the starboard engine out of action. The 110 made an erratic turn to
port, emitting clouds of smoke, and disappeared into the cloud below,
apparently out of control. This was the only occasion when my camera
gun worked and the film clearly showed all that had happened, confirm-
ing my claim. [Quoted in Bickers, p. 172]


                    -0-0-0-0-0-
```

away from the aircraft and dropping into the sea, literally by the hundreds. The formation became a shambles.' [Quoted in Jullian, p. 86]

In the first attack, two Me110s and one bomber were hit, generating panic. Some of the Me110s formed a defensive circle, others dived low and headed for home. No. 72 Squadron fought for five minutes, and then, just north of Blyth, its place was taken by the Hurricanes of No. 605 Squadron, scrambled from Drem, southeast of Edinburgh, at 12.25pm. The Luftwaffe lost four more bombers shot down and then, as the formation approached Newcastle, it was attacked by No. 41 Squadron from Catterick and no. 79 from Acklington, the latter, like No. 72 Squadron, an experienced unit.

By 12.45pm, almost all the Messerschmitts and many of the Heinkels had retreated across the North Sea. A few pressed on, scattering bombs in the Newcastle area. Several Heinkels did not survive the long journey back to their Scandinavian bases. Eight bombers and seven Me110s had been shot down, for the loss of only one British aircraft.

The same morning *Luftflotte* 5 mounted another, even riskier, attack. Around 50 Junkers Ju88 bombers from *Kampfgeschwader* 30 in Denmark set off to bomb fighter airfields at Church Fenton and Leconfield in Yorkshire. They were unaccompanied by escorts, relying instead on speed, surprise and the belief that there would be few fighters around to oppose them.

Shortly after 1pm, the raid was plotted approaching Staxton Wold radar station, overlooking the North Yorkshire coast, from the northeast. The commander of 12 Group, Air Vice-Marshal Trafford Leigh-Mallory, scrambled elements of four squadrons, but it was No. 616 and a flight of No. 73 that made the interception as the Ju88s crossed the coast at Flamborough Head. Six bombers were shot down straightaway, but the rest pressed on, swinging south to attack the airfield at Driffield. They dropped 169 bombs, which destroyed four hangars. Six RAF personnel were killed and a further twenty wounded. Ten aircraft were destroyed on the ground, but they were Whitley bombers rather than the all-important Hurricanes and Spitfires. Apart from a hit on an ammunition dump at Bridlington, the raid had no other successes.

In the two *Luftflotte* 5 attacks, the Luftwaffe had lost 20 per cent of the aircraft deployed, with more than 80 aircrew dead or missing. The attack had been a disaster for the air fleet, which would carry out no further major daylight operations.

In the south, the RAF was under more pressure than ever before. During the afternoon, there were so many raids it was almost impossible to establish where they were heading. A *Daily Express* reporter, watching from the coast, wrote that the mass of hostile incoming aircraft was so dense that they appeared 'to make an aluminium ceiling to the sky'.

At 2.15pm, Kent and Essex stations of the Chain Home radar network started picking up large concentrations of aircraft over Calais and Belgium. The sheer volume of incoming aircraft and the gaps in the radar cover made it very difficult to get a sense of the shape and size of the attacks. In fact, the raiders were three *Gruppen* of Dorniers from *Kampfgeschwader* 3. They were heading for the north Kent airfields, together with a swarm of escort fighters from bases in the Pas de Calais.

While attention was focused on this huge armada, a lightning raid on the fighter station at Martlesham Heath, Suffolk, was executed by sixteen Me110s and

continued on page 193

'How beautiful the Earth can be'

Oberleutnant Rudolf Kratz flew with *Luftflotte 5*'s *Kampfgeschwader* 30 in the unescorted attack of 15 August, which scored hits against Driffield airfield. He recorded his heady experiences that day.

The coast. The initial point. No time left for thinking - there lay England, the lion's den. But the eagles were going to attack the lion in his lair and wound him grievously.

'Fighters to starboard ...' Three specks overflew us, disappeared to the rear, and after a diving turn, hung behind us. 'Your turn now.' The words disappeared in the rattle of our machine guns. In short bursts the volleys flew towards the first fighter. He turned away and the second one took his place. This one's fire is ineffective as well and both passed below and were shot at by our ventral gunner. Like hornets they swooshed through our formation, the roundels on their fuselage looking like eyes.

'Five fighters to port above,' reported the wireless operator calmly. 'Dammit,' the pilot said, but did not get agitated. We kept on flying towards our target. Staring before us we tried to locate the airfield amidst the ragged clouds. 'There, the field, below us.'

The target at last - the fighters were beginning to be a real nuisance. The time had come now. I did not give a single Pfennig [penny] for the life of those below - drop the HEs [high explosives], away with the blessing! The aircraft went into a dive, speed rapidly building up, and the wind roared and howled around us. The hangars grew and grew. They were still standing. The AA guns were firing away at us, but they were too late.

A jolt - the bombs were free, the steel bodies out whistling down. Below all hell was let loose. Like an inferno, steel hit steel, and stones. Bomb upon bomb exploded, destroying and tearing apart what they hit. Hangar walls and roofs crumpled like tin sheets, pieces flying through the air. Aircraft were shattered by a hail of splinters. Barracks tumbled down, enormous smoke and dust clouds rose like mushrooms. Here and there explosions and flames shot up. The airfield and the hangars were already badly hit but bombs kept falling from the bombers that followed us, kept raining down in a horrible shower. Fire from exploding ammunition burst upwards like torches. The English AA artillery had been eliminated, their firing positions turned into craters.

The sun shone into our cabin. The enemy fighters had been got rid of. Below us lay the wide sea. How beautiful the Earth can be. Hands loosened their grip on the machine guns. What happened just a few minutes ago lay behind us and we relaxed. The engines were running evenly, we were flying home. The airfield didn't exist any more; that was the result. [Quoted in Ishoven, pp. 53-4]

-0-0-0-0-0-

THE BUSINESS OF KILLING

Pilots often said that they were fighting against machines rather than men. The experience of aerial warfare was certainly very different from that of the trench warfare that their fathers and uncles had endured. But it could still be a disturbingly intimate and vivid business. John Bisdee, of 609 Squadron, remembered the first time he hit an Me110: 'It had a solitary tail gunner behind the pilot in the fuselage and he was shooting at me. I let off a burst and I saw him actually collapse. I lost quite a lot of sleep that night. To see a chap die in front of you was rather unnerving. In fact it was pretty ghastly.' [Quoted in Parker, p. 419]

Each man reacted differently. On 9 July, 609 Squadron's David Crook shot down a Ju87 Stuka, killing both crew-members. 'I had often wondered what would be my feelings when killing somebody like this, and especially seeing them go down in flames,' Crook wrote in his book *Spitfire Pilot*, published in 1942. 'I was rather surprised to reflect afterwards that my only feeling had been one of considerable elation – and a sort of bewildered surprise because it had all been so easy … I also rang up home and told the family with considerable pride that I had at last been in action and managed to bag a Hun.' He later describes the episode as 'the most exciting and wildly exhilarating moment of my life'.

Other airmen, though, felt a certain emotional confusion. Peter Townsend, 85 Squadron's commander, got his first 'kill' on 3 February 1940, when his section surprised a lone Heinkel and riddled it with bullets until it crash-landed in open ground behind the Yorkshire coastal town of Whitby. He was initially elated by the 'rapture of combat' but then felt remorse, visiting the two surviving crew-members in hospital. He then returned to the mess to celebrate with champagne. It was, he later wrote, 'a horribly uncivilized way of behaving, really, when you have just killed someone. But an enemy bomber down was proof of our prowess, and that was legitimate cause for celebration.' [Townsend, *Time and Chance*, pp. 105–6]

ABOVE The end of the mission for a Stuka pilot – in a field in Sussex (1940).

nine Me109s of Experimental Group 210. The formation passed undetected only some 20 miles away from Foreness Chain Home Low radar station, 'blinded' in the morning's attacks. Only three pilots of No. 17 Squadron, which had moved to the airfield for the day, managed to get airborne. The attackers' bombs smashed equipment stores and damaged two hangars, the station workshops, the officers' mess, and water and telephone connections, putting the base out of action for two days. Nine Hurricanes from No. 1 Squadron managed to catch the raid, but were set on by the Me109s. The German planes claimed three British fighters shot down, and the raiders escaped unharmed.

Eighty-eight Dorniers, the entire available strength of *Kampfgeschwader* 3, together with 130 Me109s from *Jagdgeschwader* 51, 52 and 54, approached the coast at Deal at 3.30pm. At the same time, a further 60 Me109s from *Jagdgeschwader* 26 crossed the Kent coast either side of Dover. No. 11 Group could

continued on page 196

'He got a bullet through his bottom'

Pilot Officer David Crook, of 609 Squadron, was in action on 15 August, but his efforts against the enemy took an unexpected turn.

```
    We got off the ground only a few minutes before they arrived at the
aerodrome, and were unable to intercept them, or even to see them until
they were practically over the aerodrome [Middle Wallop] as they
[Junkers Ju88s] dived out of the sun, dropped their bombs, and then
streamed back towards the coast as hard as they could go. But we were
attacking them the whole time and shot down at least five ... There was a
Blenheim fighter squadron stationed with us; they are not fast enough
for day fighting but are used a lot for night work. Incidentally, they
are twin-engined machines and very similar in appearance to the Junkers
88. One of these Blenheims happened to be doing some practice flying
near the aerodrome when the attack started, and in a fit of rather mis-
guided valour he fastened himself on to the German formation as it ran
for the coast and started attacking the rear machines. We were rapidly
overhauling the German formation, and when I was in range I opened fire
at the nearest machine, which happened to be the Blenheim. Quite natu-
rally, it never occurred to me that it could be anything else but a Ju.
88. I hit both engines and the fuselage, and he fell away to the right
with one engine smoking furiously. I saw him sliding down and noticed a
gun turret on the fuselage which rather shook me, as I knew the Ju. 88
did not have this. Fortunately the pilot had been saved by the armour
plating behind him, and he managed to make a crash landing on the aero-
drome and was quite O.K., though the Blenheim was full of bullet holes
and looked rather like a kitchen sieve. The rear gunner was not quite
so lucky, for he got a bullet through his bottom which doubtless caused
him considerable discomfort and annoyance, but was not serious. Nothing
was said about this mistake ... . [Crook, pp. 51-2]
```

-0-0-0-0-0-

TRAFFORD LEIGH-MALLORY

The Battle of Britain would probably have been fought very differently if Air Vice-Marshal Trafford Leigh-Mallory had been in charge of Fighter Command in 1940 (as he would be two years later), or even if he had been given Park's job as 11 Group Commander at the beginning of the year (as he felt he ought to have been). Born in Cheshire in 1892, Leigh-Mallory joined a Territorial Regiment at the outbreak of the First World War, and shortly afterwards he received a commission in the Lancashire Fusiliers. He was wounded during the Second Battle of Ypres. In July 1916, he was seconded to the Royal Flying Corps, where he flew reconnaissance and bombing missions. He stayed on after 1918 in the Royal Air Force, and in 1937, after service at the Air Ministry and overseas, he was given command of 12 Group, responsible for the fighter cover over Central England.

Leigh-Mallory was intelligent and well educated, and those who worked with him found him industrious, loyal to his friends, caring of his pilots and willing to take advice. But he was also openly ambitious and prone to pomposity, characteristics that some explained by his need to escape from the shadow of his famous older brother, George Mallory, the mountaineer who had perished on Mount Everest in 1924. The appointment of Air Vice-Marshal Park, junior to him in rank and seniority, to the command of the frontline No. 11 Group clearly rankled.

Strongly influenced by one of his squadron leaders, Douglas Bader, Leigh-Mallory advocated the deployment of fighters in large numbers, and was therefore closer to Air Ministry opinion than to the Dowding and Park system of immediate forward response with small numbers. Leigh-Mallory's vigorous campaigning and intriguing during the Battle of Britain for the adoption of his 'Big Wing' tactics created strong tensions with his superior and his opposite number at 11 Group (see page 231).

With the sidelining of Dowding and Park after the Battle of Britain, Leigh-Mallory's star rose. He took over 11 Group command, where he initiated offensive and aggressive, but ultimately wasteful, fighter sweeps over France. In November 1942, he was promoted to the rank of air marshal and appointed to lead Fighter Command. He went on to play a key role in the planning and execution of air cover for the Normandy landings.

Leigh-Mallory was killed in November 1944, when the plane taking him and his wife to his next appointment as Air Commander-in-Chief, South-East Asia Command, crashed en route in the French Alps during bad weather.

Trafford Leigh-Mallory, photographed at his desk in December 1942, by which time his 'Big Wings' were making their sweeps over the Continent.

SIR CHRISTOPHER QUINTIN BRAND

Of all the Group commanders during the Battle of Britain, Quintin Brand, in charge of 10 Group, had the most distinguished record as a fighter pilot. He was born in South Africa in 1893 and served in the local defence force during the first two years of the First World War. After that, he transferred to the Royal Flying Corps. In 1917, he was one of the three pilots who carried out the first ever night-time patrol by single-seater fighters, a mission over the Thames Estuary described as 'perhaps the most important event in the history of air defence'.

By May 1918, Brand was leader of 112 Squadron. In the last German air raid of the First World War, he brought down one of the three Gotha bombers destroyed that night, only narrowly escaping with his life as the flaming bomber plunged into the sea close by. This action won him the Distinguished Service Order (DSO). On 15 September 1918, he was attacking an enemy aircraft over France. His engine's sump was punctured, covering the windscreen in oil. Despite this, he pursued his opponent, driving him down to 200 feet above ground, at which point he was forced to call off the attack. For this, he was awarded the Distinguished Flying Cross (DFC).

After the war, Quintin Brand and Pierre van Ryneveld, another ex-RFC South African, made one of the first flights from England to the South African Cape. Starting from Brooklands on 4 February 1920, they flew their Vickers Vimy bomber, named *Silver Queen*, to Cairo. On 11 February, they crashed, at night, near Egypt's Wadi Haifa. The two engines were saved, however, and fitted to a new airframe, so the pilots were able to continue their journey and reached Pretoria on 5 March, where the aircraft was destroyed in a take-off accident. The South African air force supplied them with a De Havilland DH9 and they landed in Cape Town on 20 March. For their achievement, they were both knighted.

From 1925 to 1927, Brand was Senior Technical Officer, then Principal Technical Officer, at the Royal Aircraft Establishment at Farnborough. Between 1932 and 1936 he was Director General of Aviation, Egypt, before returning to England to take up the post of Director of Repair and Maintenance at the Air Ministry. In July 1940, on the creation of 10 Group to defend Southwest England and South Wales, he was appointed its commander and promoted to Air Vice-Marshal.

Brand enjoyed a good relationship with Park and Dowding, frequently deploying his squadrons effectively to back up the efforts of 11 Group. He also supported their tactics of using small and rapidly deployed groups of fighters, rather than the 'Big Wings' favoured by Leigh-Mallory and others. Thus he found himself in the wrong camp when Dowding and Park were moved from their commands, and he was posted in late 1940 to take over a training group. He retired from the RAF in 1943 and died in Rhodesia (Zimbabwe) in March 1968 at the age of 74.

Quintin Brand (*right*) with Pierre van Ryneveld (*left*) in front of the *Silver Queen* in 1920, the year of their trans-continental adventure.

counter at first with only 12 Hurricanes of Nos 111 and 151 squadrons apiece and 12 Spitfires of 64 Squadron. Four more squadrons quickly scrambled: Nos 1, 17, 32 and 501. The Dorniers proceeded almost unmolested as far as Faversham, Kent, where they split, one group heading for Rochester, the other towards Eastchurch.

At Rochester, nearly 300 bombs fell, destroying hangars, workshops, storage sheds and six Sterling bombers under construction at the nearby Short Brothers factory. Eastchurch also received a battering. While 11 Group's fighters were tied up in a huge mêlée with Me109s, further raids hit Maidstone, Hawkinge airfield, Dover, Rye and the radar station (again) at Foreness.

In the west, Sperrle's *Luftflotte* 3 forces were also on the move. At about 5.20pm, a force of some 60 Ju88s of *Lehrgeschwader* 1 and 40 Messerschmitt Me110s of *Zerstörergeschwader* 2 was intercepted by 43 Squadron southeast of the Isle of Wight. As the formation proceeded over Southampton and the Solent, three more squadrons – 249, 601 and 609 – tried to drive it back, but the Ju88s broke through, with half of them heading for Middle Wallop and the other half for Worthy Down, near Winchester. However, little damage was done in either place and the raiders suffered heavily, with 601 Squadron downing four of the bombers.

Fighter Command's 10 Group was now thinly stretched, and when a heavily escorted raid of Ju87s from *Sturzkampfgeschwader* 1 threatened Portland, Air Vice-Marshal Brand had to call on two Hurricane squadrons – Nos 87 and 213 –

'My cockpit filled with smoke and fumes'

Squadron Leader John Dewar of 213 Squadron was in action on 15 August 1940. He was hit by Me109s while attempting to attack a defensive circle of Me110s over Portland. Then came the decision as to whether to bale out or attempt to control his damaged aircraft.

My cockpit filled with smoke and fumes, and I realised I had been hit. I dived steeply away; it was difficult to see but I knew from the sun that I was going north. I saw I was being pursued but it turned out to be Fg. Off. [Flying Officer] Strickland who, at considerable risk to himself, had come to protect me and watch where I fell. I found it impossible to sit in the cockpit and prepared to bale out; half out the cockpit, however, my head was clear of the fumes; there was no fire and the engine was running, so I decided to make for land, flying on the stick alone. Having reached Weymouth Bay the Hurricane was still flying splendidly, so I followed a Spitfire back to Warmwell. By holding my breath I managed to lower the undercarriage and flaps and make a landing, which was very fortunate as the aircraft is [sic] not seriously hit except in the engine and wings ... .
[Quoted in Mason, p. 206]

-0-0-0-0-0-

from Exeter to intercept. They met the enemy aircraft well south of Portland, but, seeing that the formation contained around 60 Me109s and 20 Me110s, as well as 40 Stukas, they called for reinforcements. The Spitfires of 234 Squadron went in, and while they engaged the German fighters, the Hurricanes attempted to down the slower Stukas and Me110s. Several enemy planes were destroyed, but, outnumbered five to one, the British fighters suffered, too.

The progress of the raids was followed by Winston Churchill during a visit to Fighter Command Headquarters at Bentley Priory. Guided by Dowding, he watched the huge map board below them in the operations room showing squadrons in action, refuelling and rearming and then taking off again. Dowding's anxieties were soothed by the apparent weakness of the Luftwaffe's intelligence picture, which led it to waste its efforts on bomber bases that were irrelevant to the survival of its real target, Fighter Command.

But the Luftwaffe had not yet finished for the day. At about 6.20pm, while free chases of Me109s from *Jagdgeschwader* 26 distracted the radar stations still in operation, a formation of Dorniers crossed the southeast coast unchecked. To the north of this formation, Experimental Group 210 was in action again, with fifteen Me110s and eight Me109s. This time the targets were Biggin Hill and Kenley, two vital Group 11 sector stations guarding the skies around London. Unlike the establishments at Bentley Priory and Uxbridge, the control rooms for the sector stations were housed in flimsy buildings above ground. A direct hit on one could paralyze the whole sector. From Biggin Hill, Nos 610 and 32 squadrons were scrambled and met the Dorniers about ten miles southeast of the airfield. Two of the bombers were shot down, but then the British fighters became embroiled in the escort and the Dorniers ploughed on. This time, however, they missed their target, bombing West Malling aerodrome instead, a base not yet fully operational.

Meanwhile, Experimental Group 210, having failed to rendezvous with an escort of Me109s as planned, pressed on towards Kenley, taking a roundabout route in the hope of fooling the defences and hitting the airfield from the north. Suddenly, a gap in the clouds showed an airfield below and they dived to attack.

Their bombing was fearsomely accurate, smashing into buildings and wrecking the airfield. Some bombs overshot the base, hitting three small factories, where workers were just starting the night shift. No air-raid warning had sounded: 62 people were killed and a further 172 were injured. But once again the Luftwaffe had missed its primary target. It was Croydon, rather than the much more important Kenley, that now lay charred and smoking. Furthermore, Croydon, unlike Kenley, was within the boundaries of Greater London, which Hitler had ordered should not be bombed. The mistake would have far-reaching consequences.

As the twin-engine Messerschmitt Me110s turned for home, they were intercepted by No. 111 Squadron, which had scrambled from Croydon just in time to avoid destruction. The pilots now took revenge, shooting down four of the Experimental Group's Me110s, including that of the formation leader, Hauptmann Walter Rubensdörffer, who was killed. A further three Messerschmitts fell to No. 32 Squadron.

At 7.30pm, a raid on Dover was driven back by 54 Squadron: it was the final action of what had been the most momentous day yet of the Battle of Britain. The Luftwaffe had flown over 2000 sorties, as compared to Fighter Command's 974. At one point, the sheer weight of the onslaught had forced Dowding to put 130 fighters in the air at the same time, multiplying the risk to his precious assets and magnifying the chances of a catastrophic loss that would prise open Britain's air defences. As it was, 11 Group just about held its own, with every pilot either in combat or at readiness or standby, waiting in their cockpits or next to their aircraft for the scramble call that would throw them back into combat.

The Luftwaffe had caused considerable damage, although in many cases the

A German propaganda photograph shows a Luftwaffe airman marking up his 32nd aerial combat, 'every line ... a stroke against England!'

ATTITUDES TO DEATH

Flying was always a dangerous business, and the prospect of death from error, weather conditions or mechanical failure was close from the moment a would-be pilot took his first flight. Flying in combat multiplied the opportunities for, and ways of, dying. Pilots perished from bullets and cannon shells, from burning, or from being dragged down into the depths of the Channel by the weight of their heavy boots, parachutes or jackets if they managed to bale out and were not entombed in their aircraft. The average life expectancy of a Fighter Command pilot was 87 hours' flying time. Of the 2917 pilots who flew combat missions during the Battle of Britain, 544 were killed. Another 795 died before the war was over. It became natural to regard death in action as inevitable. 'I thought, I am going to die,' recalled 32 Squadron pilot Peter Brothers. 'If it doesn't happen today, it'll happen tomorrow.' [Brothers, recording]

In most pilots' accounts, death is expressed in understated, euphemistic ways: smashing into the sea or ground was called 'going in'. Death was 'the chop'. So-and-so was 'lost' or 'went west'. The levity was designed to rob death of its power, but it did not always work. Richard Hillary used the same expression, 'failed to return', for all his squadron's losses; but however euphemistic, the phrase ends up ringing through his book *The Last Enemy* like a funeral bell. There were few bodies to deal with in aerial warfare. But every pilot could imagine the horror as he saw a comrade go down in a burning cockpit, particularly as sometimes cries, prayers and screams could be heard over the radio-telehone.

The tradition of insouciance in the face of death had been established by the aviators of the previous war. 'In such an atmosphere,' wrote Cecil Lewis, a veteran of the skies over the trenches, 'you grew fatalistic, and as time went by and left you unscathed, like a batsman who has played himself in, you began to take liberties with the bowling. You took unnecessary risks, you volunteered for dangerous jobs, you provoked enemy aircraft to attack you. You were invulnerable: nothing could touch you. Then, when one of the old hands, as seemingly invulnerable as yourself, went West, you suddenly got cold feet. It wasn't possible to be sure — even of yourself. At this stage it required most courage to go on — a sort of plodding fatalism, a determination, a cold-blooded effort of will. And always alone! No friends right and left, no crowd morale!' [Lewis, p. 60]

At the beginning of the war, many units were close-knit, bonded by shared training and — in the case of the Auxiliary squadrons — place and family friendships. It was the early losses in the spring of 1940 that hit squadrons hardest. By late August, the original social cohesion had loosened, and among relative strangers losses were easier to bear. There was, anyway, no time for grieving. 'You didn't spend days moping around,' said No. 19 Squadron pilot George Unwin. 'You just said, "Poor old so-and-so's bought it," and that was it.' [Unwin, recording]

But the death of a close friend was still felt intensely. Gordon Batt of 238 Squadron was already depressed at the unit's losses when in late September his best friend, Eric Bann, was killed when his parachute failed to open. 'When Bann disappeared, I was even worse,' said Batt. 'I didn't make friends at all. You do get to a point where you do not wish to be hurt any more. I just did my job, to the best of my ability, had jovial off-duty parties, but no friends, no more [of] that. I do not even know the names of many of the people I later flew with and were killed. I just blotted that out of my mind. I just concentrated hard on doing my job, and staying alive. Otherwise you'd go barmy, I think.' [Bann, private letter]

targets hit were irrelevant to the crucial work of crushing Fighter Command. The German air force had also, on occasions during the day, shown considerable tactical skill, using feint attacks and altering direction to confuse the defenders. But often the complicated procedures had broken down, and fighter escorts had missed meeting their charges or been forced to turn back through lack of fuel. The effort had cost them dearly. Seventy-five German aircraft had been shot down – and 15 August became known in the Luftwaffe as *der schwarze Donnerstag* ('Black Thursday'). Fighter Command had lost 30 aircraft, with 17 pilots killed. It had been an epic effort. Prime Minister Winston Churchill, leaving Dowding's HQ at Bentley Priory that evening, was moved to describe it as 'one of the greatest days in history'.

16 August 1940 FRIDAY

Early mist, generally clearing later.

Given the disasters of the day before, the Luftwaffe showed extraordinary resilience when it returned to the attack on Friday. At 10.45am, after the early mist had cleared, the defenders tracked three small raids approaching Kent from the south and east. Believing it to be a feint, Air Vice-Marshal Park committed only limited forces, of which even fewer managed to intercept. Two *Staffeln* of the attacking Dorniers broke through and dropped almost 80 bombs on West Malling aerodrome, where personnel had been busy repairing the damage of the day before. This time the airfield was put out of action for four days.

Shortly before noon, radar showed three large formations heading for the southeast. This time Park sent up 86 fighters to intercept. A formation of 24 Dorniers of *Kampfgeschwader* 2, together with Me109s in escort, were heading up the Thames Estuary apparently on the way to attack Hornchurch. At 12.25pm, nine Spitfires of No. 54 Squadron descended on the bombers and forced them to turn back. The British fighters were joined by two more squadrons, which harassed the bombers as they headed back across Kent.

To the west, 150 enemy aircraft had crossed the coast between Brighton and Folkestone. While 30 Spitfires from Nos 64, 65 and 266 squadrons engaged the escorting Me109 fighters, 21 Hurricanes of Nos 111 and 32 squadrons attacked the bombers head on. During the engagement, Flying Officer Henry Ferriss from 111 Squadron collided with a Dornier and was killed. Another casualty was 266's new squadron leader, Rodney Wilkinson. 'I shan't forget his engaging charm, his curious shuffle and infectious gaiety,' wrote his friend the MP 'Chips' Channon in his diary two days later. 'He had a natural elegance, but seemed fated to die: indeed, he always said so ... He was typical of the type which is serving and saving England and there will be many aching hearts when the news of his death comes out.' [Channon, p. 263]

Some of the bombers turned for home, but others split up into smaller formations and spread out to the north and northwest. Bombs were dropped at Farnborough and over the South London suburbs and the London docks, causing 66 civilian deaths.

The third German formation, consisting of more than 100 aircraft from the Cherbourg area, appeared to be heading for Portsmouth or Southampton. At 1pm,

'Take cover, take cover'

Ann Lowe, a member of the Women's Auxiliary Air Force (WAAF), narrowly survived the 16 August raid on the sector airbase at Tangmere – as did her sister, who also worked at the base and who was asleep after a night shift.

```
    The sinister sound of the air-raid warning started and loudspeakers
over the airfield said, 'Take cover, take cover, Stukas sighted over
Selsey coming towards Tangmere, take cover, take cover.' The warning
got louder and louder and then you could hear the approaching air-
craft.
    I rushed to her [her sister's] quarters, hauled her out of bed and
began to run with her. She could run faster than me and she got ahead.
The next thing, they were coming down - phrommmmm. Then the first bomb
fell nearby and I was flung about thirty feet in the air, coming down
with my stomach on a brick. But I staggered on into the trenches.
```

-0-0-0-0-0-

on a signal from the lead aircraft, the formation split into four, with the largest group heading directly for the sector station at Tangmere. Two squadrons from the base had been scrambled as well as six others from airfields to the west, but they were unable to prevent the Stukas from carrying out a textbook dive-bombing attack. Explosives fell on the quarters, the workshops and the cookhouse. In a quarter of an hour, every hangar was damaged. Seventeen planes had been caught on the ground and wrecked, including all four of the new radar-equipped night-fighting Blenheims and seven Hurricanes under repair. Fourteen servicemen and six civilians were killed.

When the survivors at Tangmere emerged from the shelters, they were greeted by the macabre sight of a body hanging from a tree. Only the operations room had survived untouched; everywhere else was shattered by bombs, and the runways were heavily cratered.

Meanwhile, a small group of Ju87s had swung to the west and now descended on Ventnor radar station on the Isle of Wight, restored since the attack of 12 August. Twenty-two bombs landed on target, putting the station out of action until 23 September. The Luftwaffe seemed to have forgotten or ignored Goering's directive that bombing radar stations was a waste of time.

Other elements of the formation attacked the anti-aircraft defences of Portsmouth harbour, while Ju88s and Me110s struck at the naval establishments of Gosport and Lee-on-Solent, where six naval aircraft were destroyed and three hangars damaged. The Gosport raid was sighted by three patrolling Hurricanes from 249 Squadron, only recently moved down from the north. It was Flight Lieutenant James Nicolson's first combat. Leading his section against a pair of Ju88s, Nicolson was hit from behind by the powerful forward guns of an Me110

continued on page 203

'I WAS CAUGHT UP WITH MY PARACHUTE IN A TREE'

Heinz Möllenbrook took part in the attacks of 16 August, piloting a Dornier Do17-Z of *Gruppe* 3, *Kampfgeschwader* 2. His luck ran out, though, when at 12.22pm he was shot down over Kent.

'On our return flight I was in the last wave of three aircraft. We were attacked a number of times. On the first attack the plane to the left of us was hit and veered off past us. We got hit in an engine so were flying on just one. Soon we were on our own. Keeping the plane in trim was taking up all my concentration. During the second and third attacks my radio operator and mechanic were both wounded. On the fourth attack my right arm was shattered but I was still able to fly the plane. Then a Hurricane attacked us from the front.' This was flown by John Thompson of 111 Squadron. 'The frontal attack wounded my left shoulder and probably also damaged our steering,' said Möllenbrook.

'The steering column fell from my hand. I baled out with my observer who thought the other two, already badly wounded, were both out of the plane. They were subsequently found dead. I don't know how they got out. We too, however, were in grave danger. The plane was spiralling down and we were caught in its centrifugal force. The observer, in extreme panic, let out the oxygen from his life-jacket kit and it caught fire. Then, suddenly there was peace. Anyway I was lucky. My legs had been shot up but I was caught up with my parachute in a tree hanging fifty centimetres above the ground.' Möllenbrook was freed from the tree by two farm workers. 'Then they took me into their kitchen and the grandmother bound my arm, and by doing so saved it. She gave me a whisky, or perhaps two, against the pain.' [Möllenbrook quotations in Parker, pp. 217–18]

Correctly attaching a parachute was potentially a matter of life and death. Here, South African pilot Albert G. 'Zulu' Lewis, of 249 Squadron, adjusts his parachute before take-off (October 1940).

and wounded. Struck again in the reserve fuel tank, his Hurricane caught fire. But as the Me110 overshot him, Nicolson, ignoring the smoke and extreme heat, which had his instrument panel 'dripping like treacle', gave chase, and eventually shot it down. The next moment, he dived head first out of his cockpit. Blinded in his left eye by blood and with his hands terribly burnt, he fell 500 feet before he succeeded in pulling his ripcord. As he drifted down, he then came under fire from members of the Home Guard on the ground, who shot him in the buttocks. Three months later, having recovered from his wounds, Nicolson was awarded the only Victoria Cross to go to a fighter pilot during the battle.

There were more raids during the late afternoon, preceded by German fighter sweeps designed to drag the exhausted Fighter Command pilots into the air, so that they would be back refuelling when the bombers arrived. One sweep descended on Manston, strafing the airfield buildings and destroying a Spitfire and a Blenheim on the ground. Meanwhile, Nos 1, 610 and 615 squadrons engaged a formation of Heinkel He111 bombers, escorted by Me110s, over the Sussex–Surrey border. Hurricanes of Nos 32, 56 and 501 squadrons took on another enemy raid, which appeared to be heading for Biggin Hill, successfully driving it back, while Spitfires from 610 Squadron engaged the fighter escort.

Flight Lieutenant James Nicolson, of 249 Squadron, photographed during his convalescence following his VC-winning action on 16 August 1940.

Following their visit to Bentley Priory the previous day, Churchill and his chief of staff, Hastings Ismay, were now at 11 Group's headquarters at Uxbridge. Smoking was strictly forbidden in the Group's underground operations room, but

continued on page 206

'I couldn't see through that eye for blood'

Flight Lieutenant James Nicolson, of 249 Squadron, recorded the moment on 16 August 1940 that earned him Fighter Command's sole Victoria Cross of the Battle of Britain.

```
    The first shell tore through the hood over my cockpit and sent
splinters into my left eye. One splinter, I discovered later, nearly
severed my eyelid. I couldn't see through that eye for blood. The second
cannon shell struck my spare petrol tank and set it on fire. The third
shell crashed into the cockpit and tore off my right trouser leg. The
fourth shell struck the back of my left shoe. It shattered the heel of
the shoe and made quite a mess of my left foot. I was just thinking of
jumping out when suddenly a Messerschmitt 110 whizzed under me and got
right in my gun-sight … I pressed the gun button for the Messerschmitt
was in nice range; I plugged him first time and could see my tracer
bullets entering the German machine. [BBC broadcast]


                        -0-0-0-0-0-
```

WOMEN'S AUXILIARY AIR FORCE (WAAF)

Women made up a large proportion of the personnel operating the vital and sophisticated communications infrastructure of Fighter Command during the Battle of Britain. The vital role played by the Women's Auxiliary Air Force (WAAF) ensured them a leading place in the mythology of the battle. Their qualities were encapsulated in images showing them in slate blue tunics, hair shiny and curled just below the neck, bosom thrust forward, looking skywards with firm determination.

A WAAF recruitment poster. The WAAF offered challenge, adventure and freedom. There was no shortage of volunteers.

The WAAF succeeded the Women's Royal Air Force (WRAF), formed at the same time as the RAF on 1 April 1918. Its personnel acted in a wide variety of jobs, from sailmakers and 'dopers' of planes to engine fitters and electricians. At its height, the WRAF contained over 24,000 members. It was disbanded after the First World War.

The Munich Crisis hastened the formation of the ATS, the Auxiliary Territorial Service, designed to engage women in service work. In June 1939, two specialist offshoots emerged: the WAAF and the Women's Royal Naval Service (WRNS). During the course of the war, the ATS, WAAF and WRNS would recruit more than 600,000 women into the services.

The WAAF's first commander was Katherine Trefusis-Forbes. She was described by one WAAF as being 'neat as a new pin, and given to roaring to work on her motorbike'. [Quoted in Escott, p. 5] Long after the war, in 1966, she would marry Sir Robert Watson-Watt, the man behind Britain's radar system.

There was no shortage of candidates for the WAAF. The glamour of the air and the 'fighter boys' meant that over half of women volunteers marked the WAAF as their first choice. It offered a chance for adventure and a stake in the struggle against a hated enemy.

The WAAF also presented a challenge to social norms. Many boyfriends, husbands or fathers were unenthusiastic at the thought of their womenfolk mixing relatively freely with men at their bases. Women in uniform had acquired a 'fast' reputation during the previous war, however unfairly. 'You used to see women in uniform, and it all seemed rather glamorous,' said WAAF NCO Vera King. 'But my father was very service-oriented and his memory for the women's services from the First World War was that they had bad reputations. His theme was, if you go into the services, no decent man will want to marry you.' [King, recording]

Hazel Williams remembers leaving home to report for duty with the WAAF: 'I shall always remember my mother, tears streaming down her face, at the door. Then she called me back and said "Don't sit on strange lavatory seats," and pointing to my bosom, "Don't let any man touch you there!"' [Quoted in Crang, p. 383]

Those taken on were supposed to be between 17½ and 43 years old, but there were few checks on age. Some as young as 15 were recruited, but the majority were 18 or 19 years old. Most early volunteers were educated and well-to-do. 'At the start, there were a whole lot of titled people in the WAAFs. It was the upper strata of society,' said WAAF Marian Orley. 'But a lot of them couldn't take it. Out of 60 of us, about 30 didn't come back after a week's leave at Christmas. I had to parcel up their effects and send them back.'

The more privileged volunteers arrived in

a world different from the one they had known at home. Accommodation was basic and cramped, with three to a billet, and discipline was strict. On their first night, many women wept into their straw pillows. 'Hair had to be kept off the collar,' said Marian Orley. 'No jewellery was allowed except a wedding ring. And no-one plastered their faces with make up.' [Orley, recording] Male NCOs treated their female charges with condescension. 'They thought we were in it for the fun,' said one WAAF.

'We all grew up very quickly in those days. We had to,' said WAAF Kay France. 'When I became a sergeant I discovered I had to be both disciplinarian, the spoil-sport sergeant, and mother, comforting girls whose boyfriends had been shot down or whose parents were killed in bombing raids.'

Initially there were limited roles for the new recruits. They worked as equipment assistants, mess and kitchen workers, cooks, drivers and clerks. But it was soon discovered that women were not only as proficient as men in almost all of the support roles, but in some cases better, particularly as radar operators and plotters, where precision and thoroughness were vital. Those operating the top-secret radar equipment were known as 'Clerks, Special Duties'. They had to have above-average educational achievement and were sworn to secrecy about their true role.

Many succeeded in alleviating some of the hardships, smuggling in non-regulation shoes and underwear as well as feather mattresses to cushion the uncomfortable straw ones they were issued with. During quiet periods, the women wrote letters, knitted, sewed and embroidered. WAAF Hazel Gregory spent much of her time making underwear: 'It was the fashionable thing to do at the time — we were all hand-stitching glamorous undies. Most of the men were very intrigued.' [Quoted in Parker, p. 122]

The WAAF's role may have seemed like a step towards equality. But to many the attitude of the authorities still seemed belittling and un-fair. After a raid on Kenley airfield in Surrey, the pilots were released to enjoy themselves. The WAAFs on the airfield, however, were sent to bed 'in case of any nervous reaction'. Women were given inferior rations and were paid only two-thirds of what their male counterparts made for doing the same job. 'I began to get a bee in my bonnet about equal pay,' said Marian Orley. 'The NCO in charge of the watch was a woman sergeant — she was paid less than an ordinary airman on the switchboard. That got under my skin a little.' [Orley, recording]

By mid-1940, WAAFs were performing virtually every role in Fighter Command, save combat flying. But some did fly in other capacities: 30 of them worked for the Air Transport Auxiliary, piloting Spitfires and Hurricanes from factories or repair yards to the squadron air-fields. Others were switchboard operators, parachute packers, plotters, RDF operators or barrage-balloon operators. A number worked with codes and ciphers, analysed reconnaissance photographs, and performed intelligence operations. During the crisis weeks of 10 July to mid-October, the plotters worked four-hour watches — four hours on and two hours off. One night in three there was a watch of eight hours during the day, giving the women a full night in bed. 'Everybody worked very hard,' said plotter Edith Kup. 'Everybody wanted to do their best. I mean, we didn't think about it, we just did it.'

Proximity between aircrew and WAAFs inevitably led to romances, so that working in the operations rooms meant that women could sometimes hear from the radio-telephone what was happening to their boyfriends in the skies above. One WAAF was working in the Debden Sector operations room when she heard that 'Blue Four' was heading into the sea, his aircraft on fire. Without having to wait for confirmation, she knew that the man she was about to marry was dead. [Interview with author]

As the Luftwaffe onslaught started hitting airfields and sector stations, the women of the WAAF found themselves in the frontline. During the war, 191 WAAFs were killed and 420 wounded. But for most of them, this danger in-creased the pride they took in their work and their contribution to the war effort. The press and public, too, took the WAAFs to their hearts.

an exception was made for the prime minister's ever-present cigar. 'There had been heavy fighting throughout the afternoon,' Ismay later wrote. 'At one moment every single squadron in the Group was engaged; there was nothing in reserve, and the map table showed new waves of attackers crossing the coast. I felt sick with fear.'

Fighter Command was now fighting on a front from Harwich to Portsmouth, and it was inevitable that some bombers would get through. Two Ju88s penetrated all the way to Brize Norton airfield in Oxfordshire. Approaching the runway, they lowered their landing gear in the hope that they would be mistaken for Blenheims. The ruse worked, and as they crossed the perimeter the wheels went up and 32 bombs were released. Inside one of the hangars was a large number of fuelled-up aircraft. A bomb set off an enormous explosion, destroying 46 planes, the majority of them training aircraft, but also including 11 Hurricanes undergoing repairs. As on the previous day, the Luftwaffe's target had been planes on the ground, and as before there had been much effort wasted on attacking non-Fighter Command airfields. But the strain of opposing them had been exhausting and costly. Many of the RAF pilots flew four or five combat sorties, and 20 aircraft were shot down.

At the end of the day, Churchill, still at Uxbridge, was told that a hundred of the enemy had been shot down, though the real figure was nearer fifty. The inaccuracy was inevitable in the swirling confusion of aerial combat. Churchill was once again deeply impressed by what he had seen. The experience seems to have inspired perhaps his most famous phrase. 'As evening closed in and the fighting died down,' wrote Ismay, 'we left for Chequers. Churchill's first words were, "Don't speak to me;

I have never been so moved." After about five minutes he leaned forward and said, "Never in the field of human conflict has so much been owed by so many to so few." The words burned into my brain.' [Ismay, p. 182]

SATURDAY 17 August 1940

Saturday at last brought some relief, both for defenders and attackers. The sky was so empty of raiders that some radar operators thought that their equipment had malfunctioned. At Biggin Hill, No. 32 Squadron's pilots caught their breath, having spent the last two days at almost constant readiness, dossing down under the wings of their aircraft. 'Not a single sausage, scare, flap or diversion of any description today. Amazing. Heavenly day too,' wrote Squadron Leader Michael Crossley in the unit's unofficial diary.

Fine in the Channel, with some cloud in the east.

The day's lull was a sign that the Luftwaffe, too, was desperate for a respite. Pilots were nearing exhaustion, and aircraft had to be repaired and patched up, a process that often involved sending the machine on a train or lorry all the way back to the Reich.

In England the work of fixing the damage of the day before continued. At Tangmere, shot-down German airmen were pressed into helping fill the airfield's numerous craters, often by hand as no bulldozers were available. Electricity supplies, crucial to the base's communications, were quickly restored; water and accommodation took longer – latrines now consisted of a plank over a ditch, and WAAFs had to sleep on benches at nearby Goodwood racetrack.

Fighter Command had lost 78 pilots killed in the last eight days, with a further 27 badly wounded. The majority of them were experienced men. Since 1 August only 70 new pilots had joined Fighter Command, many of them greenhorns, fresh from the accelerated courses that the Operational Training Units were now having to run. Dowding was forced to fill the gaps with volunteers from Bomber and Coastal Command pilots, the units that would be needed to repel any invasion. There was no other choice. Everything was being gambled on the survival of Fighter Command.

As the summer dusk fell, though, everyone felt thankful for a day of relative quiet. The lull would only be fleeting. The Luftwaffe was licking its wounds, but it was also gathering its strength for the next great effort. The following days were to be among the most desperate of the battle.

5

HARDEST DAYS

18 August to 6 September 1940

Fighter Command was now engaged in a desperate fight to survive as a serious deterrent force. Sunday 18 August would become known in Battle of Britain legend as 'The Hardest Day'. That morning the Luftwaffe had at its disposal 276 Junkers Ju87 Stukas; 768 twin-engine Heinkel He111, Dornier Do17 and Junkers Ju88 bombers; 194 Messerschmitt Me110s; and 745 Messerschmitt Me109s, as well as reconnaissance aircraft. Against them, Fighter Command could muster 419 Hurricanes and 211 Spitfires, as well as small numbers of the much less effective and now obsolescent Blenheim, Gladiator and Defiant fighters. The single-engine fighter forces were fairly evenly balanced. However, Fighter Command had the double task of shooting down bombers and fighting off their escorts. The German fighter pilots could concentrate on the single task of destroying their counterparts. The defenders had to cover a large number of potential targets. More than ever, it was vital that the RAF fighters were in the right place at the right time, and at the right height.

18 August 1940 SUNDAY ('THE HARDEST DAY')

Misty over the Channel, but otherwise fine and fair; some cloud later.

There was mist on the Channel as the first, by now routine, German reconnaissance aircraft appeared high over the south coast, tracking the movement of aircraft to the RAF's forward bases. By noon it was clear that the day was going to be a dramatic one. High-level radar at Dover reported the largest build-up yet of enemy aircraft, and every 11 Group fighter was brought to readiness. No. 501 Squadron, already in the air, was now ordered to patrol above Canterbury. Four more squadrons were sent to cover the line between Canterbury and Margate to protect the docks, the Thames Estuary and Gravesend and Hornchurch airfields. A further four squadrons, numbering twenty-three Spitfires and twenty-seven Hurricanes, were ordered to guard Kenley and Biggin Hill.

PREVIOUS PAGE

Vapour 'contrails' stretch across the sky above London, early in the morning of 6 September 1940.

Before the Hurricanes of 501 Squadron could engage any enemy aircraft, they were ambushed by a high-altitude fighter sweep of Me109s from *Jagdgeschwader*

continued on page 215

Dame Laura Knight's expressive 1940 portrait of WAAF Corporal J.D.M. (Daphne) Pearson is filled with the quiet drama of determination in the face of adversity. In August 1940, attacks on RAF airfields thrust WAAFs into the frontline. Corporal Pearson had epitomized WAAF bravery earlier in 1940, when she won the Empire Gallantry Medal for rescuing a bomber pilot from his wrecked plane as his bombload exploded.

Luftwaffe Order of Battle *Morning of 18 August*

Luftflotte 2 *Headquarters in Brussels. Commanded by Generalfeldmarschall Albert Kesselring*

PARENT UNIT	UNIT	AIRCRAFT TYPE	BASED AT/HQ	COMMANDER	SERVICEABLE AIRCRAFT
I Fliegerkorps			**Beauvais, France**	**Generaloberst Ulrich Grauert**	
Kampfgeschwader 1	Staff and KG HQ	He111	Rosières-en-Santerre	Generalmajor Karl Angerstein	5
	I Gruppe	He111	Montdidier	Major Ludwig Maier	23
	II Gruppe	He111	Montdidier	Oberstleutnant Benno Kosch	25
	III Gruppe	Do17	Rosières-en-Santerre	Major Willibald Fanelsa	19
Kampfgeschwader 76	Staff and KG HQ	He111	Cormeilles-en-Vexin	Oberstleutnant Stefan Frölich	3
	I Gruppe	Do17	Beauvais	Hauptmann Alois Lindeiner	26
	II Gruppe	Ju88	Creil	Major Friedrich Möricke	29
	III Gruppe	Do17	Cormeilles-en-Vexin	Major Franz Von Benda	23
II Fliegerkorps			**Ghent**	**General der Flieger Bruno Lörzer**	
Kampfgeschwader 2	Staff and KG HQ	Do17	Arras	Generalmajor Johannes Fink	4
	I Gruppe	Do17	Epinoy	Major Martin Gutzmann	21
	II Gruppe	Do17	Arras	Major Paul Weitkus	31
	III Gruppe	Do17	Cambrai	Major Adolph Fuchs	24
Kampfgeschwader 3	Staff and KG HQ	Do17	Le Culot	Oberst Wolfgang von Chamier-Glisczinski	5
	I Gruppe	Do17	Le Culot	Oberstleutnant Gabelmann	24
	II Gruppe	Do17	Antwerp/Deurne	Hauptmann Pilger	27
	III Gruppe	Do17	St Trond	Hauptmann Rathmann	29
Kampfgeschwader 53	Staff and KG HQ	He111	Lille-Nord	Oberstleutnant Stahl	3
	I Gruppe	He111	Lille-Nord	Major Kauffmann	17
	II Gruppe	He111	Lille-Nord	Major Winkler	20
	III Gruppe	He111	Lille-Nord	Major Edler von Braun	21
Sturzkampfgeschwader 1	II Gruppe	Ju87	Pas de Calais	Hauptmann Anton Keil	26
Lehrgeschwader 1	IV (Stuka) Gruppe	Ju87	Tramecourt	Hauptmann Bernd von Brauchitsch	16
Erprobungsgruppe 210		Me110, Me109	Marck	Hauptmann Hans von Boltenstern	15
Lehrgeschwader 2	II Gruppe	Me109	St Omer	Hauptmann Otto Weiss	34
IX Fliegerdivision			**Soesterberg**	**Generalmajor Joachim Coeler**	
Kampfgeschwader 4	Staff and KG HQ	He111	Soesterberg	Oberstleutnant Hans-Joachim Rath	6
	I Gruppe	He111	Soesterberg	Hauptmann Nikolaus-Wolfgang Meissner	20
	II Gruppe	He111	Eindhoven	Major Dr Gottlieb Wolf	23
	III Gruppe	Ju88	Amsterdam/Schiphol	Hauptmann Erich Bloedorn	25
Jagdfliegerführer 2			**Wissant**	**Generalmajor Theodor 'Theo' Osterkamp**	
Jagdgeschwader 3	Staff and HQ	Me109	Samer	Oberstleutnant Carl Viek	2
	I Gruppe	Me109	Colombert	Hauptmann Hans von Hahn	24
	II Gruppe	Me109	Samer	Hauptmann Erich von Selle	30
	III Gruppe	Me109	Desvres	Hauptmann Walter Kienitz	25
Jagdgeschwader 26	Staff and HQ	Me109	Audembert	Major Gotthard Handrick	2
	I Gruppe	Me109	Audembert	Hauptmann Kurt Fischer	24
	II Gruppe	Me109	Marquise	Hauptmann Karl Ebbighausen	29
	III Gruppe	Me109	Caffiers	Major Adolf Galland	33
Jagdgeschwader 51	Staff and HQ	Me109	Wissant	Major Werner Mölders	2
	I Gruppe	Me109	Wissant	Hauptmann Hans-Heinrich Brustellin	23
	II Gruppe	Me109	Wissant	Hauptmann Günther Matthes	25
	III Gruppe	Me109	St Omer	Major Hannes Trautloft	39
Jagdgeschwader 52	Staff and HQ	Me109	Coquelles	Major von Merhart	1
	I Gruppe	Me109	Coquelles	Hauptmann Siegfried von Eschwege	36
	II Gruppe	Me109	Peuplingne	Hauptmann Von Kornatzki	23
Jagdgeschwader 54	Staff and HQ	Me109	Guînes	Major Martin Mettig	3
	I Gruppe	Me109	Guînes	Hauptmann Hubertus von Bonin	24
	II Gruppe	Me109	Hermalinghen	Hauptmann Winterer	36
	III Gruppe	Me109	Guînes	Hauptmann Fritz Ultsch	29
Lehrgeschwader 2	I Gruppe	Me109	Marck	Major Hans Trubenbach	36
Zerstörergeschwader 26	Staff and HQ	Me110	Lille-Nord	Oberstleutnant Joachim-Friedrich Huth	2
	I Gruppe	Me110	Yvrench	Hauptmann Wilhelm Makrocki	21
	II Gruppe	Me110	Crécy	Hauptmann Ralph von Rettburg	29
	III Gruppe	Me110	Barley	Hauptmann Johann Schalk	21
Zerstörergeschwader 76	Staff and HQ	Me110	Laval	Major Walter Grabmann	2
	II Gruppe	Me110	Abbeville	Hauptmann Max Groth	22
	III Gruppe	Me110	Laval	Hauptmann Friedrich-Karl Dickoré	12

Key

Jagdgeschwader (JG) = Fighter Wing
Kampfgeschwader (KG) = Battle Wing
Küstenfliegergruppe = Coastal Flying Group

Sturzkampfgeschwader (StG) = Dive-bomber Wing
Lehrgeschwader (LG) = Teaching Wing, of mixed aircraft
Erprobungsgruppe = Experimental Group

Zerstörergeschwader (ZG) = Destroyer Wing, of heavy fighters
Note: Reconnaissance, air-sea rescue and predominantly mine-laying units are excluded.

Luftflotte 3 *Headquarters in Paris. Commanded by Generalfeldmarschall Hugo Sperrle*

PARENT UNIT	UNIT	AIRCRAFT TYPE	BASED AT/HQ	COMMANDER	SERVICEABLE AIRCRAFT
IV Fliegerkorps			**Dinard**	**Generalleutnant Kurt Pflugbeil**	
Lehrgeschwader 1	Staff and HQ	Ju88	Orléans/Bricy	Oberstleutnant Alfred Bülowius	2
	I Gruppe	Ju88	Orléans/Bricy	Hauptmann Wilhelm Kern	19
	II Gruppe	Ju88	Orléans/Bricy	Major Debratz	16
	III Gruppe	Ju88	Châteaudun	Major Dr Ernst Bormann	18
Kampfgeschwader 27	Staff and KG HQ	He111	Tours	Oberst Gerhard Conrad	3
	I Gruppe	He111	Tours	Major Gerhard Ulbrich	12
	II Gruppe	He111	Dinard	Major Friedrich-Karl Schlichting	18
	III Gruppe	He111	Rennes	Major Manfred Freiherr von Sternberg	23
Sturzkampfgeschwader 3	Staff and KG HQ	Ju87, Do17, He111	Caen	Oberst Angerstein	5
	I Gruppe	Ju87	Caen		24
	Kampfgruppe 806	Ju88	Nantes	Hauptmann W. Siegel	32
	Kampfgruppe 100	He111	Vannes	Hauptmann Friedrich Carol Aschenbrenner	19
V Fliegerkorps			**Villacoublay**	**General Robert Ritter von Greim**	
Kampfgeschwader 51	Staff and KG HQ	Ju88	Orly	Oberst Dr Fisser	0
	I Gruppe	Ju88	Melun	Major Schultz-Hein	18
	II Gruppe	Ju88	Orly	Major Winkler	17
	III Gruppe	Ju88	Etampes	Major Walter Marienfeld	20
Kampfgeschwader 54	Staff and KG HQ	Ju88	Evreux	Oberstleutnant Otto Höhne	0
	I Gruppe	Ju88	Evreux	Hauptmann Jobst-Heinrich von Heydebrock	20
	II Gruppe	Ju88	St André-de-L'Eure	Hauptmann Karl-Bernhard Schlaeger (acting)	15
Kampfgeschwader 55	Staff and KG HQ	He111	Villacoublay	Oberstleutnant Hans Korte	3
	I Gruppe	He111	Dreux	Major Joachim Roeber	27
	II Gruppe	He111	Chartres	Major Friedrich Kless	26
	III Gruppe	He111	Villacoublay	Major Hans Schlemell	23
VIII Fliegerkorps			**Deauville**	**General Wolfram Freiherr von Richthofen**	
Lehrgeschwader 1	V Gruppe	Me110	Caen	Hauptmann Horst Liensberger	24
Sturzkampfgeschwader 1	Staff and KG HQ	Do17, Ju87	Angers	Major Hagen	33
	I Gruppe	Ju87	Angers	Major Paul Hozzel	28
	III Gruppe	Ju87	Angers	Hauptmann Helmut Mahlke	28
Sturzkampfgeschwader 2	Staff and KG HQ	Do17, Ju87	St-Malo	Major Oskar Dinort	43
	I Gruppe	Ju87	St-Malo	Hauptmann Hubertus Hitschold	24
	II Gruppe	Ju87	Lannion	Major Walter Enneccerus	23
Sturzkampfgeschwader 77	Staff and KG HQ	Do17, Ju87	Caen	Major Graf von Schönborn	21
	I Gruppe	Ju87	Caen	Hauptmann von Dalwigk zu Lichtenfels	30
	II Gruppe	Ju87	Caen	Hauptmann Waldemar Pleweg	31
	III Gruppe	Ju87	Caen	Major Helmut Bode	37
Jagdfliegerführer 3			**Deauville**	**Oberst Werner Junck**	
Jagdgeschwader 2	Staff and HQ	Me109	Evreux	Major Harry von Bülow	3
	I Gruppe	Me109	Beaumont-le-Roger	Major Hennig Strumpell	27
	II Gruppe	Me109	Beaumont-le-Roger	Major Wolfgang Schellmann	24
	III Gruppe	Me109	Le Havre	Major Dr Erich Mix	20
Jagdgeschwader 27	Staff and HQ	Me109	Cherbourg-West	Oberstleutnant Max Ibel	5
	I Gruppe	Me109	Plumetot	Hauptmann Eduard Neumann	39
	II Gruppe	Me109	Crépon	Hauptmann Lippert	27
	III Gruppe	Me109	Carquebut	Hauptmann Joachim Schlichting	32
Jagdgeschwader 53	Staff and HQ	Me109	Cherbourg	Major Hans-Jürgen Cramon-Taubadel	4
	I Gruppe	Me109	Rennes	Hauptmann Blumensaat	37
	II Gruppe	Me109	Dinan	Major Günther Freiherr von Maltzahn	26
	III Gruppe	Me109	Sempy & Brest	Hauptmann Wolf-Dietrich Wilcke	21
Zerstörergeschwader 2	Staff and HQ	Me110	Toussée-le-Noble	Oberstleutnant Friedrich Vollbracht	2
	I Gruppe	Me110	Amiens	Hauptmann Heinlein	19
	II Gruppe	Me110	Guyancourt	Major Carl	23

Luftflotte 5 *Headquarters in Stavanger, Norway. Commanded by Generaloberst Hans-Jürgen Stümpff*

PARENT UNIT	UNIT	AIRCRAFT TYPE	BASED AT/HQ	COMMANDER	SERVICEABLE AIRCRAFT
X Fliegerkorps			**Stavanger**	**Generalleutnant Hans Geisler**	
Kampfgeschwader 26	Staff and KG HQ	He111	Stavanger	Oberstleutnant Karl Freiherr von Wechmar	5
	I Gruppe	He111	Stavanger	Major Hermann	28
	III Gruppe	He111	Stavanger	Major Waldemar Lerche	19
Kampfgeschwader 30	Staff and KG HQ	Ju88	Aalborg, Denmark	Oberst Herbert Rieckhoff	1
	I Gruppe	Ju88	Aalborg	Major Fritz Doensch	26
	III Gruppe	Ju88	Aalborg-West	Hauptmann Gerhard Kellewe	21
Zerstörergeschwader 76		Me110	Stavanger	Hauptmann W. Restemeyer	20
Jagdgeschwader 53	II Gruppe	Me109	Stavanger & Trondheim	Hauptmann Hentschel	35
Küstenfliegergruppe 506	3 Staffeln	He115	Stavanger & Trondheim	Major Eisenbach	22

'My shots must have hit the right place'

On 18 August 1940, Major Gerhard Schöpfel of *Jagdgeschwader* 26 engaged enemy fighters of 501 Squadron.

> Suddenly I found a squadron of Hurricanes below me in the usual British formation of tight threes, which were climbing in a spiral. I circled about 3,300 ft above them. Then I saw a pair of Hurricanes weaving behind the formation, on guard against attack from astern. I waited until they were curving north-westwards from Folkestone, then attacked out of the sun and below.

Schöpfel claimed that he shot down both weavers without the main body of the squadron realizing.

> Now I was beneath a third machine. I fired a short burst. This aircraft likewise fell apart. The British flew on, having noticed nothing. I positioned myself under a fourth machine. This time I had to get closer. When I pressed the firing button the Hurricane was so close to me that fragments from it hit my aircraft. Oil covered my cockpit so thickly that I couldn't see, and after two minutes of action had to break off. After I had broken off, Oberleutnant Sprick led No. 8 Staffel in an attack on the British, who were now aware that Germans were right behind them and dived. However, Sprick managed to shoot down two more. I think this was the first time in this war that a pilot shot down four British aircraft on the same sortie. Looking back at those anxious moments, it was not very difficult. My shots must have hit the right place, so that there was no time for the others to be warned. [Quoted in Bickers, p. 189]

-0-0-0-0-0-

'It had been a beautiful morning'

Betty McNabb was taking a cliff walk near Beachy Head when low-flying Dorniers of *Kampfgeschwader 76* crossed the coast.

```
      It had been a beautiful morning, peaceful and quiet, and as we
strolled enjoying the tranquillity of the morning, we both spoke and
agreed that it was a shame that there had to be a war on, on such a
tremendous day as this. I can remember the gentle breeze, so gentle
it hardly rustled the leaves on the trees, and all the birds seemed
to be singing quite oblivious to our presence, when suddenly we heard
a heavy rumbling sound, almost the sound of a strong wind coming to-
wards us. We could see nothing, but the sound got louder it was
so strange.
      Then suddenly, and it gave us both a fright really, these huge dark
shapes appeared over the cliffs almost as if they had come right out
of the sea. The noise was now deafening as what must have been six or
seven huge bombers disappeared as soon as they had appeared and all
was peaceful again. My God it was scary. [www.battleofbritain1940.net]


                        -0-0-0-0-0-
```

26, led by Major Gerhard Schöpfel, which shot down four Hurricanes within moments over Canterbury. Schöpfel himself sent Pilot Officer John Bland down in flames to his death. Two other Fighter Command pilots were badly wounded, and one escaped unharmed. Meanwhile, some of the bombers were approaching their targets.

First on the target list was Biggin Hill. Kesselring's plan was for two waves of high-level bombers to pound the airfield and then for a low-level attack by nine Dorniers of *Kampfgeschwader 76* to deliver the *coup de grâce*. The latter crossed the Channel at only 100 feet, avoiding high-level fighters and radar detection. They then raced northwards, following the railway lines and hugging the valleys. On the approach to Biggin Hill they flashed through Burgess Hill village in Sussex, strafing as they went, at alarmingly low altitude. From the third floor of St Lawrence's Hospital, a bewildered patient found himself looking directly into the cockpit of the leading bomber.

The German crews had been briefed to expect a mass of smoke at the target following the earlier high-level bombing. But they arrived over a peaceful and undamaged Biggin Hill, for the high-level bombers had been delayed by heavy cloud over their airfields in France. As they released their bombs, the Dorniers came under fire from the airfield's anti-aircraft guns just as the Hurricanes of 32 and 610 squadrons arrived. The gunners succeeded in bringing down the commander, Oberleutnant Lamberty. Coming down in a field near the airfield, he struggled free of his burning cockpit to face a troop of Home Guard, guns pointed. Lamberty raised his hands in surrender, and when the Home Guarders

OPPOSITE

Two Messerschmitt 109s (a *Rotte*) race across the skies. Sleek and deadly, the Me109 was the aircraft the fighter boys most feared.

saw burnt shreds of flesh falling from them, they lowered their rifles.

Moments after Lamberty's capture another wave of German raiders arrived and the British and Germans together threw themselves to the ground. Then he was led, together with his crew, along a road to the base. On the way they met a group of civilians, to whom Lamberty offered his parachute. In return he asked for help getting his cigarettes out of his pocket as his hands were too burnt to function. This request was granted, and a cigarette put in his mouth and lit. From the base he was taken to a hospital where his burns were treated.

The high-level bombers eventually arrived, but their bombs dropped to the east of Biggin Hill, doing little damage. Kenley was not so fortunate. Nos 111 and 615 squadrons were successfully distracted by a medium-level bombing raid, allowing the Dorniers to go in low. Their bombs rippled across the base, destroying all ten hangars, the stores building and ten Hurricanes. All communications and electricity and water supplies were cut. One bomb landed directly on a shelter trench, killing twelve and injuring twenty. The returning RAF Kenley squadrons looked down on smoke-hazed devastation. They landed on a strip of ground that threaded between the craters, marked out with white flags.

Work began immediately to get Kenley operational again using an emergency plan. A new operations room was set up in a disused butcher's shop in nearby Caterham High Street. Restoring all the vital telephone links took more time, however, and it was two hours before 11 Group HQ at Uxbridge was back in contact with all its sector stations.

The Luftwaffe attacks now swung westwards. At about 2pm, four formations were mapped approaching the Isle of Wight. It was the largest Stuka strike yet – though it was fated to be the last. Over a hundred Ju87s – the whole of *Sturzkampfgeschwader* 77 – each with a 550-pound bomb under its fuselage and four 110-pounders under its wings, were heading in a four-pronged formation to attack the airfields at Gosport, Thorney Island and Ford, and Poling radar station. The Luftwaffe's reconnaissance flights had led it to believe that the airfields were used by Fighter Command. In fact, Gosport was primarily a torpedo development unit, Thorney Island was the base of two Coastal Command Blenheim squadrons, and Ford was a naval air station. The bombers were protected by nearly 160 Me109s. 'It was a magnificent sight,' said one of the Stuka pilots, as the giant formation assembled. 'Cherbourg lay in the sunshine below us, with the breakers visible along the coast. The sky had a light blue tint while over the Channel there was a light haze.' [Quoted by Price, p. 114]

When the attackers reached the Isle of Wight, a formation of 22 Stukas peeled away to the west, heading towards Gosport. Before they reached their target, their top cover of Me109s came under attack from the Spitfires of 234 Squadron, which shot down three of them. But the lower-level formation ploughed on to attack Gosport unmolested, and they succeeded in damaging two hangars and wrecking four aircraft.

Near Bognor Regis, Sussex, the formation had split again, with two *Gruppen* heading to the east against Ford and Poling, while one *Gruppe* turned northwest to attack Thorney Island. At Ford, there was no warning for personnel to reach the shelters and an anti-aircraft complement of only six guns. Bombs hit the barracks hut, the hangars and the airfield's fuel storage, killing twenty-eight and wounding

OPPOSITE

A Civil Defence poster warns British school-children not to play with exotic-looking objects. The constant raids littered the land with dangerous debris.

continued on page 220

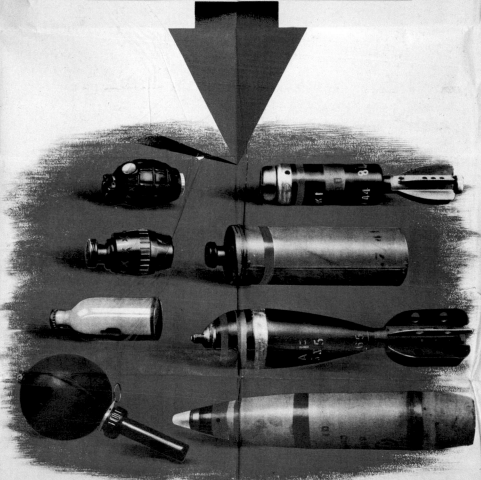

Captured German airmen, spruced up after ditching, crash-landing or baling out,
are brought to London under the escort of Military Police in August 1940.

CAPTURED AIRMEN

In the later stages of the Battle of Britain, when the Blitz was wrecking London, some German airmen who parachuted onto English soil were handled roughly. But for the most part, those Luftwaffe personnel who escaped alive from their aircraft over Britain were treated humanely.

Christabel Leighton-Porter, who modelled for the *Daily Mirror* cartoon character Jane, was in Lyme Regis, Dorset, when there was a raid over the sea. 'They shot down a German plane and I remember all the people on the beach getting in a circle and then a boat brought in the Germans that had baled out. Everybody was shouting. Even the little kiddies were encouraged to join in and boo. But when the Germans got out of the boat, people saw that these were very frightened young blond boys and everybody went very quiet.' [Leighton-Porter, recording]

For most people, such an episode was the first time they had seen a real German. A.G. Street, a Home Guarder, chased through the Wiltshire countryside trying to find an enemy airman who had been seen baling out. When captured, 'he seemed a very ordinary, decent-looking lad,' Street commented. 'As I was driving home, I realized that I, a civilian, had just experienced my first taste of war, and that I disliked it intensely. I was dead keen to hunt that fellow, felt the same exhilaration as I did when hounds were running, and would have shot him on the instant if need be. But, somehow, when he was caught I had no further quarrel with him.' [Calder, 1992 edition, p.152]

'She had the most enormous cut in her thigh'

Lillias Barr was a WAAF officer stationed at Kenley when Dorniers hit the airbase on 18 August, as she described to Ernie Burton.

```
    Someone called out that the sick quarters had a direct hit, so
I sped in that direction. I remember running over the hummocky grass.
There were lots of people badly shaken sitting about. The doctor
had been killed, and Mary Coulthard, one of the two WAAF sick-bay
attendants, was badly injured. She had the most enormous cut in her
thigh. I had never seen anything like it, she had been thrown on to
a steel helmet which had sliced through her leg. She and the other
attendant were smiling though, because they had applied a tourniquet
which had worked; and I smiled too - I, who under normal circumstances
could faint at the sight of someone's cut finger! We tied a label on
to her before she was taken to hospital. [www.battleofbritain1940.net]
```

-o-o-o-o-o-

WAAF armourers and flight mechanics service a Hurricane.

The prime minister's secretary, 'Jock' Colville, was in Southwest England on 18 August, watching the action overhead.

```
     We were sitting on the terrace looking towards Thorney Island …
Suddenly we heard the sound of AA [anti-aircraft] fire and saw puffs
of white smoke as the shells burst over Portsmouth. Then to our left,
from the direction of Chichester and Tangmere, came the roar of
engines, then the noise of machine-gun fire … shading our eyes to
escape the glare of this August day, we saw not far in front of us
about twenty machines engaged in a fight. Soon a German bomber came
hurtling towards us with smoke pouring from its tail and we lost
sight of it behind the trees ... Out of the melee came a dive-bomber,
hovered like a bird of prey and then sped steeply down on Thorney
Island. There were vast explosions as another and another followed,
and my attention was diverted from the fight as clouds of smoke rose
from the burning hangars of Thorney aerodrome. In all, the battle
only lasted about two minutes and then moved seawards, with at least
two German aircraft left smouldering on the ground. [Colville, p.225]
```

ABOVE
Coils of defensive
barbed wire contrast
with the natural land-
scape between Dover
and Folkestone, 1940,
as the south coast
beaches were turned
into frontlines.

a further seventy-five. Fourteen aircraft on the ground were destroyed.

At Thorney Island, airfield hangars and a fuel dump were hit, as well as more naval aircraft. The largest force of 31 Stukas now dived down on Poling. Radar operator Avis Parsons was working on a switchboard, feeding the information from Poling and nearby Truleigh Hill through to the filter room at Fighter Command.

'There was a scream,' Parsons recalled later, 'as the Stukas dived and then the noise of the explosions was terrific.' Parsons continued working for 15 minutes and then the lines went dead. Five minutes later, the Stukas had finished. They had dropped 87 bombs. In R Block, where Parsons was working, all the windows were smashed and the doors blown in. Outside, cars were ablaze, huge craters had been gouged everywhere, and chunks of metal from the aerial mast littered the ground.

'This duel of winged machines'

Squadron Leader Peter Townsend led No. 85 Squadron into action on 18 August, as it joined other squadrons to tackle the immense incoming Luftwaffe formations.

The squadron was flying well together as we entered cloud at ten thousand feet, heading straight towards 'a hundred plus'. We emerged from clouds somewhere over the Thames Estuary and there advancing towards us was a massive column about a mile and a half high, stepped up wave upon wave. At the base were Ju. 87s, above them Heinkels, then Dorniers and Ju. 88s, then a layer of Me. 110s, and above, at about twenty thousand feet, a swarm of Me. 109s … When they saw the British fighters KG2 closed in tight. This gave them a formidable concentration of fire especially now that they had an extra MG15 on each side … As we closed in on the bombers, the Ju. 87s and Heinkels turned away seawards. A dozen Me. 110s cut across us and immediately formed a defensive circle. 'In we go,' I called over the R/T, and a moment later an Me. 110 had banked clumsily across my bows. In its vain attempt to escape, the machine I was bent on destroying suddenly looked pathetically human. It was an easy shot - too easy. For a few more seconds we milled around with the Me. 110s. Then down came a little shower of Me. 109s. Out of the corner of my eye I saw one diving for me, pumping shells. A quick turn toward it shook it off, and it slid by below, then reared up in a wide left hand turn in front of me. It was a fatal move. My Hurricane climbed round easily inside its turn. When I fired the Me. 109 flicked over and a sudden spurt of white vapour from its belly turned into flame. Down came another. Again a steep turn and I was on its tail. He seemed to know I was there, but he did the wrong thing. He kept on turning. When I fired, bits flew off, the hood came away and then the pilot baled out. He looked incongruous hanging there, a wingless body in the midst of this duel of winged machines.
[Townsend, *Duel of Eagles*, pp. 376-7]

-0-0-0-0-0-

But the Stukas had suffered as well. At the start of the attack they had been intercepted by Hurricanes of 43 Squadron, which had caught them at their most vulnerable moment, when they were committed to their dives. Five were shot down and another two badly damaged before the high-level escort came to the rescue. The other *Gruppen* now also started to come under fierce RAF attack. While 234 Squadron Spitfires held the escort from *Jagdgeschwader* 27 at bay, fighters from Nos 152, 601 and 602 squadrons completed the massacre started by 43 Squadron. In all, the British fighters shot down 16 Stukas, with two crashing on their return to France. A further four were badly damaged.

It was a decisive defeat for the Junkers Ju87, the aircraft that had been the terror of Europe. After 18 August, Stukas would be used no more in the Battle of Britain.

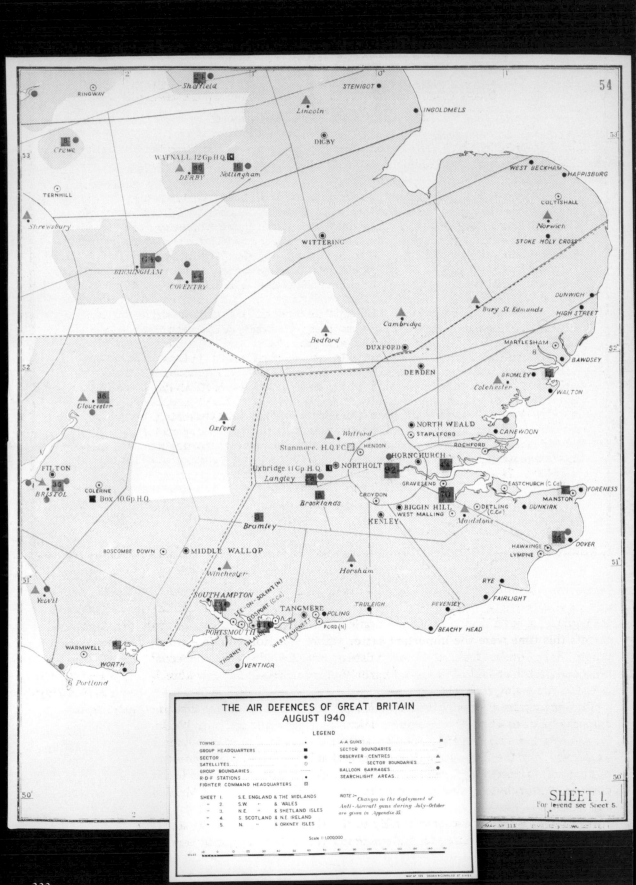

THE AIR DEFENCES OF GREAT BRITAIN
AUGUST 1940

LEGEND

TOWNS	•	A·A GUNS	■
GROUP HEADQUARTERS	■	SECTOR BOUNDARIES	
SECTOR	■	OBSERVER CENTRES	▲
SATELLITES	⊙	SECTOR BOUNDARIES	▲
GROUP BOUNDARIES		BALLOON BARRAGES	
R·D·F STATIONS	•	SEARCHLIGHT AREAS	
FIGHTER COMMAND HEADQUARTERS	▨		

SHEET I. S.E. ENGLAND & THE MIDLANDS
" 2. S.W. " & WALES
" 3. N.E. " & SHETLAND ISLES
" 4. S. SCOTLAND & N.E. IRELAND
" 5. N. " & ORKNEY ISLES

NOTE :— Changes in the deployment of
Anti-Aircraft guns during July-October
are given in Appendix 35.

Scale 1:1,000,000

SHEET I.
For legend see Sheet 5.

'Unpredictable weather cooked up some nasty surprise'

Oberst Josef Priller, a Luftwaffe fighter pilot with *Jagdgeschwader* 26, described the difficulty of calculating how long fuel would last, especially given the vagaries of the weather.

It often happened, particularly over the Channel, that the unpredictable weather cooked up some nasty surprise. Fighter aircraft had a relatively short range and sometimes had barely enough fuel left to get them home. In settled weather, one could calculate with reasonable accuracy how much to keep in hand for the return leg, but those conditions seldom prevailed in the operational zone.

Sometimes, it would be fair over England, but thickly clouded over France.

A Gruppe in our Geschwader experienced an example of this one day when tricky weather during the morning enforced an urgent change in the planned operations ... In the afternoon the sun came out and this Gruppe was ordered to take off. It penetrated about thirty or forty miles deep into England, 'free hunting', which meant looking for enemy aircraft, and low-level attack. On the way back they found that suddenly the whole French coast had become covered with cloud and fog. No fewer than eleven machines were reported missing. During the course of the evening ten others turned up one at a time. They had had to go separately far inland to look for somewhere to put down. Most of them had eventually found an airfield but one had had to make a belly landing. [Quoted in Bickers, p. 184]

-0-0-0-0-0-

By 5pm, the aircraft of *Luftflotte* 2 had returned, refuelled and re-armed, and were massing again over the Calais area. Radar accurately estimated the formation at about 250 aircraft. The Luftwaffe's aim was now improving, and the targets this time were the important sector stations of Hornchurch – which protected the London docks, the Thames Estuary and the industrial-commercial centres of Dagenham and Tilbury – and North Weald, which backed up Hornchurch as well as protecting the Home Counties.

The German plan was for 52 Heinkels of *Kampfgeschwader* 53 to take off first and cross the Essex coast north of Foulness before heading inland to North Weald. Fifteen minutes after the Heinkels, fifty-eight Dorniers of *Kampfgeschwader* 2 would take off in the direction of Deal, Kent, so that both attacks would cross the coast at the same time. The Dorniers would then follow the Thames Estuary in the direction of Hornchurch. Both bomber groups were to be protected by 140 Me109s and Me110s.

Air Vice-Marshal Park reacted quickly to the threat to his northern sector stations, ordering 13 squadrons to readiness or into the air. Following an agreement

OPPOSITE

An Air Ministry map from The National Archives shows a plan of 11 Group's fighter defences, along with parts of 10 Group and 12 Group.

made the previous day, 12 Group put four squadrons in the air to cover the airfields, which meant that 140 fighters were being deployed. Four squadrons – Nos 32, 54, 56 and 72 – were sent forward to engage the enemy before they neared the targets. The 12 Hurricanes of 56 Squadron glimpsed the Heinkel group just off the Essex coast. 'We had to go up through a bit of cloud and suddenly we saw them,' said Flying Officer Innes Westmacott. 'I must say I gulped a bit! It looked an enormous raid.' [Quoted in Price, p. 141]

As a section of the squadron targeted the bombers, the close German escort of Me110s moved to block the attack, desperately accelerating from the 180mph they had been forced to maintain to stay with the Heinkels. At such slow speeds the Me110s were sitting ducks. Five were shot down by 56 Squadron, which also

managed to fatally damage one of the He111s. Soon they were joined by No. 54 Squadron Spitfires, which shot down two further Me110s and damaged several more. Now out of ammunition, the two British squadrons peeled away, unharmed, but having failed to turn back the bombers. The Luftwaffe's intentions had been revealed, however, so Park sent up Nos 85, 151, 257 and 310 squadrons, a total of 61 Hurricanes.

To the south, 32 and 501 squadrons clashed with the Dornier formation, but they were hit hard by the escorting Me109s, losing four fighters and failing to deflect the raid. But then, as both formations closed on the airfields, the weather intervened. Thick cloud was now forming and, with the strict order still in place that no bombs should be dropped on London, the Luftwaffe crews had no option but to turn back. As they headed for home, the strong RAF forces near North Weald brought down more of the unwieldy Me110s.

British propaganda declared a great victory, claiming it was Fighter Command together with the anti-aircraft batteries that had turned back the early evening raids. The headline in The Times the next day read: 'Germany's Heaviest Air Defeat', followed by the claim that 140 Luftwaffe planes had been shot down, at least twice the actual number. The

A page from a wartime alphabet book encourages children to learn who their enemies are.

Daily Mirror's story was headed '140–16: R.A.F.'s Biggest Victory'. Fighter Command admitted to just over 20 fighter losses. The real figure, though, was 39, including the 6 Hurricanes destroyed on the ground at Kenley.

The afternoon's action, like that of the morning, had been a blow to the Luftwaffe's resources and morale. By now, the disparity was clear between what the Luftwaffe crews had been told of Britain's fighter defences and what they had themselves seen in the skies over Kent. For once, the RAF put up enough aircraft to make the fighter ratio very nearly one-to-one. 'Only a few of us have not yet had to ditch in the Channel with a badly damaged aircraft or a dead engine,' said Oberleutnant Hahn of 1 *Gruppe*, *Jagdgeschwader* 3. 'Utter exhaustion had set in. For the first time pilots discussed the prospects of posting to a quieter sector.' [Quoted in Bickers, p. 228]

After the attrition of the day before, poor weather would limit activity for the next five days, allowing both sides to rest, repair their forces and take stock.

Cloudy, with occasional showers in the east.

At a meeting at his Carinhall estate today, Hermann Goering took out his frustrations on his men. He blamed the fighter pilots for the losses affecting his bomber fleets, and he replaced several commanders with others considered more aggressive. He ordered closer escorting, even though an examination of the statistics would have revealed that it was when the Me109s were engaged in free hunts that they inflicted the most losses. Goering also decreed that the Me110 'Destroyer' would itself now fly with Me109 escorts. The Ju87 Stuka, it was confirmed, would take no further part in the battle other than in exceptional circumstances.

Fighter Command also analysed the heavy fighting of the previous six days. The strength in depth that had been created by pre-war planning was beginning to tell. Supplies of fighters, either new or patched up by the efficient Civilian Repair Organization, were steady. In fact, the numbers available were set to increase. The problem, though, was pilots. Since 8 August, 90 pilots had been killed and another 50 injured badly enough to be *hors de combat*. In the same period, only 65 novices had arrived from the Operational Training Units. It was vital that each squadron retain at least a core of experienced men to provide guidance and leadership. A high proportion of enemy 'kills' was achieved by a small number of the most aggressive and skilful pilots.

'We have reached the decisive period of the air war'

On 19 August, at his country estate of Carinhall, Goering decreed his immediate aims in the air war against Britain.

```
       We have reached the decisive period of the air war against England.
The vital task is to turn all means at our disposal to the defeat of
the enemy Air Force. Our first aim is the destruction of the enemy's
fighters. If they no longer take to the air, we shall attack them on
the ground, or force them into battle by directing bomber attacks
against targets within the range of our fighters. At the same time,
and on a growing scale, we must continue our activities against the
ground organisation of the enemy bomber units. Surprise attacks on the
enemy aircraft industry must be made by day and by night. Once the
enemy Air Force has been annihilated, our attacks will be directed as
ordered against other vital targets. [Quoted in Wheatley, p. 73]


              -o-o-o-o-o-
```

'THE FEW'

On 20 August, having been deeply stirred in the previous days by the tenacious efforts of Fighter Command to protect the nation, Prime Minister Winston Churchill addressed the House of Commons. His speech that day, with its nod to the St Crispin's Day speech in Shakespeare's *Henry V*, immortalized the epic feats being fought in the skies by 'the few'.

> The gratitude of every home in our Island, in our Empire, and indeed throughout the world, except in the abodes of the guilty, goes out to the British airmen who, undaunted by odds, unwearied in their constant challenge and mortal danger, are turning the tide of the war by their prowess and by their devotion. Never in the field of human conflict was so much owed by so many to so few.

Winston S. Churchill

New orders were given to try and minimize losses. Pilots were discouraged from engaging over the sea, where so many of them had perished after having baled out safely. Sector-station controllers were again urged to avoid combat with free sweeps of Me109s, however glaring the provocation.

Dowding's other great concern was his 11 Group sector stations – Northolt, Tangmere, Kenley, Biggin Hill, Hornchurch, North Weald and Debden. Much effort by the Luftwaffe had been wasted on other, less important, aerodromes, but now these vital nodes of Fighter Command's system were coming under heavy attack.

After a quiet morning on 19 August, a build-up of aircraft was spotted over Calais. Then, for about an hour after midday, about 100 Me109s sped over Dover and the south coast, trying to lure British fighters into the sky but encountering only rain and cloud. To the west, about 30 Ju88s were sent in the direction of Portsmouth and Southampton. Several were driven back after interception by 602 Squadron Spitfires from Westhampnett, but others pressed on as far as South Wales. Here they hit oil storage tanks at Pembroke Dock. A couple of the Ju88s also penetrated to the airfield at Bibury, which was used by a night-fighting detachment of Spitfires from No. 92 Squadron. One fighter was destroyed on the ground and three others damaged, but two of the squadron's planes got airborne and chased the raiders, downing one of the Ju88s.

That night, long-range German bombers criss-crossed the country as far north as Liverpool. They inflicted over 100 civilian casualties, but the raiders failed to locate their fighter airfield and factory targets.

OPPOSITE
The prime minister leaves 10 Downing Street to address the House of Commons, summer 1940.

TUESDAY 20 August 1940

The day started cloudy, but the morning still saw heavy German reconnaissance over the Thames Estuary and the airfields of Southeast England. A characteristic lightning raid was carried out by the Experimental Group 210, but its target – Martlesham Heath airfield in Suffolk – escaped major damage.

Generally cloudy with rain.

In the afternoon, there was only one major raid, by 27 Dorniers escorted by 30 Messerschmitt Me109s. Their target was Eastchurch, but the formation was turned back by No. 615 Squadron, which shot down two of the bombers and one fighter with the assistance of Spitfires from No. 65 Squadron.

WEDNESDAY 21 August 1940

The weather contributed to a continuation of the relative lull on the Wednesday. In addition, a reorganization of the German fighter wings, the *Jagdgeschwader* – whereby more Me109s were to be concentrated in the Pas de Calais – meant that the Luftwaffe launched only light raids. Nevertheless, determined to prevent Fighter Command from having time to rest and recuperate, Kesselring and Sperrle ordered pairs or trios of aircraft to probe all along the front, from Cornwall to Skegness. Several raiders were shot down, but bombs hit St Eval airfield, Cornwall, disturbing the rest of No. 238 Squadron (which had been sent there to recuperate), hitting a hangar and destroying four Blenheims and damaging four more.

Cloudy, with occasional rain.

22 August 1940 THURSDAY

Cloudy, with rain and winds.

Thursday followed a similar pattern to that of the previous day, with most Luftwaffe units grounded by poor weather. As if to compensate, the early morning saw the first outbreak of shelling by the heavy artillery units now established at Cape Gris Nez. Some hundred shells were fired at a convoy passing through the Straits of Dover between 8am and 9am. No vessels were hit, so Experimental Group 210 went on the attack soon after midday, protected by Me109 fighter sweeps on its flanks. As the bomb-carrying Me110s approached the ships, Spitfires from Nos 54 and 610 squadrons swung into action, and during a fierce dogfight two of the British fighters were shot down, with one pilot, Sergeant G.R. Collett, killed. But the convoy survived undamaged, and most of the rest of the afternoon saw only limited enemy incursions, by fighters.

The only other heavy raid of the day was once again carried out by Experimental Group 210. It was just after 7pm, and at Manston aerodrome the redeployment of No. 600 Blenheim Squadron away from this exposed position was almost complete, with the last of the supplies and equipment being loaded onto lorries. Suddenly the Me110s swept in from the sea and dropped some thirty bombs, destroying two Blenheims as well as hangars, offices and storehouses. Remarkably, there were no casualties on the ground.

23 August 1940 FRIDAY

Showers with bright intervals inland; cloudy over southern and eastern waters.

Sporadic Luftwaffe raids continued today across the country, including on some BBC wireless stations. Fighter Command claimed a Ju88 and a Heinkel 111 shot down while losing none of its own planes or men, either in the air or on the ground. But more than 30 civilians died as a result of air raids.

24 August 1940 SATURDAY

Fine and clear in the south.

Saturday brought perfect weather, with the skies bright and clear. From 8.30am the day would see six major attacks over ten hours, carried out by a total of more than 500 bombers and fighters. This would be the first day of two weeks of sustained air offensives on a massive scale.

At 8.30am, Pevensey radar picked up German aircraft across a broad front. Fifteen minutes later, the enemy forces had organized themselves into a close-flying formation of 40 Do17s and Ju88s, protected by 66 Me109 fighters. Twelve Fighter Command squadrons were scrambled in response, with Spitfires of No. 610 Squadron, from Biggin Hill, making the first contact. With the advantage of height and the sun behind them, they succeeded in breaking up the raid, which retired to the southeast and then split up, though some bombs fell on the streets of Dover. Spitfires of No. 54 Squadron, from Hornchurch, shot down three Me109s as they turned for home.

Shortly after the disappearance of this raid from the radar screens, another was detected crossing the Channel from Cape Gris Nez. No. 610 Squadron had only just returned to Biggin Hill when it was scrambled again, along with Nos 151 from North Weald and 501 from Gravesend, against an incoming formation of Ju88s and Me109s. No. 264 Squadron at Hornchurch, equipped with its Boulton Paul Defiants, was also ordered up. This move was a sign of Fighter Command's stretched resources, for a month earlier the massacre of No. 141 Squadron, which flew Defiants, had demonstrated painfully the aircraft's weaknesses.

The defenders managed to break up this raid too and return to their bases. For the Defiant squadron, this meant the forward base at Manston, the RAF's least popular airfield. Some of the squadron were still refuelling when, shortly after 1pm, a raid warning sounded. Most of the Defiants got airborne, taking off as bombs started to hit the base, but they were unable to gain height fast enough to avoid being pounced on by German fighters. Three were shot down, including that of the commander, Squadron Leader Philip Hunter, and all six men inside the aircraft were killed. The remainder returned to Hornchurch, only to be forced to scramble again amid falling bombs at just after 3.30pm, when the airfield came under attack. Two of the Defiants collided as they raced to take off, and another was shot down shortly afterwards.

At the same time as the Hornchurch attack a force of 46 Dornier Do17s and Heinkel He111s attacked North Weald. The raid was met by two British squadrons and, as the Me109 cover was too high to provide swift protection, 151 Squadron's Hurricanes succeeded in attacking the Heinkels, while 111 Squadron adopted its head-on charge against the Dorniers. About 20 bombers struggled through and inflicted substantial damage. Nevertheless, after these assaults both Hornchurch and North Weald were still able to function.

For the Germans, attacking to the north of London was highly risky as they were operating at the very limit of the range of the Me109 fighters. As the North Weald bombers headed for home, their Me109 escort long departed, they were only rescued from annihilation by the clever defence of accompanying Me110s.

Poor, battered Manston was once again in the firing line. It was attacked twice that day. Seventeen men were killed, the runway badly cratered and the telephone lines destroyed. The decision was taken to abandon the base except for emergency deployments or refuelling.

By 4pm, Air Vice-Marshal Park had committed almost all of his 11 Group fighters, and he called on 12 Group commander Leigh-Mallory to provide cover for his northern airfields. Seizing the chance to demonstrate his 'Big Wing' theory, Leigh-Mallory sent up three squadrons to form up over Duxford before heading *en masse* to the rescue of North Weald and Hornchurch. The experiment was, though, a débâcle. The last planes to take off, No. 19's Spitfires, never met up with the other two squadrons, though they were the only fighters to make a proper interception.

No. 10 Group was now also drawn into the day's fighting. At 3.40pm a large formation was spotted on radar approaching the Isle of Wight. Expecting Ju87 dive-bombers and another feast of kills, the intercepting fighters were positioned too low for the incoming Ju88s and Me110s. Several squadrons had been scrambled, but only No. 609 made contact, close to Portsmouth, and in the worst possible position. The raid appeared earlier than expected and 609 Squadron found itself 5000 feet directly below the formation. They were lucky to escape with

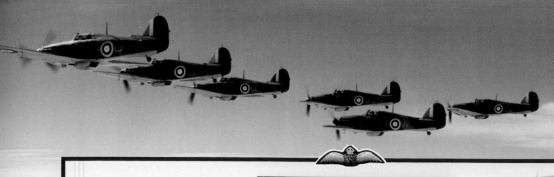

Pilot Officer David Crook, of No. 609 Squadron, was all too aware of the menacing possibility of Messerschmitt Me109s swooping from out of the sun to ambush the British fighters.

    It was always a rather tricky and unpleasant business attacking the
bombers while their fighter escort were still in position above. Often
it was almost impossible to see them because of the blinding sun, but
you always knew they were there, and as soon as they saw a favourable
opportunity, they would dive down and attack. Generally, therefore, we
had to try to get in one very quick attack on the bombers and then turn
round before the fighters arrived on the scene. [Crook, p.65]

-0-0-0-0-0-

ABOVE
Formations of No. 1
Squadron Hurricanes
speed through the air,
followed by Spitfires of
No. 266 Squadron. On
this occasion they were
not flying in anger, but as
part of an aerial display
(October 1940).

only one Spitfire shot down, and they were unable to turn the raid back. Two hundred 250-kilo bombs fell on Portsmouth, hitting shops, factories, houses and the naval dockyards. The raid inflicted more casualties on the ground than any single attack so far, with 104 killed and 237 injured.

Although the Luftwaffe had lost over 30 aircraft during the day's attacks, it had reasons to believe its fortunes were improving. The day had shown that, unencumbered by Stukas, its attacks had been numerous and fast enough to penetrate almost anywhere in Southeast England. Unlike on 18 August, when the weather had come to the rescue, the bombers had got through, even to targets north of London, as the smoking wreckage at North Weald and Hornchurch testified.

Fighter Command was having to contend with new problems and challenges. Its radar network, weakened by damage, had been tested to the limit by the sheer numbers of incoming hostile aircraft. In addition, the controllers' finely balanced decision-making had been complicated by the clever new Luftwaffe tactic of maintaining a constant stream of aircraft flying parallel to the Sussex coast about 20 miles out to sea, occasionally feinting towards the coast.

With the fall of darkness, there was no respite. From just before 11pm, nearly 200 more German bombers streamed across the Channel, this time with only searchlights and anti-aircraft guns to take them on. There was a successful interception by a Blenheim night-fighter, but mostly the bombers ranged freely over Kent, Sussex and Surrey. Bombs meant for the Thames Haven oil storage depot and Short's aircraft factory in Rochester fell on the City and at least nine other London districts. In Bethnal Green the bombs ignited fires. St Giles' Church in

THE 'BIG WING' CONTROVERSY

The 'Big Wing' was a tactical concept, which was championed by the 12 Group commander, Air Vice-Marshal Trafford Leigh-Mallory, with energetic support from his subordinate, Acting Squadron Leader Douglas Bader. At its heart was the belief that large formations of attackers were best opposed with large numbers of defenders.

The proposal was partly born out of the genuine belief that wing-sized formations of three to five squadrons stood a better chance of defeating the Luftwaffe than the one or two squadrons that Air Vice-Marshal Park in 11 Group preferred to send up. But it was also driven by service politics. In July and August 1940, the brunt of the fighting was being borne by Park's men in Southeast England. No. 12 Group was based in the Midlands, at one remove from the frontline, and Leigh-Mallory and Bader — both ambitious men — felt themselves on the sidelines. When they were called on to support 11 Group, it was often too late to make a difference. On several occasions, Park requested their help for the subsidiary role of guarding No. 11 Group airfields.

Park offered practical objections to the Big Wing tactic. Radio communications were not good enough, he argued, to be able to control more than one squadron in the air. Operating more than a dozen aircraft increased the risk of collisions and 'friendly fire' tragedies, and anyway the German raids were too widespread to make a Big Wing practicable. The short time between the detection of an attacking force and its arrival meant there was not enough time to assemble a large force before the raiders had crossed the Channel.

Air Chief Marshal Dowding supported his protégé Park, maintaining that the more aircraft sent into battle the greater the risk of drastic losses of machines and pilots. But the argument was sharpened by the deep animosity between Park and Leigh-Mallory. It has been counted as a failure of Dowding's that he did not crush the time-wasting dispute between his two key subordinates.

Much of the resistance to the Big Wing theory turned out to be justified by events. Of the 32 occasions that a Big Wing was ordered up by Leigh-Mallory, only 7 resulted in combat, and only once were the Big Wing fighters the first to intercept. But at the time the pilots of the wings returned to their bases with impressive claims for the number of enemy aircraft downed. These turned out to be exaggerated. There was little doubt, however, that better use could have been made of 12 Group to strengthen the overall defensive strategy.

Only when the Luftwaffe turned its attention to London instead of the airfields did the Big Wing really become feasible. The switch ensured Fighter Command would survive and could at last concentrate on inflicting losses rather than on its own protection.

Dowding (*left*) and Leigh-Mallory (*right*) stand to attention at a march-past celebrating the third anniversary of Battle of Britain Day (15 September 1943).

On 24 August, Pilot Officer David Crook of 609 Squadron found himself impotent in the face of the enemy bombing run against Portsmouth.

> At about 4 p.m. we took off with orders to patrol Portsmouth at 10,000 feet … on this occasion we were the luckless ones sent low down to deal with any possible dive-bombers. We hated this - it's a much more comforting and reassuring feeling to be on top of everything than right underneath. Superior height is the whole secret of success in air fighting. However, 'orders is orders' and so we patrolled Portsmouth. Very soon a terrific A.A. [anti-aircraft] barrage sprang up ahead of us, looking exactly like a large number of dirty cotton-wool puffs in the sky. It was a most impressive barrage; besides all the guns at Portsmouth, all the warships in the harbour and dockyard were firing hard. A moment later, through the barrage and well above us, we saw a large German formation wheeling above Portsmouth. We were too low to be able to do anything about it … They were now releasing their bombs, and I cannot imagine a more flagrant case of indiscriminate bombing. The whole salvo fell right into the middle of Portsmouth, and I could see great spurts of flame and smoke springing up all over the place. We spent a very unpleasant few minutes right underneath the German formation, praying hard that their fighters would not come down on us. However, the danger passed and a very disgruntled squadron returned home, having seen so many Huns and yet not having fired a single round. [Crook, pp. 56-7]

-0-0-0-0-0-

Cripplegate was damaged, and bombs also landed on Oxford Street department stores. Nine people were killed and fifty-eight injured.

When Goering found out that Central London had been hit, in contravention of the strict rules laid down by the Führer, he was furious, demanding the names of the guilty aircrafts' captains and threatening them with transfer to the infantry. But there was no calling the bombs back, and now the nature of the wider struggle had been irreversibly altered. Within 24 hours, Bomber Command would launch its first attack on the city of Berlin.

25 August 1940 SUNDAY

Fair early in the morning, later cloudy.

In spite of fine weather on the Sunday morning, the Luftwaffe continued flying *Staffel*-strength formations up and down the Channel in an effort to exhaust the British defenders and lure Fighter Command away from its bases. However, neither Air Vice-Marshal Park nor his 10 Group counterpart, Quintin Brand, was inclined to take the bait.

Then, in the late afternoon, Ventnor radar station picked up several enemy formations to the west of the Cherbourg peninsula. Soon they grouped together and began to approach Weymouth Bay. There were more than 300 aircraft, made up of nearly 100 Ju88 bombers (of *Kampfgeschwader* 51 and 54), 120 Me110 twin-engine fighters (of *Zerstörergeschwader* 2 and 3 and *Lehrgeschwader* 1) and, following behind and above, a *Gruppe* of single-engine Me109s from *Jagdgeschwader* 53.

As the formation approached the coast, it split into three, targeting Portland, Weymouth and Warmwell. All the Middle Wallop, Exeter and Warmwell squadrons had been scrambled, with the Hurricanes of No. 17 ordered to defend Warmwell. One No. 17 Squadron pilot, Flying Officer Count Manfred Czernin, a naturalized Englishman of East European descent, attacked head on and then from the rear, shooting down three Me110s in quick succession. Two more fell to other pilots of 17 Squadron. But the squadron's leader, Cedric Williams, was himself downed by return fire from one of the twin-engine fighters, which severed his port wing and almost certainly killed the pilot. Swooping Me109s accounted for another Hurricane, but its pilot was rescued safely from the sea after baling out. One of the Me109s was shot down by the squadron in return.

Two Dornier Do217s cast a shadow over the Silvertown area of London's docklands. The oval structure (near the centre) is the West Ham greyhound-racing track.

'I remember it was a bright moonlit night'

Ron Harvey, who lived in Bethnal Green, London, was among the very first to be 'bombed out' on 24 August.

I was twelve years old at the time of the bomb. My brother was away in the army, there was my mum and dad and my sister and her boyfriend. When the warning sounded I was woken up by Mum or Dad and I went downstairs through the kitchen into the back yard to the shelter where there were already some neighbours. Being sleepy, I didn't realise at the time that my sister and her boyfriend had stayed in the house. I remember it was a bright moonlit night. Being twelve years old, I wasn't taking notice of the grown-ups. I was just at the door of the shelter and I heard this German plane come over and I knew it was German because of the drone of the engine. A few seconds passed and then there was a whistle of a bomb coming down. I was just by the door. Someone shouted 'There's something coming down. Duck!' and I ducked and I must have had my face to the right because I saw the two black balls fall on the house. The bombs exploded and it wasn't like a 'boom' or a blast, more like the crack of a thunderbolt, which echoed through the street for a few seconds and that was that. The shelter was full of dust and someone said, 'Gas!' but I knew it wasn't, it was brick dust. The next thing I remember is being out of the shelter … and there was all this activity going on – I suppose it was rescue work. And there were lots of people digging out my sister and her boyfriend. They were roughed up a bit, a few bruises; all the chimneys had come down. There was no damage for miles and miles around before that. I was going to school just round the corner, it was as if there wasn't a war on. That was the beginning of the war for me, when things started happening. [Quoted in Parker, p.241]

-o-o-o-o-o-

OPPOSITE
A wartime poster urges preparation for a quick getaway or some sudden fire-dampening. The once theoretical danger of attack while you slept became ever more real as autumn approached.

All but seven of the forty-odd bombers that No. 17 Squadron encountered were turned back, but those few had a lucky strike on Warmwell. The station's sick bay and two hangars were hit, but, more importantly, a bomb that landed outside the airfield cut the station's telephone and teleprinter cables.

Meanwhile, 87 Squadron's twelve Hurricanes from Exeter went in against the Ju88s heading for Portland, while 609 Squadron's Spitfires from Middle Wallop targeted the Me110s. 'My mouth feels hellishly dry,' No. 87 Squadron pilot Ian 'Widge' Gleed later wrote of the encounter. 'There is a strong sinking feeling in my breast. Thank God a doctor isn't listening to my heart. It's absolutely banging away.' [Quoted by Adams, p. 33] No. 87 Squadron's Laurence 'Rubber' Thoroughgood shot down one of the bombers – his first and only kill of the battle – and No. 609, with the crucial advantage of height, accounted for two of the Me110s and another five damaged. The Spitfires of Pilot Officer David Crook and Flying Officer

LOOK
before you sleep

ALL WINDOWS AND INNER DOORS OPEN?

WATER IN BUCKETS?

SAND IN BUCKETS?

GAS MASK, CLOTHES AND TORCH HANDY?

GOOD NIGHT!

Printed for H.M. Stationery Office by Johnson, Riddle & Co., Ltd., Penge, S.E.20.   51-7372

Piotr Ostaszewski-Ostoja were hit, but both safely returned to Middle Wallop.

Messerschmitt Me109s then dived on the mêlée, forcing the British fighters to break off from the vulnerable bombers and Me110s. No. 87 Squadron pilot Sid Wakeling was turning to face the new threat when a cannon shell ripped into his cockpit. His comrades heard him over the R/T saying that his hand had been blown off, but that he was going to try to land his Hurricane. But the aircraft was now on fire and spiralling down towards the Dorset countryside. At the last moment Wakeling was seen jumping clear, but his parachute failed to open and he died as he hit the ground (see also page 245). Wakeling was the day's sole casualty from 87 Squadron, which quickly shot down three of the Me109s. The squadron accounted for two more Messerschmitts as the raiders turned for home. Other squadrons, arriving as the dogfight drifted west of Portland, were less successful, and a further six British fighters were lost.

Laurence Thoroughgood later summed up the spirit of the pilots at this time: 'We were fighting over our home ground and this had a great bearing on our morale. The Luftwaffe certainly had the numbers but this only seemed to spur us on. We certainly got tired but were fit and young.' [Quoted in Bickers, p. 245] In fact, some squadrons were reaching the end of their physical and mental reserves. No. 54 Squadron, down to only seven serviceable Spitfires, was desperately tired and in need of a rest. For now, though, they would have to fight on. No. 32 Squadron, based at Biggin Hill, had been in combat since May. At 6.30pm on 25 August they were in the forefront of an interception over Dover. Kesselring had sent over a raid of more than 100 aircraft, and Park had responded with six squadrons. No. 32 Squadron dived on the bombers – Dornier Do17s – shooting down one, but were in turn pounced on by Me109s, which shot down two of its number, killing a pilot. This meant that the squadron now had hardly enough pilots for a full flight. Two days later, No. 32 was withdrawn to Northumberland. 'We were down to seven pilots,' said pilot Peter Brothers. 'Funnily enough, of the original pre-war squadron, many had been shot down, wounded, some burned, but nobody had been killed. It was only the new boys who had died.' [Brothers, recording] The vulnerability of inexperienced fighter pilots would be gruesomely demonstrated as Dowding was now forced to move untried squadrons to the frontline.

26 August 1940 MONDAY

Mostly cloudy, with brighter patches in the south.

From first light on Monday, high-level Luftwaffe reconnaissance planes criss-crossed the skies over 11 Group's area, looking for concentrations of fighters on the ground. By late morning, more than 150 German aircraft were approaching from the direction of Lille, crossing the coast near Deal in Kent. Most of them headed west, while some Me109s went on a shooting spree across the Kent countryside, and a number of Heinkels turned for Folkestone, which was bombed. No. 616 Squadron, only recently moved south from Church Fenton, was vectored from Kenley to intercept, but it arrived too late to catch the bombers, encountering instead a great mass of about 50 Me109s over Dungeness. As the Spitfires desperately climbed in an effort to get the sun behind them, they were bounced by

		SINGLE-ENGINE AIRCRAFT			MULTI-ENGINE AIRCRAFT						PASS-ENGER	INSTR./CLOUD FLYING [Incl. in cols. (1) to (10)]	
		DAY		NIGHT		DAY			NIGHT					
AL	PILOT	DUAL	PILOT	DUAL	1ST PILOT	2ND PILOT	DUAL	1ST PILOT	2ND PILOT			DUAL	PILOT
)	(2)	(3)	(4)	(5)	(6)	(7)	(10)					(12)	(13)

Hitler's chief of propaganda Joseph Goebbels (in raincoat) inspects the damage done by RAF bombs dropped on Berlin in August 1940.

TARGET: BERLIN

In retaliation for the bombs dropped on London on 24 August 1940, Bomber Command launched its first raid on Berlin. Flying Officer Wilf Burnett piloted a Hampden bomber during the attack on the German capital. 'We had expected Berlin to be one of our targets at one time or another once the hours of darkness allowed us to cross the coast in safety. The orders came through on 25 August. We were given industrial targets in Berlin. All the crews wanted to have a go, purely and simply for no other reason than to refute Goering's boast that Berlin would never be bombed.' [Quoted in Parker, p. 245]

Burnett's Hampden was cold and cramped for its crew of four. Flying at 10,000 feet, together with another 80 Hampdens and Wellingtons, they followed the Dutch coastline and then headed inland, guided by moonlight falling on rivers and canals below. But as they approached Berlin, after about four hours' flying time, thick cloud descended.

The bombers' principal target was the Siemens-Halske factory, but the anti-aircraft fire kept them too high to allow them to aim their bombs accurately, so they landed on fields and woods and also on some residential areas of the city. No-one was killed, but the raid was an embarrassment to Goering, who had indeed boasted that no bomb would ever land on Berlin. 'Berliners are stunned,' wrote the American journalist William Shirer in his diary. 'They did not think it could ever happen.' Churchill was delighted, writing the next day to the Chief of the Air Staff: 'I want you to hit them hard and Berlin is the place to hit them.' The prime minister ordered further raids for 28, 30 and 31 August.

'Obviously it was going to crash'

Flying Officer Count Manfred Czernin flew with No. 17 Squadron's Hurricanes on 25 August. He recounted crisply his experience of a day's successful duelling with Messerschmitt Me110s.

```
    One broke. Chased and fired from above. Nose went down, EA [enemy
aircraft] burst into flames and crashed straight into the sea. Climbed
and resumed attack. Beam attack and 110 broke away pouring smoke and
went into a vertical dive, burst into flames and crashed into the sea.
Resumed attack and had to break off as Spitfire on its tail firing at
him. Shook him off and attacked 110 and after long burst from quarter
astern, nose dropped and it lost height … and glided down with both
engines out. Broke off as obviously it was going to crash and saw two
Spitfires attack it again. One baled out and then EA nose dived into
a wood two miles SE of Dorchester and burst into flames. [Quoted in
Franks, pp. 32-3]
```

-0-0-0-0-0-

a further 30 Me109s, which, in 30 seconds, shot down four of them, with two pilots killed and two wounded. A further two Spitfires force-landed after being hit.

The main German formation, ploughing on over Canterbury and then Maidstone, was now involved in a long dogfight with some 40 Hurricanes and 30 Spitfires. Again, Park sent up the Defiants of 264 Squadron from Hornchurch. This time they succeeded in downing one Dornier and damaging another, but they were then jumped by two *Gruppen* of Me109s. Three of the Defiants were shot down, completing the almost total destruction of the squadron's fighting ability. As the Me109s chased the survivors away, using up precious fuel, No. 1 (Canadian) Squadron rushed at the Dorniers, only to be caught in a crossfire that downed three of their Hurricanes. Three more fighter squadrons joined in and the Me109s started deserting their bombers as their fuel supplies dwindled. In the end, only a handful of Dorniers got through to bomb Biggin Hill and Kenley, where little damage was caused.

By 1pm, the raiders were flying back over the Channel. They were quickly replaced by fighter sweeps and a dummy raid north of the Thames Estuary. This consisted of Dorniers empty of bombs, but with a swarm of Me109s lurking above. No. 85 Squadron was scrambled and managed to attack the Dorniers of *Kampfgeschwader* 3 in a head-on charge without falling prey to the Me109s. Several of the bombers were damaged for the loss of one British aircraft, whose pilot baled out safely.

A new enemy raid was detected at 2pm off the coast of Belgium. This, too, headed towards the Thames Estuary, closely watched by Park, who surmised that it was aimed at Hornchurch, North Weald or London itself. This time, with the radar picture confused, the size of the German raid was overestimated, leading Park to put ten squadrons into action against what turned out to be about 80 Dorniers of *Kampfgeschwader* 2 and 3, escorted by 40 Me109s and the same number of Me110s.

South of Clacton, part of the German force – including about half of the bombers – swung east and appeared to be heading directly for Central London. Park ordered up almost all of the rest of his forces and called on 12 Group to defend his northern airfields.

Meanwhile, the northerly thrust of 40 Dornier Do17s crossed the coast just south of Colchester, where it encountered heavy flak. Most of the bombers turned back, but half a dozen Dorniers pressed on, bombing Debden. Three airmen were killed, buildings destroyed and an aircraft on the ground badly damaged. There was no sign of the promised cover from 12 Group. No. 19 Squadron, from Duxford, just ten miles away, arrived only after the bombers had departed.

The six Dorniers escaped, but the main home-bound formation was now intercepted by 310 Squadron from Duxford. It was the first combat for the Free Czech squadron. Although plagued by problems with their radio transmitters, the Czechs showed impressive aggression. One of the pilots, Sergeant Edward Prchal, chased a Dornier for 30 miles before shooting it down, only to be set upon by an Me109, which hit his Hurricane in the wing and forced an emergency landing near Upminster. Another Dornier and one Me110 were also shot down by 310 Squadron, for the loss of three Hurricanes, with all the Czech pilots baling out safely. Then, No. 111 Hurricane Squadron arrived from Martlesham, along with 56 Squadron from North Weald. Five further Luftwaffe aircraft were shot down, although both squadrons lost two fighters each.

The other part of the raid – heading, it seemed, for London – was met by a large force of fighters just north of Southend. Once again, the Me109s' dwindling fuel reserves forced them to leave the bombers to their fate. Several Dorniers and Me110s were shot down, and a signal flare from the leading aircraft aborted the raid. The German formation turned south, dropping its bombs at random over Kent, on Rochester, Maidstone, Ashford, Canterbury and Dungeness.

Following a pattern now established, the afternoon saw Generalfeldmarschall Sperrle throw his forces from *Luftflotte* 3 into the battle. At around 4pm, some 50 He111s (of *Kampfgeschwader* 5) with 107 Me109s and Me110s set off across the Channel heading towards Portsmouth and Southampton. Eight squadrons were sent up in response, but only Nos 43, 615 and 602 succeeded in intercepting, shooting down four He111s and four Me109s for the loss of two Hurricanes and two Spitfires.

Pilot Officer Harold North of 43 Squadron was one of three Fighter Command pilots wounded. Having led his Yellow Section in a head-on attack on the Heinkels, he dived down, almost being hit by the bombs being jettisoned hastily by the enemy. He then climbed back into the attack, hitting a Heinkel, which started belching smoke. At that moment he was wounded in the shoulder by cannon fire, but continued firing the rest of his ammunition into a straggling Heinkel before baling out.

Most of the Heinkels dumped their bombs into the sea, and there was only light damage to the coastal towns. It was to be the last major raid from Sperrle's *Luftflotte* for three weeks, as his bomber force was redirected to night attacks on industrial targets in the English Midlands.

continued on page 244

DOUGLAS BADER, FIGHTER ACE

Several of the most successful, top-scoring Battle of Britain pilots became instant celebrities through exposure in the press and on the BBC. The most prominent was Douglas Bader (1910–82), whose determination to fly and fight despite the handicap of being a double amputee seemed a symbol of national resolve. His ebullience and love of the limelight, however, sometimes seemed at odds with the propaganda effort to present the pilots as ordinary young men and reluctant warriors to whom fighting did not come naturally.

Bader was born in London in 1910, the son of a soldier who died in 1922 of shrapnel wounds received in the First World War. His childhood heroes were the fighter aces of the Royal Flying Corps, and he was determined to become a pilot himself.

He won a scholarship to St Edward's School in Oxford, where he excelled at sports, then qualified as a cadet at RAF Cranwell. Finishing very close to the top of his class, he was commissioned into No. 23 Squadron RAF in July 1930. A year later he was selected to fly in the elite RAF aerobatic team. Its precision stunts and choreographed displays were a highlight of the June 1931 Hendon air show, with the press describing Bader's performance as 'the day's best event'. But Bader had a strong streak of disobedience and repeatedly ignored orders forbidding low flying.

On 14 December 1931, while visiting Reading Aero Club, he attempted one of his specialities – slow rolls at very low altitude – in his British Bulldog fighter. Regulations forbade this man-oeuvre below 1000 feet; Bader attempted it, apparently on a dare, below 30 feet. His left wing clipped the ground and he crashed, suffering appalling injuries. Both legs were amputated, one above the knee and one below. Bader later recorded the incident in laconic style in his logbook: 'Crashed slow-rolling near ground. Bad show.' He was still only 21.

In 1932, after a long convalescence, he was fitted with a pair of artificial legs and, through remarkable determination and persistence, he learned to walk again. In time, he was able to drive a specially modified car, play golf and even dance. His comeback instilled in him an unshakeable self-confidence. 'Don't listen to anyone who tells you that you can't do this or that,' he said. 'Never, never let them persuade you that things are too difficult or impossible.' [Quoted in Lucas, p. 60] In the short term, however, his efforts to remain an RAF pilot were unsuccessful.

After the outbreak of war in 1939, things changed. A long campaign overcame official resistance and Bader was re-called to service. In February 1940, he was posted to No. 19 Squadron, based at RAF Duxford. George Unwin, who shared a room with him, put up with the scraping and squeaking as Bader adjusted his legs with a file and a tin of oil.

In April 1940, Bader left 19 Squadron to become a flight commander with No. 222 Squadron, also based at Duxford, and while patrolling the coast near Dunkirk in his

Spitfire he shot down an Me109. A day or two later he bagged a Dornier Do17. His confidence and aggression brought him the command of 242 Squadron at the end of June 1940. This was a Hurricane unit based at Coltishall, made up mainly of Canadians who had suffered high losses in the Battle of France. Despite their initial resistance to the new commanding officer, the pilots were won over by Bader's strong personality and perseverance.

On 11 July 1940, Bader scored his first kill with his new squadron. 'I am not one of those who see war as a cricket match where you first give anything to defeat the opponent and then shake hands,' he said. 'You knew you were flying with an ace in every sense of the word,' commented fellow pilot Alan Smith. 'A bloke who knew exactly what he was doing, who was on the ball, was afraid of nothing, and a great leader.' [Quoted in Brickhill, p. 44] But Bader's bombastic nature and tendency to dramatize was in many ways the antithesis of the 'fighter boy' ethos of ironic understatement. Many found him easier to admire than to like. His forceful character inevitably attracted criticism, and he was not universally popular with his comrades. 'He made me sick,' said John Freeborn, who flew with No. 74 Squadron. 'I've never met such a self-opinionated fool in all my life.' But for every one who hated him, there was another who adored him. 'I never met anyone with such charisma,' said Max Williams, one of the groundcrew for Bader's squadron. 'He was awesome, marvellous.' [Quotations above from www.channel4.com]

As a leading advocate, along with Air Vice-Marshal Leigh-Mallory, of the Big Wing tactic, Bader was able to put his theory into practice in the last phases of the Battle of Britain. In 1941, he was promoted to wing commander. Stationed at Tangmere, Bader led his wing of Spitfires on sweeps over northwestern Europe throughout the summer campaign. By August 1941, Bader had claimed 22 German aircraft shot down, the fifth-highest total in the RAF; but that same month his Spitfire was hit, and he was forced to bale out over occupied France.

His German captors treated him with great respect. General Adolf Galland (see page 133), the German flying ace, offered the RAF safe passage to drop off replacements for Bader's damaged 'tin leg'. Nevertheless, Bader tried to escape from the hospital where he was recovering, and over the next few years he made so many attempts at escape that the Germans threatened to take away his legs. In August 1942, he was finally dispatched to Colditz Castle, where guards outnumbered prisoners. Liberated in April 1945, he requested a return to action but was turned down.

Bader was given the honour of leading a victory fly-past of 300 aircraft over London in June 1945. He left the RAF soon afterwards and died in 1982.

OPPOSITE
Douglas Bader, in October 1940.

RIGHT
The indomitable Bader swings one of his 'tin legs' into a Spitfire at North Weald on 15 September 1945.

LESLIE CARR

TEMPER DASH with DISCRETION

Do
atta

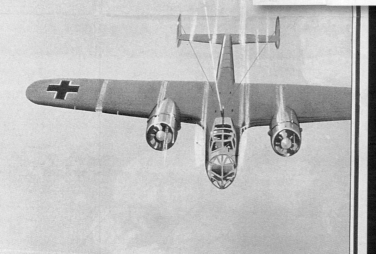

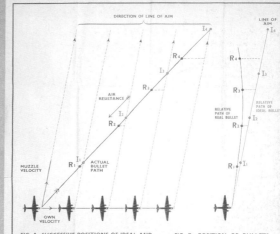

DIRECTION OF LINE OF AIM

LINE OF AIM

AIR RESISTANCE

MUZZLE VELOCITY

ACTUAL BULLET PATH

RELATIVE PATH OF REAL BULLET

RELATIVE PATH OF IDEAL BULLET

OWN VELOCITY

FIG. A—SUCCESSIVE POSITIONS OF IDEAL AND REAL BULLETS FIRED SIMULTANEOUSLY

1. SINCE BULLETS ARE FIRED FROM A MOVING GUN, ACTUAL BULLET PATH IS FOUND BY COMPOUNDING MUZZLE VELOCITY WITH OWN VELOCITY. BOTH IDEAL AND REAL BULLETS MOVE ALONG THIS SAME STRAIGHT PATH.
2. IDEAL BULLET IS UNRESISTED BY AIR AND TRAVELS WITH CONSTANT VELOCITY. IDEAL BULLET, THEREFORE, REMAINS ON LINE OF AIM.
3. REAL BULLET IS RETARDED BY AIR AND LAGS BEHIND IDEAL BULLET. REAL BULLET, THEREFORE, DEPARTS FROM LINE OF AIM BY RAPIDLY INCREASING AMOUNTS.

FIG. B—POSITION OF BULLETS RELATIVE TO GUNNER

1. IDEAL BULLET APPEARS TO TRAVEL IN THE DIRECTION OF FIRE AND REMAINS ON LINE OF AIM.
2. REAL BULLET APPEARS TO HAVE A CURVED PATH, TRAILING BEHIND THE LINE OF AIM.
3. TO ALLOW FOR THIS TRAIL, LINE OF AIM MUST BE TURNED TOWARDS NOSE OF OWN AEROPLANE.
4. AMOUNT OF ALLOWANCE DEPENDS ON RANGE, LAYING OF GUN, HEIGHT AND AIR SPEED OF OWN AEROPLANE, AND TYPE OF BULLET.

PRINCIPLES OF DEFLEXION FIRE (FREE GUN)—

BULLET TRAIL

See also A.P. 1730 B, Vol. I, Chap. I

ABOVE

An Air Ministry graphic suggests how aircraft gunners, when aiming, need to compensate for air resistance and the speed of their own aircraft.

LEFT

Another Air Ministry poster warns against the dangers of over-exuberance in taking on the enemy.

Drawing by THE AEROPLANE

MAY. 1940	AIR DIAGRAM 1304			
ISSUE NO.	1			
DATE	MAY. 1940			

FOR OFFICIAL USE ONLY

eagerness spoil a combined entally make you a 'sitter' the enemy.

'One lives and one learns – if lucky'

On 25 August, Pilot Officer David Crook's eagerness to engage the enemy in his Spitfire almost proved fatal. It was a salutary lesson.

We sighted a very big German formation coming over the coast below us, and the C.O. swung us into line astern and manoeuvred into a good position for the attack. Then, down we went. I happened to be almost last on the line, and I shall never forget seeing the long line of Spitfires ahead, sweeping down and curling round at terrific speed to strike right into the middle of the German formation. It was superb!

The great weight and fierceness of this onslaught split up the Huns immediately and they scattered all over the place, with Spitfires chasing them right and left. I saw an Me110 below me and dived down on him going very fast indeed. Unfortunately I was going too fast and in the heat of the moment I forgot to throttle back with the result that I came up behind him at terrific speed and overshot him badly. I got a good burst of fire at practically point blank range as he flashed by and then I had to turn away very violently or I should have collided with him. His rear gunner took advantage of my mistake and fired a short burst at me, and put several bullets through my wing, very close to the fuselage and only a few inches from my leg.

When I turned round to look for the Hun he had disappeared. Though there was a lot of fighting in progress and machines were turning and diving all over the sky, I had dived down below them all and couldn't do much about it … I returned to base absolutely furious with myself for having missed that Me110. He was right in front of me, and if only I had not gone at him so wildly I should have had him easily.

Anyway, it taught me to be a little more cool in future. One lives and one learns - if lucky. [Crook, pp.59-60]

-0-0-0-0-0-

It had been a hard day for both sides. The Luftwaffe had lost 41 aircraft more than the RAF. But Fighter Command had suffered badly too, with 26 fighters destroyed and 3 very badly damaged, against a total loss of only 17 Luftwaffe fighters. Air Vice-Marshal Park's greatest concern that evening, however, was the failure of 12 Group to protect Debden, which placed a further strain on his working relationship with Leigh-Mallory. The next day he reported: 'Thanks to the friendly co-operation afforded by 10 Group they are always prepared to detail two to four squadrons to engage from the West mass attacks ... Up to date 12 Group ... have not shown the same desire to co-operate by dispatching their squadrons to the places requested ... When 12 Group offered assistance and were requested by us to patrol our aerodromes, their squadrons did not in fact patrol over our aerodromes.' [Quoted in James, p. 356] Park was already inclined to blame Leigh-Mallory for the attack on North Weald on 24 August. Now Debden was added to his list of grievances.

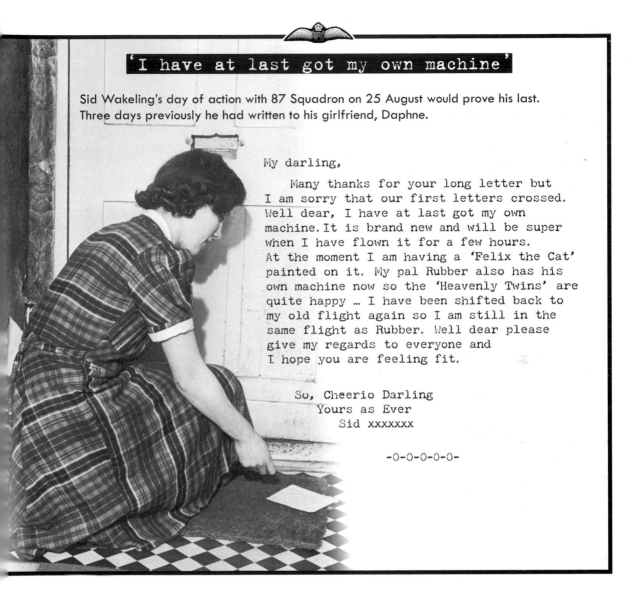

'I have at last got my own machine'

Sid Wakeling's day of action with 87 Squadron on 25 August would prove his last. Three days previously he had written to his girlfriend, Daphne.

My darling,

Many thanks for your long letter but I am sorry that our first letters crossed. Well dear, I have at last got my own machine. It is brand new and will be super when I have flown it for a few hours. At the moment I am having a 'Felix the Cat' painted on it. My pal Rubber also has his own machine now so the 'Heavenly Twins' are quite happy … I have been shifted back to my old flight again so I am still in the same flight as Rubber. Well dear please give my regards to everyone and I hope you are feeling fit.

So, Cheerio Darling
Yours as Ever
Sid xxxxxxx

-0-0-0-0-0-

TUESDAY 27 August 1940

During the night of 26/27 August, more than 200 bombers raided Bournemouth, Plymouth, Coventry and Birmingham. But bad weather on the Tuesday morning brought a respite, and the Germans flew only reconnaissance sorties. Meanwhile, at the German bases in northern France and the Low Countries, plans were being drawn up for ever tighter escorts for the bomber fleets. It was apparent that British fighters had struggled to get at the bombers when they were surrounded on all sides by Me109s. However, Luftwaffe fighter pilots vigorously protested that this policy meant that they would never surprise Fighter Command's Spitfires and Hurricanes. Instead of going after them, they would have to wait for the enemy to come to them. The policy confirmed that the destruction of RAF airfields and planes on the ground had taken priority over destroying Fighter Command's planes in the air.

Rain in central and eastern parts; cloudy over Channel.

continued on page 248

The Czech pilots of 310 Squadron and their British flight commanders gather in front of a Hurricane at Duxford (7 September 1940).

'The Czechs really did a fine job'

Squadron Leader G.D.M. Blackwood of 310 Squadron had to bale out on 26 August, but some of the Czech pilots he was leading had better luck.

    The Czechs really did a fine job despite their aggressive attitude.
I think their only problem was that as soon as they saw an enemy that
would make for a possible target, nothing else mattered. On that day,
I picked out a Dornier that was not in formation and made him my
target. I fired a short burst, then another, and the bomber started
to wobble a bit. Just then, I smelt burning, and it wasn't long before
the starboard fuel tank burst into flame. I undid my harness and the
oxygen tube, opened the hood and turned the aircraft upside down and
fell out.
    One of the Czechs, Emil Fechtner, managed to get in one of our
first successes of the day. By all accounts he started his firing way
too early, but kept his finger on the button, and at about 100 yards
a [Messerschmitt] 110 belched smoke from one of its engines. But then
he was jumped on by half a dozen 109s, so discretion being better
than valour, he went up into the cloud cover and disappeared from
sight. [www.battleofbritain1940.net]

-0-0-0-0-0-

'A searing pain in my right leg'

Flight Lieutenant Charles MacLean, of 602 Squadron, survived the aerial battles of 26 August, over Portsmouth, but not without consequences.

```
     On August 26, there was a heavy attack on Portsmouth. I was leading
A flight … I followed the formation back over the Channel and was en-
gaged in doing head-on attacks on the leading aircraft of this big
wave of bombers … on the second one, I'd slowed down to about 160 mph
to increase the amount of time for shooting. Suddenly there was a
frightful bang and a searing pain in my right leg about six inches
above the ankle. I looked down to find my right foot hanging loose,
all messed up with blood and sinews. I was at 16,000 feet, the pain
was fiendish and I thought I'd have to bail out. I threw back the
hood, took off my mask and looked down at the sea. It looked beautiful
- blue and inviting. Then I tried my throttle and the engine was an-
swering … I flew back to Tangmere as fast as I could. I was worried
about the amount of blood that I was losing but it didn't seem to be
coming out very fast and I thought there'd be enough to last. Indeed
there was and I landed back at Tangmere with the wheels up … I retired
to hospital where it was the usual old story. They tried to pretend
that they hadn't taken the leg off but    it was pretty obvious that
they had. [MacLean, recording]
```

-0-0-0-0-0-

A forlorn Hurricane lies in a field near Great Yarmouth, Norfolk, after its pilot crash-landed following a dogfight (1940).

Air Chief Marshal Dowding took the opportunity of the lull to rotate some of his squadrons. No. 65, down to 12 pilots and only 9 aircraft, was moved from Hornchurch, Essex, to Church Fenton in Yorkshire; it was replaced by 603 Squadron, currently at Turnhouse in Scotland. No. 54 Squadron looked on enviously, but instead of being moved it was supplied with fresh aircraft, bringing its number back up to 12 Spitfires.

28 August 1940 WEDNESDAY

Mostly fine and fair, with cloud in Dover Straits.

Wednesday would be very busy for the exhausted pilots of 54 Squadron. The cloud and drizzle of the previous day had cleared, and at first light came the now-familiar reconnaissance sorties. At 8am a raid was plotted building up over the Pas de Calais. Thirty-two Hurricanes from Nos 79, 85, 501 and 615 squadrons were sent up to intercept, along with 12 Defiants from No. 264 Squadron. All made contact as two heavily escorted formations – one of Heinkels and one of Dorniers – crossed the coast northwest of Dover. Twenty-three Dorniers of *Kampfgeschwader* 3 made for Eastchurch, Kent, while twenty-seven Heinkels from *Kampfgeschwader* 53 headed for Rochford in Essex.

No. 79 Squadron attacked the Heinkels but was engaged by the escorting fighters. In the meantime, No. 264's pilots went in on the attack against the bombers, claiming one shot down and another damaged; but they were pounced on by Me109s lurking above. Their Boulton Paul Defiants were slow and vulnerable, and their gun turrets could not fire forwards, rendering the aircraft vulnerable in daytime action. Four of them were downed, and a further three damaged. It was the end of the road for the Defiant. After today's events, the aircraft was withdrawn from daylight duties.

One of 264's pilot officers, Jim Bailey, aged 21, had a lucky escape when the Me109s 'bounced us from behind. My engine stopped and I had to dive for the ground whilst pretending to be in a spin ... I had to crash land. As this was August the ground was hard and the field I chose had a double hedge. The fields of Kent were obstructed by wooden poles to prevent German glider troops landing, so I had to weave my way between (them) before hitting the hedge. As I climbed from the cockpit, my super air gunner Sgt Oswald Hardy said to me "Did you see this?" He pointed out that a number of the poles had connecting electric cables. I had flown underneath without even having noticed!' [Bailey, 'Defiant Survivor']

The Heinkels ploughed on to the Rochford area, but heavy flak disrupted their bombing runs and they inflicted little damage. The Dorniers got through to Eastchurch, protected from the attacks of 501 and 605 squadrons by their escort of about 60 Me109s from *Jagdgeschwader* 1 and 51. Several RAF bombers were hit on the ground and buildings destroyed, but the airfield, which was primarily used by Coastal Command, remained operational.

A few hours later, bombers were back over Rochford. A mass of Dorniers of *Kampfgeschwader* 3, heavily escorted by Me109s and Me110s, had approached from the Thames Estuary. No. 54 Squadron was scrambled, as well as No. 1 Squadron. 'They covered the whole sky ahead,' said 54 Squadron's Al Deere, 'a solid mass of aircraft from about 15,000ft up to 32,000ft at which height a dozen or so 109s

weaves along in the wake of hundreds of escort fighters below.' [Deere, p. 133] One of the Me109s was shot down, and the airfield again escaped serious damage, although Al Deere was shot down for the third time – this time, he believed, by a Spitfire.

At around 4pm, radar plotters tracked a third incoming raid and, with several flights protecting the sector stations, Nos 85, 54, 56, 151 and 603 squadrons were vectored to intercept near the coast. But this time there were no bombers to be found. Instead, the raid consisted of five *Gruppen* of Me110s and six of Me109s. It was the sort of fighter-to-fighter combat that the controllers were anxious to avoid. The defenders, though, were in an advantageous position. No. 85 Squadron, led by Peter Townsend, was at 18,000 feet above Dungeness when they saw Me109s below them. Although ordered to ignore fighters and go for the bombers, they had height and the sun behind them. The temptation was too strong. Squadron Leader Peter Townsend called out, 'Down we go! Pick your own.' 'It was as if we had flushed a covey of partridges,' he later wrote. 'One pulled across me in a steep left hand turn, giving me a perfect shot. It rolled over belching white smoke – a hit in the cooling system.' He fastened onto another Me109, but it dived and the Hurricane could not keep up even at full boost. Townsend followed, firing short bursts in the hope of slowing the Me109 down. 'But in the heat of the chase I forgot

Churchill watches the Luftwaffe's attacks in progress on 28 August, from an observation post at Dover Castle.

the basic rules, until suddenly, wham! A bullet splintered in the cockpit. Never did I get out of anybody's way so fast. Stick forward, bottom rudder, engine cuts, clouds of black smoke.' Townsend made it back to his base at Croydon. [Townsend, *Duel of Eagles*, p. 400]

Sam Allard, another 85 Squadron pilot, shot down an Me 109 about three miles off Folkestone. As the Me109s raced for home, the squadron followed, shooting down three more into the sea. The action, 85 Squadron's most successful of the Battle of Britain, was watched from below by Winston Churchill, who was visiting Dover.

The other intercepting squadrons were less fortunate. No. 603, in action on the very day of its arrival in the south, lost three of its Spitfires, with two pilots killed. Richard Hillary, who would later write *The Last Enemy* about life and death as a fighter pilot, was one of three of the squadron who arrived late to the fight after repairs to his aircraft. 'We landed at Hornchurch at about seven o'clock to receive our first shock,' he wrote. 'Instead of one section there were four Squadrons at readiness; 603 were already in action. They started coming in about half an hour after we landed, smoke stains along the leading edges of the wings showing that all the guns had been fired. They had acquitted themselves well although caught at a disadvantage of height.' In all, the day's combat had cost Fighter Command 17 aircraft.

That night saw the first mass raid of about 150 bombers by the Luftwaffe. The target was the port of Liverpool, where vital supplies from the United States were being unloaded. The bombing was inaccurate, falling on a wide area and doing little

OPPOSITE

A striking depiction of anti-aircraft guns (1940) by C.R.W. Nevinson (1889–1946). An official war artist during the First World War, Nevinson's output during the second war was to be severely limited by the stroke he suffered in 1942.

'Stand by for head-on attack'

Squadron Leader Peter Townsend led 85 Squadron on its head-on attack into a pack of Dorniers on 26 August.

```
     There was one way to get at the bombers without getting mixed up
with the fighter escort. 'Stand by for head-on attack and watch out
for those little fellows above,' I called. Then I brought the squadron
round steadily in a wide turn, moving into echelon as we levelled out
about two miles ahead on a collision course. Ease the throttle to
reduce the closing speed - which anyway allowed only a few seconds'
fire. Get a bead on them right away, hold it, and never mind the
streams of tracer darting overhead. Just keep on pressing on the but-
ton until you think you're going to collide - then stick hard forward.
Under the shock of 'negative G' your stomach jumps into your mouth,
dust and muck fly up from the cockpit floor into your eyes and your
head cracks on the roof as you break away below. [Townsend, Duel of
Eagles, p. 392]


               -0-0-0-0-0-
```

'The usual mad rush to cockpits'

By 28 August, Al Deere, of No. 54 Squadron, had become used to the frantic routines of scrambling; but once in flight that day, he experienced a novel sensation.

```
    The telephone bell: orders to scramble; the usual mad rush to cock-
pits; a feverish pushing of starter buttons; a roar as twelve Merlins
sprang into life; a jostling for places at the take-off end; and the
squadron was airborne for another combat. Up and up we climbed; first
Gravesend was left behind, then Chatham, then Canterbury, and finally
Dover, plainly visible to twelve pairs of eyes which gazed down as it
passed below the squadron, now at 33,000ft. This was the highest we
had been and, in the jargon of the fighter pilots, 'we were hanging
on our airscrews'. It was cold, extremely cold; my feet were like
lumps of ice and tiny prickles of cold stabbed at my legs, just
above the knees. [Deere, p.147]
```

-0-0-0-0-0-

Another day, another scramble, as pilots rush to get airborne in summer 1940.

Eric Kennington painted this intense portrait of Richard Hillary, the dauntless 603 Squadron pilot who suffered terrible burn injuries to his hands and face on 3 September 1940. Hillary struggled back into flying, and told his story in *The Last Enemy*, but a second crash killed him in 1942.

damage to the docks but causing casualties. Smaller forces hit Birmingham, Bristol, Bournemouth, Coventry, Derby, Manchester and Sheffield. Civilian deaths and injuries were mounting. All over the country air-raid sirens dragged people out of bed and into the shelters, and shut down factories and workshops. The raiders had little to fear from night-fighters. Blenheims were sent up, but only one enemy bomber was sighted.

THURSDAY 29 August 1940

This morning saw blank radar screens everywhere. The survivors of 264 Squadron flew out of Hornchurch, to be replaced by No. 222 Squadron from Kirton-in-Lindsey. The newcomers had much to learn. They parked their Spitfires wingtip to

Showers, with bright intervals; cloudy over Channel and Straits of Dover.

THE GYRO GUNSIGHT

From the 1930s the Royal Aircraft Establishment at Farnborough, Surrey, worked to devise a gunsight that would automatically aim the fighter's guns at a point ahead of the enemy so that the rounds and the target would arrive at the same place at the same time.

In 1937, the design of the Gyro gunsight (GGS) was completed. A rapidly spinning mirror was mounted on a Hooke's universal joint, which connected it to a hemisphere of thin copper rotating between the poles of two powerful magnets.

Although the GGS was used to great effect during the Battle of Britain, there were only a few of them available. In 1940, the standard gunsight was the reflector sight, which projected an illuminated ring, usually with a central cross, onto an oval glass behind the windscreen. The pilot adjusted the ring to fit the target size.

King George VI tries out a reflector gunsight as he tours an Operation Training Unit of Bomber Command (19 July 1940).

wingtip, peacetime style, and had to be told that this was inadvisable in the current circumstances. At Kenley, 615 Squadron left and 253 Squadron came with 18 Hurricanes from Turnhouse.

It was not until about 3pm that the first large build-up of enemy aircraft was plotted over the French coast. Park reacted forcefully, sending up nine squadrons to join the four already patrolling in the air. The pilots were under instructions to avoid the attritional fighter-versus-fighter combat of the day before. But the radar picture was deceptive. There was actually only a small number of bombers among the mass of German aircraft; it was mainly composed of fighters – more than 500 Me109s of *Jagdgeschwader* 3, 26, 51, 52 and 54, together with 150 Me110s from *Zerstörergeschwader* 26 and 76.

No. 85 Squadron spotted the enemy formation as it crossed the coast just before 4pm. 'I had sighted eighteen Heinkels coming in over Beachy Head several thousand feet above us,' wrote Squadron Leader Peter Townsend. 'As we climbed, hanging on our propellers, the blue above glinted with little silver flashes. Me109s! As I watched, they grew in number until there were myriads of them – we thought some two hundred in all ... Labouring up painfully beneath the Heinkels, our twelve Hurricanes were sitting ducks ... Then the inevitable – down came the Me109s and it was each one for himself. When my Me109 came, firing, I whipped

HIGH-OCTANE FUEL

RAF aircraft gained a very significant power increase from using 100-octane fuel, while the Luftwaffe had to make do with 60- or 70-octane. Achieving an octane rating of 100 required a very complicated process and a large and expensive refinery plant. The necessary 'alkylation' process was pioneered by scientists at the Anglo-Iranian Oil Company's (AIOC) laboratory at Sunbury-on-Thames, but it was the US Army Air Corps that first produced 100-octane aviation fuel. In 1937, engine-specialist Air Commodore Rod Banks urged the RAF to adopt engines able to use it, 'even if the supply of such fuel were limited, because the use of high-duty equipment might prove decisive in the air in the early stages of a war'. [Quoted in Bickers, p. 111] So two British engines, one of them the Merlin, were tested and developed to run on 100-octane.

In June 1939, the first cargo of 'BAM.100' (British Air Ministry 100) was shipped from the Lago (Esso) refinery on the island of Aruba, part of the Dutch West Indies. The valuable fuel was dyed a distinctive green and secretly stockpiled by the Air Ministry. In May 1940, the RAF began to use the special fuel in the Merlins of the Hurricanes and Spitfires. At a stroke the maximum boost was doubled from 6 pounds (in metric pressure measurements, 1.36ata) to 12 pounds (1.82ata), resulting in an increase in maximum power from 1130 horsepower to 1310 horsepower. This made a major difference to the Hurricane and Spitfire, bringing the former broadly up to the level of the Me109E and delivering to the Spitfire a vital edge.

round and caught him doing that fatal turn across my sights. Tighten the turn, nose up a little, and I had him. The Me109 staggered, like a pheasant shot on the wing. A big piece flew off, maybe the hood. A plume of white smoke trailed. I had a split-second impression of the pilot, seemingly inert during those last dramatic moments. Then the aircraft stalled and dived to earth near Hastings.' Another Me109 was shot down, but 85 Squadron lost two aircraft itself. The other squadrons were quickly ordered to avoid combat. [Townsend, *Duel of Eagles*, pp. 404–5]

Early in the evening, Kesselring sent over several fighter sweeps, but it was clear that Park was not to be drawn into a pointless fight. One Staffel of Me109s did, however, catch 501 Squadron patrolling near Hawkinge airfield. The squadron had been in action since 10 May, and its pilots included the flying ace 'Ginger' Lacey and experienced men such as John Gibson. But previous heavy losses meant that it also included its fair share of novice fighter pilots. Bill Green, who described himself as 'probably the most inexperienced pilot in the RAF', did not even see the enemy before his aircraft was hit. Gibson was also shot down, but it was his fifth time baling out, and he was by now well used to parachuting. Lacey downed one of the Me109s and another was damaged. Green and Gibson shared a lift back to Hawkinge.

On the night of 29/30 August the bombers were back over Merseyside to unload more explosives on the docks area, still smouldering from the night before. But this time the activity did not lead to a falling off of raids the next morning. The coming days looked ominous for the defenders. An extensive anticyclone covering northwestern Europe promised several days of fine weather. The Battle of Britain was now entering a decisive phase, in which the Luftwaffe would have to break the power and the will of Fighter Command or accept that it was never going to create the conditions of air superiority that would allow an invasion to take place. The clock was ticking, as the date set for Operation Sea Lion hurried closer. It was the time for Goering to muster all the forces at his disposal and attempt to crush the British air defences by concentrated and relentless assaults.

Bristol Blenheims were used as bombers and night-fighters. This particular one served as a reconnaissance plane before being lost with all its crew during a raid on invasion barges at Ostend on the night of 8 September 1940.

30 August 1940 FRIDAY

Generally fair, but some low cloud.

On Friday, for the first time, the Luftwaffe attacked with everything it had. Soon after dawn the first of several probing moves began. No. 111 Squadron's Hurricanes ran into a *Gruppe* of Dorniers, near Manston, escorted by about 30 Me110s of *Zerstörergeschwader* 75. They reported the formation and then went into the attack, damaging one of the heavy fighters. The Hurricanes were quickly joined by three of No. 54 Squadron's Spitfires, which managed to hit (but not shoot down) two of the bombers.

At about 10.30 am, the first sizeable formation rolled towards the Kent coast. It was the vanguard of three waves, spaced at only half-hourly intervals. Low cloud made the job of the Observer Corps watchers especially difficult, but they identified the force correctly as consisting of 60 Me109s. Air Vice-Marshal Park declined the challenge but put his fighters at readiness – at Kenley, Biggin Hill, Northolt, Croydon, North Weald, Rochford and Hornchurch – in the expectation that bombers would follow.

Sure enough, at 11am Observer Corps posts reported 40 He111s, 30 Do17s, 60 Me109s and 30 Me110s approaching the Kent coast at three different points. Nine squadrons were scrambled. No. 85 Squadron had been sent to patrol over Dungeness at 18,000 feet. 'I could see the enemy circling at Cap Gris Nez like a swarm of gnats,' wrote Peter Townsend. 'We waited up-sun in the English sky – eleven Hurricanes ready to pounce ... Escorted by scores of Me109s and Me110s,

'I really thought my number was up'

Bill Green's slim experience of aerial warfare matched his name. Flying with 501 Squadron, he was shot down by an invisible opponent on 29 August.

There was a crash of glass, and a hole appeared in the middle of the supposedly bullet-proof windscreen about the size of a tennis ball, or a little larger. I heard bits falling into the cockpit and I was immediately covered in glycol liquid coolant. The aircraft was finished, the stick was just like any old bit of stick. I realised I had to get out and I already had the hood back and I got as far as just taking the weight on my feet and I was gone. I think my head must have been exposed to the wind and I was just sucked out. I found myself in space and I started to roll around trying to find the parachute release and thought to myself, I'm never going to find this ripcord.

He eventually located the cord and pulled it, but nothing happened.

I was going through the air at one hundred and forty miles per hour, terminal velocity, and the wind noise was quite terrific … I really thought my number was up.

His parachute pack was trapped between his legs. Suddenly, at just 300 feet above the ground, a gust of wind opened the parachute folds.

There was a jolt when the parachute kicked me backwards … after the noise of the freefall, I was struck by the sudden quiet. It made more impact on me than any noise I'd ever heard. I thought, Gosh, I'm all right.
I'd picked up some cannon splinters in my leg, and it was swollen and in the centre there was a hole, just as though you'd stuck a pencil right through it. When I got back to Hawkinge I went to sick quarters and the doctor laid me out and started probing around with what looked like a steel knitting needle. I fainted. That really put me out of action then for the rest of the Battle of Britain.
[Quoted in Parker, pp. 255-6]

-0-0-0-0-0-

A scene of unusual calm pervades the Hawkinge forward airbase, the closest Fighter Command outpost to enemy-occupied France (1940). The base is now the site of the Kent Battle of Britain Museum.

a score of Heinkels advanced further towards the English coast.' As the Heinkels and Me110s crossed the shoreline, Townsend ordered a head-on attack. 'I took my little band of Hurricanes down in a shallow dive, slipped them into echelon and turned in well ahead of the Heinkels, heading straight at them. Our attack, I wrote later in my combat report, "had the desired effect".' [Townsend, *Duel of Eagles*, p. 407]

The German formation was scattered, and two Me110s were shot down for the loss of one Hurricane, although the pilot baled out unhurt. Elements of the formation pushed on towards Ashford, Kent, where they were intercepted by Nos 43, 79 and 603 squadrons, and a huge dogfight developed. While it raged, another enemy wave was crossing the skies over the Channel. The radar screens were showing something that had never been seen before. They were clogged with a continuous flow of white blips, bombers and fighters streaming in an unbroken line towards England. All of 11 Group's squadrons were now at readiness or in the air. Among them were the new boys from 222 Squadron, and 30 August would prove a bad day for them. Patrolling over Gravesend at about 11.25am, they were bounced by ten Me109s. One Spitfire was shot down, but the wounded pilot managed to put down at Hornchurch. It appeared that the squadron was still flying in the regulation 'vic' formation, which had long been abandoned by frontline squadrons in favour of looser tactics that allowed quick responses to ambushes.

From Kenley, the other 'green' squadron, No. 253, was scrambled when it seemed the airfield was about to be attacked. The attack failed to materialize, and the fighters were instead vectored south to take on the third wave of bombers, which was crossing the coast near Hove and already being harried by No. 43 Squadron from Tangmere. Three of the 253 Squadron Hurricanes got separated from the rest and were sent east and told to climb as fast as they could.

Just south of Maidstone, Squadron Leader Tom Gleave saw that 'stretching as far as the eye could see were rows of Me109s riding above the haze ... it was a fantastic sight'. Gleave led his three Hurricanes into their flank. 'I turned with the tide and took a bead on the nearest Me109,' he wrote later. On a slight right-hand turn he shot from 175 yards, hitting the engine cowling and cockpit. 'The hiss of

Four Messerschmitt Me109 fighters sit lined up ready for action, as two Dornier Do17s pass overhead.

'We were more nimble in a turn.'

Squadron Leader Peter Townsend, flying a Hurricane with No. 85 Squadron, summed up the best evasive measures when Messerschmitt Me109s were on the prowl.

The Me109. It had the legs of the Hurricane and, thanks to fuel-injection, could jump straight into a dive without the engine cutting, as did our carburettor-fed Merlins. But we had one great advantage: we were more nimble in a turn. So everyone knew what to do: 'If the Me. 109s interfere and it's each one for himself - never climb, never dive. Just turn. Since you haven't got eyes in the back of your head, keep weaving and bear in mind: you're always in danger. Attack from the sun if possible, but never forget to "beware the Hun in the sun".' [Townsend, *Duel of Eagles*, p. 376]

-0-0-0-0-0-

Pilots of 303 Squadron with of one of their Hurricanes
at RAF Leconfield (October 1940).

SQUADRON 303 BLOODED

At 4.15pm on 30 August, Polish Squadron 303 left Northolt for a training flight. It was due to meet up with a squadron of Blenheims to practise dummy attacks on them north of St Albans, Hertfordshire. As the Hurricanes circled above the Blenheims, a large group of German planes came into view. It was one of the many formations that had penetrated 11 Group's forward defences and now ranged over Southeast England. Ludwik Paszkiewicz — 'Green 1' — spotted the enemy aircraft first and reported over the radio to his squadron leader, Ronald Kellett, that he wanted to attack. But Kellett was keen to get his Hurricanes and the vulnerable Blenheims out of danger, and he made no reply.

Paszkiewicz then saw a lone Dornier, which was below the formation, banking towards him. 'When enemy aircraft was almost head on,' reads the Squadron's intelligence report,

'he saw the Hurricane and dived steeply, followed by Green 1. When enemy aircraft straightened out, Green 1 closed and fired a burst at 250 yards at the fuselage from dead astern — no effect apparent. Green 1 closed to 100 yards and, getting under the enemy aircraft, fired a long burst at the starboard engine, closing to point blank range. Engine stopped and caught fire. Green 1 broke away … Enemy aircraft crashed and exploded.'

Paszkiewicz then returned to Northolt, where the rest of the squadron had already landed. In front of his fellow pilots he was given a severe reprimand for leaving the formation without authorization. Kellett privately congratulated Paszkiewicz for his skilful and deadly attack, and he announced that on his personal recommendation the squadron was now fully operational. There was wild applause.

pneumatics, the smell of cordite in the cockpit and the feel of the nose dipping slightly under the recoil all lent excitement to the first real combat in my short-lived career at Kenley.' After firing for about four seconds, he saw 'sunlit pieces of the shattered Perspex spiralling after like a shower of tracer. The Hun slewed slightly on while on his back, his nose dropped and he dived beneath out of my sight – going straight down.' [Quoted in Mason, p. 256] By now, Gleave's two wingmen had disappeared – both had been quickly shot down – and Gleave had an Me109 on his tail. He dipped to the right and then pulled up in a sharp climb to his left, which brought him back into the centre of the formation. Another Me109 appeared in his sights, and he fired, seeing the German fighter dive spewing black smoke. As he looked down, he almost collided with another Me109, which streaked past his nose, but then turned into his sights. Gleave fired again, and once more saw his bullets hit home. 'I seemed now to be in the midst of a mass of 109s. They were all over the place but still trying to keep some semblance of a formation. Tracers passed above and below, curing downwards and giving the impression of flying in a gigantic cage of gilt wire.' Another Me109 passed in front of him, and Gleave fired from only 75 yards (67 metres). After only a few seconds he heard a series of 'feeble clicks' as his ammunition supply expired; but it was another 'kill', his fourth in a matter of minutes. As three further Me109s attached themselves to his tail he made his exit, 'flicking the Hurricane on its side at the same time sticking the nose well and truly down, skidding and turning until I was going flat out'.

Elsewhere, ten squadrons from 11 Group were in combat over Kent, with the remainder of Gleave's 253 Squadron losing another Hurricane over the Isle of Sheppey. By 11.45am, sector controllers were confronted with a picture of whirling confusion, with 48 Observer Corps posts reporting combat overhead.

With almost all his forces now in the air, Park called on 12 Group to defend Kenley and Biggin Hill. Once again, the group's response was to create controversy and bad feeling. Instead of guarding the airfields, the 12 Group pilots went looking for the enemy, missing a *Staffel* of Ju88s, which detached itself from the third bomber wave coming over at midday to attack Biggin Hill. More than thirty 250-kilo delayed action bombs were dropped from 18,000 feet, most of them falling on neighbouring villages. At the same time, nearby Kenley was also hit, with buildings destroyed and aircraft on the ground crippled. Croydon and Detling suffered minor damage.

For the first time, there was no precious pause in which to refuel, reflect and recuperate between raids. Shortly after 1pm, three more waves of attacks by bombers, Me110s and Me109s poured across the Channel at 20-minute intervals. A lucky strike on the main electricity grid shut down the radar stations at Rye, Pevensey, Foreness, Dover, Fairlight, Beachy Head and Whitstable, knocking them out for three hours. The loss of cover meant that only five Squadrons succeeded in intercepting the next raid. One of these was No. 222 Squadron, in the air again and learning once more the harsh lessons of combat. Another Spitfire was lost and two more badly damaged. Kenley, Tangmere and Shoreham were all hit.

At around 4pm, the defenders were starting to hope that the German effort would now slacken. But the worst was still waiting. For the next two hours, nineteen Gruppen of enemy aircraft crossed the Channel, racing to Biggin Hill, Kenley and North Weald as well as to aircraft and component factories at Oxford,

'I suppose one feels like this in an earthquake'

Felicity Peake, aged twenty-six and already a war widow, commanded the twenty-five WAAFs stationed at Biggin Hill. She described how 'on 30 August, the storm broke', as sirens sounded and she ran to the shelter trench, which rapidly filled with people 'packed like sardines, with tin hats on waiting'. Soon, they could hear:

```
    Bombs falling at the far side of the aerodrome, each one seeming to
come nearer until one fell just outside our trench. I remember think-
ing, I suppose one feels like this in an earthquake. The vibration and
blast were such that one felt that one's limbs must surely come apart.
Bombs fell pretty continuously, the noise was indescribable.
```

As soon as the bombing had finished, she:

```
    … climbed over the earth and rubble that had been blown into our
trench and out into that lovely summer day. All was strangely quiet.
I wound my way back the way I'd come towards the WAAF guard room.
As I approached I saw a woman lying on the ground on the other side of
the road into the station. When I started to walk across a voice said
to me, 'Don't bother, she's dead.' I distinctly remember saying to
myself and thinking to myself, This is the first dead person I have
ever seen. I've got to get used to this. So I made a point of standing
and looking at her and then I did find that my feelings were at least
controllable. When I arrived at the guard room, or what was left of
it, I found that the airwomen's trench had had a direct hit … Many
airmen were already digging to reach the airwomen who had been trapped
in their trench. The dry summer had made the ground unusually hard
and their task was no light one. As the work went on, we must all
have had the same thought: What shall we find when we reach them?
Ambulance and stretcher parties were standing by, a way was cleared,
and gradually, one by one, the airwomen were brought out.
```

Miraculously, although many of the twelve airwomen buried were badly injured, only one, New Zealander Corporal Lena Button, had been killed. [All quotations from Parker, pp. 249–50]

-o-o-o-o-o-

Luton and Slough. Although they had been in almost continuous combat since 10.30am, Nos 1, 56, 79, 222, 253, 501 and 603 squadrons were sent up again to intercept. The Oxford raid was turned back, but a formation of 30 Heinkels from *Kampfgeschwader* 1, escorted by Me110s, had crossed the coast north of the Thames at about 5pm and broke through to Luton. There it hit the Vauxhall works, killing fifty-three people on the ground and injuring another sixty. Bombers that had missed their primary targets struck Detling airfield, setting oil tanks ablaze, damaging hangars and runways and cutting electricity and telephone lines.

Then, at around 6pm, ten Ju88s, flying low at under 1000 feet, feinted towards

continued on page 267

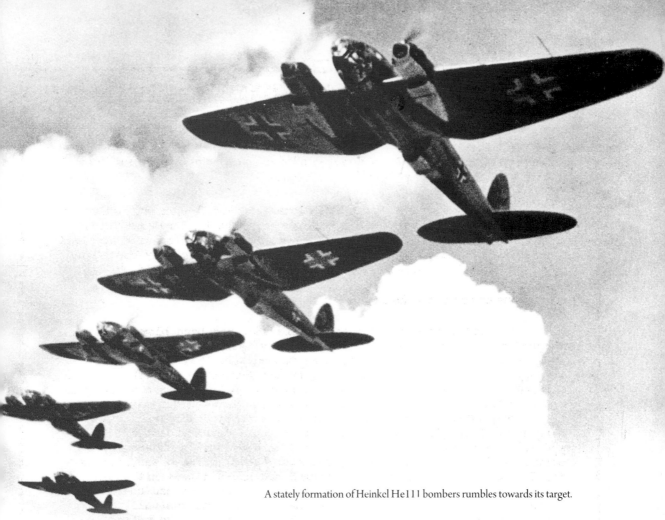

A stately formation of Heinkel He111 bombers rumbles towards its target.

'I was attacked by several 110s'

The highly competent Sergeant 'Ginger' Lacey, of 501 Squadron, was scrambled on 30 August and soon found himself in the midst of Messerschmitt Me110s as he tried to get to the German bombers.

```
      Collision was imminent. So I broke underneath and when I pulled up
I saw that the Me. 110 had left the formation and was going east with
smoke coming from its port engine. Climbing, I found a He. 111 just
ahead, also going east, rather slowly, as though it had been damaged.
I attacked, opened fire at 250 yards and saw the undercarriage drop
and the port engine catch fire. As I closed, long flames and thick
black smoke made vision difficult. I had to break off, as I was
attacked by several 110s. I continued fighting until I had no
ammunition left. [Quoted in Coonts, p.50]


                        -o-o-o-o-o-
```

'LACK OF MORAL FIBRE'

A very small number of soldiers and airmen felt little fear and indeed enjoyed the war. But the vast majority faced a constant battle between the impulse for self-preservation and the compulsion to follow orders and not to let comrades down. 'When it comes to the point, a sincere desire to stay alive is all too likely to get the upper hand,' wrote 616 Squadron's Hugh Dundas, who experienced a sickening panic during his first combat mission. 'Certainly, that was the impulse which consumed me at that moment that day. And that was the emotion which I had to fight against, to try and try and try again to overcome, during the years that followed.' [Dundas, pp. 2–3]

Combat flying left pilots drenched in sweat. The grinding tension of constant readiness shredded nerves, and mental and physical exhaustion lowered their defences against fear. Al Deere explained that: 'The dangerous state is reached in battle when one is so tired mentally and physically that the ever present urge of self-preservation overrules the more normal urge to do one's duty.' [Deere, p. 103]

Most pilots leaned heavily on the support of their peers. In Fighter Command culture, anxiety was masked by banter and ironic humour and an admirable, but artificial, insouciance. What Pilot Officer James Goodson, an American flying with 43 Squadron, remembered was 'the jokes, the fun in the mess, the camaraderie. If people were frightened, tired, neurotic, disillusioned and despondent there was an

Members of 601 Squadron exude the insouciance and good humour that was *de rigueur* among pilots – and a way of keeping fear at bay. (The tractor was the squadron's means of transport across their muddy airfield at Exeter.)

unwritten law in Fighter Command that you did anything rather than show it. Probably those cracking the jokes the most, who were making silly schoolboy pranks in the mess, they were probably the most frightened but they never, never showed it.' [Goodson, recording]

Not everyone could prevail in the constant battle with fear. Peter Brothers was posted to 257 Squadron in early September 1940 and found a unit with its morale in tatters. On one occasion its pilots had been ordered to patrol Maidstone at 20,000 feet, when they saw a horde of German aircraft. The squadron piled in but the commanding officer remained behind, insisting that the orders were to patrol and he was sticking to them. 'On the third occasion of this happening,' said Brothers, 'we decided that he just didn't like combat. He was avoiding it, I think.' [Quoted in Parker, p. 262]

Sergeant Stanley Wright, an NCO at Manston, told the story of a Blenheim air gunner: 'He went off one morning in one of twelve aircraft. He went off later that morning in one of the six that remained. In the afternoon, he was told to go up in one of the three that was left – and he said "NO!"' [Wright, recording]

It was impossible to maintain a constant *sang froid*. Tempers frayed and snapped. Brothers remembers a young pilot at Biggin Hill who lost his cool when his boiled egg was not properly cooked. He threw it at the WAAF waitress. Some became emotionally numb, morose, withdrawn, and avoided companionship. Others became unusually animated, smoking incessantly, forcing themselves to laugh loudly, feigning high spirits.

'You could sometimes see a deterioration in one of your pals,' said Sergeant Maurice Leng of No. 73 Squadron. 'They're not quite the same person that you knew. Morose, quiet, non-talkative – they're losing the motivation to carry on. Although they probably wouldn't know that themselves. And you'd think, "Poor old George. I don't think he's going to last long." And very often, he didn't.' [Leng, recording] Many pilots had regular nightmares, and some developed physical symptoms, such as excessive sweating, shakes and facial twitches. Edith Kup, a WAAF plotter, remembered seeing a young pilot 'out of the corner of my eye, and he sort of sagged down the wall. I said, "Would you like to lie down? We have some beds in the Ops Room." He said, "Yes," so I asked someone to keep an eye on him. The boy had cracked but nobody said anything. Later, I went back into the Ops Room, and he was asleep. We tried to wake him and we couldn't, so we rang the medical officer and asked him to come. And when they picked him up, he was stiff, from head to toe, you know, he didn't sag in the middle. And the medical officer said to me, "You're looking at some one who's literally scared stiff." Nobody saw him again – he was whisked off.' (Kup, recording)

The decision as to whether a crack-up was due to breakdown or cowardice was always complicated, as Al Deere explained: 'In the case of fighter pilots, in particular, it presented squadron and flight commanders with a really difficult problem and one with which they were being continually faced. Up till the moment the air battle is joined, each pilot is a member of a team and should he be inclined to cowardice the presence of other aircraft serves as an anti-dote to his feelings, the more so when he knows that for the initial attack he is under the censorious eyes of the other pilots in the formation. It is immediately subsequent to this first attack that the opportunity occurs for the less courageous to make their get-away without seeming to avoid the issue.' Deere himself admitted that once, alone in the sky, 'temporarily isolated from the main battle', he had to grimly 'talk himself into going back'. Deere was one of the most confident and aggressive pilots in Fighter Command; if he struggled, then certainly many others would have taken the opportunity to avoid further combat. As Deere went on, 'under just such circumstances it is most difficult to prove that a particular pilot has not pulled his weight. After the initial attack it is almost impossible to observe the actions of any one pilot, and unless a watch has been set on a suspect – it has been done – there can be no positive proof of cowardice.' [Deere, pp. 102–3]

The experienced 'aces' themselves were not immune to nerves. 'Ginger' Lacey, of 501 Squadron, recorded how 'Towards the end of the Battle I had just taken about as much as I could bear. My nerves were in ribbons and I was scared stiff that one day I would pull out and avoid combat. That frightened me more than the Germans and I pleaded with my C.O. for a rest. He was sympathetic but quite adamant that until he got replacements I would have to carry on. I am glad now that he was unable to let me go. If I had been allowed to leave the squadron, feeling as I did, I am sure that I would never have flown again.' [Quoted in Hough and Richards, p. 202]

The RAF approached the issue with wartime ruthlessness. 'We had one case who just refused to fly and he was stripped down to the lowest rank,' said Sergeant Charlton Haw of 504 Squadron. 'His wings were taken away from him and he was put on to cleaning latrines. He was taken out of the sergeants' mess so we didn't have any more contact with him and then he was posted away and I never heard of him again.' [Haw, recording] Such men were branded by the RAF as suffering from 'LMF' (Lacking Moral Fibre). Officers deemed guilty of the condition were stripped of their rank, dismissed from the service and lost their flying wings. Because LMF was thought to be 'dangerously contagious', such men would then be posted to menial jobs on other bases, where it was made sure that everybody knew what had happened.

"LET US
GO FORWARD
TOGETHER"

the Thames Estuary before heading directly for Biggin Hill. The attack achieved almost total surprise. No. 79 Squadron was on the ground, with No. 610 patrolling too far away to help. As the pilots of 79 Squadron rushed to get airborne, the station's personnel hurried to the shelter trenches. Sixteen 500-kilo bombs fell with devastating accuracy. One landed on an airmen's shelter trench, killing everyone huddled inside. Another buried a dozen airwomen in their trench. One of the four remaining hangars was smashed, along with barracks, storehouses, the armoury and workshops. Three Spitfires were destroyed on the ground and a further two were badly damaged. Thirty-nine ground staff died, twenty-six were wounded, and telephone, electricity, water and gas lines were cut. Hornchurch sector station was now forced to take over control of the Biggin Hill sector while Post Office engineers worked frantically to reconnect the base's communications.

Night closed on a day of desperate fighting. Fighter Command had flown 1054 sorties, an unprecedented number that would remain the highest daily tally for the entire battle. Twenty-two squadrons had been in action, many up to four times. One squadron, No. 56, went up seven times. The Germans had also had an exhausting day. The crews of Kesselring's *Luftflotte* 2 flew 1310 sorties. As darkness fell, Sperrle's *Luftflotte* 3 took over, sending 130 bombers to Liverpool and South Wales, as well as single-bomber sorties against North Weald, Debden, Biggin Hill, Hornchurch, Detling, Eastchurch, Thorney Island, Calshot, Rochford, Broxbourne, Derby, Norwich and Peterborough. Damage to the airfields was light, but the constant alarms and alerts wore down civilian and Fighter Command personnel alike. And the German assault was far from spent.

OPPOSITE
The two icons of British resistance in 1940 – Churchill and the fighter plane – combine in a morale-boosting poster of that year, though it was a little premature to show tanks advancing.

SATURDAY 31 August 1940

At 8am on Saturday, reports from the now-restored radar stations signalled four waves of enemy aircraft forming up, one on the way to Dover and the other three heading up the Thames Estuary. The Dover raid turned out to be Me109s only, flying at 25,000 feet, where they were more than a match for the British fighters. When they were identified by the Observer Corps, Park hurriedly recalled the two squadrons – Nos 501 and 1 (Canadian) – which had been sent to intercept. The order, however, came too late for the Canadians, who were jumped by the Messerschmitts and lost three fighters, with two of the pilots receiving serious burns to face and hands. With no other opposition in the sky, the Me109s set about the Dover balloon barrage.

Meanwhile, the formation racing up the Thames Estuary had been confirmed as a mixture of He111s, Do17s and Me110s. Park ordered up 13 squadrons from 7 airfields around London, leaving himself very little in reserve. As the British fighters closed on the raiders, the latter broke into several groups, each targeting, again, the Fighter Command airfields. Near Clacton, Essex, 12 Hurricanes from 257 Squadron at Martlesham engaged 50 Me110s. Two of the raiders were shot down, but the Me110s also took down two British fighters, killing a pilot.

As other raiders approached North Weald, they were met by No. 56 Squadron near Colchester. The Me109 escort shot down four of the squadron, killing one pilot and wounding two more. The Hurricane pilots, exhausted after their exertions the

Generally fair with some haze over the Thames Estuary and Dover Straits.

previous day, retreated and the bombers ploughed on to North Weald, where they caused considerable damage.

While North Weald was under bombardment, another formation of 40 Dorniers, with a heavy Me110 escort, was heading further north, making for 12 Group's sector station at Duxford. The attack came as a surprise, and with no fighters at readiness Leigh-Mallory was forced to call on 11 Group for assistance. Fortunately for the airfield, Park had 111 Squadron on patrol nearby. Speeding northeast, the squadron succeeded in manoeuvring into a position to launch another head-on attack. The Luftwaffe formation scattered, and the Me110s went into a defensive circle. Abandoned by their escort, the Dorniers jettisoned their load over the fields and turned for home. One bomber and one Me110 were shot down for the loss of one of 111 Squadron's Hurricanes.

Staff at the Duxford
Operations Room.
The sector station had
a narrow escape from
bombing on 31 August.

Duxford had been spared, but bombers made their way unchecked to Debden. There they dropped a hundred 250-kilo bombs, causing eighteen casualties, destroying three barrack blocks and the sick bay, and severely damaging four Hurricanes caught on the ground. No. 19 Squadron's Spitfires from Fowlmere had been scrambled shortly after 8am to intercept this raid, but they caught up with the bombers only after the damage was done. Over Little Shelford, they spotted the retreating formation of about 20 Dorniers and some 50 Me110s. The Spitfires went into the attack, but the Me110s had the advantage of height. When the No. 19 pilots opened fire, they found that their newly fitted cannons were jamming again. Four of the squadron were shot down for only one Me110 in return.

Shortly after 9am, two further groups, one of about 20 Dorniers escorted by fighters, the other of Me109s and Me110s, swept up the Thames Estuary. The Dorniers dropped 80 bombs on Eastchurch airfield, causing limited damage, while the fighters strafed Detling.

Further waves of Me109s over Kent were ignored by Park, but when two new formations of bombers – Heinkels and Dorniers – were mapped heading for Croydon and Biggin Hill, he had to react quickly. No. 85 Squadron's pilots at Croydon were sent to their aircraft, whose engines had already been started. Leading the squadron, Peter Townsend glanced back at his men, whose fighters had formed up behind him. 'They looked superb, all those Hurricanes,' he later wrote, 'straining against the brakes with their long, eager noses tilted skywards and the sun glinting on their whirling propellers. Every pilot was watching me, waiting for the signal. At last it came: "Off you go," called Kenley, and we were racing forward with a bellow of twelve thousand horsepower.' It was the last time Townsend would lead his squadron into battle by day. 'The bombs were already on their way down. I had just moved the lever to raise the undercarriage, when my engine faltered, faded, and picked up again. Blast had struck the motor like a punch in the wind. Turning in the cockpit, I saw the rest of the squadron emerging from a vast eruption of smoke and debris.' Overhead, thousands of feet above, Me110s were 'wheeling in the blue, with Me 109s swarming above'. [Townsend, *Duel of Eagles*, p.148]

'Asleep with exhaustion'

Aircraftman Charles Cooper, a squadron armourer, witnessed an incident involving Canadian Pilot Officer J.A. 'Johnny' Walker of No. 111 Squadron which testifies to the exhaustion of the surviving pilots.

On one of our busy days at Croydon we were watching the return of our Hurricanes, and ready to rearm quickly, when we noticed one aircraft [had] landed and taxied a short distance only to stop some way off with the engine still turning over. Thinking the pilot had been wounded, we dashed over to the aircraft, only to find the pilot, Johnny Walker DFC, a Canadian, was leaning forward with his body held by the Sutton harness, head on his chest and asleep with exhaustion. [Quoted in Hough and Richards, pp. 237-8]

-0-0-0-0-0-

At a severe height disadvantage, No. 85 Squadron did well, 'flogging their Hurricanes mercilessly during the climb' and shooting down at least two Me110s, but losing three aircraft shot down, including the squadron leader's. 'A blast of shot suddenly splattered my Hurricane,' recalled Townsend, 'my left foot was kicked off the rudder-bar, petrol gushed into the cockpit. The shock was so terrific that for a few instants I lost control and went into a steep dive ... then I straightened out. By some miracle, my Hurricane had not burst into flames ... My windscreen was starred with bullets ... I baled out and watched my poor Hurricane dive into the trees and blow up.' Injured in the foot, Townsend would be out of action for

A Spitfire pilot is taken on an evening promenade as he recuperates from a leg wound (10 September 1940).

| YEAR | | AIRCRAFT | | PILOT, OR | 2ND PILOT, PUPIL | DUTY |
| MONTH | DATE | Type | No. | 1ST PILOT | ~~ENGER~~ | (INCLUDING RESULTS AND REMARK |

TOTALS BROUGHT FORWAR

A BAD DAY FOR NO. 19 SQUADRON

Flying Officer James Coward, No. 19 Squadron's 'Green' Section leader, was in action on 31 August. He was on the point of firing at the enemy bombers when he was hit in the leg by a cannon shell. He felt little but, looking down, 'I could see my foot hanging loose on the pedal, but you thought you were invincible and I still went in to open fire.' However, the cannon armament in his wings jammed. Still heading directly for the Dornier, Coward ducked as the top of his Spitfire grazed the underside of the bomber. The hood of his plane was ripped off and the Spitfire spiralled downwards, out of control and spraying its pilot with petrol. 'I baled out at 22,000 feet,' said Coward, 'and got caught on the back of the cockpit as I went.' Thrashing about on top of his aircraft, suddenly he was free.

```
     I was going to free-fall for a bit in case they shot up my
parachute, but my foot was thrashing around up by my thigh and the
pain was too much. I pulled the ripcord and I swung there in a great
figure of eight. The blood was pumping out of my leg - it was amazing
how bright it was so high up. I thought I'd bleed to death so I used
the radio wire from my helmet to put a tourniquet round my thigh.
After that, I felt no pain, apart from the petrol that had drenched
me and was stinging my armpits and crotch. I drifted across Duxford
towards Fowlmere and then the wind took me back again.
```

Luckily for Coward, a doctor was at hand when he landed painfully in a field. He was taken to Addenbrooke's Hospital, where his leg was amputated below the knee. [Coward quotations from Parker, pp. 259–60]

One other No. 19 pilot who had been shot down had baled out unhurt. The Spitfire of young Pilot Officer Ray Aeberhardt had also been hit, but he attempted to get his struggling aircraft back to ground at Fowlmere. Armourer Fred Roberts was watching: 'He went up on his nose on landing and the plane caught fire, we were there and we watched him burning, we couldn't do anything, we couldn't get near him. We hadn't got the fire-fighting facilities at Fowlmere and that sort of thing, you know.' [Roberts, recording] Aeberhardt, at nineteen, had been the youngest man in the squadron.

The tension and stress of the summer days shows in this famous image of No. 19 Squadron pilots Walter Lawson (*left*), Brian Lane (*centre*) and George 'Grumpy' Unwin (*right*) at Fowlmere after a sortie (September 1940). Only Unwin survived the war.

'Jerry hadn't broken our spirit'

Sergeant Gunner Ben Elswood was one of those manning the anti-aircraft gun battery at Biggin Hill when it was attacked on 31 August.

```
     Anyone would think that we were the only important aerodrome
protecting London. Day after day, raid after raid. As soon as the
bombers come over and make bloody holes in the ground, we go out and
fill 'em up again. Everything is in poor shape, but Jerry hadn't
broken our spirit. Hangars continued to operate even with no roofs
on. There was always a steady stream of ambulances to take the injured
to hospital, in fact it got to a bloody state where they queued up
waiting for the next raid. If there were heroes though, then it had
to be the women. They just don't know how to bow to defeat. Bloody
marvellous they were, stuck to their posts like glue, each one
deserved a medal. [www.battleofbritain1940.net]
```

-0-0-0-0-0-

weeks, one of several highly experienced pilots lost from the frontline today.

There was some damage to Croydon, but it was Biggin Hill that was worst hit. Two Staffeln of He111s broke through to bomb from 12,000 feet, hitting two Spitfires on the ground, as well as two of the remaining hangars and other buildings. Most serious was a further hit on the vital operations room, severing the communications and power lines again, thus undoing all the hard work since the raid of the previous day.

As they left Biggin Hill, the Heinkels were attacked by 253 Squadron, which shot down two of their number. But Squadron Leader Tom Gleave, the destroyer of four Me109s the previous day, was hit by fire from his blind spots behind and below him. His reserve fuel tank, between the instrument panel and the engine, burst into flames, splashing Gleave with burning fuel. With the cockpit on fire, he struggled to bale out. He groped among the flames in front of him to disconnect his radio lead and oxygen tube, but in vain. As his clothes and hair caught fire, he squirmed out of his harness, yanked open the hood, and wrenched off his helmet. He shot from the cockpit like a projectile and then steeled himself to pull the ripcord with his blistered hands.

Landing in a field, Gleave surveyed his legs and arms, on which the flesh now hung in charred strips. He had feared being burned more than anything. As well as his legs and arms, his hair, eyelids and nose had also been consumed by the heat of the burning cockpit. A WAAF, Igraine Hamilton, who worked at Orpington Hospital remembered: 'When Tom Gleave's wife came to see him for the first time after his crash, she said, "I don't know! Playing with matches again?" Anyone who had a wife like that was very lucky.' [Hamilton, recording]

Ten minutes earlier, the sector station at Hornchurch had also come under attack. The Luftwaffe had learned to focus and coordinate their attacks with

A crashed Spitfire from 152 Squadron lies in a Dorset field in September 1940, its pilot having escaped unharmed.

devastating effect. There was little warning. No. 54 Squadron's Al Deere was lined up with his comrades on the runway, when 'a wildly gesticulating voice' started shouting over the radio transmitter, 'Hornet aircraft get airborne as quickly as you can, enemy in the immediate vicinity.' [Deere, pp. 142–3] Below, Richard Hillary of 603 Squadron was watching. 'I looked up again, and this time I saw them – about a dozen slugs, shining in the bright sun and coming straight on,' he wrote. 'At the rising scream of the first bomb I instinctively shrugged up my shoulders and ducked my head.' [Hillary, pp 100–1, and below]

'I was not quite airborne, when a bomb burst on the airfield, ahead of me and to my left,' wrote Al Deere. For a moment, he thought he had made it. Then 'a tremendous blast of air, carrying showers of earth, struck me in the face and the next moment [I was] thinking vaguely that I was upside down'. 'I saw the three Spitfires,' wrote Hillary. 'One moment they were about twenty feet up in close formation; the next catapulted apart as though on elastic. The leader [Deere] went over on his back and ploughed along the runway with a rending crash of tearing fabric; No. 2 put a wing in and spun round on his airscrew, while the plane on the left was blasted wingless into the next field.' Hillary saw no more as he dashed for the shelter.

Deere's Spitfire hurtled down the runway on its back. 'Finally the aircraft stopped its mad upside-down dash leaving me trapped in the cockpit, in almost total darkness, and breathing petrol fumes, the smell of which was overpowering,' wrote Deere. 'Bombs were still exploding outside, but this was not as frightening as the thought of fire from the petrol now seeping into the ground around my head. One spark and I would be engulfed in flames.' Miraculously, none of the three pilots had been killed, and one now came to the aid of Deere, freeing him from the cockpit. They helped each other across the airfield to the shelter as machine-gun bullets hit the ground around them.

When the pilots and airmen and women emerged from the shelter, they found that 'Gaping holes and great gobbets of earth were everywhere,' Hillary wrote, '... the runways were in something of a mess'. Six airmen had been killed and many more wounded. 'Sick quarters bore all the signs of a casualty clearing station, a queue of injured airmen and stretcher cases filling the passageway,' wrote Deere. Sixty bombs had been dropped in a line across the airfield, from just outside the perimeter through the 54 Squadron dispersal area and beyond into a housing estate. Hangars and the operations room, however, had not been hit. The station commander ordered that every available man and woman, including officers, should immediately repair the aerodrome surface, and by 4pm, says Hillary, 'there was not a hole to be seen'.

At Biggin Hill, too, furious work was under way to restore communications, infrastructure and runways. But both sector stations would be hit again before the end of the day. At about 5.50pm, Ju88s and Me110s of Experimental Group 210 dropped thirty bombs each on Biggin Hill and Hornchurch, where two Spitfires were destroyed on the ground. The Biggin Hill raiders were engaged by the Hornchurch squadrons, Nos 222 and 54, with losses on both sides.

It was now clear that the Luftwaffe's tactics had changed from mass attacks across a wide front to incessant, concentrated assaults at the approaches to London held by 11 Group. The last two days had seen 2800 enemy sorties against the sector stations, hitting the vital organs of Fighter Command. Without the incalculable benefit of radar and the early warning system in operation, Fighter Command would have been overwhelmed.

As it was, it had still been a grim day. Most of the Fighter Command losses were the result of fighter-versus-fighter combat. With the concentration of Me109s in the Pas de Calais, the enemy bombers now had a thick phalanx of escorts, which the Hurricanes and Spitfires were having great difficulty penetrating. And that night, the bombers were over England again, with most of the force concentrated, once more, against Liverpool. At the same time, the invasion itself was taking visible shape in the form of the huge build-up of shipping gathering in the French Channel ports.

Today, Fighter Command had suffered 37 aircraft destroyed, 9 pilots killed and 18 others badly wounded. Fighters had also been destroyed on the ground. The Luftwaffe had lost 39 aircraft in combat. The margins were shrinking to nothing.

A two-man team operates an anti-aircraft Bren gun in August 1940, at an undisclosed coastal location. It would likely have had little effect against the Luftwaffe.

1 September 1940 SUNDAY

The morning of 1 September started quietly. Dowding assumed that the Luftwaffe would be exhausted after the efforts of the previous two days, and he took the opportunity to pull two shattered squadrons out of the frontline. No. 151 Squadron, with only ten aircraft and twelve pilots left, moved from Stapleford to Digby and was replaced by 46 Squadron, rebuilt since its destruction in the Norwegian campaign. No. 56 Squadron, leaderless and down to seven aircraft, retired to the comparative calm of Boscombe Down, with 249 Squadron taking over its duties at North Weald.

Biggin Hill was battered and only semi-functioning, now able to accommodate only one squadron rather than the four it had housed previously. So, No. 72 Squadron moved to Croydon, while 79 Squadron alone remained at Biggin Hill to provide airfield defence.

Fair with some cloud, clearing in the afternoon.

continued on page 276

CLASS DISTINCTIONS

Before the Second World War, there were sharp distinctions among the ranks in the RAF. In October 1936, Peter Brothers arrived at his squadron as a pilot officer. 'Back then you were a "bog rat", just a pilot officer, lowest of the low, unwanted, and underpaid,' he remembered. 'Nobody spoke to you except when a flying officer or a flight lieutenant would tell you to go and press the bell so a waiter would come in to get him a drink.' [Brothers, recording]

Between officers and other ranks, there was an even sharper divide, which persisted even when the fighting started – when officers and sergeant pilots were doing the same job and sharing the same dangers.

Flight Sergeant George Unwin of 19 Squadron, a pre-war regular, leaps out of his Spitfire after a sortie, as one of his groundcrew looks on (September 1940).

'There was no familiarity or anything like that,' said Flight Sergeant George Unwin of No. 19 Squadron. 'You never mixed at all, you were trained like that, the RAF built it into you.' [Unwin, recording] This was partly a hangover from before the war, when the majority of sergeant pilots were ex-apprentices who had been accepted for flying training but might at any stage be required to return to their old trades.

Unwin remembered that by an unspoken agreement the officers and NCOs drank in different pubs. This was not the case in every squadron, but all units had different messes, with the officers' one superior in comfort to that of the NCOs. Officers also had a smarter, more comfortable uniform, and a batman or orderly to make their tea and clean and maintain their uniforms. NCOs had to polish their own buttons.

Nearly a third of the 'fighter boys' in the summer of 1940 were NCOs and almost all those who survived would eventually be given commissions. But, to begin with, in order to become an officer it helped greatly to have gone to the right school, or to have the bearing of an officer and gentleman.

This culture of division could lead to practical inefficiencies. 'When I became an officer,' said Cyril 'Bam' Bamberger of 610 Squadron, 'the controller and the wing commander would drop into our mess and we were up to date with what was going on. We were very well briefed. But the sergeant didn't know what was going on. This separation was a big weakness.' [Bamberger, recording] Even among the sergeants there was a pecking order, with those from the RAF Volunteer Reserve looked down on by the regulars who had come up through apprenticeships.

That men doing the same job should have such different levels of status and privilege was unremarkable at the time. As the battle wore on, many of the distinctions were eroded by the fighting and by the shared danger. Also, the technical nature of a pilot's job meant that the RAF had to become more meritocratic – and thus more socially egalitarian – than the other services, and the culture of mickey-taking, along with the consciousness that all pilots belonged to an elite, helped blur the distinctions. Auxiliary squadrons lost their exclusive character as the original men were killed, wounded or posted away, and as more NCOs arrived at squadrons, so the social mix was also diluted. By the end of the Battle of Britain, even the squadrons that, pre-war, had been the most exclusive now contained men from every conceivable background.

GRAND TOTAL [Cols. (I) to (10)]
...............Hrs...............Mins.

274

Totals Carried Forward

EQUIVALENT RANKS OF THE RAF AND LUFTWAFFE

ROYAL AIR FORCE	LUFTWAFFE
Marshal of the Royal Air Force	Generalfeldmarschall
Air Chief Marshal	Generaloberst
Air Marshal	General
Air Vice-Marshal	Generalleutnant
Air Commodore	Generalmajor
Group Captain	Oberst
Wing Commander	Oberstleutnant
Squadron Leader	Major
Flight Lieutenant	Hauptmann
Flying Officer	Oberleutnant
Pilot Officer	Leutnant
Warrant Officer	Stabsfeldwebel
Flight Sergeant	Oberfeldwebel
Sergeant	Feldwebel
Corporal	Unteroffizier
Leading Aircraftman	Obergefreiter
Aircraftman First Class	Gefreiter
Aircraftman Second Class	Flieger

Reichsmarschall Goering mingles with some of his Luftwaffe subordinates.
The rank of *Reichsmarschall* had no equivalent in British military hierarchy.

On the evening of 31 August, Air Chief Marshal Dowding had dinner with Winston Churchill at the prime minister's official country residence, Chequers. Churchill's secretary, Jock Colville, recalled the conversation.

```
    Dowding is splendid. He stands up to the P.M., refuses to be
particularly unpleasant about the Germans, and is the very antithesis
of the complacency with which so many Englishmen are afflicted.
He told that he could not understand why the Germans kept on coming
in waves instead of concentrating on one mass raid a day which could
not be effectively parried. Ismay suggested that they might be short
of planes and have to use bombers twice daily. There was a great
discussion about the ethics of shooting down enemy pilots landing
by parachute, Dowding maintaining it should be done and the P.M.
saying that an escaping pilot was like a drowning sailor.
Otherwise he was in a very ruthless frame of mind. [Colville, p.235]
```

-o-o-o-o-o-

OPPOSITE
Churchill pores over a map with Vice-Admiral Sir Bertram Ramsey at Dover (28 August 1940).

At 10.20am, the first raid was reported assembling over France. Half an hour later, the German aircraft were advancing towards Dover on a five-mile front. Fourteen squadrons were scrambled, intercepting the raiders as they crossed the coast between Dungeness and Margate. On reaching land, the force split into two groups, each of about thirty bombers and fighters, with one formation heading for the Thames Estuary.

A fierce dogfight now developed over northeastern Kent. No. 85 Squadron had been in action the previous evening, shooting down four Me109s over the Channel. It was now back in combat, downing two more of the single-engine Messerschmitts. No. 1 Squadron from Northolt and No. 54 from Hornchurch joined the combat, while No. 72 Squadron was sent up from Croydon. The latter lost three Spitfires when it was jumped by Me109s.

While the defenders were engaged by the Me109s, however, the bombers got through, hitting Detling, Eastchurch and the London docks. At Biggin Hill, 79 Squadron was caught on the ground, and at least one Hurricane was destroyed.

The defending fighters hardly had time to refuel before the aircraft of Nos 1, 54, 72, 85 and 616 squadrons were scrambled again, as 170 Luftwaffe planes crossed the Kent coast shortly after 1.30pm. Three squadrons – Nos 72, 253 and 616 – engaged the attackers over Folkestone and Hastings, and No. 85 Squadron ran into them near Lympne. One of 85's Hurricanes developed engine trouble and the pilot landed at Lympne airfield, only to see his aircraft wrecked when bombs started falling on the runways and hangars.

No. 85 Squadron stayed with the Luftwaffe formation as it ploughed north, but the Hurricanes could not penetrate the escort to break up the bombers, which stayed on a course for Biggin Hill and Kenley. As the fighting moved closer to

A PRIME MINISTER'S MODUS OPERANDI

Winston Churchill's working routines, as prime minister and steward of Britain's war effort, were certainly unorthodox. He frequently spent part of the working day in bed. With his black cat Nelson nestling at his feet, and a large chromium-plated spittoon at his side in which to throw his cigar stubs, he would emit a steady flow of memoranda. He did not so much discuss ideas as exhort and harangue his colleagues, concerning himself with all sorts of issues large and small, from the spelling of foreign names to the size of the jam ration.

But the strain was beginning to tell. 'He did not shout … nor did I ever see him drunk,' his private secretary, Colville, wrote. 'But never notably considerate except to those in pain or in trouble, he was more than normally inconsiderate and demanding during the last months of 1940. He complained of delays when there were none; he changed carefully prepared plans at the last minute; he cancelled meetings and appointments without caring for anybody's convenience but his own; and he was continually insisting on personal amenities which gave much trouble to overworked people and were, in a small way, divisions from the war effort.'

FIGHTER COMMAND LOSSES *IN AUGUST 1940*

Aircraft type	Numbers destroyed	Numbers damaged	Pilots killed	Pilots missing	Pilots wounded
Hurricane	211	44	85	1	68
Spitfire	113	40	41	3	38
Blenheim	13	10	6	3	0
Defiant	7	3	7	0	4
All types (total)	**344**	**97**	**139**	**7**	**110**

London, the defenders started to suffer badly. Four Hurricanes were shot down. One of the pilots was killed in his cockpit, a second died when his parachute failed to open, and a third, already badly burned, suffered a broken back, leg and arm when his parachute only partially opened. Sergeant Glendon Booth would die of his injuries five months later, aged only twenty.

No. 85 Squadron had now been in action seven times in four days and had lost its wounded squadron commander, Peter Townsend, and a total of nine aircraft. As its diary laments, 'only six Hurricanes, all that remained of the squadron, landed at Croydon, with one landing wheels up'. Two days later, the squadron was withdrawn from the frontline.

As the German formation neared the sector stations, the aircraft remaining there for airfield defence were sent up, including No. 79 Squadron from Biggin Hill. But they were unable to turn back the raid, and three 79 Squadron aircraft were shot down. The bombers arrived at Biggin Hill while a funeral service was under way for those killed in previous raids. First, the twin-engine Me110s came in low, bombing with great accuracy and destroying buildings and infrastructure; then, Dorniers dropped high explosives from on high. Kenley suffered too, with Do17s bombing during a low-level run over the airfield.

At 5.30pm came the last wave of attacks, as seven distinct formations were plotted approaching across the Channel. Most of these turned out to be fighters, which raced across the southern part of Kent, strafing balloon barrages and other targets of opportunity. With the defences distracted, a formation of bombers and Me110s hit the forward airfields of Hawkinge and Lympne, and then moved on to Biggin Hill. It was the third attack of the day, and the worst. A direct hit wrecked the operations room, forcing its move to a shop in the village, and four Spitfires

LUFTWAFFE LOSSES *IN AUGUST 1940*

Aircraft type	Numbers destroyed	Numbers damaged	Pilots killed	Pilots missing	Pilots wounded
Dornier Do17	71	31	70	129	57
Heinkel He111	89	15	113	204	35
Junkers Ju88	89	32	94	182	19
Junkers Ju87	57	16	35	58	19
Messerschmitt Me109	217	45	54	91	39
Messerschmitt Me110	119	40	80	113	22
Other types	27	4	17	27	10
All types (total)	**669**	**183**	**463**	**804**	**201**

were destroyed on the ground. Biggin Hill's last remaining squadron, No. 79, was moved to Croydon.

On 1 September, the Luftwaffe had flown only half the number of sorties it had flown the day before; but the German planes had still succeeded in hitting vital airfields. Fighter Command had failed to stop them and had suffered 16 fighters shot down and 4 damaged. The Germans had suffered similar losses, but they must have felt they were at last making headway in their plan to wreck the infrastructure of Fighter Command and destroy its ability to defend the British homeland.

MONDAY 2 September 1940

Overnight, 120 German bombers ranged across England against scattered targets. The morning light of 2 September saw an attack at 7am, when a *Gruppe* of Dorniers from *Kampfgeschwader* 3 and one *Geschwader* of Me109s assembled over Calais. Sixty fighters were scrambled in response, as the raid approached Deal, but only twenty of them made contact; the others were kept back to patrol over the vulnerable airfields.

Above Maidstone the formation split up and fanned out to attack Biggin Hill, Rochford, Eastchurch and North Weald. The latter was saved from damage by the intervention of 222 Squadron from Hornchurch and 249 Squadron from North Weald. No. 249 lost three aircraft, but managed to break up the bomber formation sufficiently to disrupt the targeting of the airfield. But the raids on Eastchurch and Rochford were more successful for the Germans. At Rochford, an ammunition dump was hit and five planes destroyed on the ground. Spitfires of 72 Squadron

Generally fine and warm after early mist patches.

RAF Fighter Command Order of Battle *1 September 1940*

SECTOR	SQN	AIRCRAFT	BASED AT	COMMANDER
11 Group				
Biggin Hill	79	Hurricane	Biggin Hill	S/L Hervey Heyworth
	501	Hurricane	Gravesend	S/L Harry Hogan
North Weald	56	Hurricane	North Weald	Temporarily unfilled
	151	Hurricane	Stapleford	Temporarily unfilled
	25	Blenheim	Martlesham	S/L W.W. Loxton (acting)
Kenley	72	Spitfire	Croydon	S/L A.R. Collins
	85	Hurricane	Croydon	S/L Peter Townsend
	253	Hurricane	Kenley	Temporarily unfilled
	616	Spitfire	Kenley	S/L M. Robinson
Hornchurch	54	Spitfire	Hornchurch	Temporarily unfilled
	222	Spitfire	Hornchurch	S/L J.H. Hill
	600	Blenheim	Hornchurch	S/L David Clark
	603	Spitfire	Hornchurch	Temporarily unfilled
Tangmere	17	Hurricane	Tangmere	S/L A.G. Miller
	43	Hurricane	Tangmere	S/L C.B. Hull
	602	Spitfire	Westhampnett	S/L Sandy Johnstone
Debden	111	Hurricane	Debden	S/L John Thompson
	257	Hurricane	Debden	S/L H. Harkness
	601	Hurricane	Debden	S/L Sir Archibald Hope
Northolt	1	Hurricane	Northolt	S/L David Pemberton
	1 (Can)	Hurricane	Northolt	S/L E.A. McNab
	303	Hurricane	Northolt	S/L R.G. Kellett / S/L Z. Krasnodesbski
10 Group				
Pembrey	93	Spitfire	Pembrey	S/L F.J. Sanders
Filton	87	Hurricane	Exeter	S/L R.S. Mills
	213	Hurricane	Exeter	S/L H.D. McGregor
St Eval	236	Blenheim	St Eval	S/L G.W. Montagu
	238	Hurricane	St Eval	S/L Harold Fenton
Middle Wallop	152	Spitfire	Warmwell	S/L Peter Devitt
	234	Spitfire	Middle Wallop	S/L J.S. O'Brian
	249	Hurricane	Boscombe Down	S/L J. Grandy
	604	Blenheim	Middle Wallop	S/L Michael Anderson
	609	Spitfire	Middle Wallop	S/L Horace Darley
12 Group				
Duxford	19	Spitfire	Fowlmere	S/L Philip Pinkham
	310	Hurricane	Duxford	S/L G.D.M. Blackwood
Coltishall	66	Spitfire	Coltishall	S/L Rupert Leigh
	242	Hurricane	Coltishall	S/L Douglas Bader
Kirton-in-Lindsey	264	Defiant	Kirton	S/L G.D. Garvin
Digby	29	Blenheim	Wellingore	S/L S.C. Widdows
	46	Hurricane	Digby	F/L A.D. Murray
	611	Spitfire	Digby	S/L J. McComb
Wittering	74	Spitfire	Wittering	S/L A.G. Malan
	229	Hurricane	Bircham Newton	S/L H.J. McQuire
	23	Blenheim	Wittering	S/L G.F.W. Heycock
	266	Spitfire	Wittering	Temporarily unfilled
13 Group				
Church Fenton	73	Hurricane	Church Fenton	S/L M.W.S. Robinson
	64	Spitfire	Leconfield	S/L A.R.D. MacDonald
	302	Hurricane	Leconfield	S/L W.A.J. Satchell / S/L M. Mumler
Catterick	32	Hurricane	Acklington	S/L N.M. Crossley
	41	Spitfire	Catterick	S/L H. West
	219	Blenheim	Leeming	S/L J.H. Little
	610	Spitfire	Acklington	S/L J. Ellis
	607	Hurricane	Usworth	S/L J. Vick
Turnhouse	141	Defiant	Turnhouse	S/L William Richardson
	605	Hurricane	Drem	S/L W. Churchill
Dyce	263	Hurricane	Grangemouth	S/L H. Eeles
	145	Hurricane	Dyce	S/L T.P. Pugh
Wick	3	Hurricane	Wick	S/L S.F. Godden
	504	Hurricane	Castletown	S/L John Sample

Key S/L = Squadron Leader; F/L = Flight Lieutenant; W/C = Wing Commander

managed to intercept the Biggin Hill raid, having recently arrived south from Acklington. While they were at 13,000 feet and tussling with Me110s, Me109s and Dorniers, nine bombers flew in at low level, causing further damage.

No. 603 Squadron from Hornchurch had been scrambled when it looked, for a moment, as if their airfield were about to come under attack. As the bombers headed away, 603 was ordered to give chase and succeeded in downing three Me109s over the sea. One fell to the guns of Richard Hillary.

By noon, another large formation was approaching Dover. This time, Park sent up his fighters earlier, ordering them to hit the main formation before it split up into groups heading for individual targets. No. 72 Squadron, flying from Croydon, sighted and engaged the 250-strong body of planes to the north of Rochester, and No. 603 Squadron joined the mêlée just east of Sheerness. Three of the 603 pilots were shot down, but all of them survived. The German formation did succeed in breaking into separate attacks, and once again a huge dogfight broke out over the Kent countryside, involving 70 Fighter Command aircraft. Nos 111 and 222 squadrons both sustained losses, while above Ashford No. 43 Squadron shot down two Me109s but lost three aircraft itself. Pilot Officer Tony Woods-Scawen had successfully baled out on four previous occasions, but now he found himself in a stricken Hurricane only 1000 feet above the ground. He jumped nonetheless, but at that moment his aircraft exploded above him, killing him.

'A beautiful Riley car'

In a laconic snapshot of transient mortality, Peter Morfill of 501 Squadron remembered how on 2 September he and his comrades lost a pilot but gained a car.

> One lunchtime, at Gravesend, a chap came in a beautiful Riley car and as it stopped, we looked in and saw squash rackets, tennis rackets and golf clubs, I think. The CO asked the newcomer, 'Where have you come from?' He replied, 'So-and-so Spitfires.'
>
> 'Hurricanes here,' said the CO. 'Same thing, anyway. Grab yourself some food but forget sleeping quarters at the moment, we'll do that later on. We're on readiness in quarter of an hour so you've just got time to grab something. We lost three blokes today, so you're on.'
>
> 'Yes, sir!' he replied. I will always remember his face. Anyway, we took off at about two o'clock and he was dead at quarter past. So after the day was over, the CO phoned his mother, and she didn't want to know anything, not the car, nothing, so now we had a squadron car. We used to go from Gravesend down the hill to the pub down the bottom there and could get seven people in this car. [Quoted in Parker, pp. 262-3]

-0-0-0-0-0-

His brother Patrick, a pilot in No. 85 Squadron, had been lost the previous day.

As before, the Hurricanes and Spitfires found themselves dragged away in a high-altitude fight while the bombers ploughed on unmolested beneath. Bombs targeted Biggin Hill, Kenley and Hornchurch, where a successful last-ditch defence by No. 603 Squadron saw many of the bombers driven to jettison their loads wide of the aerodrome.

Then, at 5.30pm, 250 more enemy aircraft were over Kent, leading to another huge fracas between 160 Me109s on the one side and fighters from Nos 46, 72, 111, 222, 501, 603 and 616 squadrons on the other. No 501 was hit hard, losing four Hurricanes, with two pilots wounded and one killed.

The early evening raids targeted Detling and Eastchurch, where the bomb dump was hit. Everything within 400 yards (365 metres) – buildings, drainage pipes, power and telephone cables and five aircraft – was destroyed. It was the final straw for Eastchurch; like Manston before it, the airfield was declared non-operational.

The most worrying development was that bombers were now reaching aircraft factories. At Brooklands the Vickers works that produced Wellington bombers was struck, and at Rochester the Short Brothers factory was hit, with civilians killed and buildings demolished. Fortunately for Fighter Command, the raiders missed the Hawker factory at Brooklands, which had been their primary target.

It had been another gruelling day for Fighter Command. Over 700 sorties had been flown and 25 fighters had been destroyed, with another 4 badly damaged. Seven airfields had been hit, for which effort the Luftwaffe had lost twenty-two planes shot down and nine damaged.

Once again, Dowding was forced to shuffle his forces. At Croydon, No. 111 Squadron from Debden took the place of 85 Squadron. The replacements were hardly rested and fresh. The pilots had been averaging four hours' sleep a night and they were down to seven aircraft. At Hornchurch, No. 54 Squadron was reaching the end of its endurance. Even Al Deere, famously calm, found himself twitching and snapping. One 54 Squadron pilot fell asleep into his breakfast plate.

3 September 1940 TUESDAY

Fine and warm, with some haze in the Channel and Straits of Dover.

Today, the utterly fatigued No. 54 Squadron was replaced at Hornchurch by No. 41 Squadron, which had been re-forming at Catterick. The new squadron commander had a shock. 'We were amazed at the eagerness of you chaps to get away from Hornchurch, but we soon learned why,' he said. 'None of you looked as if you had slept for a week.' Al Deere calculated that during August his squadron had received 18 replacements, but now only 16 pilots remained for the transfer north.

Also today, No. 66 Squadron arrived at Kenley from Coltishall. Both Nos 41 and 66 squadrons would suffer a painful first few days in the south. 'After the hard lessons of the first two days, we became more canny and determined not to let ourselves be caught from above,' wrote Richard Hillary [Hillary, p. 98], whose 603 Squadron had suffered over the previous few days.

Today was the first anniversary of the start of the war, and Britain found herself in a grim situation. Across the Channel, nearly 2000 barges, 1600 escort

A remarkably clear British reconnaissance photograph shows the early build-up of barges for the German invasion plans that were ripening in the first days of September 1940.

vessels, 419 tugs and 168 transports had been assembled. On the same day, Feldmarschall Wilhelm Keitel ordered the embarkation of invasion materials to begin in eight days' time, on 11 September, the date set for Invasion Day minus ten.

In the meantime, Fighter Command's sector stations were targeted once again. The largest raid of the day started appearing on British radar at around 8.30am. Three squadrons went to meet the attackers, but they were ordered to disengage once it was realized that the enemy formation consisted almost entirely of fighters. However, by 9.30am a large formation of 54 Do17s, 80 Me110s and 40 Me109s was flying up the Thames, heading, it seemed, for North Weald or Debden, or perhaps even London itself. Park scrambled 249 Squadron from North Weald, 17 from Debden and 603 from Hornchurch, and they joined battle.

No. 603 Squadron climbed to meet the raiders. As its pilots moved into line astern, Me109s dived on top of them. The Spitfires turned to meet them, and a fierce dogfight ensued. Richard Hillary managed to fire two bursts at an Me109, seeing smoke start to appear, but was then shaken as his aircraft was struck. Within seconds, the cockpit was on fire. Hillary wrenched at the hood, but it stuck fast. He undid his harness to free his arms, but now the flames were licking around him and he passed out. Then, the Spitfire flicked into a spin and rolled onto its back, at which point Hillary, still unconscious, fell from the plane. The cold air brought him round. He grabbed at his ripcord, the canopy blossomed overhead and he drifted down into the sea off Margate. It was three hours before he was picked up and taken to hospital to be treated for serious burns to his face and hands.

No. 603 Squadron lost one other Spitfire, with another wounded pilot, and No. 17 Squadron suffered as well. One of its pilots, Sergeant Desmond Fopp, was badly burned but managed to bale out after being hit by an Me110. Flying Officer David Hanson shot down a Dornier but was struck by return fire. By the time he had struggled free of his cockpit, he was only a hundred feet off the ground and was killed when he plunged to earth. A third No. 17 pilot managed to force-land his stricken aircraft at North Weald.

These efforts could not prevent an attack on North Weald, where 200 bombs, many delayed-action, were dropped. Four of the base personnel were killed on the ground and the runways were cratered. Hornchurch and Debden were also hit, but both remained operational.

As the bombers departed, Hurricanes from six squadrons attacked in waves. A number of Me110s were shot down, with successes for Nos 46 and 303 squadrons. But the former accidentally shot down two Blenheims near North Weald (as well as losing three of its Hurricanes), and the latter, for all its aggression, saw one aircraft lost and one damaged for its one kill. In other squadrons, losses were surprisingly high against the retreating formation of Dorniers and Me110s. Four aircraft of 257 Squadron were shot down, with one flight commander killed and another very badly burned.

Don Finlay (*centre*) with some of his No. 41 Squadron pilots at their Hornchurch base, December 1940. The squadron's arrival in the south, on 3 September 1940, saw them blooded quickly, including the loss of their squadron leader at the time, Hilary Hood, on 5 September.

'I was sitting in a ball of fire'

Sergeant Desmond Fopp, of No. 17 Squadron, thought he had evaded his Messerschmitt Me110 pursuers on 3 September, until a burning cockpit told him otherwise.

```
     We were scrambled late and did not get sufficient altitude to
achieve a favourable attacking position from above, with the result
that we had to attack head-on at about 20,000 feet, and hope to break
up the large formation of Do 17s, with guns blazing which did separate
them considerably. I had just put a Dornier's engine out and he was
smoking badly when I saw three Me 110s coming in behind me in line
astern. By this time I had run out of ammunition but decided that as
I could not match them for speed I would turn into them and simulate
an attack. This I did and to my astonishment and joy they broke
all round me so I immediately half rolled and dived for the deck.
Unfortunately for me one of them was also below and behind out of
sight and managed to put a cannon shell into the radiator, with the
result that all I heard was a thump and the next second I was sitting
in a ball of fire. [Quoted in Franks, p.38]

                    -0-0-0-0-0-
```

Two squadrons from the Duxford sector were also called on, and having had a longer time to climb they found themselves in a better attacking position. No. 310 Czech Squadron fell on the Me110s, shooting down four of them, and Spitfires of 19 Squadron hit a further three. They were hampered, though, by continuing problems with their cannons recently fitted, in place of the usual machine-guns.

The afternoon would see only one half-hearted raid, as the Luftwaffe drew breath for the next phase. In The Hague, Goering and his senior commanders debated the next move. Goering sensed that Hitler was losing faith in the invasion plan. It would require a huge new effort by the Luftwaffe to restore confidence. The Luftwaffe's intelligence reports suggested that Fighter Command was running out of aircraft and that its bases around London were in ruins. What better way to lure the rest of Dowding's forces into the air than to attack London itself? Otherwise, Dowding could simply move his forces north, out of range of Me109s, to preserve them for deployment against an invasion. Hitler, furious with the continued Bomber Command attacks on Berlin, was ready now to countenance such a move.

Sperrle was more cautious and distrusted the optimistic assessments of Fighter Command's supposedly paltry resources. But Kesselring, who spoke with the authority of having overseen the aerial destruction of Warsaw and Rotterdam, pressed for an all-out offensive on the British capital. 'If you can pull off these attacks,' he told the Luftwaffe commanders, the invasion would be unnecessary and 'you will have saved the lives of 100,000 German soldiers'.

continued on page 289

SINGLE-ENGINE AIRCRAFT				MULTI-ENGINE AIRCRAFT						PASS-ENGER	INSTR/CLOUD FLYING [Incl. in cols. (1) to (10)]	
DAY		NIGHT		DAY			NIGHT					
DUAL	PILOT	DUAL	PILOT	DUAL	1ST PILOT	2ND PILOT	DUAL	1ST PILOT	2ND PILOT		DUAL	PILOT
(1)	(2)	(3)	(4)	(5)	(6)	(7)	(8)	(9)	(10)	(11)	(12)	(13)
56·50	311·55	4·10	10·25							10·05	6·00	3·30
·45												
	·35											
1·20											·10	
	1·00											
	·30											·30
	·45											
·30												
	1·00											·30
	1·00											
·35												
	1·40											1·40
·40												
·45												
·40												
12·15	13·20	1·00	2·15								·45	2·55
5·00	12·00											
62·05	318·25	4·10	10·25							10·05	6·10	6·10
(1)	(2)	(3)	(4)	(5)	(6)	(7)	(8)	(9)	(10)	(11)	(12)	(13)

Readiness, September 1940.

Shorty, Geoff, and D.M.C.

P61.

SINGLE-ENGINE AIRCRAFT				MULTI-ENGINE AIRCRAFT							PASS-ENGER	INSTR/CLOUD FLYING [Incl. in cols. (1) to (10)]	
DAY		NIGHT		DAY			NIGHT						
	PILOT	DUAL	PILOT	DUAL	1ST PILOT	2ND PILOT	DUAL	1ST PILOT	2ND PILOT			DUAL	PILOT
(1)	(2)	(3)	(4)	(5)	(6)	(7)	(8)	(9)	(10)		(11)	(12)	(13)
50	226.40	3.10	6.55								10.05	5.25	3.15
	.40												
	.20												
			1.15										
	.20												
	.30												
	1.10												
	.30												
	1.15												
	.55												
	1.00												
2.00	.50												
2.00	1.05												
	1.30												
	.40												
	1.00												
	.45												
	1.10												
	.10												
	1.00												
	.55												
	1.10												
	.30												
	.50												
0	248.55	3.10	8.10								10.05	5.25	3.15
	(2)	(3)	(4)	(5)	(6)	(7)	(8)	(9)	(10)		(11)	(12)	(13)

Taking off for one of the London battles. September. 1940.

'We are now on the brink of victory'

On 3 September 1940, an (as ever) self-confident Herman Goering informed his senior lieutenants in the Luftwaffe that victory was at hand, and that he had a plan for the final destruction of Fighter Command.

My fellow commanders, we are now on the brink of victory. An assault and an invasion of England is now more promising than ever before. Our intelligence has now informed us that the RAF is now down to less than a hundred fighter aircraft, the airfields protecting London are out of action because of the superb and accurate bombing of our bomber forces, their communications are in disarray, and now we are told, their air commanders are arguing with each other.

Gentlemen, another phase is now almost complete. The RAF is now no longer the great threat that it used to be, and we can now draw every available fighter plane that the RAF has into the air, because the next target must be London itself.

-0-0-0-0-0-

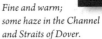

WEDNESDAY 4 September 1940

On Wednesday, Hitler announced the change of German strategy in a speech at the Reichstag. 'Just now ... Mr Churchill is demonstrating his new brainchild, the night air raid,' he said. 'When they declare that they will increase their attacks on our cities, then we will raze their cities to the ground. We will stop the handiwork of these night air pirates, so help us God!' [Shirer, pp. 779–80]

Fine and warm; some haze in the Channel and Straits of Dover.

Bombs had been falling on British civilians for three months. Over a thousand had been killed by the end of August, and as many again injured. But to switch the whole weight of the German bombers against London, rather than the RAF airfields, was a decisive change of strategy by the Luftwaffe.

London was an obvious strategic target. Heavily populated, it was the hub of national road, rail and water transport and of the country's commerce, industry and finance. It was the nation's biggest port and the centre of the government, legislature and judiciary. Primary targets would still be industrial and commercial, in particular the docks. But the Luftwaffe command was fully aware that many civilians would be killed. It was part of the plan to cause terror and chaos and create pressure from a panic-stricken public on Britain's rulers to seek terms with Hitler. The threat of invasion loomed in the background. During his speech, Hitler made a menacing joke. 'In England they're filled with curiosity and keep asking "Why doesn't he come?" Be calm. Be calm. He's coming! He's coming!'

For three more days, though, the attacks on Fighter Command would press on relentlessly. The weather stayed bright and fair, ideal conditions for the attackers. As on the preceding days, RAF losses were equal to, or greater than, the Luftwaffe's.

On the morning of 4 September, 70 He111s and Do17s with 200 Me109s approached the Kent coast between Dover and Hastings, then split up to attack Eastchurch and Lympne. Just after midday a formation of 300 aircraft approached Folkestone, while another raid homed in on the Poling radar station and yet another formation approached Brighton. Park put up 14 squadrons, including newly arrived No. 66 and two borrowed from other sectors. During fierce fighting, 66 Squadron lost five Spitfires. Apart from one formation that got through to damage the Short Brothers factory in Rochester, the raids were driven back.

Under cover of the larger raids, 20 bomb-carrying Me110s had crossed the coast near Littlehampton and were flying northwards at low altitude, following the railway lines. At 1.15pm they were spotted 6000 feet over Guildford, Surrey, by the Observer Corps. No. 253 Squadron, patrolling from Kenley, was alerted and intercepted them, diving on the low-flying Messerschmitts, shooting down five and leaving a trail of wreckage across the Surrey countryside. But some of the heavy fighters made it to their target, Brooklands, where they again hit the Vickers works rather than the Hurricane-producing Hawker factory. The raid was still devastating. Six 500-kilo bombs landed on the machine shops and Wellington assembly sheds, killing eighty-eight people and wounding many more. The factory was wrecked, and it was four days before bomber production restarted.

Churchill inspects bomb damage to shops in Ramsgate, Kent, on 28 August 1940.

5
SEPT
1940

Continuing fine and warm, with some cloud later.

5 September 1940 THURSDAY

On Thursday, No. 66 Squadron lost a further three aircraft. The day saw Kesselring abandon his established pattern and instead launch smaller raids, over a period of eight hours starting at 10am. The first formations were intercepted by four squadrons, including the newly arrived No. 41 Squadron, which engaged Dorniers and Me109s over the Thames Estuary, shooting down two of the fighters and damaging two bombers for the loss of one Spitfire. At the same time, No. 79 Squadron was scrambling to defend its Biggin Hill base, while eight Hurricanes of 111 Squadron took on a hundred enemy aircraft just north of Dungeness.

Soon afterwards, No. 19 Squadron, now back in standard Spitfires armed with machine-guns, hit a raid of more than 100 aircraft heading for Hornchurch. The formation was turned back, but the squadron lost its commanding officer, shot down and killed, and had two other Spitfires badly damaged.

Lympne and Eastchurch airfields suffered some minor damage, and at about 3.30pm a raid was plotted again over the Thames Estuary. No. 73 Squadron had landed at Debden from the north only at 11.05am, but it was ordered up against the formation of He111s and Ju88s. After damaging one Heinkel, the squadron was 'bounced' by Me109s, and within moments had lost four Hurricanes shot down, with one pilot killed and another wounded. But then the Me109s were themselves 'bounced' by Hurricanes from the Polish 303 Squadron, which accounted for three of them. While the fighters slugged it out, the bombers hit oil-storage facilities at Thameshaven, starting an immense blaze.

This raid turned out to be the Germans' most successful of the day, and once more Fighter Command lost as many aircraft as the Luftwaffe. No. 41 Squadron did not repeat its success of the morning. During the afternoon it lost four aircraft

This famous photograph shows Hermann Goering (sixth from left) and assembled Luftwaffe officers gazing out across the Channel towards their as yet unobtained object.

and the squadron commander and a flight commander were killed. The deaths of senior men were particularly alarming for the inexperienced pilots. Peter Brothers, veteran of No. 32 Squadron, was one of those selected from 'resting' squadrons to bolster 'green' units, and on 5 September he arrived at 257 Squadron. Two of the squadron's flight commanders had been killed the previous day. 'The squadron morale was absolutely zilch,' said Brothers. 'Obviously the young chaps thought, well, if the flight commanders can get shot down, what chance have we got?' [Quoted in Parker, p. 262]

During the afternoon, Goering's special train, *Asia*, complete with private bedroom, study and cinema, carried him across Germany and the Low Countries to Cap Gris Nez, within sight of the White Cliffs of Dover. With Hitler having given the order that day for London to be attacked, Goering was eager to be present for the final phase.

FRIDAY 6 September 1940

On the morning of 6 September Kesselring reverted to staggered raids, sending over substantial formations from first light. Early in the morning, No. 303 Polish Squadron was hit while trying to disrupt a bomber formation over Kent. Five of its aircraft were shot down, and both squadron commanders were wounded.

Fine but cooler. Some haze over the Straits of Dover and Thames Estuary.

There were further attacks on Thameshaven, still burning from the day before, and Brooklands was raided again. This time, the Hawker factory was bombed, but the damage was slight. Throughout the day, squadrons were kept busy just defending their home aerodromes, and losses were again steady. No. 601 had four of its pilots shot down, with two killed, and in all twenty-three RAF fighters were destroyed during the day. The Luftwaffe sustained similar losses.

continued on page 295

'I circled around and waved to him'

The aerial duelling occasionally offered opportunities for chivalry. Flight Lieutenant Michael Robinson of 601 Squadron recorded one such, on 6 September.

```
     Having attacked two Me 109s at the mouth of the Thames Estuary,
I saw a third Me 109 flying past me. I followed him down to ground
level and chased him southwards. He never rose above 100 feet until
well south of Maidstone and then throttled back. I overtook him and
formated [flew at a fixed distance] on him, pointing downwards for him
to land. He turned away so I carried out a dummy quarter attack,
breaking very close to him. After this he landed his Me in a field
at about 140 mph some 25 miles south-east of Maidstone. The pilot got
out apparently unhurt and held up his hands above his head. I circled
around and waved to him, and as he waved back I returned and threw
a packet of twenty Players at him and returned to base. He picked
up his cigarettes. [Quoted in Gelb, p. 114]
```

-0-0-0-0-0-

Captured Luftwaffe airman Werner Voigt lights up, relieved to have escaped a watery grave after ditching his Me109 into the sea off Dover.

A SQUADRON DIARY

Nine Hurricanes left Northolt at 08.40 hours [on 6 September 1940]. Four Hurricanes landed Northolt 08.35 [sic] - 09.50 hours. After various patrol orders the [303 Polish] Squadron was over Western Kent and saw very large formations of enemy aircraft moving up from the coast to the east of them and above. Their lack of height forced them to attack climbing and at only 140 mph. This contributed largely to our heavy casualties. S/Ldr Kellett destroyed one Do215 and force-landed at Biggin Hill slightly wounded. F/O Urbanowicz reports: 'I was Yellow 2 with S/Ldr Krasnodebski, the second section. I saw a raid a mile away travelling westward - about 40 Dorniers. Red Section went in to attack. I saw Me109s and Hurricanes flying across from left to right on each other's tails. One Me109 then attacked me from starboard. We had a short dogfight. I fired 3 or 4 seconds at 200 yards. The engine caught fire and E/A fell vertically to earth. I lost my section and orbited. I saw bombs dropping in one place and Me109s circling round that place and much AA fire. I circled there and attacked a bomber. One Me 109 was in the way and two more attacked me. I had to dogfight with the three Me's. I had no chance to fire. I escaped over some balloons by the sea, and the Me's climbed up. I heard "All Apany Pancake" calling the squadron in to land and I came home.' F/Lt Forbes shot down one Me109 and damaged another. He was forced down by petrol pouring in to the cockpit. He tried to land but overshot the field and was slightly wounded by splinters. The aircraft was damaged by shellfire and the landing and was Cat 3. [i.e. destroyed] F/O Feric destroyed one Me109 and probably another. Sgt Frantiszek shot down one Me109 and his aircraft was hit in the tail by a shell. He landed at Northolt and his aircraft has been repaired here. S/Ldr Krasnodebski's aircraft a/c was hit by a shell before he had engaged the enemy and immediately caught fire. He was taken to Farnborough Hospital suffering from burns and shock. Sgt Karubin claims to have shot down one He111. He crashed near Pembury, shot down by a Me109, and was admitted to Pembury Hospital, slightly injured.

Summary:

Enemy casualties -

1 Do215, 5 Me109s and 1 He111 destroyed. 2 Me109s probable.
Own casualties - 5 Hurricanes Cat 3, 1 Hurricane Cat 2. [i.e. badly damaged], Two pilots wounded and two pilots slightly wounded.

-0-0-0-0-0-

AIR VICE-MARSHAL PARK'S ASSESSMENT –
6 SEPTEMBER 1940

Contrary to general belief and official reports, the enemy's bombing attacks by day did extensive damage to five of our forward aerodromes and also to six of our seven sector stations. There was a critical period when the damage to sector stations and our ground organization was having a serious effect on the fighting efficiency of the squadrons, who could not be given the same good technical and administrative service as previously … The absence of many essential telephone lines, the use of scratch equipment in emergency operation rooms, and the general dislocation of ground organization, was seriously felt for about a week in the handling of squadrons by day to meet the enemy's massed attacks, which were continued without the former occasional break of a day.

-0-0-0-0-0-

'It seems a funny way to run a war'

Squadron Leader A.V.R. (Sandy) Johnstone, of 602 Squadron, knew from his own experience exactly how stretched the supplies of trained pilots and replacement aircraft had become.

```
    Two further pilots have come to us straight from a Lysander
squadron with no experience whatsoever on fighter aircraft. Apparently
demand has now outstripped supply and there are no trained pilots
available in the Training Units, which means that we will just have
to train them ourselves. However, it remains to be seen whether we
can spare the hours, as we are already short of aircraft for our
own operational needs. It seems a funny way to run a war …
[Sandy Johnstone, p. 113]

                    -o-o-o-o-o-
```

Fighter Command was approaching a crisis. During the previous two weeks it had seen 295 of its fighters destroyed and 171 seriously damaged. Even with the improvements in production, the aero factories were struggling to keep up with the rate of attrition. Workers were tiring and productivity was slowing. During August, just over 300 pilots had been lost and only 260 had arrived to replace them, many inadequately prepared by the shortened training time now in operation. Six of the seven sector stations of 11 Group were now bombed almost to the point of collapse. Five of its advanced airfields were seriously damaged.

Dowding began to consider withdrawing the remainder of his forces to northern England to be thrown into the fight when the actual invasion began. The British Army was tensing for action, in the belief that command of the air was about to be lost and invasion was imminent.

But then, just as it seemed the final blows were about to fall, the Luftwaffe changed direction.

6

CULMINATION

7 September to 31 October 1940

Hermann Goering was confident that 7 September 1940 would be one of the greatest days of his life. He spent the morning touring airfields in the Pas de Calais and then proceeded to Cap Gris Nez, from where the White Cliffs of Dover could be seen clearly across the sparkling waves of the English Channel. He had dressed for the occasion in his comic-opera powder-blue uniform encrusted with yards of gold braid. A lavish picnic was laid out to sustain him while he watched the show, and photographers were on hand to record his moment of triumph.

Across the water, the defenders looked up at the clear skies with heavy hearts and prepared themselves for another desperate day. After days of relentless pounding, the fabric of Fighter Command was battered and torn. Its pilots were strung out with fatigue and strain, and the replacements coming to fill the gaps caused by losses and exhaustion were novices flying into an intensely lethal environment where inexperience equalled death.

Park wrote later that the damage to 11 Group's airfields was now so bad that it 'greatly reduced the defensive power of our fighter squadrons. The destruction of numerous telephone lines ... using emergency sector Ops. Rooms ... and an almost complete disorganization of the defence system made the control of our fighter squadrons extremely difficult ... had the enemy continued his heavy attacks against Biggin Hill and the adjacent sectors ... the fighter defences of London would have been in a perilous state.' [Quoted in Moss, p. 294]

PREVIOUS PAGE
Rolling banks of
smoke swirl over
London as the Blitz
begins in earnest on
7 September 1940.

OPPOSITE
A German bomber crew
is briefed on its target
for the day (1940).

But following the meeting on 3 September, and unbeknownst to Fighter Command, the Luftwaffe's tactics were about to change radically. The target on 7 September would be *Loge*, the German codeword for London. Goering's decision to shift the weight of the attack to the capital was driven by his natural impatience rather than rational calculation. The primary aim of the Luftwaffe was to achieve air superiority. In the preceding days it had undoubtedly done great damage to bases and infrastructure, but there were still many aircraft coming up to oppose the raids. Rather than accept that this was evidence that their intelligence services had underestimated the strength of Fighter Command, the German leadership

chose to regard each robust response as the last rally before collapse. Once London was threatened directly, the RAF would have to put 'the last fifty Spitfires' into the fight, which Kesselring confidently assessed were all that were left, and the German fighters could dispose of them in one final action.

There were also now good political reasons for attacking London. Hitler had made his wishes clear in his 4 September speech. Britain's gall in bombing Berlin would have to be avenged, and Goering was anxious to please his master.

7 September 1940 SATURDAY

Fair with some haze. The morning dawned sunny, clear and hot. It was perfect bombing weather. But the drama was slow to begin. A German reconnaissance plane checking on bomb damage to Liverpool was intercepted and shot down, after a long chase. Just before midday, radar picked up a small formation just off the coast. Spitfires of No. 66 Squadron on a routine patrol were vectored to intercept, but they broke off when it turned out the intruders were only Me109s trying to provoke a fight. Otherwise, there was an ominous quiet. Squadrons were stood down, and pilots dozed in the sunshine. It was hard, though, to relax. It seemed clear that the lull was only a pause for breath, and the longer the wait, the more time the Luftwaffe had to assemble its forces.

Across the Channel, Luftwaffe airfields were busy arming and fuelling an enormous host of aircraft for the great assault to come. Just before 4pm, the quiet spell over southern England was broken as the first radar reports were processed at Bentley Priory and counters started appearing on the situation map. All over the south, fighter squadrons were brought to readiness.

An air armada of nearly 1000 Luftwaffe aircraft was building up over the French coast. It was the greatest collection of aircraft ever seen. There were 348 bombers in the fleet, stacked up in towering layers from 14,000 to 20,000 feet, while above and behind them, outnumbering them almost two to one, buzzed 617 fighters, charged with protecting the formations and intent on destroying every Hurricane or Spitfire that attempted to penetrate the ranks. The vast aerial formation rolled across the Channel on a front that was 20 miles wide.

The first Observer Corps reports of the enemy's massed ranks reached the Maidstone centre at 4.16pm, 'many hundreds of aircraft' having been sighted approaching the coast between Deal and North Foreland. At 4.17pm, eleven Fighter Command squadrons were ordered to scramble, and six minutes later all the remaining fighter squadrons in 11 Group were brought to readiness. Calls went out to 10 Group and 12 Group to stand by to help.

Air Vice-Marshal Park was away from 11 Group's Uxbridge headquarters, so decision-making fell elsewhere. It was judged that the assault must be another attack on the hard-pressed sector stations, on the oil terminal at Thameshaven, or on aircraft factories. Squadrons now raced to guard these locations.

Once across the coast, the Luftwaffe force split up, and, at varying altitudes, changed direction, criss-crossing the flight paths of the formations above and below them. For the British, tracking the huge number of aircraft was extremely difficult, but it was clear that one large group was heading north towards the Essex coast,

A Heinkel He111 bomber makes its way across the Channel for an attack (1940). Visible through the glass of the forward gunner's position is the island of Jersey, already under German occupation.

threatening North Weald, while another, made up of more than 200 bombers, was veering west towards Biggin Hill and Kenley. But when the northerly group reached the Thames Estuary, it suddenly swung to the west and headed directly up the river. The westerly group, meanwhile, had bypassed the sector stations, passed over Central London and then turned towards the East End and the docks. When a third group, following behind, headed on a direct line from the coast to the East End of London, the target was at last clear.

The convergence on the capital was a surprise. Frantically, the order went out to the squadrons in the air to leave their airfield and factory patrols and rush to the capital. Although Dowding had 23 squadrons airborne by the time the first bombs started to fall, only a few were able to intercept the bombers before they struck the city.

The first four squadrons to be scrambled – Nos 1 and 303 (Polish) from Northolt, 504 from Hendon, and 501 from Gravesend – were in the air by 4.20pm, but had been sent to patrol airfields and the oil depot at Thameshaven. Joined in the air by No. 249 Squadron from North Weald five minutes later, they now hurtled towards the stream of enemy aircraft, to be confronted with an awesome sight. In the words of Francis K. Mason, the great chronicler of the Battle of Britain, they 'found themselves on the edge of a tidal wave of aircraft, towering above them, rank upon rank, more than a mile and a half high ... covering the sky like some vast irresistible migration'. [Mason, pp. 359–60]

No. 249 Squadron intercepted a forward part of the enemy force over Maidstone, but was hugely outnumbered by the escorting fighters and soon found itself surrounded by more than 60 Messerschmitt Me109s. During a fifteen-minute dogfight, six of No. 249 Squadron's Hurricanes were lost, one pilot (Pilot Officer R.D.S. Fleming) was killed and three were wounded, and

'The whole sky to ourselves'

Helmut Staal, flying in the leading flight of bombers on 7 September (*Gruppe* 2, *Kampfgeschwader* 76), described the experience.

     It had been an easy flight up from the Thames Estuary and along the
Thames. There was no opposition and we felt that we had the whole sky
to ourselves. We were at 5000 feet. The docks at Woolwich stood out
almost as if beckoning for us to release our bomb load. Through the
glass canopy I could see tall cranes and the long square shape of
the three main docks. I lined them up carefully, and as I pressed the
release button I looked elsewhere at the huge mass of buildings and
warehouses below, then just caught a glimpse of the sticks of bombs
as they kinked from side to side as they fell towards earth.
[www.battleofbritain1940.net]

                            -0-0-0-0-0-

all without having any impact on the enemy armada – there was not a single 'kill'.

No. 303 Squadron ran into a layer of the bomber stream over Loughton in Essex – 40 Dorniers at 20,000 feet, with a formation of Me110s above and behind, and above them, at about 25,000 feet, the Me109s. The Polish squadron was about 4000 feet above the bombers and dived, turning their whole force broadside. 'We gave them all we'd got,' said their English squadron leader, Ronald Kellett, 'opening fire at 450 yards and only breaking away when we could see the enemy completely filling the gunsight. That means we finished the attack at point-blank range. We went in practically in one straight line, all of us blazing away.' [Quoted in Wood and Dempster, p. 346]

The squadron claimed ten bombers destroyed or damaged, for the loss of two aircraft. It was a sweet revenge for men who had been driven from their homes and loved ones by the German invasion. Nos 1 and 63 squadrons also had early successes, sending several bombers tumbling away from their formations. But the German fighter screen proved very hard to penetrate.

In the city, the sirens had sounded at 4.43pm. Londoners were used to alarms by now and ambled rather than ran to the shelters. At Upton Park football ground, West Ham fans enjoying a 4–1 lead over Tottenham Hotspur grumbled as they trooped out of the ground. Eighteen-year-old Betty Roper was in the East End, near Victoria Park: 'We heard the sirens. Nobody went into the shelters at first.' But the sky was clear, and soon fingers were pointing upwards at the ominous black dots approaching from the east. 'There were hundreds of them,' said Betty. 'The sky was black and you could see the bombs falling. They were like silver. Soon the docks were alight.' [Quoted in Parker, p. 269]

Eighteen-year-old Fire Watcher Robert Barltrop was on the flat roof of Sainsbury's grocery in Walthamstow. Shoppers ignored the air raid warning, but 'this time the all-clear didn't come ... I had a view across to the east and I saw the planes coming from the Dagenham and Barking directions. They were following the Thames like a little swarm of flies. They puffed some anti-aircraft fire all around them and as I sat there watching, the planes got more and more numerous. Then clouds of smoke began to rise from the East End. Then the clouds gradually became one huge cloud.' [Quoted in Parker, p. 270]

The first wave included more than 150 He111s and Do17s, flying three miles high. An onlooker from below couldn't help admiring the 'majestic orderliness' of the bomber fleet. At about 5pm, the aircraft arrived over the docks, warehouses and crowded terraces of the East End. Incendiaries fell, and within moments huge fires sprang up and a massive pall of smoke climbed upwards, blinding the anti-aircraft gunners and acting as a beacon for the bombers following.

Oberstleutnant Paul Weitkus, commanding a *Gruppe* of *Kampfgeschwader* 2, had orders to attack the docks near Tower Bridge. 'We all had sketches of our targets,' he said. 'When we reached [the] Docks there were not many fighters but the guns seemed quite good.' They 'placed the bombs very well and large fires started.' [Letter, RAF Museum]

But now Fighter Command forces were at last arriving in strength, over London, the Thames Estuary and the Isle of Sheppey, attacking both incoming and returning bombers. 'They dived through the bomber formation from a terrific height,' remembered 45-year-old veteran General Fink, the commander of

OPPOSITE
In a classic photograph from 7 September, a Heinkel He111 looms threateningly over Wapping and the Isle of Dogs in London's East End.

Kampfgeschwader 2. 'We had the impression that each fighter had chosen one bomber and was diving to attack it … It was a horrible feeling when they came down on you.' Fink's Dornier Do17 was hit. He was the only one of the four-man crew to escape unhurt, and it was a tribute to the sturdiness of their aircraft that it managed to struggle back to the base at Arras.

By 5pm, Dowding had 23 squadrons in the air, all racing towards the Thames Estuary. Soon an epic dogfight involving over 1000 aircraft developed over London and the estuary, criss-crossing the sky with 'contrails' and the sinister glitter of tracer bullets. Now and then an aircraft would dissolve into flame and slide earthwards, trailing smoke. Sometimes parachutes would appear and sway down through the chaos and the smoke rising from the fallen bombs. Sometimes they would not, and a stricken machine would glide to its doom, accelerating – it seemed to watchers – as it went, to erupt with a flash followed by a deep, final boom.

'You couldn't tell a 109 from a Spitfire in the chaos of diving machines and bursting flak,' Paul Weitkus remembered (in a letter). 'Whoever saw who first was the victor.' No. 41 Squadron, scrambled from Hornchurch, hit the northern flank, but lost three aircraft. No. 43 Squadron, scrambled from Tangmere at 4.40pm, came across a formation of 30 Dorniers over the Thames, guarded by 80 Me109s. In command was Squadron Leader Caesar Hull, a popular South African who had won a DFC in Norway. He ordered one section, under Flight Lieutenant John 'Killy' Kilmartin (a handsome and enigmatic Irishman who had been fighting since the Battle of France), to engage the escort. Hull joined the other section under Flight Lieutenant Richard Reynell, a Hawker test pilot before the war, in attacking the bombers. They climbed until they were about 1500 feet above the Dorniers, then attacked from astern. The bombers took evasive action, and each Hurricane picked out its own target. Several of the bombers were hit, but Kilmartin's section, hopelessly outnumbered, could not keep the Me109s away. One dived down on the squadron leader, whose Hurricane took a hit and went out of control, spiralling earthwards with no sign of Hull escaping. Man and machine together hit the

'My father shouted at me to get down'

For Horace Davy, a London resident, the war truly came home to him on the first day of the Blitz.

The sirens went and we went to a local air raid wardens' post to shelter. I can remember looking up in the sky to see the German bombers and seeing some of our aircraft, the puffs of smoke from the anti-aircraft guns and the barrage balloons which seemed to be pretty useless. I climbed up an exterior fire escape to get a better view and I clearly remember some pinging noises. It was the shrapnel from exploding shells that was beginning to fly around. Then my father shouted at me to get down. [Davy, recording]

-0-0-0-0-0-

earth in the grounds of Purley High School. Dick Reynell was hit as well. With his Hurricane trailing smoke, he succeeded in getting out of the cockpit and jumping moments before the fighter exploded into flames, but his parachute failed to open. His body hit the ground at Blackheath.

No. 234 Squadron, from 10 Group, was ordered up from Middle Wallop at 5pm. It lost its CO, Joe O'Brian, over Biggin Hill, as well as its senior flight lieutenant, Pat Hughes, five minutes later over South London. Hughes had been attacking a Dornier when its wing ripped off and smashed into his Spitfire, causing him to crash. An Australian who had claimed 16 victories over the past two months, he was a severe loss. His aggression and cheerfulness had made him an inspiration for the rest of the squadron. As Pilot Officer David Crook, of 609 Squadron, later wrote: 'However many fighters we lost or damaged, replacements always turned up immediately. This must have demanded the most terrific efforts from both the factories and the ground crews, and though we couldn't see the efforts we did appreciate the results. But experienced pilots could never be replaced. You could only train the new ones as best you could, keep them out of trouble as much as possible in the air, and hope they would live long enough to gain some experience. Sometimes they did.'

Another squadron racing from Middle Wallop had more success. Spitfires of No. 609 Squadron caught a formation of bombers as they turned southwest of London, and they claimed the destruction of three Me110s, two Do17s and one Me109, all without loss.

A large number of the escorting Me109s had by now been forced to turn back for lack of fuel, and British fighters harassed the bombers as they returned home,

A hazy still from a Spitfire's gun camera captures the daunting sight of a large formation of Heinkel He111s (September 1940).

continued on page 308

Factories, warehouses and docks in East London's industrialized Silvertown area erupt into flames on 7 September 1940, as shown in this Luftwaffe photograph. Casualties included the Tate & Lyle sugar refinery, Knight's soap factory and the Silvertown Rubber Works.

'I went for the nearest bomber'

Flight Lieutenant J.H.G. McArthur flew with 609 Squadron on 7 September and accounted for one of their 'kills' of the day.

```
    I went for the nearest bomber and opened fire from about 400 yards,
meanwhile experiencing heavy return cross fire from the bomber forma-
tion. After about twelve seconds smoke started to come from the port
motor and it left the formation. I then waited for it to go down to
3000 feet and then dived vertically on to it and fired off the rest of
my ammunition. It kept on going down seemingly still under some sort
of control, until it hit the water about ten miles out from the centre
of the Thames Estuary. [Quoted in Franks, pp. 42-3]
```

-o-o-o-o-o-

many of the Luftwaffe pilots nursing damaged aircraft and wounded crew. But although their formations were ragged, they still held together, and many of the RAF's fighters were now also short of fuel following the dogfights of the twenty minutes after 5pm.

A call had gone out to 12 Group, which sent into action a 'Big Wing' comprising Nos 19, 242 and 310 squadrons. But, again, they had taken so long to assemble that they had failed to intercept over Maidstone as planned. Some made their way independently towards the Isle of Sheppey, with the Spitfires of 19 Squadron about 3000 feet above the two Hurricane squadrons. While still climbing, 242 Squadron was 'bounced' by about 60 Me109s and lost 2 aircraft, with 1 pilot, Flying Officer John Benzie, killed. The fighters at last made contact with some bombers over the Thames Estuary. Later they claimed to have shot down 11 aircraft, although this turned out to be a gross overestimation of their impact.

By 5.45pm, the whole Luftwaffe formation had turned south, and the 'all clear' sounded in London at 6.15pm. In just over half an hour of bombing, immense destruction had been inflicted on the city. The first wave had, with great accuracy, bombed Woolwich Arsenal on the south side of the River Thames as well as the entrance to London's dockland. The gunpowder storage bins at the Woolwich munitions factory were hit, sending great sheets of flame hundreds of feet into the air. Soon the whine and crash of high explosive and incendiary bombs shook the docks at Rotherhithe, Millwall and Limehouse. The gas works at Beckton was hit, then the West Ham power station. The cheaply built working-class terraces huddled between the docks and factories were pounded to dust and rubble, and whole streets were obliterated.

On the Surrey Docks 1.5 million tons of timber were set alight. The warehouses and stores around the Port of London had been stacked with combustible goods. The flames bloomed as the bombs landed, then leaped hungrily from each dry, flammable structure to the next. The Thameside Tate and Lyle refinery disgorged a

OPPOSITE
Cecil Bacon's 1939 poster *Air Raid Wardens Wanted* depicts an ARP volunteer looking authoritative and self-assured. As the Blitz unfolded, wardens would be sorely tested.

CODEWORD 'CROMWELL'

Britain's senior military men, the Joint Chiefs of Staff, met at 5.20pm on 7 September, just as the first wave of bombers was turning home, having plastered London's East End. Together, the top brass surveyed the situation facing the country. Photographic evidence showed a huge build-up of barges at Ostend and all along the continental Channel coast. Radio decrypts indicated that all German army leave had been cancelled from 8 September. Dive-bombers had now been moved to the Pas de Calais to cover the Straits of Dover. The chiefs also heard that the tides in the Channel would be 'particularly favourable' for shipping between 8 and 10 September. The conclusion was that invasion was 'imminent', and all forces in the UK were now ordered to 'stand by at immediate notice'. The General Headquarters Home Forces, on their own initiative, issued at 8.07pm the codeword 'Cromwell', to bring all their forces to 'immediate action'. Many thought that this meant that the invasion was already under way. Church bells were rung, and several bridges blown up as the Home Guard dragged itself out of bed to man checkpoints all over southern England. The night of 7/8 September was, for much of the country, a miserable, sleepless one.

A British reconnaissance photograph shows invasion barges gathering in Boulogne, September 1940, as fears of an impending onslaught intensified.

torrent of molten sugar that covered the river in burning sheets. A rum store caught fire, the barrels exploding like bombs, and the streets ran with blazing spirit. The air was choked with soot, oil, chemicals, burning paint and rubber, bound together into a slimy, viscous vapour by the water of hundreds of hoses, which played on the inferno as ineffectually as a shower of rain on a volcanic eruption. Firemen found themselves surrounded, cut off, suffocated and vaporized by the superheated oxygen. Whole areas of the docks were abandoned to burn themselves out.

Bert Martin, then 16 years old, had joined his Civil Defence unit in Homerton, East London. That afternoon he was working the stirrup pumps and handling the hoses with their 14-pound brass nozzles. 'I was terrified and resigned,' he said. 'I would be holding a hose amid burning buildings – I couldn't touch the buttons on my tunic because they were so hot. My face blistered. I don't think you ever get immune to it – the wreckage, the dead bodies. It was a kaleidoscope of hell.' [Quoted in Parker, p. 272] Every available fire engine was in action. Fireboats, three hundred yards away on the opposite side of the river, found their paint blistering from the heat of the inferno, the massive conflagration now extending all along the riverside.

The worst-hit areas were the working-class districts of West Ham, Bermondsey, Stepney, Poplar, Bow, Shoreditch and Whitechapel. At Silvertown, bordered by the Thames, the River Lea and the docks, over 13,000 people were trapped. The City, where banks and businesses abutted the East End, also suffered.

When the 'all clear' sounded, the fires were still raging, with nine miles of waterfront ablaze. Fire crews were summoned from as far away as Coventry. Auxiliary Fireman George Wheeler was called to a brick-built shelter in Wick Road, Hackney, at around 7pm, which had received a direct hit. 'The bomb had blown out a wall and the concrete roof had come down on the people inside. There were men, women, children; some alive, most dead. Everything was covered in this thick grey dust ... I think there were about thirty dead. It was a terrible sight. As darkness came the whole of the skyline on the river as far as you can see was one big, red glow.' [Quoted in Parker, p. 272]

The raids went on and on. In the fading light, guided by the firestorm, came the specialist night-bombers of Sperrle's *Luftflotte* 3, more than 200 of them, unescorted and relying on the darkness for protection. From 8pm to nearly 5am the next morning, an almost continuous stream of He111s, Ju88s and Do17s dropped high explosive and incendiary canisters into the dockland fires. By midnight, nine huge conflagrations, each three times the size of the biggest blaze seen in peacetime, were raging across the East End.

American journalist Ben Robertson, watching from high ground south of the city, reported 'the most appalling and depressing sight any of us had ever seen ... It almost made us physically ill to see the enormity of the flames that lit the entire western sky. The London that we knew was burning – the London which had taken thirty generations of men a thousand years to build – and the Nazis had done that in thirty seconds.' [Robertson, p. 106]

One Mr Kyle, of West Ham, remembered how 'Our brave warden, who for months had been swaggering about in his uniform, tin helmet cocked to one side, was cringing against the wall under the concrete steps, sobbing. I never saw him again.' [Quoted in Philip Ziegler, p. 114] After months of practice and false alarms, ARP Wardens, firefighters, medics and other officials were now on the frontline. So too was the civilian population. In the crypt of a church in Bow, 'people were kneeling and crying and praying. It was a most terrible night. I became unconscious,' remembered Gladys Strelitz, from East Ham. The shelters provided for civilians proved at once to be totally inadequate. Near Liverpool Street, a goods station covered by flimsy railway arches was supposed to shelter 3000. Soon there were 14,000 inside, with only basic sanitation. In Victoria Park, 1450 people crammed into a shelter and had to stand shoulder to shoulder all night as water lapped around their ankles.

None of the shelters was capable of withstanding a direct hit. During the afternoon attack, Civil Defence Volunteer Emma Fredericks had been called out to help at a shelter in Limehouse that had become engulfed in flames, but little could be done while the raid was still in progress. The Volunteers returned at about four o'clock the next morning to be told that there were still people alive inside. They started pulling out of the way the collapsed roof of heavy beams, but had to stop while an unexploded bomb was defused by the Royal Engineers. 'It was about midday before we again went in and tried to excavate the area around the shelter,' said Fredericks. 'We knew that there was now no hope of finding anybody alive, but one never knows. Stranger things have happened. When we finally got down to the shelter, we found body over body, people almost burnt to a cinder, the air smelt of burning flesh that had gone rotten, I could take no more and had to get out. I was proud of the job I was doing, but on this occasion I was not afraid to call myself a coward, I just could not do it, but like so many others I plucked up courage to go back later. But the situation was absolutely shocking.' [Quoted in www.battleofbritain1940.net]

Many London civilians sought shelter in the Underground from the nightly Luftwaffe visits.

'On the edge of an inferno'

George Wilkins, serving with the Auxiliary Fire Service on 7 September, witnessed for himself the conflagration that erupted on London's dockside.

```
     Saturday September 7th was sunny with a light westerly breeze. At
4pm, we on our Emergency Fireboat were ordered down to Tilbury. As we
approached Tower Bridge we saw vast volumes of smoke on its eastward
side rising white into the sunlight. We passed under Tower Bridge and
soon were on the edge of an inferno. Everything was alight, tugs and
barges were flaming and sinking in the river. All the timber of Surrey
Commercial Docks was blazing furiously.
     The sun had disappeared and darkness was as of night. A strong wind
was whipped up by the great fire heat which caused small flaming
planks of wood to be blown about like matchsticks, and the river
itself was as turbulent as a whipped-up small sea. Small crowds of
people were here and there at the water's edge crying out for rescue.
Warehouses and all sorts of buildings were burning on both sides of
the river. Not until we were near Greenwich did we see the sun again
and then only as a pale disc through the great ceiling of smoke. There
I saw a gasometer alight. To my surprise it did not explode but went
as one great blue flame, like an enormous gas jet lasting only a
minute. [www.battleofbritain1940.net]
```

-o-o-o-o-o-

SUNDAY 8 September 1940

Fair early in the morning, turning cloudy later.

'At six o'clock the next morning, the sun tried to come out but it couldn't,' remembered Walter Marshall, a Reserve Policeman. 'The intensity of the smoke over the docks wouldn't allow it. It was the nearest I'd ever seen to hell.' [Marshall, recording] Fires were still raging around the warehouses in North Woolwich, the Royal Albert Docks, Queen Victoria Dock and George V Dock.

The East End was wrecked. Telephone and electricity lines had been cut, gas, water and sewage pipes ruptured. Streets were choked with debris and burnt-out vehicles. Unexploded and delayed-action bombs were everywhere. Some 430 civilians had been killed. Another 1600 were seriously injured. Thousands were homeless. Many greeted the dawn staring, bewildered and desolate, at the wreckage of what had once been their homes. Unknown to them, this was just the beginning of what would become known as 'the Blitz'. With one night's exception due to bad weather, the bombers would return for seventy-six consecutive nights.

But after that first day and night, for all the terrors and losses, there was still a fragile consensus that it could have been worse. Interwar theories and popular fears had suggested that an attack on London would result in thousands of deaths, mass panic and civil breakdown. This had not happened. There had been no terrible new weapon. None of the bombs had produced poison gas, apart from the fumes from

F/Lt.FORBES.

J7/8

39

FORM F

COMBAT REPORT.

Sector Serial No. .... (A) ....

Serial No. of Order detailing Flight or Squadron to
    Patrol .... (B) ....

Date .... (C)   7/9/40

Flight, Squadron .... (D) Flight : B Sqdn. : 303 Polish

Number of Enemy Aircraft .... (E)   40 DO 215 & 50 ME 109

Type of Enemy Aircraft .... (F)   Bombers & Fighters

Time Attack was delivered .... (G)   1700

Place Attack was delivered .... (H)   Essex

Height of Enemy .... (J)   20,000 ft.

Enemy Casualties .... (K)   1 DO 215 destroyed

Our Casualties   Aircraft .... (L)   1 Hurricane Cat.2.

                 Personnel .... (M)   Pilot slightly wounded

GENERAL REPORT .... (R) ....

We were ordered into the air to rendez-vous with No.1 Squadron who took off first. We were sent up to 15,000 ft and then to 20,000 ft, and proceeded North and then East. No.1 Squadron remained below us to starboard and in front. I led the Squadron up to 24000 ft, determined after my experience yesterday not to be caught napping at too low an altitude. It is easy to get down to the enemy and impossible to attack climbing when the slow speed makes one an easy prey to the ME 109's. I sighted a formation of about 40 enemy bombers flying Northwards. Their rearguard of ME 109's were engaged with Spitfires at 25,000 - 30,000 ft. No.1 Squadron went in to attack the enemy's tail and drew off most of the remaining fighter escort. It was a perfect combination of circumstances. We were flying in Vics line astern. The enemy was flying also in Vics line astern with 3 and 5 A/C in each Vic. The A A fire had loosened their formations. As soon as No.1 Squadron attacked, the enemy wheeled Eastwards, and we caught them on the turn. We reformed towards the enemy and launched the attack in Vics abrest, striking the formation a little to the rear of centre. They were easy meat. We came at them from partially up sun and at great speed as they turned away from us. I led in, and attacked a DO 215, hitting the starboard wing. Great chunks fell off the wing and engine, which stopped. I gave another good burst into the cockpit and more stuff fell off. E/A fell away sideways in a long glide and hit the sea. I broke away, and whilst in a steep turn, a shell hit my starboard wing root and exploded. I felt my leg was wounded and there were 3 or 4 glycol and hydraulic system leaks in the cockpit. I decided to try to return to an Aerodrome and get the machine down whole. I succeeded in regaining Northolt and landing without mishap.

                 Signature   *A.D.Forbes.*

                               Forbes F/Lt.

               O.C.   {   *Section*   Blue 1
                         Flight   B
                         Squadron 303 Squadron No. Polish.

Flight Lieutenant Athol Forbes's combat report for 7 September records a successful interception as he led 'B' Flight of 303 (Polish) Squadron's Hurricanes into action against an enemy formation.

the fires. Many bombs had failed to explode. Casualties had been significantly fewer than expected.

There had been no mass hysteria among the working class, as had been feared. 'People gathered their possessions together and piled them into perambulators. With children in their arms, they started their walk to friends or relatives,' a *Daily Telegraph* journalist reported (on 9 September). 'Their morale was astonishing. As they were walking to their new homes many were laughing and joking among themselves ... they have taken it on the chin.'

There was refuge in humour, as there would be in every bombed city of the war. In Chelsea on the Sunday morning, the pubs were packed. 'Jokes were made to relieve the tension,' wrote Theodora FitzGibbon, 'beer mugs were put down more noisily to shut out other sounds. We were glued together by dread. All our eyes were rounder, the pupils enlarged, and although we laughed, our lips twitched with alarm.' [Quoted in Philip Ziegler, pp. 114–15]

Churchill visited the City during the morning of 8 September, cheered on all sides, according to his account, with cries of 'Good old Winston', 'Good Luck' and shouts of 'Are we downhearted?', eliciting the loud response from all sides: 'No!' Whatever the inner feelings, the collective outward display was one of defiance, unity and resolution.

Soon afterwards 11 Group's commander, Keith Park, flew over London in his personal Hurricane. 'It was burning all down the river. It was a horrid sight,' he said. 'But I looked down and said, "Thank God for that," because I realized that the methodical Germans had at last switched their attack from my vital aerodromes on to cities.' [Quoted in Calder, p. 155]

Park's relief was justified. The decision by Goering to alter strategy to bomb London would be one of the most decisive of the war. The change of tactics granted a reprieve to Fighter Command, which, if the attacks on its bases had continued, might at last have been forced to retreat and regroup beyond the reach of German bombers and fighters. As it was, with London taking the force of the Luftwaffe's attacks, stations and infrastructure could be repaired. The frantic tempo of the preceding days, when pilots were fighting out of airfields that were simultaneously under attack, slackened slightly.

Satisfaction at the turn of events was tempered by the fact that the fighters had been unable to shield London. They had inflicted only 38 losses on the Luftwaffe, a small total considering the huge number of aircraft deployed. Fighter Command had seen 28 of its aircraft shot down, 19 pilots killed, and the capital battered. By contrast, Luftwaffe crews could see the huge pall of smoke over London all the way from their bases in northern France. To them it looked like a great victory. 'I personally have taken over the leadership of the attacks against England,' Goering announced in a radio broadcast on 8 September. 'For the first time we have struck at England's heart ... this is an historic hour.'

The Saturday had been as exhausting for the Germans as for the British. The Luftwaffe had to pause before it could strike again. On Sunday 8 September, the fine weather faded and the clouds rolled in, to the huge relief of the defenders. 'The weather was bad today, thank goodness, so we had a reasonable rest,' reported Richard Barclay (in his diary), whose Squadron, No. 249, had been mauled the previous day. 'I think we are all still a bit shaken after yesterday.'

continued on page 318

Dowding took advantage of the lull to rotate some of his most battered units. Exhausted and now leaderless, No. 43 Squadron retired to Usworth and was replaced by No. 607 Squadron, which had seen little action since France, apart from the abortive attack on the north by *Luftflotte* 5. No. 111 Hurricane Squadron was moved from Croydon to the relative safety of Drem, in Scotland; No. 79 Squadron was relocated from Biggin Hill to the South Wales airfield of Pembrey, from where No. 92 Squadron re-entered the fray, eager for more action.

Until about 11.30am on 8 September, there was little enemy activity. But the quiet was followed by two hours of sustained attacks. Spitfires of No. 41 Squadron were on a routine patrol when they were vectored towards Dover, where they encountered a formation of Dorniers, heavily escorted. Severely outnumbered, the British fighters struggled against the Me109s. The aircraft of Flying Officer William Scott was seen trailing smoke and diving away from the battle. Neither pilot nor machine was seen again.

The Spitfires were reinforced by Hurricanes of 46 Squadron, and others, and soon the German formations began to break up. This success was partly the result of two new tactics on the part of Park. First, he deployed several fighter squadrons in pairs, which gave them a better chance of breaking into the bomber ranks. Second, he had ordered that the chain of command follow rigidly their orders as far as height was concerned. Park was well aware that in order to avoid being 'bounced' from above, sector controllers had been adding a few thousand feet to their ordered altitude. The squadron leader would then add a few more thousand for safety. The result was that the intercepting fighters were arriving among the high-flying Me109s, leading to fighter-versus-fighter combat of the type that Park was determined to avoid, while the bombers sailed on below. With Park's new discipline, the Hurricanes and Spitfires were arriving at the level of the bombers and were able to down several of them before the Me109s could dive to defend them.

Some elements of the German armada pressed on to London, where three bombers were downed by flak, and the attack was blunted. Bombers ditched their loads over Gravesend, Dover and Sevenoaks before turning back over the coast. The airfields were mostly left alone, giving 11 Group another priceless day in which to repair facilities and replenish supplies and aircraft.

During the daylight tussle, the RAF lost four fighters, with two pilots killed and two wounded. The Luftwaffe lost seven to combat, three of which were Me109s. The fact that only eleven squadrons had been used, and only just over a quarter of the sorties flown as compared to the previous day, gave many of Fighter Command's pilots a welcome day of rest. It had been the first time in ten days that Park's 11 Group squadrons had not been at readiness the whole day.

There would, though, be no respite for the people of London that night. The sirens sounded at 7.30pm, and soon afterwards the bombers were overhead. This time, many civilians spurned the crowded and unsanitary public shelters, instead heading for Liverpool Street, the nearest Underground station to the East End in 1940. After being barred from entry at first, they spent the night on the platforms and in a tunnel that was under construction.

The authorities had feared that the use of the Underground might lead to a 'deep shelter mentality', that people would be reluctant to re-emerge and that vital war

PREVIOUS PAGE
The abrupt ending to this particular bus journey provides a graphic example of the havoc wrought on the lives of ordinary Londoners in September 1940.

work would be neglected. But they were forced to relent, and by the end of the month more than 150,000 people were using the Underground network as shelter. The live rail was switched off and people found space wherever they could, accepting the stench caused by the absence of sanitation as the price of safety.

Nevertheless, 400 civilians were killed on the night of 8/9 September, as 200 bombers dropped 1700 high-explosive bombs and countless incendiaries. By morning, 12 new areas of fire were blazing out of control. Six hospitals were damaged as well as docks, railways and warehouses. In one block of flats, 50 people died as a result of one bomb. A direct hit on the Columbia Market shelter also caused very heavy casualties. The next day, there were no trains running in or out of South London.

MONDAY 9 September 1940

This morning's *Times* carried an article reflecting on the events of two days previously. In the words of the special correspondent, 'Because of the dogged spirit of those manning our defences, Service and civilian, the Germans failed on Saturday to perpetrate a second Rotterdam in London. It was not for want of trying on their part, for they sent over hundreds of bombers which "pasted" wide areas indiscriminately.'

For Fighter Command, Monday began quietly. Apart from a couple of nuisance raids and the customary reconnaissance flights, there was little activity in the morning. Park had noticed that attacks on aerodromes had usually taken place before noon, and he guessed correctly during that morning's lull that the Luftwaffe would continue to ignore his sector stations in favour of metropolitan targets,

Scattered showers, thundery in the east; Channel fair.

Squadron Leader Douglas Bader (centre, hands in pockets) stands with other members of No. 242 (Canadian) Squadron, which formed part of 12 Group's Duxford Wing, sent out against the German raiders as the mass attacks of September got under way.

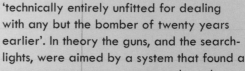

ANTI-AIRCRAFT COMMAND

The formation of an anti-aircraft corps was announced in June 1938 and it became operational in April 1939. By that time the stimulus provided by the 1938 Munich Crisis had ensured that guns to supply it were rolling off the production lines. Even so, at the beginning of the war Anti-Aircraft Command remained one of the worst-equipped branches of the forces, with only 4000 heavy and light guns and the same number of searchlights at its disposal. The quality of its personnel was questionable. Its leader, Sir Frederick Pile, complained that 'AA Command were to get the leavings of the Army intake after every other branch of the Services had had their pick.' During the winter of 1939–40, out of the twenty-five who arrived at a fairly representative battery, wrote Pile, 'one had a withered arm, one was mentally deficient, one had no thumbs, one had a glass eye which fell out whenever he doubled to the guns, and two were in the advanced and more obvious states of venereal disease'.

Pile was also exasperated by the selfish public reaction to the positioning of new batteries. 'It was only necessary to suggest siting a gun anywhere near a golf-course, a building-estate, a park, on a farm, or even close to a polo-ground for everyone to demand through their M.P. that the guns be removed at once from that neighbourhood and put in some other neighbourhood,' Pile wrote. 'In nearly all the cases the protests were entirely successful.' Pile admitted that 'London was inadequately defended' and his guns

Anti-aircraft searchlights scan the skies on the hunt for intruders (1940).

'technically entirely unfitted for dealing with any but the bomber of twenty years earlier'. In theory the guns, and the searchlights, were aimed by a system that found a target through sound location, but it was slow and inaccurate and many batteries simply blazed away at the skies. The sound of the guns was welcome, though, giving at least the illusion of defence.

The majority of the gun sites, wrote Pile, 'were several feet deep in mud, and the gunners lived in crude dug-outs built by themselves by the emplacements. Blast from the guns … soon caused these hastily constructed living quarters to collapse, and nearly all of them became so warped from bombs and gunfire that it was futile to bale out the rain-water.' [All quotations from Pile's 1949 book *Ack-Ack*]

Heavy anti-aircraft guns consisted mostly of 3.7-inch and 4.5-inch pieces that were fixed in place. Light, moveable guns included 40-mm Bofors, Vickers Mark VIII 2-pounder and 3-inch guns. Machine-guns included the 0.303-inch Lewis, 0.303-inch Bren and 20-mm Hispano. While high-flying bombers were almost impossible to hit, at lower levels 'light flak' was very effective, but weapons were in very short supply. Bofors guns were slow, loaded by hand and could get off only a few rounds against fast, low-flying enemy aircraft. Britain had no equivalent of the deadly light flak batteries that travelled with the German army, the twin-37mm and quad-20mm guns.

As civilians took shelter, the German bomber crews and fighter pilots were also tasting fear in their incursions over England's capital. Oberst Josef Priller was a pilot with *Jagdgeschwader* 26.

It was no easy task over England in September 1940. Sometimes the youngsters were the victims of their inexperience and over-enthusiasm. There were times when we heard a plea from someone who was confused and disoriented, and nothing could be done about it. I remember one occasion when a lad who hadn't, as we used to say, tasted much English air, lost sight of our formation after some frenzied twisting and turning about the sky. But we could see him: he had dived steeply and was over the outskirts of London. He should have stayed with the Staffel instead of chasing off on his own. When he grasped the situation he called for help: 'Come quickly! I'm on my own over London.' [Quoted in Bickers, p. 183]

-0-0-0-0-0-

which – the pattern so far suggested – they preferred to attack later in the day. He nevertheless took the precaution of lining up fighters from Nos 12 and 10 Groups to protect airfields and aircraft factories, and moved some of his forces forward to prepare for the expected afternoon attack.

The first signs of a big raid were picked up after 4pm. Formations were massing over Calais and Boulogne. They reached the coast between the North Foreland and Dover just before 5pm. The raid was led by Me109s, a tactic designed to lure up the British fighters early, so that they would be short of fuel when the bombers arrived. Park did not take the bait, but when the 109s were followed by large groups of bombers, Fighter Command rose to meet them. Over Surrey, No. 607 Squadron from Tangmere intercepted a formation of He111s and Do17s and, with the help of 605 Squadron, drove back the attack, although at the cost of six of their Hurricanes shot down and three pilots killed. No. 605 Squadron lost two aircraft, with one pilot killed. To the east, a raid approaching London was intercepted over Dartford by Spitfires of No. 222 Squadron.

The Coltishall and Fowlmere squadrons of Group 12, which had been detailed to guard North Weald and Hornchurch, now arrived, having taken the unilateral decision that they were needed further south. The 'Wing' (consisting of Nos 19, 242 and 310 squadrons) reached the battle in some disarray and short on fuel, but, if its pilots' claims are to be believed, it had a huge impact, shooting down 21 aircraft. (German records for the day are incomplete, and nothing like the wreckage of 21 aircraft was ever found.) Certainly, the mass of fighters caused a scene of utter confusion in the air, with pilots having to avoid friendly fire as well as the enemy's bullets and cannon shells. Douglas Bader, leading 242 Squadron, reported that he was chasing a Dornier when suddenly two Hurricanes dived down from each side in front of him. So intent were the Czech pilots of 310 Squadron on their target that they collided, the left wing of the Hurricane on the right

'POOR LONDON!'

Unteroffizier Peter Stahl was an experienced pilot, having flown as a civilian weather forecaster before the war. But 9 September was his first flight over England.

> Over Lille is our agreed meeting point with units from other Geschwader. Eventually there is an assembly of at least 200 bombers that gathers into some sort of order and sets course for London. Soon afterwards we are joined by an escort of Me109s and Me110s. There were 500-600 aircraft with me in tight formation. Wherever one looked, one saw our aircraft, all around, a marvellous sight. Among us we estimate that the total load destined to fall on London soon afterwards amounts to at least 200,000 kg. And this had been going on for some days already. Poor London!

Guided to the target by 'black smoke pillars' from fires still burning in the capital, the formation released its first bombs.

> Then it is my turn to press the red release button … The aircraft makes its usual jump of relief and we look down. The Thames bends, the docks and the whole colossal city lie spread out before us like a giant map. Then come the explosions of our bombs which we observe while banking in a wide turn eastwards, then south … the effect of our attack is an enormous cloud of smoke and dust that shoots up into the sky. One cannot imagine that a town or a people could endure this continuous crushing burden for long.

But then the formation started to break up as British fighters were suddenly among it.

> At first I take them for our own escorts and wonder about their tactics, twisting around among bombers in such a foolhardy way. Then I realize that they are British ... there is tracer all around us, and a wild twisting turning air combat has broken out between our 109s and the Spitfires and Hurricanes. Now everything is happening right underneath us! I get away to hide in the thickest bunch of our bombers I can spot nearby.

One of Stahl's engines was hit and started leaking oil, but he managed to get his Ju88 back to his airfield near Amiens. [All quotations in Stahl, pp. 60–2]

-0-0-0-0-0-

folding and ripping away, sending the aircraft into an instant spin.

Nine fighter squadrons, attacking simultaneously in pairs, met one of the biggest raiding groups over South London. The twenty or so Me110s immediately adopted their defensive circle, and many bombers dumped their loads and turned for home. But most of them found themselves swept into a nearby battle, where 40 Ju88s were being ruthlessly and successfully attacked by 9 Hurricanes of No. 253 Squadron and 12 aircraft of 303 (Polish) Squadron.

For the Luftwaffe pilots, who had been led to believe that Fighter Command was all but finished, the strength of the opposition was a shock. Far from weakening, the British resistance seemed to have stiffened. One large raid did manage to penetrate Central London, but most bombers were blocked from reaching their targets and ended up dropping their loads on the residential areas of Purley, Norbiton, Surbiton and Kingston-upon-Thames, as well as over Canterbury.

Twenty-eight German aircraft were shot down, compared to Fighter Command losses of twenty-one aircraft (with six pilots killed and several severely wounded). Yet the day's fighting had been a tactical victory for the British, who managed to drive back most of the raiders short of their targets, and a blow to the morale of the Luftwaffe.

The events of Monday night, though, showed once again that Fighter Command was all but powerless to stop the bombers in the darkness. The sorties flown by British pilots were more of a risk to themselves than the enemy. Another 370 people were killed on the ground and 1400 injured, as 170 bombers from *Luftflotte* 3 showered explosives and incendiaries over a large area. The bombardment was moving westwards. In Central London, Somerset House by the side of the Thames and the Royal Courts of Justice were both bombed. Madame Tussaud's waxwork museum was hit and set on fire, as was the Natural History Museum in South Kensington. (During the firefighting at the museum, some of the seeds in the herbarium were soaked and would later begin to germinate, including samples collected nearly 150 years earlier.) A school in Bethnal Green, East London, which was being used as a shelter, took a direct hit.

TUESDAY 10 September 1940

Tuesday saw poor weather, with rain and storms keeping Luftwaffe activity to a minimum. Until about 5pm, there were only reconnaissance and weather sorties by the Germans. Then, small numbers of single aircraft or small formations, using the clouds as cover, carried out a series of nuisance raids on Tangmere, West Malling, Poling and Portsmouth. The only interception of note was by No. 72 Squadron, which caught a small number of Ju88s and shot down two of them over East Grinstead, Sussex. For the first time in two weeks, Fighter Command suffered no combat losses, though two pilots of No. 602 Squadron crashed at Tangmere that night after a patrol. In both cases, the men had no experience of night flying.

At this time, the darkness presented far more difficulties for the RAF pilots than it did for the incoming Germans. Night-flying was dangerous and it was almost impossible for the British fighters to make the visual contact necessary to attack the bombers. 'I flew a number of night sorties from Biggin Hill,' said No. 501

Cloudy, with rain and thunderstorms.

Squadron pilot John Bisdee. 'Of course it was awful to see, particularly the dockland area and the East End of London, absolutely in flames ... the trouble was that it was practically impossible to locate a German bomber at night if you didn't have radar.' [Quoted in Parker, p. 281] A handful of Blenheims and Bristol Beaufighters had been equipped with the new airborne radar, but they were too few in number and the equipment was far from reliable.

The response of the anti-aircraft batteries to the night-time raids was unimpressive, partly because they were holding their fire to leave the skies clear for RAF fighters. But after the destruction that occurred on 7 September, Sir Frederick Pile, in command of the nation's anti-aircraft defences, ordered every available gun to London and decreed that 'every gun was to fire every possible round'. On the night of 10 September, the raiders were met by more than twice the previous amount of firepower, and the attackers were forced to fly higher. The resulting inaccuracy of the falling bombs meant more damage to residential areas, but the noise of the British guns raised civilian spirits. As the US military attaché Raymond Lee mused that night, 'It is a pleasure to reflect that so much metal is going up instead of coming down.' [Quoted in Lee, p. 54]

That night saw the worst fire yet. At St Katherine's Dock, paraffin, wax and animal skins were set ablaze. Flames shot 200 feet into the air. Soon the whole area was without gas, electricity or water. In one shelter nearby, 300 people huddled for most of the night, with only two buckets for sanitation. 'People are tight-lipped and strained,' wrote a teacher to a friend the next day, 'no longer ashamed of their fear, and the shelters are full to suffocation.' [Quoted in Philip Ziegler, p. 115]

Despite the spectacle and the destruction, the bombing of London was doing little to bring the goal of German air superiority closer. The orders for the launching of Operation Sea Lion had been due to be given the next day, 11 September.

The prime minister is greeted by onlookers as he inspects bomb damage in the City of London on 10 September 1940. The warm welcome he received suggested that domestic fears (and German hopes) of a collapse in civilian morale under the bombing were mistaken.

They were to be followed by a ten-day period of minelaying and embarkation, with the landing assault scheduled for 21 September. There were now more than 2000 barges assembled to carry the attacking force to the British coast, and Grossadmiral Raeder informed Hitler that the invasion fleet would be ready on 15 September. But the unexpectedly strong British resistance during the daytime fighting of the previous days had forced a pause for thought. Hitler told Raeder that although the Luftwaffe had achieved 'tremendous success', the crucial condition for invasion – daylight air superiority – had not been met. His view was backed up by a report in the German Naval Staff Diary for 10 September: 'There is no sign of the defeat of the enemy's Air Force over southern England and in the Channel area,' it stated. 'We have not yet attained the operational conditions which the Naval Staff stipulated to the Supreme Command as being essential for the enterprise, namely, undisputed air superiority in the Channel area and the elimination of the enemy's air activity in the assembly area of the German naval forces and ancillary shipping.' The *Kriegsmarine* could not understand how the focus on London was helping the cause of the invasion: 'It would be in conformity with the timetable preparations for Sea Lion, if the Luftwaffe now concentrated less on London and more on Portsmouth and Dover, as well as on the naval ports in and near the operational area.'

The date on which the decision would be made was moved to 14 September. But time was slipping away. The longer the invasion was delayed, the greater the risk of bad weather and difficult sailing conditions in the Channel. The fate of the operation now depended on the Luftwaffe delivering a devastating and decisive attack.

WEDNESDAY 11 September 1940

Unaware of the equivocation among the Nazi political and military hierarchy, Britain was now gripped by the sense that the climax to a historic crisis was approaching. The population braced itself for a landing that, it seemed, could surely only be days away. Churchill pointed out in a speech today that if Hitler was going to send his troops across the Channel, he would have to do so soon. 'The invasion is expected at any moment now,' wrote 'Chips' Channon in his diary the next day, 'probably some time during the weekend.'

Showers over Thames Estuary and Channel, clearing later.

Poor weather this morning limited the Luftwaffe to tactical reconnaissance, but by the afternoon the skies had cleared. A small German force approached the English coast near Dover at 3.05pm and then headed north. Accurate reports from the Observer Corps meant that Air Vice-Marshal Park was able to react proportionately, allowing him to have assets available when the main attack came in half an hour later. Most of the bombers were He111s from *Kampfgeschwader* 1 and 26, escorted by about 200 Me109 and Me110 fighters. By the time they crossed the coast at Folkestone and headed northwest towards Maidstone, Park had almost all of his 11 Group squadrons in the air, as well as support from Nos 10 and 12 Groups.

Over Kent, No. 1 (RCAF) Squadron from Northolt, No. 222 from Hornchurch and No. 238 from Middle Wallop swooped to attack. By now a standard technique had evolved, with the Spitfires clashing with the enemy fighters while the

THE NATIONALITIES OF FIGHTER COMMAND

A substantial contingent of more than 500 pilots from countries other than the United Kingdom flew with their British counterparts in the Battle of Britain. The international mix of participants – defined by their flying at least one authorized operational sortie with an eligible unit between 10 July and 31 October 1940 – is as follows.

Nation	Number of pilots	Nation	Number of pilots
Great Britain	2353	Ireland	10
Poland	139	United States	7
New Zealand	98	Jamaica	2
Canada	86	Egypt	1
Czechoslovakia	84	Austria	1
Belgium	29	Iceland	1
Australia	21	Palestine Mandate	1
South Africa	20	Southern Rhodesia	1
France	13	Unknown	4

Hurricanes went for the bombers. But the British fighters were too few and, having been scrambled late, too low. Five were lost, and the bombers and their escorts ploughed onwards, turning into the Thames Estuary, bound, surely, for the capital once again. But as they realigned over the broad mouth of the River Thames, they were met by a massed force of six squadrons (Nos 17, 46, 72, 73, 249 and 266). Over the estuary between Herne Bay and Shoeburyness, and between Gravesend and Tilbury, a huge, swirling high-altitude battle developed. Two of the No. 12 Group squadrons – Nos 19 and 74 – also threw themselves into the mêlée, even though they had been detailed as usual to protect Hornchurch and North Weald. The Me109s, many at the limit of their fuel, were mostly checked by the fighters, but the bomber formations butted through the defenders and pressed on for London.

Meanwhile, a second wave of bombers and escorts had crossed the coast between Dungeness and Dover and was also heading up the Thames to London. Park had further squadrons in the air patrolling over sector stations and aircraft factories, which he now vectored to intercept. They swept into the edges of the Luftwaffe formation, whittling at its flanks, but still it ploughed on.

At about 4.20pm the raiders reached London, and high explosive and

THE 'Y SERVICE'

Radio had been a valuable source of intelligence since the First World War, and by the Second World War an organization known as the 'Y Service' was established to listen in on the enemy. In the first three months of the war, the only messages picked up were in Morse code using the W/T (wireless telegraphy) method. Encrypted messages were sent to the Government Code and Cypher School established at Bletchley Park in Buckinghamshire. Soon, ham radio operators reported picking up voice messages in a foreign language they could not understand on the 40-megacycle band using R/T (radio telephony). RAF Intelligence purchased some American Hallicrafter 510 units, which could be tuned to the 40-megacycle band. By March 1940, these were set up at Hawkinge aerodrome, and their operators could hear the same transmissions.

However, none of the RAF personnel at Hawkinge understood German. Luckily, an army anti-aircraft gun operator stationed there did, and he was transferred to new duties.

The RAF mounted a rapid recruiting drive within the WAAF to find women with an expert knowledge of idiomatic and regional German. By the beginning of the Battle of Britain, half a dozen had been identified and were installed as intelligence operators at a new base at Fairlight in East Sussex.

The WAAFs eavesdropped on conversations among German aircrews that showed little respect for operational security. The airmen would often mention the number of aircraft in their formations and their destinations, information that was very valuable to RAF Intelligence. Soon, more branches of the 'Y Service' were set up around the country.

incendiaries started raining on the East End. As the bombers did their work, the Me110s that were still with them retreated to the south and formed a defensive circle, waiting to help them home. But that was all the protection the Heinkels could hope for. The Me109s were either still engaged or had headed back across the Channel before their fuel ran out. As the bombers sought to link up with the Me110s, the defenders saw their chance and took it. Sixty fighters from Nos 17, 56, 73, 222, 249 and 303 squadrons fell on the as yet unprotected Heinkels of *Kampfgeschwader* 26. No. 303 (Polish) Squadron, which had just seen two of its aircraft shot down by Me109s over Kent, once more demonstrated its aggression, downing three of the He111s in ten minutes. Before the bombers could reach their escorts, the Me110s were attacked by Nos 17 and 73 squadrons, which shot down four of them. Five more bombers were downed, and many more damaged. In the clashes of the afternoon, *Kampfgeschwader* 26 lost more than 50 aircrew.

The Germans suffered, but the defenders paid a high price, too, in men and machines. Despite claims that 80 enemy aircraft had been destroyed, the figure was actually closer to 25. Fighter Command had lost 29, with 17 pilots killed.

Across the Channel there was nothing to suggest that the German timetable was slipping. Aerial reconnaissance was showing a continual build-up of invasion

'A HEAVY, FULL-SCALE INVASION OF THIS ISLAND IS BEING PREPARED'

On 11 September Winston Churchill broadcast to the nation, warning that the approaching winter could mean an invasion sooner rather than later. [Quoted in Gilbert, pp. 778–9]

'We cannot tell when they will try to come. We cannot be sure that in fact they will try at all, but no one should blind himself to the fact that a heavy, full-scale invasion of this Island is being prepared with all the usual German thoroughness and method, and that it may be launched at any time now ... We must regard the next week or so as a very important week for us in our history. It ranks with the days when the Spanish Armada was approaching the Channel and Drake was finishing his game of bowls or when Nelson stood between us and Napoleon's Grand Army at Boulogne. Every man and every woman will therefore prepare himself to do his duty, whatever it may be, with special pride and care ... These cruel and indiscriminate bombings of London are, of course, part of Hitler's invasion plans. He hopes, by killing large numbers of civilians, women and children, that he will terrorise and cow the people of this mighty imperial city, and make them a burden and anxiety to the Government ... Little does he know the spirit of the British nation, or the tough fibre of Londoners, whose forebears played a leading part in the establishment of Parliamentary institutions.'

Winston S. Churchill

shipping in the ports. That night, Bomber and Coastal commands put up every available aircraft to attack Calais, Dunkirk, Le Havre and Boulogne. For over three hours, more than a hundred aircraft dropped eighty tons of bombs, destroying at least a hundred barges, but losing 15 machines in the process. The RAF bombers were, on the whole, five years out of date, slow and lacking in armour compared with their Luftwaffe equivalents. Six further *Staffeln* of Me109s had recently been withdrawn from offensive action to guard the invasion preparations, and effective German flak units were now thick on the ground.

That night, 200 bombers pounded London, and Merseyside was also hit hard. Throughout the hours of darkness, there were harassing raids over Scotland, Bristol, Lincolnshire and Norfolk, while along the east and south coasts mines cascaded into the sea to hamper the Royal Navy's ability to block the invasion.

THURSDAY 12 September 1940

On Thursday, deteriorating weather relieved the pressure on Fighter Command. The skies over the Channel were a solid mass of cloud as heavy rain swept over Southeast England. During the morning, radar picked up only isolated aircraft high above the seas off Britain's east and south coasts. Fighter Command left them alone. It was not worth the risk of attempting to intercept single intruders in such poor flying weather.

Unsettled, with heavy cloud and rain in most parts.

Around noon, small incoming formations were detected. They broke up into dispersed raids, sometimes of only one or two aircraft each, and none of them close to London. The weather made both interception and accurate bombing extremely difficult, but in several places cat-and-mouse games took place among the clouds. In the west, No. 152 Squadron was sent up from Warmwell and the pilots briefly sighted a Ju88, but before they could attack, it vanished back into the murk. No. 238 Squadron had more luck, damaging another Ju88 and in the process killing one and wounding two of its crew. Another raider off the coast of Scotland was shot down, while at the other extreme of the country a squadron from Exeter claimed another lone enemy aircraft.

The Luftwaffe's night raids were much smaller today, with only 54 bombers over London and single aircraft scattered over the rest of the country. By the standards of the developing Blitz it was a night of comparative calm in the capital. Bombs fell on the City, in Aldgate, Mansion House and Holborn. An 800-pound bomb landed right in front of the steps of St Paul's Cathedral, and penetrated 26 feet into the ground. It took three days to dig it out. When it emerged, looking, in the words of one newspaper report, 'like a vast hog about 8 feet long', it was driven by lorry to Hackney Marshes. When detonated, it blasted a crater a hundred feet across, an explosion that would have been powerful enough to reduce the façade of Sir Christopher Wren's masterpiece to rubble. It was Lieutenant Robert Davies of the Royal Engineers, the bomb disposal officer, and his assistant, Sapper George Wyllie, who neutralized the bomb. They became the first recipients of the new George Cross award for 'acts of the greatest heroism or the most conspicuous courage in circumstances of extreme danger', which could be awarded to civilians as well as soldiers.

OPPOSITE
Radiating confidence, Churchill visits a coastal defence position near Hartlepool, in the north-east, a few days before the onset of the Blitz.

CIVILIAN AIR RAID CASUALTIES

Month of 1940	Men killed (injured)		Women killed (injured)		Children* killed (injured) *under age 16		Total killed (injured)	
July	178	(227)	57	(77)	23	(17)	258	(321)
August	627	(711)	335	(448)	113	(102)	1,075	(1,261)
September	2,844	(4,405)	2,943	(3,807)	1,167	(2,403)	6,954	(10,615)
October	2,791	(4,228)	2,900	(3,750)	643	(717)	6,334	(8,695)
November	2,289	(3,493)	1,806	(2,251)	493	(458)	4,588	(6,202)
December	1,838	(2,962)	1,434	(1,775)	521	(307)	3,793	(5,044)
TOTAL	10,567	(16,026)	9,475	(12,108)	2,960	(4,004)	23,002	(32,138)

On the same night, Bomber Command hit the German invasion ports again. Seventy barges were reported destroyed, with two British aircraft lost to flak. Concentrations of German troops around the Channel ports, massing for the invasion, were also targeted, causing heavy casualties.

13 September 1940 FRIDAY

Generally unsettled and cloudy.

Hitler met with his senior army and air force commanders today to review the invasion preparations. The results of the fighting on 11 September gave grounds for optimism. There was a feeling that the air assault could be poised on the brink of success. The commander-in-chief of the army, Walther von Brauchitsch, even suggested that the invasion might be unnecessary, and that the air campaign alone would be enough to bring about victory. Hitler himself remained oddly detached from events, sometimes seeming to accept Goering's glowing accounts of progress and predictions of impending victory, sometimes appearing doubtful and sceptical of Sea Lion's feasibility. He allowed the planning to continue at the same intense pace, however. There was no indication that the go-ahead would not be given the next day as planned.

In the meantime, it was another relatively quiet day in the cloudy and unsettled skies over Britain. Early-morning reconnaissance planes, reporting back on the weather and on Fighter Command dispositions, were left alone. Then, from 9.30am to 11.30am, there was a stream of single aircraft crossing the coast near Hastings at the rate of about one every eight minutes. Most headed for London on a variety of different courses. Cloud and the high altitude of the raiders made interception almost impossible. The bombs were landing in the centre now, amid the symbols of British power, in Downing Street, Whitehall and Trafalgar Square. Buckingham Palace was bombed for the third time, and the royal chapel wrecked. The cloud allowed these single aircraft to penetrate deep inland, bombing an aluminium factory in Banbury, Oxfordshire, a railway junction outside Reading and buildings requisitioned by the Air Ministry in Harrogate.

Soon after midday, radio intercepts from German weather reconnaissance aircraft warned of further attacks. Park ordered key airfields to put at least one squadron at readiness. Soon, radar reported intruders heading towards mid-Kent, aiming, it seemed, for Biggin Hill, Kenley or London. Hurricanes from No. 501 Squadron were scrambled from Kenley, and they intercepted a small force of He111 bombers from *Kampfgeschwader* 27. Sergeant James 'Ginger' Lacey shot one down, before himself being hit by return fire. He baled out unhurt as most of the bombers turned back, having aborted their mission. Three small raids around Tangmere to the west were also driven away.

That night, the raids were heavier. At 8.45pm aircraft were reported building up over the Cherbourg area, and for the next three hours bombers streamed in from Cherbourg, Dieppe, Calais and Boulogne. The main target was London, but East Anglia was also hit. Four raids were flown from the Channel Islands to the Bristol Channel and South Wales.

There was a lull after midnight, but around 2am a wave of aircraft, which had taken off from the Dutch islands, approached London from the northeast and pounded the capital until just before dawn. Only two of the attackers were shot down, one by a night-fighting Blenheim, the other by anti-aircraft fire.

The pattern of damage was becoming depressingly familiar. There was widespread destruction of the rail network, of the gas, electricity and water supply, and of houses and offices. In West Ham, Ravenshill School, which was occupied by families evacuated from their homes, was demolished by high explosive bombs, killing and injuring more than 50 people.

Hitler and many of his military men believed that such incidents would produce a clamour among civilians that would force Britains politicians to seek negotiations. Credence was given to reports reaching Berlin from, among other sources, US Ambassador Kennedy in London that British morale was crumbling. In the imagination of the German press, social cohesion was dissolving. In London, the rich were avoiding their military duties and living in luxury while ordinary women and children went unprotected. In East London, the main target of the bombs, anti-war feeling ran through the rhetoric of the two most vociferous political groups, the Communists and the British Union of Fascists. On 11 September, the political insider Harold Nicolson, then working as parliamentary secretary to the Ministry of Information, wrote in his diary: 'The people in the East End are still frightened and angry.' But the intervention of the weather, which reduced visibility, and the technological inability

BELOW
Groundcrew load a Fairey Battle with 250-pound bombs at an RAF training station (13 September 1940). While Britain's cities and fighter bases were receiving a pummelling in August and September 1940, Bomber Command remained active against continental targets, including the invasion forces building up in the Channel ports.

Workmen fill a bomb
crater at the gates of
Buckingham Palace on
14 September 1940.
The fact that even the
highest in the land were
vulnerable to German
bombs created an
atmosphere of solidarity
in class-riven Britain.

to land bombs efficiently had made the Blitz a communal experience. Instead of hitting only the docks and industrial targets and, inevitably, the poor quarters that surrounded them, the circle of destruction widened to include the smart, western parts of London, including the seat of the king and queen. The rich and the poor were suffering alike. Eastenders who had flocked westwards to avoid the attacks on the docks now returned home. Queen Elizabeth declared, now that her own home had been bombed, that she 'could look the East End in the eye'. Rather than deepening class faultlines, the bombing was creating, at least temporarily, a feeling of solidarity.

The hoped-for political effects of the bombing were, though, a subsidiary part of the German purpose. The main aim remained to destroy Fighter Command, and the attacks on the capital were intended to hasten that end by drawing the British fighters into a defensive war of attrition that would end with German control of the skies. Only then could the invasion safely go ahead.

<h1 style="text-align:center">SATURDAY 14 September 1940</h1>

On Saturday, Hitler held another meeting with his senior military commanders in Berlin. It was, in theory, the day of decision, the date on which Operation Sea Lion would be launched, to strike before the late-autumn weather in the Channel made an amphibious landing too perilous to attempt.

Hitler accepted, however, that daylight air superiority had not been achieved, and he delayed the decision once more. Now orders would be issued on 17 September, with the operation starting ten days later. In spite of the delay, he was full of praise for the Luftwaffe and his mood towards the operation had swung back to optimism. Bad weather was blamed for the slackening of progress. In an echo of Goering's predictions of the *Adlertag* offensive, Hitler declared that all that was required was five days' good flying weather to complete the elimination of Fighter Command. The Luftwaffe was primed for another maximum effort.

But throughout the morning the weather continued to thwart the German plans. The dense, murky cloud of the previous two days continued, restricting the Luftwaffe to a few minor raids. However, Ju88 bombers from *Kampfgeschwader* 1 attacked south coast radar stations and caused enough disruption to allow raids to arrive over Brighton and Eastbourne almost unopposed. A combination of small groups of He111s and Do17s killed or injured 60 people and caused substantial damage.

Showers, local thunder, and dense cloud over southern waters and southeast.

LEFT
Queen Elizabeth and King George VI look an East Ender in the eye, as they visit a bomb-ravaged part of the capital in 1940.

YEAR 1940		AIRCRAFT		PILOT, OR	2ND PILOT, PUPIL	DUTY
MONTH	DATE	Type	No.	1ST PILOT	OR PASSENGER	(INCLUDING RESULTS AND REMARKS)
—	—	—	—	—	—	— TOTALS BROUGHT FORWARD
SEPT.					(cont).	Got one of Me 110's on fire whereupon the other left his charge & ran for home! Played with He 111's for a bit & finally got one in both engines. Never had so much fun before!
	14	Spitfire	X4170			Patrol.
	15		X4170			Party. 242 leading wing. Ran into ~~the~~ the whole Luftwaffe over 10/10 over London. Wave after wave of bombers covered by several hundred fighters. Waded into escort as per arrangement & picked out a 109. Had a hell of a dog fight & finally he went into cloud in inverted dive patty obviously crashed as he appeared out of control.

GRAND TOTAL [Cols. (1) to (10)]

843 Hrs 10 Mins.

TOTALS CARRIED FORWARD

In the afternoon, and with no change in the weather, the Luftwaffe decided to risk the elements and mount two sizeable raids, and aircraft approached London from Kent and the Thames Estuary. The poor conditions hampered the defenders as much as the attackers. Twenty-two squadrons from 11 Group were sent up and five squadrons from 12 Group, but most failed to locate the raiders. Those that did came off worst in their clashes with the escorts. Four of 73 Squadron's Hurricanes were shot down by Me109s and two damaged, one of them a victim of mis-identification by a Spitfire. The thick cloud made accurate bombing impossible. Explosives were scattered over the suburbs, killing 49 people in the Richmond and Wimbledon areas of Southwest London.

A second attack began after 6pm, with seven formations, each comprising between twelve and thirty aircraft. They crossed the coast at Dover and Lympne, heading for London and, it appeared, the fighter bases that had been providentially left largely alone since the attacks on the capital began. But ten fighter squadrons were in the air when the lead German aircraft crossed the coast, and the bombers were headed off. There were more scattered raids along the coast and inland later in the evening.

Fourteen British fighters had been shot down during the day, while the Luftwaffe had lost only half as many. To the Germans, looking for positive signs, it appeared that the British defences had been scrappy and disorganized. The message passed up the line to Goering was that the RAF seemed close to defeat.

'We had now learnt our lessons'

At the beginning of the Battle of Britain, a Luftwaffe that was combat-hardened from fighting in Spain, Poland, France, the Low Countries and Norway faced a largely 'green' collection of British squadrons. But during the fighting the 'experience gap' closed. In the words of Pilot Officer David Crook, of 609 Squadron:

We had now learnt our lessons, though the price for this experience had been the death of several members of the squadron. We realized now the vital importance of getting above the enemy before going into action; we knew that cool thinking and the element of surprise can more than compensate for inferior numbers, and can sometimes produce astonishing results. We knew ... that if you attack out of the sun the enemy will hardly ever see you until the last moment; and vice versa, how essential it is to maintain the most intense vigilance always in order to prevent being surprised oneself. [Crook, pp. 61-2]

-0-0-0-0-0-

15 September 1940 SUNDAY ('BATTLE OF BRITAIN DAY')

Fine, with some cloud patches.

The truth of the claims about Fighter Command's weakness would be tested today. Orders were issued for a massive Luftwaffe attack on London. But the piecemeal and rather chaotic response of Fighter Command the previous day was misleading. Contrary to appearances, the German bomber crews and fighter pilots were going into battle against a force that was in considerably better shape than it had been just one week before. By switching the weight of their attacks away from the airfields and onto London, the Germans had achieved the opposite effect from the one they sought. The new circumstances reduced the time the British pilots had to spend in the air. In the six days before the start of the Blitz, Fighter Command had flown 4667 sorties. In the six days after, it flew only 2159. The decision to move the airfields and sector stations down the target list and concentrate on London resulted in two highly beneficial consequences for the RAF. It had allowed Fighter Command not only to repair its infrastructure, but also to refresh and restore its pilots. The business of defending London was intense, but the danger periods were short and intermittent. It was less exhausting and required less effort than the constant activity of the preceding period.

The result was that by 15 September Fighter Command had remustered its strength. New Polish pilots brought a valuable injection of aggressive and skilful personnel, while combat experience made veterans of pilots who were novices only weeks before. Heroic effort had returned all but the hardest-hit Fighter Command bases to something close to full operational efficiency. Since 7 September, Dowding had been able to rotate his battered squadrons and introduce new pilots to those

outfits worst hit by losses. A large number had enjoyed whole days of rest without being called to readiness. New pilots had even been able to fly a few training sorties before going into action. Fighter Command met the dawn of 15 September with high spirits and renewed energy.

It was the Luftwaffe crews now that were tired from incessant attacks and, as the days passed and the defenders unfailingly came up to meet them, who began to doubt their mission. As the fighter ace Adolf Galland recorded: 'Failure to achieve any notable success, constantly changing orders betraying lack of purpose and obvious misjudgment of the situation by the Command, and unjustified accusation had a most demoralizing effect on us fighter pilots, who were already overtaxed by physical and mental strain.' [Quoted in Hough and Richards, p. 275]

The night of 14/15 September was ominously quiet. Although the weather had cleared, only 50 bombers appeared over London. At bases on either side of the Channel, the airmen tried to sleep as groundcrew repaired, refitted and rearmed the aircraft. They could not know it, but the dawning day would pose the supreme test of their skill, their courage and their aggression.

Park was ready. Radio intercepts and reconnaissance had indicated that a very heavy attack was imminent. When the morning of 15 September dawned clear and bright, he knew that in all probability this was to be a crucial day. Yet he remained almost superstitiously disinclined to dramatize. He had important visitors at his headquarters in Uxbridge, the prime minister and his wife. 'I do not know if anything will happen today,' he told them as they looked down from the control room gallery at the map tables, which showed only a few counters indicating aircraft in the air.

The chalky scribble of 'contrails' is written across the sky after a dogfight in September 1940.

'There was not one squadron left in reserve'

With his usual instinct for locating the dramatic centre of events, Winston Churchill was at 11 Group headquarters at Uxbridge on 15 September, during the crucial hours of the battle that day. He recorded how:

```
   Presently the red bulbs showed that the majority of our squadrons
were engaged … A subdued hum arose from the floor, where the busy
plotters pushed their discs to and fro in accordance with the swiftly
changing situation … The Air Marshal himself [Park] walked up and
down behind, watching with a vigilant eye every move in the game,
supervising his junior executive hand, and only occasionally inter-
vening with some decisive order, usually to reinforce a threatened
area. In a little while all our squadrons were fighting and some had
already begun to return for fuel. All were in the air. The lower line
of bulbs was out. There was not one squadron left in reserve.
[Churchill, Vol. 2, pp. 295-6]
```

-0-0-0-0-0-

The clear dawn had ripened into a glorious late summer day. The conditions were perfect for the Luftwaffe to finish its task. Yet they were taking their time in coming. From first light, Park had a full squadron at each sector station kept at readiness, while small patrols were mounted along the east and south coasts from Harwich to Land's End. Occasional Luftwaffe reconnaissance flights were shot down or chased away. Near Exeter, a lone He111 on a weather patrol was destroyed by Hurricanes from No. 87 Squadron.

Soon after 10.30am, unambiguous reports began to arrive of a massive build-up of aircraft over the Pas de Calais. Preparing a huge air armada was a slow and laborious process. While it went on, the Me109s wasted fuel buzzing in attendance and the British gained precious time to organize their defences.

The bomber force was made up of about a hundred Do17s from *Kampf-geschwader* 3 and 76. They were escorted by twice as many Me109s. When formed up, the fleet was almost 2 miles wide, and stacked up in layers between 15,000 and 26,000 feet. Shortly after 11am, the aircraft started crossing the coast near Dungeness. They flew in 'vic' formations of three, five and seven aircraft each, making a giant herringbone pattern in the sky.

Watching the build-up and trying to guess the Germans' intent, Park ruled out a decoy or airfield attack and decided that the enemy target was London. It seemed clear that this was a repeat of the great attack of 7 September. He knew that such a powerful force could not be turned back altogether. But if the escort could be held and engaged in fuel-sapping combat on the way to the capital, and the formation disrupted, it would become progressively less and less able to defend itself and the conditions would be created for his fighters to wreak heavy punishment on the raiders. But his plan required the most acutely judged timing if he was to provide

a continuous defence and avoid his squadrons being caught on the ground.

By 10.55am, all of 11 Group's squadrons had been put at readiness. Park had also alerted Nos 12 and 10 Groups and requested reinforcements. Aircraft on patrol were ordered to return to base for refuelling. As the horde of German aircraft crossed the coast, Spitfires of 92 and 72 squadrons from Biggin Hill raced to meet them, making the first interception between Dungeness and Canterbury. Park waited ten minutes and then sent up his second wave, consisting of nine more squadrons from bases around London: Nos 229 and 303 from Northolt, 253 and 501 from Kenley, 17 and 73 from Debden, 504 from Hendon, 257 from Martlesham, and 603 from Hornchurch. Five minutes later, No. 609 Squadron took off from Warmwell to guard the southwestern approaches to the city, while from 12 Group the Duxford Wing, now bolstered to five squadrons, prepared for action. Just over ten minutes later a further ten squadrons were ordered up into defensive positions above London.

The Spitfires in the vanguard, some 20 aircraft, swung into the giant formation over Maidstone just after 11.30am. Some of the escort peeled off to engage. Moments later, No. 603 Squadron arrived to hit them while they were still trying to deal with the initial assault, quickly shooting down two Me109s. While more of their escorts were dragged into the dogfights, the Dorniers flew on, straight into the path of Nos 501 and 253 squadrons from Kenley. No. 501 shot down two of the bombers, but lost two of its own in the fight. The giant formation, its shape more ragged now, rumbled on through the brilliant Kent skies. At every stage of the journey more fighters were closing to meet it – a clutch of Hurricanes from Nos 303 and 229 squadrons, then three more Spitfire squadrons, which intercepted over the Medway, then another four squadrons of Hurricanes.

An unusual close-up photograph taken in flight shows clearly the forward gunner in the nose of a Heinkel He111 bomber, peering out *en route* to England in autumn 1940. Surrounded by a fragile skin of glass, he seems to inhabit an especially vulnerable space.

15 SEPT 1940

By the time the Luftwaffe armada had London in sight, just before midday, 15 Hurricane squadrons and 8 Spitfire squadrons were in the air, a force of over 250 fighters. All over northern Kent spectators looked up in awe and fascination at the chalky vapour trails being scribbled in the perfect blue by the rolling and tumbling dogfights. Above the southern suburbs of the city, the German aircrews found, for the first time, that they were outnumbered. As they set course for their targets, scanning the homely Victorian terraces, the parks, commons and railway lines, fixing on the river to lead them in, six squadrons of 11 Group were waiting for them and the Duxford Wing was on its way. No. 504 Squadron had been scrambled from Hendon at 11.20am. Just before that, two US Army Air Corps generals and a US rear-admiral had arrived at the airfield to see 'the life of a fighter squadron'. The visitors noted that the time taken from the order to all 12 Hurricanes being airborne was 4 minutes and 50 seconds.

South of Fulham, 504 Squadron saw hostile aircraft. 'The bombers were coming in towards London from the southeast and at first we could not tell how many there were,' said Squadron Leader John Sample. 'We opened our throttles and started to climb up towards them, aiming for a point well ahead, where we expected to contact them at their own height. As we converged, I saw that there were about twenty of them, and it looked as though it was going to be a nice party, for the other squadrons of Hurricanes and Spitfires also turned to join in. By the time we reached a position near the bombers, we were over London – Central London, I should say. We had gained a little height on them, too, so when I gave the order to attack we were able to dive on them from their right.' The first attack 'broke them up pretty nicely,' said Sample. 'The Dorniers didn't fly particularly tight which was to their disadvantage,' reported 504 pilot Sergeant Ray Holmes. 'If they had done, they'd have had better firepower to beat off the fighters. But our CO went at them in a quarter attack and more or less went through them and spread them out a bit.' [Holmes, recording]

BELOW
The wispy vapour trails from a dogfight over Horse Guards Parade in Central London, during the early weeks of the Blitz.

A FIGHTER PILOT'S HAT-TRICK

On 15 September, the London skies were more crowded than ever before, but Sergeant Ray Holmes, of 504 Squadron, suddenly spotted three Dorniers in 'vic' formation, separated from their fellows but still stubbornly pressing on to the centre of London. Choosing the nearest of the three, he dived on it. 'I made my attack on this bomber and he spurted out a lot of oil, just a great stream over my aeroplane, blotting out my windscreen. Then as the windscreen cleared, I suddenly found myself going straight into his tail. So I stuck my stick forward and went under him, practically grazing my head on his belly.' He saw the Dornier fall away, and then went in from the stern on a second bomber. 'I was shooting at him when suddenly something white came out of the aircraft.

I thought that a part of his wing had come away but in actual fact it turned out to be a man with a parachute coming out. I was travelling at 250 miles per hour, it all happened so quickly, but before I knew what had happened this bloody parachute was draped over my starboard wing. There was this poor devil on his parachute hanging straight out behind me, and my aeroplane was being dragged. All I could do was swing the aeroplane left and then right to try to get rid of this man. Fortunately his parachute slid off my wing and down he went.' [Quoted in Parker, p. 292] Holmes attacked the third Dornier, colliding with its tail. He lost control of his Hurricane, but baled out safely to arrive to a hero's welcome on the streets below.

Douglas Bader, with five squadrons of the Duxford Wing, arrived with the sun behind him. From an ideal tactical position, 3000 feet above the bombers, the wing smashed into the flank of the formation just as the bombers released their loads and turned for home. The bombers scattered in all directions, making it impossible for the dwindling number of Me109s to protect them.

The British pilots were cheered on in the streets below, where thousands were watching, enthralled by the twisting evasions and pursuits. The diarist of 609 Squadron recorded that one piece of a Dornier they had destroyed 'reached the ground just outside a Pimlico public house to the great comfort and joy of the patrons'.

The Germans had no chance to aim accurately. They scattered their bombs over South and Central London – over Beckenham, Westminster, Lambeth, Lewisham, Battersea, Camberwell, Crystal Palace, Clapham, Tooting and Wandsworth. Then the bombers wheeled sharply to the east or west, desperate to get away. Those fleeing westwards were caught first over Weybridge, then again further south. Those heading for the Thames Estuary were picked up by a swarm of four squadrons and harassed and hounded every mile of the way. The few Me109s left over England could offer little protection. Their fuel warning lights were glowing, and they too were heading homewards.

As the bullet-riddled Dorniers limped to earth at their bases around Antwerp, and the British fighters returned to their airfields to refuel and rearm, another force

'It seemed that the whole of the RAF was there'

Hans Zonderlind, a front gunner in a Dornier Do17, was astonished at the numbers of aircraft ranged against him on 15 September.

From the time that we had been over Maidstone until reaching the outskirts of London, we had been under extreme pressure. The British fighters had been with us since we had first crossed the English coast and had gathered in intensity all the time. Our escort had been doing a grand job with the Spitfires at keeping them away from us, and we thought that should things remain like this, then this bombing run would be made easy …

We saw the Hurricanes coming towards us and it seemed that the whole of the RAF was there, we had never seen so many British fighters coming at us at once. I saw a couple of our comrades go down, and we got hit once but it did no great damage. All around us were dogfights as the fighters went after each other, then as we were getting ready for our approach to the target, we saw what must have been a hundred RAF fighters coming at us ... where were they coming from? - we had been told that the RAF fighters were very close to extinction. We could not keep our present course, we turned to starboard [doing] all that we could to avoid the fighters and after a while I am sure we had lost our bearings, so we just dropped our bombs and made our retreat.
[www.battleofbritain1940.net]

-o-o-o-o-o-

was assembling over northern France. At 1.30pm radar reported German bombers massing west of Calais. The formation took shape more quickly than the morning air fleet, and half an hour later it was crossing the Channel. This time there was a huge phalanx of 400 German fighters to protect 150 bombers. The force was staggered in three waves.

On airfields across Southeast England, pilots bolted down sandwiches and drained cups of tea, while the armourers, fitters and riggers worked frantically on their machines. Goering had hoped that his afternoon attack would catch Fighter Command on the ground, but the speed of the turnaround meant that all the squadrons involved in the actions of the morning were at readiness when the assault began. At 2pm, Park scrambled eight squadrons to patrol in pairs above Sheerness, Chelmsford, Kenley and Hornchurch. Five minutes later he ordered up four more squadrons, then a further eight, and reinforcements were called in from 12 Group.

At 2.15pm, the first German wave crossed the coast, again near Dungeness. Two more followed, separated by ten minutes. The force advanced on London across a ten-mile front. Park and his controllers hoped to engage the German fighters early, luring them away from their charges, gradually stripping the bombers of their bodyguards, and opening them up to the attentions of the squadrons that would be waiting for them around and above London. As the German aircraft arrived over Romney Marsh, Spitfires from Nos 41 and 603 squadrons (from Hornchurch) dived into the mass, shooting down two Dorniers before being jumped by the escorting Me109s. Just south of Maidstone, No. 73 Squadron ran into a group of unescorted bombers and destroyed three of them. Over Dartford, Spitfires of No. 66 and No. 72 squadrons fastened onto a large body of bombers, and fierce dogfights broke out with the escorts. Four more squadrons arrived to join in. The formation wavered. Some of the pilots banked off to the right or left to try to escape the attacks or to turn back.

No. 303 (Polish) Squadron had been ordered up from Northolt and sent to cover the Kent coast along the Thames. Soon afterwards, the nine Hurricanes led by

ABOVE

Hurricanes in their 'vic' formations – on this occasion, from No. 85 Squadron led by Peter Townsend – slide above the clouds near their base at Church Fenton, Yorkshire (October 1940).

OPPOSITE

An unknown pilot glances skywards from his cockpit after returning from a sortie (summer 1940).

303 SQUADRON INTELLIGENCE REPORT
15 SEPTEMBER 1940

S/L Kellett [commanding 303 'Polish' Squadron] was ordered to patrol
Northolt at 20,000 ft. and took off with the nine serviceable machines.
The other Squadrons had left sometime previously and 303 operated
throughout alone ... when still 2,000 ft below their patrol level, they
sighted coming head on from the southeast a very large formation of
bombers and fighters. The Bombers were in vics of three sections line
astern with Me110s in sq formation between the vics of Bombers. To the
flanks and stepped up above to 25,000 ft. were many formations of Me109s.
Blue Section had got rather in front of the others, and wheeling round
to let them come up. S/L Kellett had to deliver a quarter frontal attack
instead of head on. This he did initially with only the other two members
of Blue Section - Sgt. Wojciechowski and P/O Zak. Probably as there were
a lot of clouds about, the enemy imagined that this was the advance guard
of a large force and began to wheel towards the east, and when the other
two sections came in they turned completely to the east. After the first
rush the Me110s and the 109s fell upon the nine Hurricanes which were
compelled to defend themselves individually as best they could, and
escaped destruction in the clouds. As it was, four of the aircraft which
returned were slightly damaged by enemy fire, one, Sgt Adruszkow's, was
destroyed, the pilot baling out unhurt at Dartford, and Sgt Brzezowski
is missing.

Squadron Leader Kellet came across a large formation over Gravesend. In the
fight that followed, two Hurricanes were shot down, but the Poles managed to
destroy at least two Me110s and a number of bombers.

From the west, a force of about 80 bombers was heading across the outskirts of
Surrey towards Central London. They were met by Hurricanes from Tangmere –
213 and 607 squadrons – which tore into them, shooting several down and
throwing more off course.

The size and fierceness of the defending force were dismaying to the Luftwaffe
crews, who had been told that Fighter Command was in its death throes. Over Kent
they had been assailed by a total of 170 fighters, and 50 bombers had lost heart
and turned back before reaching Chatham. But the huge numbers of escorting
Me109s were fighting hard, too, and doing their job of fending off the full weight
of the British fighters.

On reaching the outskirts of London, the German aircraft came under heavy
anti-aircraft fire from the new batteries that had been brought in from elsewhere
to defend the city. As the planes emerged from this barrage, they were faced with
the biggest concentration of British aircraft they had yet encountered. There were

fifteen squadrons facing them – ten from 11 Group and five from the Duxford Wing. For the second time that day, German aircrew were presented with the alarming sight of a mass of British fighters, aggressive, determined and well organized.

Bader later complained that his force had been scrambled too late. The Spitfire squadrons, although flying above the Hurricanes, came in too low and had to climb to drive off the Me109s. But the sheer weight of his wing's charge still had the desired effect, forcing the enemy out of formation so that its defensive arcs dissolved into small desperate groups, whose concern was no longer to attack but to survive. 'This time, for a change, we outnumbered the Hun, and believe me, no more than eight got home from that party,' Bader later declared. 'At one time you could see planes going down on fire all over the place, and the sky seemed full of parachutes. It was sudden death that day, for our fighters shot them to blazes.' [Quoted in Turner, p. 87]

Thickening cloud and the relentless fighter assault spared the German target for the day – the Royal Victoria and Surrey Commercial Docks – from serious damage. Instead, the bombs fell over a wide area, on Hammersmith in West London, on Islington and Kilburn in the north, in the very centre on the Strand, and as far south as Croydon and Mitcham. This broad spread was testimony to how widely the formation was scattered and contrasted tellingly with the concentrated destruction the Germans had achieved eight days before.

'I must have had a guardian angel with me'

Sergeant George Unwin, of No. 19 Squadron, strayed into the massed ranks of enemy planes on 15 September. He was very lucky to survive.

```
    I got lost from my squadron and when I looked, there was not a
soul in the sky. Then in the distance, I saw some ack-ack and I went
towards it and I saw these waves upon waves of German bombers coming
in. It was a fascinating sight. There seemed to be hundreds of them
and I forgot about anything else. Suddenly, I found aeroplanes
whizzing all around me. I'd flown smack into the middle of the fighter
escort. Without thinking. Damn fool. I went into a tight turn and shot
at several 109s as they went through my sights - and I actually shot
two of them down. I got the first one and he bailed out. When I went
to sight the next one, the light in my reflector sight failed. The
bloody bulb failed. I was still in a tight turn and I shot the second
one down without a sight. His petrol tank went up. It was probably the
turn that saved me - the Messerschmitt couldn't turn like a Spitfire.
It frightened me - I was all on my own in the middle of I don't know
how many Messerschmitts but I didn't get a hole in me. I must have
had a guardian angel with me. [Unwin, recording]


                    -o-o-o-o-o-
```

The attacks on bombers continued relentlessly all the way to the coast, with three or more British fighters sometimes raking a single stricken bomber. Over Kent, a force of 50 Me109s arrived to shepherd the bombers home, but by then the damage had been done.

Long before nightfall it was clear that a great battle had been won, perhaps the decisive encounter of the summer air war. The Air Ministry announced that 183 enemy aircraft had been shot down. The real figure was 56, considerably fewer but still the heaviest daily loss the Luftwaffe had suffered so far in the campaign and a severe blow to its strength and morale. The German air force was fighting a war of attrition, but its enemy's numbers seemed to be growing. In the space of 90 minutes, 28 squadrons had been in action and the skies had been filled with more than 250 British fighters. Goering's claim that Fighter Command was down to its 'last fifty Spitfires' was now a sour joke.

In contrast, the pilots of Fighter Command ended the day filled with elation. Their losses had been much lighter than the Luftwaffe's – 26 aircraft downed, with 13 pilots killed. For the first time they began to feel that they were controlling events. 'What about the RAF yesterday?' Sergeant Eric Bann wrote to his parents the next day. 'My gosh, for every bomb dropped upon the King and Queen old 238 gave them hell. We got 12 Huns in one scrap. We just went in as one man and held our fire until very close range and then blew them right out of their cockpits.'

For Fighter Command, almost everything had gone right – detection, interception and destruction. The whole intricate organization, from radar station to Observer Corps look-out post, to Group and sector station commands, to the 'sharp end' of a pilot with his thumb on the fire button, and the entire communications infrastructure linking them – all had functioned exactly as they should. All but one of the squadrons sent up had made contact in the morning, and all 28 had tangled with the enemy in the afternoon, Fighter Command's best 'hit' rate of the Battle of Britain. Improved coordination with Anti-Aircraft Command, and Park's masterful depletion of the enemy fighter force and careful management of his assets, had made the skies over London a place of doom for the German air force.

The RAF had been helped, too, by the Luftwaffe's poor performance. The first offensive was slow and predictable. After the early morning, there were fewer feints or dummy raids to confuse the defenders, and the huge attack had been made across a relatively narrow corridor, making effective interception easier. The slow second attack had allowed crucial time for Fighter Command to get back to readiness, and both raids had demonstrated the Me109's debilitating lack of fuel-carrying capacity. The main clash, in the skies over London, had been in a place of Park's choosing too, at the extreme limit of the German fighters' range.

The British press seized on the erroneous but irresistible claim of 183 enemy aircraft shot down. The *Daily Express* crowed that 'Goering may reflect that this is no way to run an invasion'. Churchill had become concerned at the inflation of the figures. He wanted the Americans to believe Britain was winning the battle, but it was also important that the figures remained credible and backed up by evidence. But, for once, the hyperbole, if inaccurate in terms of the numbers, was right in its tone. The fine flying weather, longed for by the Germans to deliver their final blow, had ended up benefiting the RAF's fighter interceptors more than the Luftwaffe. Wreckage of German aircraft was lying smashed in fields, lanes and streets all over

OPPOSITE
T.F. (Thomas) Neil
as a flight lieutenant
with 249 Squadron,
May 1941.

'September 15 was a very special day'

For Pilot Officer Thomas Neil, of No. 249 Squadron, his second sortie on 15 September proved an unforgettable one.

September 15 was a very special day. 249 Squadron, North Weald, had taken off in the morning and we'd intercepted about 30 Dorniers over Maidstone but we hadn't done very well. I shot at something but nothing happened. Then at about three o'clock in the afternoon, we were sent off again. We intercepted another group of Dorniers over Maidstone and this time everything went swimmingly. I found myself behind a Dornier and as I was firing at it, the crew suddenly bailed out. I was so close behind it that as one of the bodies came out, I ducked in the aeroplane, thinking, 'My God, he's going to hit me.' Their parachutes were undeveloped, they fell out. And then I remember breaking away and being attacked by some German fighters. They set about me furiously and I defended myself. And then, as so often happened in combat, you're surrounded by aeroplanes like bees round a honey pot, and suddenly everything is quiet and there are no aeroplanes. It happens instantaneously.

Then I saw another Dornier flying across my bows, about a mile away, which I immediately followed. It was going down the estuary, by this time we'd got up roughly over Gravesend. It took some time for me to catch it up because it was going in a slight dive. Eventually I caught it up and I suddenly found that a Spitfire was to my left. And thereafter it was fairly straightforward, a single aeroplane, on its own, two of us, we took it in turns to fire, it went down and down and down, out to sea, across a convoy of ships … I thought, 'Oh God, we're going to lose this one, he's going to get home.' The Spitfire and I had run out of ammunition but we flew alongside it. I could read all the letters on the cockpit, and I could see the damage that had been done. And then it got slower and slower and slower and the nose came up and up and up, and suddenly the tail hit the sea and it splashed down. I felt satisfaction - total satisfaction. The pair of us flew around and usually when an aeroplane hits the sea, it goes down and then comes to the surface. We flew around and nobody surfaced. As we flew back over the convoy the ships all blew their whistles.
[Neil, recording]

-o-o-o-o-o-

Southeast England. 'We must take September 15 as the culminating date,' Churchill later wrote in his account of the battle. Indeed, it was the decisive day and has since been observed as 'Battle of Britain Day'. As the government's Official History of the battle noted, if 15 August had shown the Germans that air superiority was not to be won quickly or easily, then 15 September showed them that it could not be won at all. The Luftwaffe's attempt to assert daylight superiority, essential for invasion, had failed. No-one, neither the pilots heading to the pubs in a mood of jubilation and hilarity born of relief, nor the earthbound civilians who had cheered them on, dared yet hope that the ordeal was over. And nor was it, for the fighting and dying would continue for some time yet. But on 15 September the moment of greatest danger passed. Though it was far from obvious at the time, the Battle of Britain was won.

Another one bites the dust. A British soldier exults in the downing of a German fighter. On 15 September, Luftwaffe losses may have represented a small fraction of the vast armada sent across the Channel, but they were a testament to Goering's failure to achieve air supremacy.

MONDAY 16 September 1940

The pilots of Fighter Command awoke on the morning of 16 September and looked up at the blessed sight of a carpet of thick rain clouds obscuring the sun. The German bombers stayed away for most of the day, and the Luftwaffe licked its wounds. It seemed, though, like a short respite rather than the beginning of the end, and in the days that followed few of the 'fighter boys' felt that the end was in sight.

Cloud and rain.

Despite the Luftwaffe's daytime losses, London had been hit hard again on the night of Sunday 15 September, with bombs falling on Hammersmith, the Strand, Westminster and the East End. Reconnaissance of the continental Channel ports showed a continued build-up of German barges, despite the now nightly bombardments by Bomber and Coastal commands. That build-up led some in the British High Command to believe that invasion was now imminent. The prime minister was more sceptical, and he even introduced a note of cautious optimism into his rhetoric. On 17 September, Churchill told Parliament that 'Sunday's action was the most brilliant and fruitful of any fought up to that date by the fighters of the Royal Air Force ... We may await the decision of this long air battle with sober but increasing confidence.' [Churchill, Vol. 2, p. 297]

Today, Goering summoned his *Luftflotten* and *Fliegerkorps* commanders for a dissection of the action of 15 September. It was clear, at last, that Dowding was not down to his 'last fifty Spitfires', and Goering reverted to his original plan. Fighter Command airfields and aircraft factories were to be targeted once again, while attacks on London continued. The big losses of 15 September forced a change in tactics. Large formations of bombers would no longer be deployed, unless circumstances were exceptional. The new approach would team bomber groups with huge fighter escorts. Bitter experience could not, though, quench Goering's taste for hyperbole. Fighter Command could still be destroyed in 'four or five days', he predicted. His claim was based on another greatly inflated battle-damage assessment. The Germans believed they had destroyed 79 Fighter Command aircraft on 15 September, rather than the real figure of 26. In fact, Fighter Command numbers were on the increase. At the beginning of July, Dowding could deploy 44 Hurricane and Spitfire squadrons. By the end of the year, there would be 71, many equipped with more powerful Mark 2 Spitfires and Hurricanes.

The Luftwaffe compensated for the relative inactivity of 16 September with a vigorous effort during the night of 16/17 September. The attacks continued until 5.30am. In all, 170 aircraft dropped 200 tons of bombs, and much of the population was forced into air-raid shelters for another exhausting and fearful night.

TUESDAY 17 September 1940

The night-time alarms were becoming routine but the daylight action was entering a new phase, with Kesselring and Park locked in a tactical battle of bluff and counter-bluff. As the weather brightened during the afternoon of 17 September, waves of Luftwaffe fighters roared in from the Channel. Park was informed that few, if any, bombers were among them, and so he was inclined to ignore the incursions as the Me109s could cause little damage except to other fighters.

Squally showers with thunder and bright intervals.

A game of chess was as good a way as any to get through the anxious hours. Inclement weather in the third week of September brought Fighter Command pilots a little more time for such pursuits.

Nevertheless, No. 501 Squadron did clash with fighters from *Jagdgeschwader* 53 near Ashford, Kent, losing two of its Hurricanes, with one of the pilots, Sergeant Edward Egan, killed when he failed to escape from his burning cockpit. Spitfires of 41 Squadron were then pulled into the combat over East Kent, followed by the Duxford Wing, whose 19 and 303 squadrons both had successes. As would often be the case in the weeks ahead, British and German fighter losses were roughly equal, on this occasion about five each.

On 14 September, Hitler had postponed making up his mind about launching the invasion until 17 September. But now that the day had arrived, he once more delayed the decision. The reason, according to the entry for the day in the War Diary of the German Naval Staff, was that the RAF 'was by no means defeated'. [Quoted in Ray, pp. 104–5] Hitler nonetheless insisted on the maintenance of a high state of preparedness.

That night, 268 bombers streamed in over Dungeness and Selsey Bill to hit London. The John Lewis department store on Oxford Street was all but burned down. Merseyside also suffered. At the same time, Bomber and Coastal commands took advantage of the full moon to attack enemy shipping concentrations, and at Dunkirk 500 tons of ammunition for the invasion armies were blown up.

WEDNESDAY 18 September 1940

Daylight on 18 September saw a continuation of the cat-and-mouse game between Kesselring and Park. The weather was unsettled, relieved by bright intervals. At around 9am, radar reported considerable numbers coming in fast between Folkestone and North Foreland. Park ordered up 15 squadrons, but such was the speed of the attack that only six of them, from Biggin Hill and Hornchurch, intercepted. They found a swarm of fighters, with no bombers to target. Those that could followed their orders to avoid fighter-to-fighter combat and disengaged, but five Fighter Command aircraft were shot down.

Two hours later, another large attack was mapped. Fearing a repeat of the earlier action, Park held back. This time, though, Kesselring had added a small

Generally unsettled, occasionally bright.

continued on page 354

'The feeling in the East End'

Two contemporary diarists, Henry 'Chips' Channon and Harold Nicolson, recorded some telling observations in their respective entries for 16 and 17 September. Channon found himself travelling through London's debris.

```
    I drove back to London via the East End, which is a scene of desolation.
House after house had been wrecked, debris falls from the remaining
floors, windows are gone, heaps of rubbish lie in the pavements.
A large hospital and a synagogue still stand, but they are windowless.
Some streets are roped off because of time-bombs. The damage is immense,
yet the people, mostly Jewish, seemed courageous.
[Channon, p. 266, entry for 16 September]
```

The next day, Harold Nicolson noted the political significance of the unfolding Blitz.

```
    Everybody is worried about the feeling in the East End, where there
is much bitterness. It is said that even the King and Queen were booed
the other day when they visited the destroyed areas. Clem [Attlee,
the Labour Party leader in the Coalition government] says that if only
the Germans had had the sense not to bomb west of London Bridge there
might have been a revolution in this country. As it is, they have
smashed about Bond Street and Park Lane and readjusted the balance.
[Nicolson, p. 116, entry for 17 September]
```

-o-o-o-o-o-

| YEAR | | AIRCRAFT | | PILOT, OR | 2ND PILOT, PUPIL | DUTY |
| MONTH | DATE | Type | No. | 1ST PILOT | OR PASSENGER | (INCLUDING RESULTS AND REMAR... |

TOTALS BROUGHT FORW...

AIRCRAFT WASTAGE

The Battle of Britain was fought not only in the air, but also in the aircraft factories of Great Britain, where the machines were forged to defend the nation. In a war of attrition, it was vital that supply kept up with losses. The damage was graded according to severity. 'Category 3' meant the aircraft was destroyed or missing. 'Category 2' losses were severely damaged aircraft that, nonetheless, might be repaired or used for parts. 'Category 1' aircraft (not included below) were usually quickly reparable, or even capable of being patched up by the maintenance facilities at the aerodromes themselves.

Week ending	HURRICANE production	Losses Cat. 2	Cat. 3	Net gain/loss	SPITFIRE production	Losses Cat. 2	Cat. 3	Net gain/loss	TOTAL net gains/ losses for both types
6 July	65	3	4	+58	32	1	5	+26	+84
13 July	57	6	22	+29	30	6	15	+9	+38
20 July	67	5	13	+39	41	5	6	+30	+69
27 July	65	3	12	+50	37	8	14	+15	+65
3 August	58	4	7	+47	41	7	11	+23	+69
10 August	54	4	16	+34	37	4	12	+21	+55
17 August	43	21	82	-58	31	11	40	-20	-78
24 August	64	9	53	+2	44	3	21	+20	+22
31 August	54	4	70	-20	37	7	50	-20	-40
7 September	54	8	84	-38	36	8	53	-25	-63
14 September	56	6	47	+3	38	10	26	+2	+5
21 September	57	8	34	+15	40	11	21	+8	+23
28 September	58	11	40	+7	34	5	35	-6	+1
5 October	60	16	29	+15	32	5	10	+17	+32
12 October	55	3	28	+24	31	4	22	+5	+29
19 October	55	10	28	+17	25	2	9	+14	+31
26 October	69	7	34	+28	42	2	9	+31	+59
2 November	56	9	16	+31	41	2	14	+25	+56

Armourers ensure guns on a Spitfire are properly lined up, part of the continual pattern of servicing, replenishing and repair.

......Hrs........Mins.

TOTALS CARRIED FORW...

SINGLE-ENGINE AIRCRAFT				MULTI-ENGINE AIRCRAFT						PASS-ENGER	INSTR/CLOUD FLYING [Incl. in cols. (1) to (10)]	
DAY		NIGHT		DAY			NIGHT					
								1ST PILOT	2ND PILOT		DUAL	PILOT
AL	PILOT	DUAL	PILOT	DUAL	1ST PILOT		DUAL	1ST PILOT	2ND PILOT			
1)	(2)	(3)	(4)	(5)	(6)		(7)	(8)	(9)	(10)	(11)	(12)	(13)

A PILOT'S NIGHTMARE

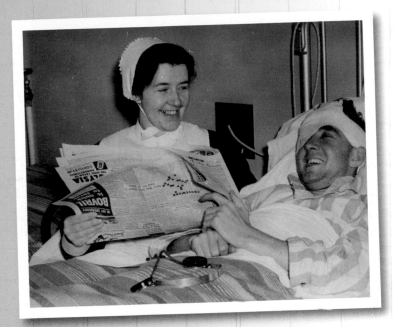

A nurse cheers a wounded pilot, supposedly by reading out the tallies of recent aerial skirmishes as recounted in the press (17 August 1940).

It was every fighter pilot's greatest fear — burning alive in his cockpit, unable to escape. Some pilots reportedly even carried revolvers with them to end the agony. 'I always wore goggles and gloves,' said Pilot Officer Thomas Neil, of 249 Squadron. 'The Hurricane got to two to three thousand degrees centigrade in a matter of seconds after being set on fire and that's why so many people were terribly burned.' [Neil, recording]

Sergeant Ralph Carnall of 111 Squadron was shot down in flames on 16 August. Another burns victim, No. 49 Squadron's George Bennions, a schoolfriend of Carnall's, found himself in the same hospital. 'His hair was burnt off,' said Bennions, 'his eyebrows were burnt off, his eyelids were burnt off. You could just see his staring eyes. His nose was burnt, there were just two holes in his face. His lips were badly burnt. Then, when I looked down, his hands were burnt. I looked down at his feet also. His feet were burnt ... I thought, "What have I got to complain about?"' [Bennions, recording]

A special burns unit was opened at the RAF hospital at Halton, Buckinghamshire, to deal with the large number of cases. Alongside this facility was the civilian special burns unit at the Queen Victoria Hospital in East Grinstead, Sussex, led by Sir Archibald McIndoe. A New Zealander, McIndoe had started out specializing in tropical diseases and liver complaints but had become a plastic surgeon under the patronage of his cousin, Sir Harold Gillies. McIndoe was a highly skilful and imaginative surgeon, developing new techniques for treating badly burned faces and hands. From observing airmen shot down into the sea, McIndoe discovered that immersion in saline promoted healing as well as improving survival rates for victims with extensive burns.

Crucially, McIndoe also recognized the terrible psychological effects of disfigurement and did what he could to ameliorate them, hand-picking the prettiest nurses for the wards, abandoning rules about 'lying to attention' and, above all, exuding confidence and calmness. He also understood the importance of social reintegration back into normal life, encouraging locals in the hospital vicinity to invite the patients to their homes.

contingent of bombers to the formations, and they were free to pound Chatham and Rochester unopposed. Over Tilbury, two Ju88 bombers from *Kampfgeschwader* 77 were shot down after the belated intervention of No. 19 Squadron's Spitfires from Fowlmere, and No. 41 Squadron caught two of the Me109s as they sped back over Maidstone.

After this miscalculation, Park put up a strong force against the next raid, which arrived mid-afternoon. This time, it was the right call. The formation contained a number of Ju88s, the Luftwaffe's fastest bomber, and as it approached Gravesend more than 100 British fighters attacked in waves. Nos 92 and 302 squadrons came in first with a head-on attack, and then, over the Thames Estuary, the Duxford Wing swept down in an almost vertical dive. The wing's claim of thirty aircraft destroyed was a wild overestimation, the real figure being nearer four. But the spectacle was further evidence for the hard-pressed Luftwaffe bomber crews that the RAF was neither depleted nor demoralized.

During the day's fighting, Fighter Command lost 12 aircraft, but with only 3 pilots killed. About half of the pilots shot down would be back flying with their squadrons within 24 hours. On the same day, the Luftwaffe lost 15 aircraft and more than 50 airmen were killed or taken prisoner.

THURSDAY 19 September 1940

Rain all day.

The day was wet and the skies were quiet, with only 70 intruders crossing the coast, most of them flying singly. But on the ground a momentous decision was taken. The previous night, nearly 200 British bombers had pounded the German invasion fleet and its nearby troop concentrations. In the morning, Hitler ordered that the build-up of shipping, which had accelerated over the previous week, should be halted. The invasion barges were now to be dispersed to prevent losses, and the soldiers moved away from the coast. The decision marked the effective end of Operation Sea Lion. There would now no longer be time to assemble an invasion force in what remained of the year. The order was swiftly implemented by seamen eager to escape the nightly attacks by Bomber Command. A week later, reconnaissance photos showed a 40-per-cent reduction in vessels in the Channel ports.

FRIDAY 20 September 1940

Generally fair, with some showers.

The suspension of the German invasion plan did not, however, lead to the diminution of the air campaign. The dim hope remained that the Luftwaffe could force victory either through the destruction of Fighter Command or by its new strategy of bombing the cities. The morning of 20 September saw another dangerous attack by waves of Me109s. This time Park responded with only four squadrons, and the British came off worst. Nos 92 and 72 squadrons from Biggin Hill intercepted between Ashford and the coast and engaged the first formation. The Hornchurch squadrons, Nos 41 and 222, rushed to assist but were bounced by the second German wave and badly mauled. In all, the RAF lost seven Spitfires, with four pilots killed, while only two Me109s were hit.

Shorn of its escort duties, and thus freed from the frustration of wasting time and fuel by endlessly throttling back or weaving, the Me109 was now a very dangerous enemy. Above 25,000 feet the Me109's two-stage supercharger gave it a better performance than the Mark 2 Hurricanes and Spitfires coming into service. Dowding and Park had decided as early as July that German fighter forces were best left alone. But radar could not tell the type of aircraft producing a blip on its screens. The Observer Corps also had difficulty in identifying whether enemy formations contained bombers. Identification was made particularly difficult by hazy conditions or when the intruders were at a great height, a tactic used increasingly by the Luftwaffe.

SATURDAY 21 September 1940

Mainly fine.

Today, the Luftwaffe began implementing Goering's order of 16 September to concentrate the offensive again on Fighter Command, and in particular the aircraft plants, now humming with activity. The effort, though, was scattered and half-hearted. The most significant sortie was against Brooklands aircraft factory in Surrey, which was targeted by a lone Ju88 raider flying in low at treetop height, having followed the railway north from Guildford. Three of its bombs fell harmlessly, but the fourth, a delayed-action 250kg high explosive, landed on the main Hurricane assembly shop. A courageous Canadian engineer, Lieutenant J.M.S. Patton, loaded the unexploded bomb onto a hastily cobbled-together sled and tipped it into a crater made by one of the other bombs, where it blew up harmlessly.

22 September 1940 SUNDAY

Dull, with fog in the morning, clearing by the afternoon.

Worsening autumn weather was beginning to come to the relief of Britain. Today, fog blunted the Luftwaffe attack, requiring Fighter Command to mount only 158 sorties in response, the smallest number since the beginning of the battle on 10 July. When, during the night, one of Churchill's private secretaries was woken to receive a message from US President Roosevelt expressing concern that the invasion was imminent, it was not thought necessary to wake the prime minister.

23 September 1940 MONDAY

Generally fine.

OPPOSITE
Fatal accidents happened not only in the air but also at the aerodromes. This Air Ministry poster puns on the wartime catchphrase 'careless talk costs lives' to get the message across.

The day dawned bright and clear, and by 9am there was a large build-up of enemy aircraft over Calais. Park reacted vigorously, sending up 24 squadrons. But the raiders were all Me109 fighters, and few British aircraft were able to gain enough height in time to intercept. Just after 10am, as the raiders crossed the coast and fanned out, they were intercepted by Spitfires from Nos 72 and 92 squadrons from Biggin Hill and No. 73 Squadron's Hurricanes from Debden. In a torrid eight minutes, four of the Hurricanes, caught still climbing, were shot down. All four pilots were wounded, two of them suffering bad burns, but all survived. The Spitfire squadrons fared better, losing two machines and no pilots and downing three of the German fighters. Only seven other squadrons made contact, and, in all, eleven British fighters were shot down, with similar losses on the German side. The night, though, witnessed the heaviest raid yet on London, by over 250 bombers. Blenheims and Defiants were sent up to try to intercept, but without success.

24 September 1940 TUESDAY

Some cloud; hazy in the Straits of Dover and Thames Estuary.

On Tuesday, calmer weather in the English Channel once again raised fears of invasion – worries that had already been exacerbated by the heavy raids of the night before. During the day a force of 200 aircraft was successfully repulsed 20 miles short of London. Experimental Group 210 also raided the Supermarine Spitfire works at Woolston, Southampton. The factory sat right on the waterfront, making it an easily identifiable target. Two *Staffeln* of Me110s dived on the factory, scoring five direct hits. The works itself sustained minor damage, but one of the bombs hit a shelter, killing almost 100 of the company's personnel. The whole attack lasted only eight minutes, but there was no Fighter Command

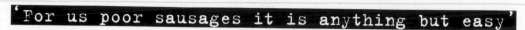

'For us poor sausages it is anything but easy'

On 25 September, Unteroffizier Peter Stahl, of *Gruppe 2*, *Kampfgeschwader* 30, was sent on a lone raid in his Ju88. His earlier confidence (see page 322) had by now waned.

```
    We're a bit more modest. It's not so much a matter of achieving
some kind of success, but mainly to ensure there's at least an air-
raid warning in London. However, for us poor sausages it is anything
but easy. During the previous large-scale raids one could to some
extent hide inside the large formations, but flying alone one is
always exposed like a practice target to a well-coordinated defence
organization.
    All four of us are anxiously searching the sky around us for
Spitfires. Sure enough, exactly at the spot where we could assume the
sirens would begin announcing an approach raid on London, we see them:
four fighters below us in a steady climb in our direction. It does not
take us long to decide that there is nothing to be done here now. I
break off our approach, tipping the aircraft on a wing and whipping
round in the fastest turn of my life. [Stahl, p. 65]
```

-0-0-0-0-0-

interception. The force of Me110s had been flying too low or too fast for detection and interception. In the absence of friendly fighters, the local anti-aircraft forces blazed away furiously, shooting down one raider and damaging two others.

25 September 1940 WEDNESDAY

Fair and cool in most areas.

On Wednesday, German attacks focused once more on aircraft factories. At 11.20am, a large force crossed the Channel. While fighter bombers carried out diversionary attacks on coastal towns, sixty He111s of *Kampfgeschwader* 55 with Me110s of *Zerstörergeschwader* 26 and Experimental Group 210 crossed the coast at 11.15am and headed northwards. Air Vice-Marshal Brand, 10 Group's commander, judged that the raid was heading for the Westland works at Yeovil, Somerset, and put up three squadrons to protect it. In fact it was heading for the aeronautical factory at Filton, near Bristol, and reached it unopposed. This factory produced Blenheims as well as aero engines for several other aircraft. Once the leading Me110s had marked the factory site, the Heinkels followed. Damage was extensive. More than 250 people were killed or injured, 8 completed aircraft badly damaged, and production severely curtailed. Belatedly, Nos 238 and 152 squadrons arrived and downed five of the bombers as they retreated back across the Channel.

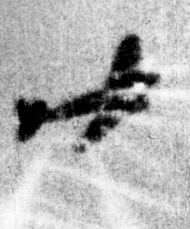

THURSDAY 26 September 1940

No. 504 Squadron was moved from Hendon to Filton today. But the Heinkels of *Kampfgeschwader* 55 had another target, the Supermarine works at Woolston near Southampton, which had been only slightly damaged by an earlier attack. The raid arrived at 5.45pm, and 70 tons of bombs hit the factory. Thirty people were killed, and production was completely stopped. Three completed Spitfires were destroyed and over twenty damaged. Six squadrons engaged the raiders, though only after the bombing, shooting down three aircraft but losing six fighters themselves.

Had this attack on the key Spitfire factory occurred earlier during the battle, it might have had a severe impact. But 'shadow' factories at Cosford, Desford and Castle Bromwich were now on stream to make up the lost capacity.

FRIDAY 27 September 1940

Today, the Luftwaffe turned again to Filton. This time, Brand was ready. Five squadrons met the formation of Heinkels from *Kampfgeschwader* 55, preceded by Me110s from Experimental Group 210 and further protected by more Me110s from *Zerstörergeschwader* 26. Over Yeovil, the British fighters swept down on the bombers, breaking up the formation and forcing them to ditch their bombs before they reached the target. The Heinkels hurried for the protection of the Me110s of *Zerstörergeschwader* 26, which were waiting over Swanage to shepherd them home, but they themselves had come under fierce attack from No. 609 Squadron (from Middle Wallop) and others. The Me110s of Experimental Group 210 pressed on to Bristol, but lost four of their nineteen aircraft, including that of their commanding officer.

It had been a punishing day for the Luftwaffe. It was about to get worse in the London area, where Kesselring launched one of his last great daylight offensives on the capital. At 8am, the first raid appeared on the plotting tables, and soon the radar screens along the southeast coast showed a number of aircraft approaching on a 50-mile front. These turned out to be bomb-carrying Me110s, escorted by Me109s. They were hit by pairs of squadrons and driven back from London, scattering their bombs haphazardly.

ABOVE
Gun camera film shows tracer fire from a Spitfire hitting a Heinkel He111 of *Kampfgeschwader* 55, after the German formation had bombed the Bristol aero works at Filton, 25 September 1940. The Spitfire was flown by Flight Lieutenant James McArthur, of 609 Squadron.

continued on page 362

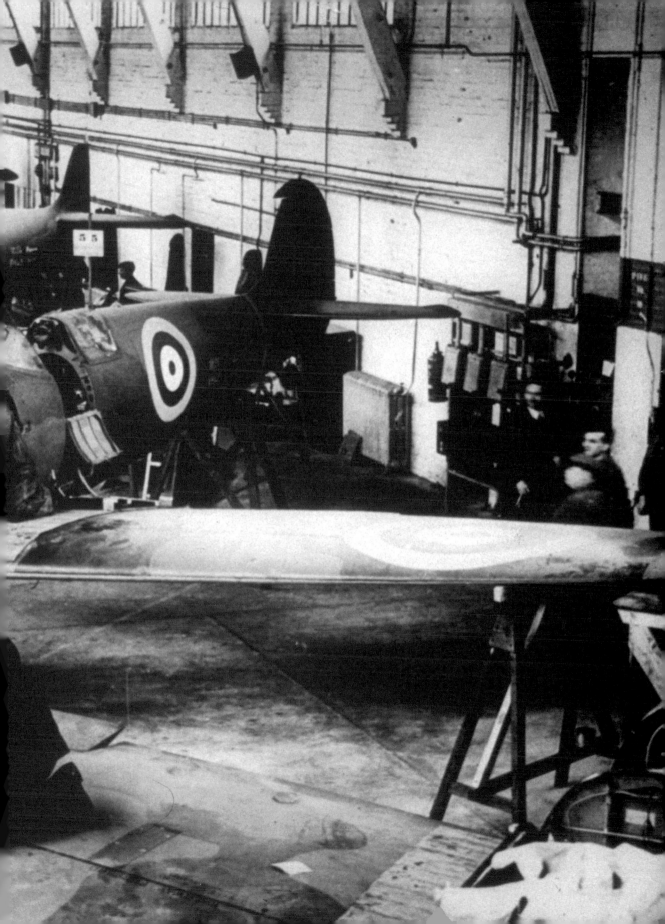

'The most gloriously exciting moments of life'

Pilot Officer David Crook took part in 609 Squadron's assault on the enemy aircraft menacing Swanage on 27 September.

> Soon we saw a squadron of Me110s circling over Swanage at 25,000 feet, waiting to protect their bombers on their return. We immediately turned towards the enemy fighters and started to climb above them … this was the first time in this war that we had met the enemy on even terms. Generally we were outnumbered by anything from three to one up to ten to one. But on this glorious occasion there were fifteen of them and twelve of us, and we made the most of it.
>
> We were close to them now and we started to dive. I think that these moments just before the clash are the most gloriously exciting moments of life. You sit there behind a great engine that seems as vibrant and alive as you are yourself, your thumb waits expectantly on the trigger, and your eyes watch the gun sights through which in a few seconds an enemy will be flying in a veritable ball of fire.
>
> All around you, in front and behind, there are your friends too, all eager and excited, all thundering down together into the attack! The memory of such moments is burnt on my mind for ever. [Crook, pp. 74-5]

-o-o-o-o-o-

Some of the Me109s remained in the London area to protect a following wave of 55 Ju88s of *Kampfgeschwader* 77. But the bombers had been late forming up, and before they could make the rendezvous they were intercepted by a strong force of over 100 British fighters. The formations were shattered and the bombers forced to ditch their loads and turn back. In the meantime, the Me109s had taken a mauling and now dived low to race for home.

Fighter Command sustained losses as well. Nos 72, 73, 92 and 303 squadrons all suffered. In a huge dogfight over East Sussex, No. 249 Squadron lost three aircraft. Sergeant George Palliser witnessed the demise of the South African Pilot Officer Percival Burton: 'I saw his contortions,' he later wrote, 'then I saw him straighten and fly straight into the German aircraft. Both crashed and Percy was killed. I was close enough to see his letters, as other pilots must have been and who also confirmed this incident, which in itself caused me to realize my young life and its future, if any, had jumped into another dimension.' [Quoted in Hough and Richards, p. 233]

Just before midday, another 300-strong German force approached London. Most were turned back by intercepting fighters, and only about 20 bombers succeeded in reaching the centre. By the end of the day, 28 Fighter Command aircraft had been shot down, but the Luftwaffe had lost 54, with all crews killed or captured.

Prime Minister Winston Churchill was delighted with the day's results, declaring that 'the heavy losses of the enemy … make 27th September rank with 15

PREVIOUS PAGE
Workers tend a Spitfire production line at the Supermarine factory near Southampton, which was targeted by bombers of Kampfgeschwader 55 on 26 September 1940.

362

September and 15 August, as the third great and victorious day of the Fighter Command during the course of the Battle of Britain.' [Quoted in Wood and Dempster, p. 366]

SATURDAY 28 September 1940

Today, Kesselring changed his tactics, sending smaller formations against London and Portsmouth. Their escorts included Me109s flying at heights of up to 30,000 feet. Here, only Spitfires could touch them, and even then at a performance disadvantage. The Hurricanes, particularly the older Mark 1 models, were unable to operate effectively at such heights, to the worry and frustration of their pilots. Hurricane pilot Richard Barclay, of No. 249 Squadron, noted in his diary two days later: 'We had hundreds of 109s above us. We were too high for the Hurricane anyway ... an awful trip as we were quite helpless, just waiting to be attacked.'

Both of the Luftwaffe raids were beaten back, but with severe losses. Sixteen British fighters were shot down and nine pilots killed, all for a return of only three

Cloud over the Channel, the Straits of Dover and Thames Estuary.

'He died from a fractured skull'

No. 238 Squadron, after a much-needed rest at the quiet posting of St Eval in Cornwall, had returned to the fray at Middle Wallop on 16 September. On 28 September, Macclesfield-born Eric Bann did not return from his mission over the Isle of Wight. His parents, to whom he had written regularly, spent months trying to find out the circumstances of his end. Eventually, they received a letter from W. Butcher of the Isle of Wight constabulary.

```
    The machine your son was piloting was seen flying at great speed
towards Portsmouth, probably hoping to regain its base as I believe
that it was on fire although not to any great extent. When at a good
height over Brading Marshes your son was seen to bale out quite safely
but watchers who saw him come down say that his parachute did not open
and this was found to be correct when Police and Military recovered
his body shortly after ... As far as I could see your son was not
wounded by the enemy as no gunshot wounds could be found on him at
all but it was perfectly obvious that he died from a fractured skull.
There was no chance of life when found I am sorry to say. Had there
been I would have worked hours as also would my men to have brought
him round, but, under the circumstances, I could see that it was
perfectly hopeless from the start ... I agree with you that at that time
these gallant men must have been very much overworked but they have
performed a most marvellous feat against overwhelming odds and have
earned the gratitude of all the civilised world and such is the spirit
of the British RAF that their names will live for ever as the saviours
of our country of which we are all so proud.

                        -0-0-0-0-0-
```

German planes. Kesselring's use of his *Luftflotte* 2 bombers as 'bait' to bring up Fighter Command against his Me109s had worked well.

29 September 1940 SUNDAY

Fine early on, with cloud later.

After yesterday's mauling for Fighter Command, the fine weather that began today might have threatened yet more damaging attacks. Luckily for the defenders, that was not to be. Cloud accumulated as time wore on, and the day witnessed only nuisance attacks on convoys and several high-flying sorties over Southeast England.

30 September 1940 MONDAY

Generally fair, with some cloud and light winds.

The last day of September dawned very bright. At Middle Wallop, 'the weather was brilliantly clear', remembered 609 Squadron's David Crook, 'and when we got up we shook our heads dismally, as we knew there would be a lot of trouble'.

In contrast with the previous day, the Luftwaffe was mounting a big effort. Soon after 9am, 200 aircraft crossed the coast in two waves. Twelve squadrons went up to meet them, and most of the bombers were turned back over Maidstone. While dogfights continued over the Thames Estuary, a free chase of Me109s and Me110s was plotted near Weymouth. David Crook's 609 Squadron was among the squadrons vectored to intercept. They were at 27,000 feet over Swanage, Dorset, when they saw their prey. The squadron flew over Weymouth Bay and then in towards land to approach the enemy out of the sun. When six Me109s appeared in front of them, the British fighters latched onto their tails and followed them down as they tried to plunge away. 'God, what a dive that was!' Crook wrote. 'I have a sort of dim recollection of the sea coming up towards me at an incredible rate and also feeling an awful pain in my ears ... I pulled out of the dive as gently as I could, but the strain was terrific and there was a sort of black mist in front of my eyes ... the Messerschmitt was now just ahead of me. I came up behind him and gave him a terrific burst of fire at very close range.' Crook's victim 'rocked violently, then turned over on his back, burst into flames and dived straight down into the sea ... the pilot made no attempt to get out and was obviously dead'. Crook returned to the mêlée to find 'a nice little massacre' in progress, and soon the surviving Germans broke off and raced for home. [Quotations in Crook, pp. 80–1]

From midday, Kesselring sent about 100 bombers and 200 fighters in another attempt on London. Again, it was driven back and an intense fighter battle developed over Kent. A number of Ju88s reached South London, but the Luftwaffe sustained heavy losses.

The final attack of the day was against the Westland factory at Yeovil. Once again, it was carried out by Heinkels from *Kampfgeschwader* 55, which arrived with a strong escort. Four squadrons attacked them on the way in, and another four on the way out, after the bombers had found their target obscured by clouds and had scattered their bombs ineffectually.

Nearly 50 Luftwaffe aircraft were shot down on this last day of September. Fighter Command lost 20, with 8 pilots killed.

In the light of the accumulating evidence and the events of 30 September, Kesselring and Sperrle now decided that all twin-engine bombers should be withdrawn from daylight action unless there was thick cloud cover to protect them. During October, they would be used almost exclusively on night-time raids.

Instead of mass attacks in daylight, the Luftwaffe concentrated on infiltrating in small numbers and at great heights, mainly with Me109s and Me110s. Frustrated by Park's targeting of the bombers and avoidance of his fighter-only sweeps, Kesselring converted a third of his Me109 force to carry 250kg bombs. In theory this would mean that they could not be ignored by the defenders. If they came under attack, the raiders could simply jettison the bomb and revert to pure fighter mode. But the extra load brought significant disadvantages also, as the additional weight further reduced the Messerschmitt's range.

Workers at a wrecking yard take their lunch break in the remains of a German bomber (summer 1940).

The new tactic caused considerable headaches for Park. A well-placed 250kg bomb could cause extensive damage. October became known in Battle of Britain folklore as 'Messerschmitt month'. Almost all the southern airfields were hit, as well as Portsmouth, Southampton and London. On 15 October, bomb-carrying Me109s hit London's Waterloo station, closing virtually all its lines out of London.

Me109s crossing the coast at 30,000 feet were beyond the reach of the Hurricane, which made up two-thirds of Fighter Command's strength, and even the Spitfire struggled to get at them. Interception was a patchy business. On one occasion it took only 17 minutes after radar detection for a formation of Me109s to reach Central London. A Mark 1 Spitfire needed 27 minutes to climb to 30,000 feet. Thus, many Spitfires missed the attackers or were caught 'on the climb'. High-altitude flying in an unpressurized, unheated cockpit was particularly debilitating. Pilots reported stomach pains and sharp aches in the joints from tiny bubbles of oxygen in their blood. The accident rate rose. Park's solution was to detail two 'spotting flights' to act as look-outs, flying high, avoiding combat and concentrating on reporting to Uxbridge any approaching aircraft.

But for all the physical wear-and-tear and the losses suffered by Fighter Command pilots during October, the new Luftwaffe tactic was never going to be decisive. There was now no shortage of British pilots or aircraft, and however fast and accurate the fighter-bombers were, their bombs were too small to affect the course of events that was revealing itself.

On 4 October, Count Galeazzo Ciano, the Italian foreign minister, was present at a meeting between Hitler and Mussolini. Later that day he wrote in his diary that 'there is no longer any talk about landing in the British Isles'. [Ciano, p. 298]

BELOW
The skeleton of Coventry cathedral (bombed on 14 November) would become the most powerful expression of the destructiveness of the Blitz outside London.

✠ AIR RAIDS ON GREAT BRITAIN

Tonnage of bombs dropped on British targets in July – December 1940

Target	High Explosive (including land mines) Tons	Incendiaries Tons	Number of Bombs
London	23,716	2,918	2,951,000
Liverpool and Merseyside	2,114	274	278,300
Birmingham	1,780	141	143,000
Coventry	965	231	234,700
Manchester	933	105	107,000
Bristol	360	112	113,500
Southampton	421	106	108,000
Plymouth	362	95	96,000
Airfields	1,710	28	28,100
Other raids	4,303	211	205,000
Total	**36,664**	**4,221**	**4,264,600**

'The Battle of Britain was all over'

During the Battle of Britain, Me109 pilot Gunther Büsgen, of *Lehrgeschwader* 2, had shot down six British fighters and flown nearly eighty sorties. On 12 October, over London, he flew his last.

```
    I copped it. On the way home I was attacked by a Hurricane and the
hits were unfortunately in the cooling system and when that was hit
you had perhaps ten minutes' flying time before you had to bale out.
We were told at that stage that if you were hit over England you had
to get back over the Channel. What a nonsense! It was quite impossible.
I was shot at 3,000 metres and, not following orders, went into a
glide, but noticed that the plane was losing height rapidly. I lifted
my cockpit roof and started to get out, but made a mistake and banged
my left arm, cutting it. After a few more flying minutes I landed the
plane at an aerodrome at Chatham. There were two Home Guards there
immediately with weapons, it seemed, out of the Tower of London.
'Hands up!' they said. I was quite good at English during my school
days and explained, 'I can't take my hands up because one is broken.'
```

As Büsgen ruefully reflected later:

```
    The flights to London we regarded as completely unnecessary …
They brought no results for us. In October the Battle of Britain
was all over - the first part of a lost war.
```

-0-0-0-0-0-

A Messerschmitt Me109 comes in to land. Heavy bombers gave way to bomb-carrying Me109s and Me110s during October 1940, but the new tactics failed to tip the balance in the Luftwaffe's favour.

On 12 October, Generalfeldmarschall Keitel, head of the German armed forces, recorded that 'The Führer has decided that from now until the spring, preparations for Sealion shall be continued solely for the purpose of maintaining political and military pressure on England. Should the Invasion be reconsidered in the spring or early summer of 1941, orders for renewal of operational readiness will be issued later. In the meantime military conditions for a later invasion are to be improved.' [Quoted in Bickers, p. 242]

On 29 October, the Luftwaffe launched its last substantial daylight effort of the Battle of Britain. By now, a small contingent from the Italian air force had joined the campaign on the insistence of Mussolini, and while its outdated bombers attacked Ramsgate, the Luftwaffe raided Portsmouth and London. Most of the enemy aircraft were intercepted and driven back, but a small number got through. The next day came a more half-hearted effort, easily repulsed by the ten squadrons Park now had in the air on patrol. On the following day, 31 October, officially deemed the end of the Battle of Britain, for the first time neither side lost an aircraft.

The Luftwaffe turned its depleted strength to the night-time bombing campaign. The Blitz would continue, with hardly a night's respite, until May 1941, when the German bomber fleets were sent east to prepare for Hitler's invasion of the Soviet Union. By then, some 43,000 British civilians had been killed, about half of them in London, and more than a million homes destroyed or damaged. But the Battle of Britain – the battle to avert invasion and defeat of the British homeland – had been won.

AFTERMATH

By November 1940, as Fighter Command's ordeal by fire eased, Britain's civilian population had taken its place in the frontline. In the autumn of 1940, daylight attacks by the Luftwaffe faded out to be replaced by relentless night-time raids, which the RAF could do little to deter. The Blitz, which was to last from 7 September 1940 until 10 May 1941, was Germany's last attempt to try to end the war in the west before beginning her campaign against the Soviet Union. It was a strategy that depended on terrorizing the British people into rising up against their leaders and demanding peace. In Southeast England and in cities across the country, ordinary people had to get used to a life of constant danger and fear.

Gwen Arnold, a young woman living near Bournemouth, remembered the experience vividly: 'Throughout that long winter the dreaded siren sounded at dusk every night, and the all clear was not heard until three, four, five or even six o'clock the next morning. Mother, Peggy and I crouched in the tiny cupboard under the stairs all those hours. We sat on boxes with only a candle to lighten the gloom. It was the worst period of the war for me. For hour after hour we listened to the distinctive throb of the German bombers (we could always tell if it was "one of ours" or "one of theirs"), the gunfire and an occasional earth-shattering explosion. At times I physically shook with fear. It was not so much fear of harm to our persons, but fear of losing our home. Home meant everything to us and I could not imagine how we would ever make another home, if we lost the house and our possessions.' [Arnold, p. 77]

OPPOSITE
St Paul's Cathedral looms majestically amid the bruised and battered buildings around it, having narrowly escaped serious damage.

Gioya Steinke, a welfare adviser with London County Council Rest Centre Service, remembered that the German bombs levelled not only houses but also class distinctions: 'As soon as the "all clear" went you had the wardens and the firemen bringing all these people into the rest centres and they were in a pretty terrible state, covered in bomb dust. Everyone was reduced to the same level. You didn't know who was a street market person and who was from the posh flats. They were all reduced down and this I think was the reason for the wonderful camaraderie of the Blitz.' [Steinke, recording]

continued on page 373

'PADDY' FINUCANE, FIGHTER ACE

Brendan Finucane, known as 'Paddy' to his comrades and admirers, was born in Dublin on 16 October 1920. After his family moved to Richmond in Surrey, he joined the RAF on a short service commission aged eighteen. Finucane was posted to No. 65 Squadron at Hornchurch on 13 July 1940, and the following month shot down two Me109s in two days. With his crinkly hair, square jaw and faraway look he seemed to exemplify the youth and low-key idealism of the pilots, and he was extensively promoted by official propaganda. After he broke his ankle in a non-military accident, Finucane was inundated with get-well letters. 'I guess you've received tons of fan mail from hero-worshipping dames all over the country,' wrote a Land Girl who gave her address as 'Amongst the turnips, Wiltshire'. She signed off: 'Boy, don't I wish I'd been a nurse.' [Imperial War Museum Archive Dept, No. 97/43/1]

During 1941, Finucane was a prolific destroyer of German aircraft, shooting down 18 Me109s between August and the end of October. In June 1942, he took over the Hornchurch wing, becoming the youngest wing commander in the RAF. On 15 July 1942, after leading a raid against shipping at Ostend and on German airfields, his Spitfire was hit by fire from a machine-gun post near Le Touquet. He was too low to bale out and the aircraft crashed into the sea. His last words over the radio were 'This is it, chaps.' He was not yet 22.

The proud Irishman Brendan Finucane sits in his 452 Squadron Spitfire,
emblazoned with a shamrock, at RAF Kenley (13 October 1941).

As Steinke suggests, civilian morale stayed firm – and the German strategy failed. Thus, Britain was saved in 1940–1 not only by the 'fighter boys' and the skill, equipment, organization and leadership of Fighter Command, but also by the refusal of ordinary people, many of them poor, to succumb to hysteria or recriminations against their political leaders under the weight of the Luftwaffe's bombing.

As for the men of Fighter Command, the Battle of Britain made some of them into celebrities. As the year 1940 wore on, the BBC leaned heavily on pilots to make broadcasts harking back to the great events of the summer. The old reluctance to promote fighter aces, which had been thought bad for group morale, was gone. Certain pilots were pushed towards the newspapers. 'Paddy' Finucane, a good-looking flying officer with No. 65 squadron, became a notable favourite with women readers.

Many of the cast of heroes, though, would not survive the war. Of the 2917 pilots who took part in the air battles of the summer of 1940, 544 had died.

Another 795 would be killed in the remaining years of the conflict. On 25 November 1940, Air Chief Marshal Dowding, originally due to retire in June 1939, was replaced as head of Fighter Command by Air Vice-Marshal Sholto Douglas. Park was also moved to a training command, and his old adversary Leigh-Mallory took over command of 11 Group. It was a victory for the proponents of the 'Big Wing' and of taking the fight to the enemy. Most of the fighter pilots in 11 Group felt that Park and Dowding were the victims of jealousy and intrigue. It seemed to one, Al Deere, that they had 'won the Battle of Britain but lost the battle of words that followed, with the result that they ... were cast aside in their finest hour'. [Deere, p. 172]

Douglas ordered Fighter Command into the offensive. Now Spitfires and Hurricanes roared over the Channel, hitting targets of opportunity such as bridges and railways, and trying to lure the enemy's fighters into the air in operations known as 'Rhubarbs' and 'Circuses'. They were expensive and wasteful. The pilots had lost the home advantage they had enjoyed during the Battle of Britain, and more pilots were killed during these continental missions than during the summer of 1940. Fighter Command and the Luftwaffe had changed places. Fighters were now called on

A victory of the spirit, reflected in the smiling faces of some of 'the Few', May 1941 – pilots of 601 County of London ('Millionaires') Squadron.

to escort British bombers on their raids on targets abroad, and British pilots experienced all the difficulties their Me109 adversaries had faced. Pilots disliked, even hated, their new duties.

Fighter Command's military significance began to decline immediately after the Battle of Britain. It was the contest it had been designed for. It went into the fray supported by a superb system of detection and interception, using aircraft that had been bred to excel at their task, which were flown by a body of men fighting for their families, their country and their ideals with skill and courage. These men were led by commanders who, while outwardly apparently unexceptional, had huge inner reserves of resolve, fortitude and intelligence.

The 'fighter boys' would never be at centre stage again. But they had given a performance that was unrepeatable. Its brilliance was matched by its significance. The Battle of Britain had immense strategic and symbolic importance. In victory, Britain lived on in freedom to provide a base for the heavy-bomber offensive against Germany and, eventually, a launch pad for the Allied invasion of Europe. The Luftwaffe, which had terrorized Europe, had been humbled. Hitler had suffered his first defeat.

AIRCRAFT OF THE BATTLE OF BRITAIN

HAWKER HURRICANE MK 1

SUPERMARINE SPITFIRE MK1

MESSERSCHMITT ME109E

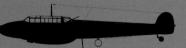

MESSERSCHMITT ME110C-4

JUNKERS JU87B-2

DORNIER DO17Z

HEINKEL HE111

JUNKERS JU88A-1

The Hawker Hurricane Mk 1 flown by Flight Officer A.V. Clowes of No. 1 Squadron, based at Wittering, October 1940.

HAWKER HURRICANE MARK 1

No fewer than 1715 Hurricanes flew in the Battle of Britain – more than all other fighter types combined – and their pilots were credited with some four-fifths of enemy aircraft destroyed during the summer of 1940.

By the end of the 1920s, advances in aircraft and engine design signalled the end of the age of the biplane. In 1930 the Air Ministry issued specification F.7/30, inviting bids from private companies to build a new generation of fast fighters. By 1933 Sydney Camm (1893–1966, right), chief designer for Hawker Aircraft Ltd at Kingston-upon-Thames, Surrey, had started work on a prototype. It would eventually become the Hurricane – the plane that Fighter Command relied on most and which won the Battle of Britain.

The new aircraft benefited from the advances made in the early 1930s in aero engineering and aerodynamics. It was to be a monoplane, powered with the proposed new Rolls-Royce 12-cylinder aero engine, and incorporating a sealed cockpit and retractable undercarriage. In other ways it was more traditional – the frame was of metal tubes and wooden 'formers' and 'stringers' (vertical frame struts and horizontal strips), covered by a fabric skin, painted with 'dope', a lacquer or varnish to reduce drag. This would make the new plane cheaper and easier to make than the metal-skinned Spitfire.

The first flight of the as yet unnamed Hurricane was on 6 November 1935 at Brooklands aerodrome in Surrey. The RAF tested the plane the following February and was impressed. Hawker pressed on with improvements and was rewarded

with an order for 600 Hurricanes from the Air Ministry in the summer of 1936.

By October 1937, the first production-Hurricane was ready for testing, fitted with an early example of the Rolls Royce Merlin II engine, which could produce 1030 horsepower at 16,000ft. The following January, the first Hurricanes were delivered to 111 Squadron Fighter Command. For pilots used to biplanes, the Hurricane looked extremely heavy and it seemed to take an age to get airborne. But the power was hugely exhilarating – it was like nothing they had ever flown, and they found it a surprisingly easy plane to control.

At the beginning of 1939, production switched to a new version with a Merlin III engine and pressed metal, rather than fabric, covering the wings. These now held eight Browning machine-guns, positioned far enough away from the propeller disc to make complicated synchronization gear unnecessary. By the beginning of the war, a little under 500 Hurricanes had been delivered to Fighter Command.

Further improvements were made, including self-sealing fuel tanks, as well as modifications to the canopy, which was often difficult to open when baling out. Two 'fixed pitch' propellers were replaced with constant-speed propellers, improving the handling qualities and increasing the ceiling at which it could operate. A Hurricane Mark 2, delivered in small quantities from August 1940, featured a 1300hp engine, the Merlin XX, and could reach 342mph. Other changes continued after the end of the Battle of Britain.

The Hurricane has entered popular mythology as the plain older sister to the

glamorous Spitfire. Certainly, it was 1000 pounds heavier, and so it was not as fast, particularly in the climb and at higher altitudes. But it could turn more tightly, and its weight and sturdy construction meant that it was a better gun platform and harder to shoot down. 'The Hurricane was absolutely viceless provided you treated it right,' said 151 Squadron's Flight Lieutenant Hugh Ironside. 'I think from the point of view of fighting, I would have preferred it to a Spitfire, because it was so much stronger … you just couldn't fuss the Hurricane.' Many pilots would be grateful for the Hurricane's rugged construction as they success fully landed their badly damaged aircraft.

FACTS AND FIGURES

Wing span	40ft
Length	31ft 4in.
Height	13ft 1in.
Power plant	One Rolls-Royce Merlin III 12-cylinder liquid-cooled engine
Horsepower	1130hp
Maximum speed	328mph at 20,000ft
Climbing rate	2750 ft/min.
Range	505 miles
Service ceiling	34,200ft
Armament	Eight 0.303in. Browning machine-guns mounted in the wings

SUPERMARINE SPITFIRE MARK 1

In successive versions, the Spitfire was the only Allied fighter aircraft to be produced from the beginning of the Second World War until the very end – and beyond. Extraordinarily photogenic and a supreme achievement in aeronautical engineering, the Spitfire has earned its place as one of history's most famous and beautiful fighter aircraft.

No combat aircraft can have inspired such depth of feeling among those who fought in it as did the Spitfire. The Hurricane was trusted for its solidity, strength and manoeuvrability; but the Spitfire was, in the words of pilot George Unwin, 'the perfect flying machine … it was so sensitive on the controls. There was no heaving or pulling and pushing and kicking. You just breathed on it.' [Unwin, recording] Although many more Hurricanes than Spitfires were flown during the Battle of Britain, it was the faster, more beautiful and altogether more glamorous Spitfire that seized the public's imagination, becoming, in the words of one of its test pilots, Jeffrey Quill, 'a symbol of defiance and of victory in what seemed a desperate and hopeless situation.' [Quill, recording]

The Spitfire evolved from the Supermarine Company's efforts to win the Schneider Trophy. This prestigious competition, held 11 times between 1913 and 1931, tested the speed and endurance of sea-planes (once thought to be the future of long-distance travel) and offered an excellent shop window for aircraft manufacturers. Supermarine had won in 1922, with an aircraft achieving 145mph. Then, the prize went for two successive competitions to the United States with a sleek, streamlined aircraft powered by a Curtiss liquid-cooled D-12 engine. This had already been used in an RAF light bomber and may have inspired Rolls Royce's milestone F.XI engine, the precursor to the Merlin.

The final three competitions, however, all went to the Supermarine Aviation Works Ltd of Southampton, with a succession of monoplane designs by Reginald J. Mitchell (1895–1937, *above right*), each of which, if the large floats are blanked out, looks more and more like the familiar, lithe shape of the Spitfire.

Supermarine's second victory was in 1929, when the S6, powered by a Rolls-Royce engine, was measured over the course flying at an average speed of 328.63mph. This led directly to the Air Ministry's 1930 specification F.7/30, for a new generation of fast fighters.

Although Mitchell and Supermarine – the company was now taken over by Vickers – won the Schneider Trophy again in 1931 in spectacular style, they struggled for a long time with the different requirements of a fighter aircraft. Mitchell's first effort was a severe disappointment, only reaching some 230mph. In 1934 both Mitchell and Sydney Camm at Hawker (working on the Hurricane prototype) were asked to incorporate into their designs the proposed new Rolls-Royce 12-piston Merlin engine as well as the facility for eight machine-guns. Mitchell's team continued to struggle with problems with the propeller and the aerodynamics of their new plane, but on 5 March 1936, two days before Hitler marched into the demilitarized Rhineland in defiance of the terms of Treaty of Versailles, the as yet unnamed Spitfire prototype took its first flight from Eastleigh airport near Southampton.

Three months later, 310 Spitfires were ordered at the same time as 600 Hurricanes. The disparity in numbers was due to concerns that the technologically well-advanced Spitfires would be more difficult to manufacture. This, indeed, turned out to be the case. It was only in

A Spitfire Mk 1A of No. 609 (West Riding) Squadron, based at Middle Wallop, late September 1940.

August 1938 that the first Spitfires were delivered to 19 Squadron at Duxford, and production rates remained low compared to the Hurricane.

As with the Hurricane, further improvements were made to the propeller, to the cramped cockpit – giving the Spitfire its distinctive bubble – and by the addition of armour around the pilot's seat and the insertion of supposedly bullet-proof glass.

The Spitfire had the same engine as the Hurricane, but it was lighter and therefore faster. What had emerged was a more modern and sophisticated aircraft than its Hawker sister. With thin, elliptical wings, and an all-metal fuselage, it was, in effect, half a generation more advanced, as its longer service life would later demonstrate.

The Spitfire's sophistication made it a more difficult and expensive fighter to build than the Hurricane. It was also more complicated to maintain and rearm. Its high nose gave the pilot poor visibility while taxiing, and its forward centre of gravity meant that it was easy to tip it onto its propeller; its narrower wheel base made it harder to land than the Hurricane. But the Spitfire was deemed worth it for its superior performance.

Up against the Messerschmitt Me109 – its great rival – it more than held its own. The German fighter was, with its fuel-injected engine, better in the dive and at very high altitudes. But the Spitfire was sharper In the turn, though not as sharp as the Hurricane, and much more agile at all altitudes. Luftwaffe fighter pilots were said to admire the Spitfire's qualities – and to be shot down by one was no dishonour. In the end, the different strengths and weaknesses of the Me109 and the Spitfire probably cancelled each other out. The contest would be decided by the tactical positioning of the aircraft and by the skill and endurance of the opposing pilots.

Most of the Spitfires deployed during the Battle of Britain carried the same eight-machine-gun armament as the Hurricane, although experiments were made with cannon-firing Spitfires. A Mark 2 model, with a slightly more powerful engine, was introduced in June 1940, though most Spitfires that fought in the summer of 1940 were Mark 1A.

Airmen talked about the aircraft in the language of love. The American pilot James Goodson, who flew with No. 43 Squadron, said: 'Once you got used to the Spitfire, of course you loved it. It became part of you. It was like pulling on a tight pair of jeans. It was a delight to fly. I used to smoke a cigar sometimes – against all rules and regulations – but if I dropped my cigar lighter, instead of groping around on the floor, I'd move the stick a fraction of an inch, the Spit would roll over and I'd catch the cigar lighter as it came down from the floor. That was the kind of plane it was. Everybody had a love affair with it.' [Goodson, recording]

FACTS AND FIGURES

Wing span	36ft 10in.
Length	29ft 11in.
Height (to tip of propellor)	12ft 8in.
Power plant	One Rolls-Royce Merlin III 12-cylinder liquid-cooled engine
Horsepower	1175hp
Maximum speed	362mph at 18,500ft
Climbing rate	9.04 min. to 20,000ft
Normal range	395 miles
Service ceiling	31,900ft
Armament	Eight 0.303in. Browning machine-guns mounted in the wings

MESSERSCHMITT ME109E

The Messerschmitt Me109 was, in various succeeding versions, produced in larger numbers than any other fighter of the Second World War. It was, according to fighter pilot Hans-Ekkehard Bob, 'an extremely beautiful aircraft. A handsome, racy machine. It handled impressively in the air.' It was the Me109 that shot down most of the 1172 British aircraft lost between July 1940 and October 1940, and which posed the most serious threat to the survival of Fighter Command.

The Me109, like its British rivals the Hurricane and Spitfire, was the brainchild of one man. Willy Messerschmitt (1898–1978) was a designer of extraordinary versatility, whose creativity ranged across gliders, fighters and, later, jets. His aim was simple: to marry the largest engine with the smallest airframe possible. His first 109 was one of four designs submitted in response to a request from the Luftwaffe for a new fighter aircraft to replace its outmoded biplanes. As with two of the other competing designs, the initial Me109, first flown in May 1935, was powered by a Rolls-Royce Kestrel V engine imported from Derby. But in other ways it was radically different, with its enclosed cockpit, all-metal stressed skin, wing-leading edge slats and narrow-track retractable undercarriage. There were faults with the design, some of which were never removed – such as its steep

upwards angle when on the ground, which made for poor pilot visibility while taxiing – but the Me109 won the competition and went into further development and production.

The first production-model left the assembly line in February 1937, equipped with a Junkers Jumo 210A inverted-vee 680hp engine, and the following month 16 were flown direct from the factory to Seville during Spain's Civil War, where they were issued to Wolfram von Richthofen's *Jagdgeschwader* (fighter wing) of the German Condor Legion to replace their Heinkel 51 biplanes.

The fighting in Spain proved a useful testing ground for the Me109 in combat. Its three light machine-guns were found to be inadequate, leading to the development of the 20mm Oerlikon cannon. Successive improved versions were produced, with the four-gunned Me109E-1 the first to be fitted with the all new Daimler-Benz DB601A engine with direct fuel injection. This was closely followed by the E-3, equipped with cannon at the expense of two of the machine-guns. By the end of 1939, some 1500 Me109Es had been built.

The new engine, with a maximum of 1150 horsepower, was more powerful than the Rolls-Royce Merlin, then being fitted into Hurricanes and Spitfires. The Me109 was also smaller and lighter than its rivals. This would give the Me109

awesome performance but create difficulties as well. There was little space for fuel or ammunition. Its thin, narrow wings, which delivered superb performance in the air, were not so effective as a gun platform and meant that the undercarriage had to be supported by the fuselage; this created a narrow and unstable wheel base and led to numerous crashes on landing.

Unlike the British fighters, the Me109 had an excellent view to the rear; it could out-climb the Spitfire to 20,000 feet and always out-dive it, thanks to its fuel injection. It was less agile than its rivals, but at over 20,000 feet it was undoubtedly the superior aircraft.

FACTS AND FIGURES

Wing span	32ft 4in.
Length	28ft 8in.
Height	11ft 2in.
Power plant	One Daimler-Benz DB601A 12-cylinder, direct-fuel injection, liquid-cooled engine
Horsepower	1150hp
Maximum speed	357mph at 12,300ft
Climbing rate	3510ft/min.
Range	412 miles
Service ceiling	36,000ft
Armament	Two 7.9mm machine-guns in upper nose (E-3 and E-4) decking with 1000 rounds per gun; two 20mm MG FF cannon in wings with 60 rounds per gun

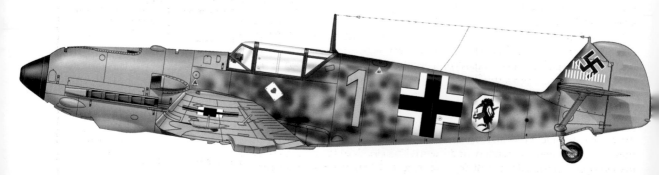

The Messerschmitt Me109E-3 flown by Oberst Josef Priller of Jagdgeschwader 51, *autumn 1940.*

The Messerschmitt Me110 flown by Hauptmann Martin Lutz during the Battle of Britain.

MESSERSCHMITT ME110C-4

Known in the Luftwaffe as the *Zerstörer* ('Destroyer'), the Messerschmitt Me110 was the best twin-engine fighter in the world and markedly superior to the British equivalent, the Bristol Blenheim. It was portrayed in propaganda, and regarded by Hermann Goering, as the Luftwaffe's most devastating modern weapon, manned by the force's best crews. However, as with the Stuka, the Battle of Britain would see its fortunes and reputation wrecked.

The first Me110 prototype was flown in May 1936. Further tests showed it to be fast and comparatively manoeuvrable for a heavy twin-engine aircraft. The plane went through successive test versions with more powerful engines and did not go into large-scale production until 1939. By the beginning of the war, only some 159 Me110s had been delivered to the Luftwaffe. But the aircraft was given production priority, and by the time of the Battle of Britain there were some 300 of the model lined up against RAF Fighter Command.

Designed for the dual roles of long-distance escort and ground-attack, the Me110 had a top speed only marginally slower than a Spitfire and faster than a Hurricane. Its basic design was highly versatile – amenable to changes in power plant and armament – and it carried three times the fuel of an Me109. Its front-firing weapons – cannon and machine-gun – produced the most devastating effect of any Battle of Britain

fighter, as Flying Officer Harold Bird-Wilson testified: 'We had a squadron commander who believed in the head-on attack. So he attacked an Me110 head-on and I'm afraid Jerry got the better of him – all we found of him was his shirt.' [Bird-Wilson, recording]

At the beginning of the war, the Me110 was producing as much fearful speculation as the Me109, and one air marshal offered a smart dinner in Paris to the first fighter-pilot to shoot one down. On 29 March 1940, Hurricanes from No. 1 Squadron took the prize, reporting in the squadron's diary that the much-feared German aircraft was 'very fast and manoeuvrable for a twin-engine aircraft, [but] can be easily out-manoeuvred by a Hurricane.' The rear gunner of an Me110, it was discovered, became ineffective during a dogfight because steep turns either caused him to black out or made it impossible for him to aim his armament effectively.

Fighting during the early weeks of the Battle of Britain showed that up against Hurricanes and Spitfires the Me110 had insufficient manoeuvrability and inadequate defensive armament. In spite of its high top speed, its poor acceleration counted against it in a dogfight or when taken by surprise. In a short time, the 'Destroyer' had become a liability. In August alone, 120 were lost on operations. The elite Me110 pilots took to forming a defensive circle when confronted with interceptors. This raised

their chances of survival, but it was a sterile manoeuvre as they could play no further part in the battle.

Goering was forced to order that his favourite aircraft, designed in part as an escort fighter, should itself have an escort of Me109s. In spite of this, and despite its much-reduced operational use, a further 83 Me110s were downed before the end of September 1940.

Nevertheless, in the hands of the very best pilots, the Messerschmitt Me110 could still be effective. Experimental Group 210, a combination of Me109s and bomb-carrying Me110s, carried out a number of spectacular set-piece raids, achieving surprise by flying at high speed not much off ground level and thereby avoiding radar detection.

FACTS AND FIGURES

Wing span	53ft 5in.
Length	39ft 8in.
Height	11ft 6in.
Power plant	Two Daimler-Benz DB601A 12-cylinder liquid-cooled engines
Horsepower	1150hp
Maximum speed	349mph at 22,960ft
Range	530 miles
Service ceiling	32,000ft
Armament	Four 7.9mm MG17 machine-guns and two 20mm MG FF cannon in the nose; one rear-firing 7.9mm MG15 machine-gun in the rear cockpit
Bombload	1100lbs

JUNKERS JU87B-2

The *Sturzkampfflugzeug* – better known as the 'Stuka' – quickly gained a fearsome reputation. Roaming ahead of the Panzer tank columns, acting as long-range artillery, the dive-bomber hit bridges, communication centres and troop concentrations with impressive accuracy. It was a key component of *Blitzkrieg*. In Poland, then in the Low Countries and France, the aircraft's steep, almost vertical dive and screaming whistles had a shattering psychological effect on those it attacked. With its distinctive shape – pointed nose, cranked wings and prominent fixed undercarriage – it was soon the element of the German armed forces most hated and feared by its enemies and most admired by its friends.

The *Sturzkampfflugzeug* was the Luftwaffe's prime weapon until the summer of 1940. The tactic of dive-bombing had been widespread during the First World War, but the first aircraft specifically designed as a dive-bomber was not developed until the 1920s. To avoid postwar restrictions on German aircraft development, Hugo Junkers had established facilities in Sweden, and from here in 1928 emerged the Junkers K47. The aircraft was tested in secret in Berlin, and soon after the Nazis came to power in 1933 a requirement was issued for a new generation single-engine dive-bomber.

Junkers continued developing his aircraft, and in 1935 the first Ju87 was tested, powered with a Derby-built Rolls-Royce Kestrel engine. At trials held the next year, the Ju87 held off competition from three other dive-bomber prototypes

to win the contest, and by the spring of the following year the Ju87A, now powered by a 635hp Jumo 210 engine, was in service with the Luftwaffe.

Tested in Spain, the aircraft was improved by the addition of diving brakes and a more powerful engine. The Ju87B series was powered by the Jumo 211A direct-injection engine that produced 1200 horsepower, had more streamlined spats over the landing gear, and was now equipped with an automatic dive control. At the beginning of 1939, the Ju87As were sent to training units and all the *Stukageschwader* (Stuka wings) were equipped with the more powerful Ju87B series. At the beginning of the war, there were 360 available to the Luftwaffe.

In operation, the Ju87 was something of an endurance test. In the dive, the Stuka crew of two could feel the blood draining from their heads. At 1000 metres an alarm rang in their headphones to alert them in case they had blacked out. At 700 metres (765 yards) above the ground they released their bombs and levelled off. Their wings were fitted with whistles that shrieked as the planes dived, and the bombs themselves had cardboard whistles on their tail rudders. 'That gave quite a psychological effect,' said Stuka pilot Werner Roell, 'but all these things worked only at the beginning of the war.'

The Ju87 had considerable success during the early stages of the Battle of Britain, particularly against shipping and naval targets. But its slow top speed and poor manoeuvrability and rate of climb were its downfall. Whole *Staffeln* (squadrons) were

wiped out by the faster and more nimble Hurricanes and Spitfires, and by mid-August 1940 the Ju87 was deployed only rarely. By the end of the month the main units had been withdrawn from combat.

Werner Roell, who flew Stukas, called them 'the sharpshooter amongst the bombers. Whereas the horizontal bombers dropped an enormous amount of bombs on an area, the Stuka had a small target and with a small number of bombs, it could erase a target of importance … Of course Stukas were slow. They had to be sturdy because they came out of the dive sharply.' [Roell, recording]

For Fighter Command's pilots, Stukas were a welcome sight and 'very easy to get out of the sky,' according to Teddy Donaldson of 151 Squadron. 'We tackled them from the back end and the poor bastards just fell out of the sky.'

FACTS AND FIGURES

Wing span	45ft 3in.
Length	36ft 1in.
Height	13ft 10in.
Power plant	One Junkers Jumo 211A-1 12-cylinder liquid-cooled engine
Horsepower	1100hp
Maximum speed	223mph at 13,500ft
Range	370 miles
Service ceiling	26,500ft
Armament	Two 7.9mm MG17 machine-guns in the wings, one 7.9 MG15 machine-gun on a rear cockpit mounting
Bombload	One 1100lb bomb carried under the fuselage; four 110lb bombs under the wings

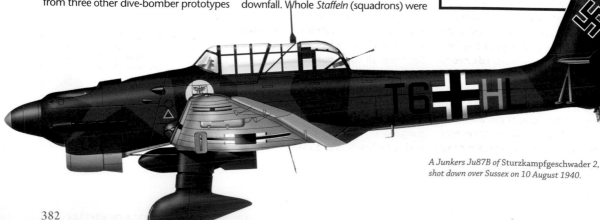

A Junkers Ju87B of Sturzkampfgeschwader 2, shot down over Sussex on 10 August 1940.

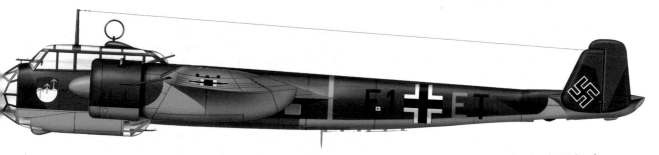

A Dornier Do17Z *of* Kampfgeschwader 76, *based at Cormeilles-en-Vexin, France, July 1940.*

DORNIER DO17Z

The Dornier Do17 was designed originally, on the face of it, as a fast passenger and mail transport for the German carrier Lufthansa; but it was easily adapted to become a Luftwaffe medium bomber and reconnaissance aircraft. Its slim fuselage, which suggested its 'Flying Pencil' nickname (*Fliegender Bleistift*), in fact made it totally unsuitable for carrying passengers.

Benefiting from the latest improvements in aeronautics and aerodynamics, the Dornier Do17 was a highly advanced design for its time. A prototype made its maiden test flight in 1934, and the following year a new version, with two 750hp BMW engines, was tested and recorded a top speed of 230mph. This qualified it as a 'fast bomber' and plans for large-scale production were completed by 1936. The following year, the aircraft caught the eyes of the world when, at a military aircraft competition in Zurich, a specially adapted Dornier displayed a speed of 248mph, almost as fast as any of the fighters competing. The same year Do17-E and F series aircraft entered service with the Luftwaffe. Both were close in design to the 1935 prototype, with the F Series adapted for reconnaissance purposes.

Dorniers fought in the Spanish Civil War, where they proved to be faster than any of the fighters put up against them. Weaknesses were discovered, however. The cockpit, where all the four-man crew was stationed, was cramped. More seriously, the bomber, which at this time carried a defensive armament of only two machine-guns, was shown to be dangerously vulnerable to attack from behind and below. To remedy this, new versions were developed with a more bulbous cockpit. This sacrificed some of the plane's aerodynamic qualities, but allowed room for a rear-facing gunner, lying down in the 'ventral position' (on the underside of the fuselage). By the time of the start of the Battle of Britain, most of the Luftwaffe's Dornier fleet were Do17Zs, each with with two 1000hp engines and six machine-guns.

The Do17 was the most reliable of the German bombers, popular with air and ground crews, but it lacked the load-carrying capabilities of the Heinkel He111 and the speed of the Junkers Ju88. During the Battle of Britain it was probably most effective coming in low over a target and bombing with accuracy.

Experience of fighting in the early weeks of the battle led the Dorniers to increase their defensive armament to eight guns, and, when the bombers were flying in tight formation, the cross-fire from all their guns made them a dangerous target. George Unwin of No. 19 Squadron recalled seeing a 'lone Dornier going home ... so I went after him. He had a rear gunner in a dustbin hanging below the fuselage and you had to fix him first and then close in on the aircraft. I could see him shooting at me and I gave him a burst and shut him up. At least I thought I had. As I closed right in again, I suddenly saw the rear gunner shooting back at me with little red sparks ... suddenly a hole appeared in this glass directly in front of my face. I thought, "Good God. I must be dead!"' [Unwin, recording]

But the Dorniers suffered too, and a lack of armour around the crew led to a high casualty rate during the Battle of Britain. The oldest of the three main bombers, unlike the He111 and the Ju88 it largely disappeared from frontline units by 1942.

FACTS AND FIGURES

Wing span	59ft 1in.
Length	52ft
Height	14ft 11in.
Power plant	Two Bramo 323P 9-cylinder air-cooled engines
Horsepower	1000hp
Maximum speed	265mph at 16,400ft
Range	745 miles
Service ceiling	26,400ft
Armament	Four to eight 7.9mm MG15 machine-guns in front, rear and beam cockpit mountings and ventral (underside) position
Bombload	2200lbs

HEINKEL HE111

The Heinkel He111 bomber was from the same generation as the Dornier Do17, and it too was facing obsolescence in 1940. Another of the Luftwaffe's 'fast bombers', the He111 had a top speed of 270mph – faster than anything it had faced while operating in Spain, but too slow against modern fighters. In fact, it was marginally slower than the Dornier and less manoeuvrable. Against that disadvantage, it could carry as much as twice the bombload. Nevertheless, as with the other bombers in the Luftwaffe, it was in essence a tactical weapon rather than a strategic bomber, designed for speed and flexibility rather than weight of armament.

Designed by twin brothers Siegfried (1899–1969) and Walter Günter (1899–1937), who joined Ernst Heinkel's company in 1931, the Heinkel He111 started life as a hybrid civil-military aircraft, as did the Dornier. Ostensibly a fast mail and passenger aircraft, the He111 was designed from the outset to be able to carry armament and a bombload. It was an elegant and efficient design, and in the mid-1930s it was pretty much the best of its kind in the world.

The first He111 bomber prototype flew in February 1935, and the aircraft went through many different versions, usually involving changes to the power plant, which became progressively more powerful. The greatest design change came with the 'P' variant, the first with the trademark streamlined fuselage and streamlined 'ventral' gondola (i.e. on the underside of the fuselage). This model started leaving the factories in 1938 and saw service in Poland. By the beginning of the Battle of Britain, many of the 'P' series Heinkels had been replaced by the improved 'H' series. Early experience of coming under attack from Fighter Command led to more and more defensive armament, as with the Dorniers. In common with other Luftwaffe bombers, the Heinkels would attempt to stay in rigid formation, the better to deploy crossfire from their guns.

Flying a Heinkel He111 required a completely different approach to that required of a fighter pilot, said Ernest Wedding. 'I flew my Heinkel 111 bomber in formation and I had to keep to my station. Even when the British fighters started attacking me, I couldn't do any intricate manoeuvres within the formation or else I would crash into the other bombers. It was a tedious job. All I was doing was watching the aircraft in front and on the left and right and hoping the chap behind was doing the same so that he wouldn't take my tail off. A bomber pilot had to be as steady as a bus driver.' [Wedding, recording]

It was Heinkels that bombed Rotterdam on 14 May 1940, and later in the war the aircraft would carry V-1 flying bombs to the English coast. By then, though, He111s had largely reverted to their role as transport aircraft, and nearly 200 were to be lost trying to carry supplies and ammunition to the German pocket at Stalingrad.

FACTS AND FIGURES

Wing span	74ft 1¾in.
Length	53ft 9½in.
Height	13ft 1½in.
Power plant	Two Junkers Jumo 211-F engines
Horsepower	1350hp per engine
Maximum speed	270mph at 16,400ft
Range	1212 miles
Service ceiling	27,890ft
Armament	Four to eight 7.9mm MG15 machine-guns in nose, dorsal and ventral (underside) positions
Bombload	4410lbs

A Heinkel He111 of Kampfgeschwader 53, based at Lille, France, September 1940.

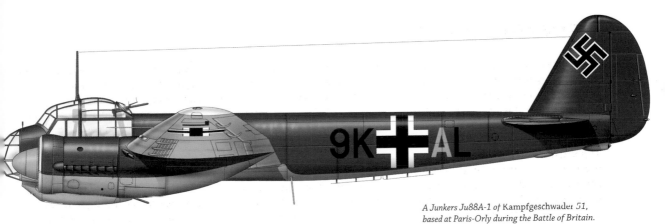

A Junkers Ju88A-1 of Kampfgeschwader 51, based at Paris-Orly during the Battle of Britain.

JUNKERS JU88A-1

The Junkers Ju88 was the newest aircraft in the Luftwaffe's armoury in 1940 and its outstanding bomber, able to carry a greater load but still outpace and out-range the Dorniers and Heinkels. It was also capable of dive-bombing with great accuracy. It is likely that had the Luftwaffe possessed more of these machines, its assault on Britain might have been more effective.

The Junkers Ju88 was conceived by W(ilhelm) H(einrich) Evers and the American designer Alfred A. Gassner – the latter a consultant from the Fairchild Company working in Europe at the time – in response to the Luftwaffe's call in 1935 for a new fast bomber. The first prototype flew in December the following year, but it took a comparatively long time to go into production, with the first test models delivered in spring 1939. By August, the Luftwaffe was taking delivery of the bomber, but only 12 saw action in Poland; the first models were beset with difficulties in the air brakes and undercarriage, problems largely ironed out by the summer of 1940.

The Ju88 was sturdily built and, like the Heinkel, could withstand a lot of combat damage but still make it back to base. Experience against Fighter Command led to an expansion of its defensive armament to as many as six machine-guns – two in the rear fuselage, one underneath, and the rest in the cockpit, where there was even one that could be operated by the pilot. The other forward-firing guns had to be operated by the flight engineer, a weakness of the aircraft.

Flight Lieutenant Charles MacLean had firsthand experience of the Ju88's capacity to soak up punishment. 'I caught up with a Junkers 88 and fired every round I could into it and it kept on flying. I flew alongside it and I could see that everyone was killed in it except for the pilot and he was obviously wounded. There were bullet holes everywhere but somehow this old thing plodded on.' [MacLean, recording]

The Ju88 achieved several notable successes during the Battle of Britain, particularly in its guise as a dive-bomber. It was also shot down at a lower rate than the other German bombers, partly because it could dive out of trouble, and not even the Spitfire could keep up with it.

Highly versatile, the Ju88 would serve with distinction throughout the war as dive-bomber, level bomber, torpedo bomber, night-fighter, reconnaissance aircraft and minelayer. Some 15,000 of them were built before 1945, a greater quantity than for any other Luftwaffe twin-engine bomber.

FACTS AND FIGURES	
Wing span	59ft 10¾in.
Length	47ft 1in.
Height	15ft 5in.
Power plant	Two Junkers Jumo 211B-1 12-cylinder liquid-cooled engines
Horsepower	1200hp per engine
Maximum speed	286mph at 16,000ft
Range	1553 miles
Service ceiling	26,500ft
Armament	Six to eight 7.9mm MG15 machine-guns in nose, rear cockpit and ventral (i.e. underside) gondola
Bombload	5510lbs

Page numbers in *italics* denote illustrations.

Page numbers in **bold** denote principal feature boxes.

Adlerangriff (Attack of the Eagle) 144, 147, 150, 158, 163, 171
Adlertag (Eagle Day) 144; first attacks 176, 178; postponement of and failure of some groups to receive message 170–1, 175
Advanced Air Striking Force 18
Aeberhardt, Pilot Officer Ray 270
Aeronautical Research Committee 60
AI (Airborne Interception) 122
Air Component 18
Air Ministry 94, 111, 156; map 222; memo 148; posters and graphics 243, 357; 'Spot at Sight' chart 111; takes control of Observer Corps 63
Air Raid Precaution (ARP) **20**
air raid wardens 308, 309
air raids: casualties of (table) **330**; precautions taken against **20**; tonnage of bombs dropped on targets (table) 366; *see also* Berlin; Blitz
Air Sea Rescue (ASR) service 112
Air Transport Auxiliary 205
Air Transport Commission (Germany) 114
aircraft, German 380–5; *see also* individual aircraft types
aircraft, RAF 377–9, armaments for 172–3; damaging of through mishap 91; fighter versus bomber debate 25, 40; fixing of damaged **94**; increase in production of **94**, 95, 106, 225; production figures 352; technical improvements 22, 94; use of high-octane fuel 255; wastage **352**; *see also* individual aircraft types
aircraft factories **94**, 95; bombing of 282, 289, 291, 355–6, 358, 359; losses of aircraft 352; 'shadow' 177, 350
aircraft mechanics 186–7
airfields, RAF 73; raids on 168–9, 170, 190, 191, 193, 196, 198, 201, 227, 229, 261, 262, 290, 366; *see also* sector stations; individual names of airfields
Allard, Sam 250
Allen, J.H.L. 86
Allen, Pilot Officer Johnny 85, 125
American pilots serving with RAF **182**
Amiens, fall of 34
Anderson, Sir John 19, 20
Anderson shelters 20, 21
Anglo-Iranian Oil Company 255
anti-aircraft batteries 137, 224, 271, 320, 324, 344
Anti-Aircraft Command **320**, 346
anti-aircraft guns 273, 320
anti-invasion preparations **108**, 108, **110**, 110, 148, 150, **310**, 310
Arandora Star (liner) 33
armaments, fighter aircraft **172–3**, 376–80 (aircraft 'facts and figures'); *see also* individual aircraft types

armaments factories 52
Armitage, Dennis 171
armourers **186–7**, 352
Arnold, Gwen 370
Ashfield, Flying Officer Glynn 124
ASR (Air Sea Rescue) service 112
ATS (Auxiliary Territorial Service) 204
Attlee, Clement 52
Austin Motor Company (Oxford) 177
Auxiliary Air Force (AAF) **80**, 274; *see also* RAF squadrons Nos 601, 602 and 603
Auxiliary Territorial Service (ATS) 204
Avro Tutors 89

'Bacon' convoy 128–9
Bader, Squadron Leader Douglas 41, 81, 121, 133, 194, 231, **240–1**, 240, 241, 319, 321, 341, 345
Bailey, Jim 248
Baldwin, Stanley 19
Ball, Albert **79**, 79
Bamberger, Sergeant Cyril 'Bam' 69, 274
Banks, Air Commodore Rod 255
Bann, Sergeant Eric 42, 113, 161, 176, 199, 346, 363
Barclay, Richard 315, 363
Barking Creek, Battle of (1939) 18, **23**, 23
Barltrop, Robert 303
Barr, Lillias 219
barrage balloons 124–5, 136, **137**, 137
Barran, Flight Lieutenant 'Pip' 81
Batt, Sergeant Gordon 175, 179, 199
Battle of Britain: end of 368; first day of 70–1, 74–8; impact of 9–10; role of in getting United States to enter the war 10–11; strategic and symbolic importance of 10–11, 375
'Battle of Britain Day' (15 Sept.) 336–48, 348
Battle of France 30–2, 30–1, 34, 132
Battles, Fairey 177, 331
Bawdsey, HMS (radar station) 6, 7
BBC broadcasts 91, 92, 156
BBC Home Service 156
beaches, holiday 151
Beaufighters, Bristol 324
Beaverbrook, Lord 28, 94, 95, 173
Beckton gas works: bombing of 308
BEF (British Expeditionary Force): and Dunkirk evacuation 7, 38–9, 38–9, 42–6, 45, 46, 100, 102, 107; in France 18, 32; withdrawal from France 34
Belfast: attack on 178
Belgium 29, 30; surrender to Germany 43
Bennett, Winnie and Dolly **94**
Bennions, George 353
Bentley Priory (Fighter Command HQ) 68–9, 69, 76
Benzie, Flying Officer 308
Berlin raid 232, **237**, 237
Bertram, Vice-Admiral Sir 277
Bethnal Green: bombing of 230, 234
Bibury, RAF: bombing of 227
'Big Wing' tactics 194, 195, 229, **231**, 241, 374

Biggin Hill, RAF 75, 197; bombing of 215, 261, 262, 267, 271, 273, 276, 278
Bird-Wilson, Flying Officer Harold 382
Bisdee, Flight Lieutenant John 120, 120, 128, 129, 166, 192, 324
'Black Thursday' (*der schwarze Donnerstag*, 15 Aug.) 181–5, 188–91, 193, 196–200
Black Velvet (film) 151, 154
blackouts 18, 20
Blackwood, Squadron Leader G.D.M. 246
Bland, Pilot Officer John 215
Blenheims *see* Bristol Blenheims
Bletchley Park 327
Blitz, the 122, **296–7**, 300–34, 316–17, 368, 370; and anti-aircraft guns 324; attempts to relieve tensions during 315; bombing of Central London 331, 345; bombing of East End and destruction caused 308–11, 313, 327; civilian deaths and injuries 313, 319, 323, 368; destruction caused by 319, 323, 331, 332, 351, 354; driving back of raiders short of their targets by British 323; fires and attempts to put out 311, 313, 324; first day of (7 Sept.) 300–13, 306–7; night-time raids 250–1, 311, 318, 323, 324, 329, 331, 349, 368, 370; sheltering in London Underground stations 312, 318–19; and shelters 311–12, 324; tonnage of bombs dropped during 366
Blitzkrieg 28, 50, 153, 382
Blücher (German cruiser) 27
Bob, Hans-Ekkehard 36, 59, 172–3, 380
Boelcke, Oswald 132
Bofors guns 320
bombers 237; 'bomber will always get through' theory, **19**; versus fighter debate 25, 40
Booth, Sergeant Glendon 278
'Booty' convoy 86
Borealis (balloon ship) 154, 155, 158
Borner, Werner 84
'Bosom' convoy 117, 119
Boulton Paul Defiants *see* Defiants
Bowen, Edward 122
Bowring, Ben 76
Boy Scouts 120
Brand, Air Vice-Marshal Sir Christopher Quintin 56, 160, **195**, 195, 258
Brand, Stanley 35
'Bread' convoy 71, 74, 76–8
Bren gun 273, 320
Brighton: bombing of 333
Bristol Beaufighters 324
Bristol Blenheims 177, 210, 256, 324, 381; losses (July) 140; losses (Aug.) 278
British Balloon Command 137
British Expeditionary Force *see* BEF
British Union of Fascists (BUF) 156, 331
Brize Norton, RAF 89; bombing of 206
broadcasts, BBC: radio 91, 92, 156; television 156

Brooke, General Sir Alan 38, 108
Brooklands aircraft factory: bombing of 282, 289, 291, 355–6
Brothers, Peter 8, 34, 41, 187, 199, 236, 264, 274, 290–1
Brown, Pilot Officer De Peyster 182
Brown, Pilot Officer Ronald 197
Browning machine-guns 172, 173, 377
Buchanan, James 'Buck' 128–9
Buckingham Palace: bombing of 118, 331, 332, 332
bullet trail diagram 243
bullets 172
Burnett, Flying Officer Wilf 237
burns units **353**
Burton, Pilot Officer Percival 362
Büsgen, Gunther 135, 367
Button, Corporal Lena 262
Byrne, Flying Officer 'Paddy' 23

Camm, Sydney 9, 60, 377, 377, 378
cannon **172–3**
Cap Gris Nez 129, 228
'Careless Talk Costs Lives' campaign 156, 157
Carnall, Sergeant Ralph 353
Castle Bromwich Spitfire factory 178, 359
casualties: civillian 227, 228, 230, 232, 253, 289, 313, 319, 323, **330**, 333, 368; pilot 373
Chain Home radar stations *see* radar stations, Chain Home
Chamberlain, Neville 20, 27, 28
Channel: convoys *see* convoys; German objective of blockading 56–7, 104; tightening of grip on by Germans 125
Channel Islands: German occupation of 50; He111 over 301
'Channel Sickness' 135, 136
Channon, Henry 'Chips' 27, 158, 176, 200, 325, 351
children, evacuating of **21**, 21
Church Fenton, RAF 182, 190, 236, 248
Churchill, Winston 8, 24, 27, 28, 52, 156, 226, 249, 266, 277, 328, 362; becomes prime minister 28; and 'Battle of Britain Day' (15 Sept.) 348, 349; and Berlin raid 237; and 'Black Thursday' 200; dinner with Dowding 276; formation of new Cabinet 28; and France 32–3, 34; inspection of bomb damage in Ramsgate 289; and invasion scare 111; 'so much owed by so many to so few' phrase 207, 226; and Soviet Union 144; speeches and broadcasts to the nation 45–6, **47**, **53**, **226**, 325, 328; 'their finest hour' phrase 53; tours London streets 315, 324; and United States 44–5, 102, 103; visits 11 Group HQ 337, 338; visits Fighter Command HQ 197; visits Dover 249, 277; working routine **277**
Ciano, Count Galeazzo 366, 368
'circle of death' Me110 formation 88, 166
City of Benares (liner) 21
Civil Defence poster 217
Civil Defence Volunteers 312
Civilian Repair Organisation (CRO) 94, 225

civilians: casualties 227, 228, 230, 232, 253, 289, 313, 319, 323, **330**, 333, 368; getting used to life of constant danger and fear 370; morale of 373
Clark, Percy 108
class distinctions: in RAF squadrons **274**; removing of among citizens 370
Clayton, Eric 168–9
Clowes, Dudley S. 9
Codrington, HMS 129
Coler, Generalmajor Joachim 181
Colerne, RAF 180
Collett, Sergeant G.R. 125, 228
Coltishall, RAF 70, 241, 282, 321
Columbia Market shelter 319
Colville, Sir John ('Jock') 34, 52, 94, 147, 220, 276, 277
combat report 314
Communists 331
condensation trails ('contrails') 208–9; *336–7*, *340*
Condor Legion 19, *19*, 49, *49*, 132, 380
convoys, Channel: 'Bacon' 128–9; 'Booty' 86; 'Bosom' 117, 119; 'Bread' 71, 74, 76–8; CW8 126, 154; E-boat attacks on 126, 154; 'Peewit' 154–5; raids on 64, *64–5*, 65, 71, 74, 81, *82–3*, 86–8, 90–1, 106, 119–20, 125–6, 128–9, 129, 131, 135, 151, 154–5, 158, 163, 228
Cooke, Pilot Officer Charles 70, 71
Cooper, Charles 269
Cosford factory 359
Coventry Cathedral: bombing of 366
Coward, Flying Officer James 270
Cowsill, Sergeant James 91
Cranwell, RAF cadet college at 89
Cripps, Sir Stafford 144
'Cromwell' codeword **310**
Crook, Pilot Officer David 67, 81, *165*, *175*, 180, 183, 192, 193, 230, 232, 234, 236, 244, *286*, 305, 335, 362, 364
Crossley, Squadron Leader Michael 207
Crowley-Milling, Denis *41*
Croydon, RAF: bombing of 197, 198
CW8 convoy 126, 154
Czech pilots 239, **246**; *see also* squadrons, RAF: No.310
Czernin, Flying Officer Count Manfred 233, 238

Daily Express 346
Darley, Squadron Leader H.S. 'George' 78, 163
Davies, Lieutenant Robert 329
Davis, Flying Officer Carl 182
Davis, Flying Officer Charles 128
Davis, Group Captain Edward 178
Davy, Horace 304
De Havilland Tiger Moths 89
Debden, RAF: 122, 205; bombing of 239, 244, 268, 284
Deere, Al(an) 62–3, 85, *86*, 125, 126, 248–9, 252, 264, 265, 271–2, 282, 374
Defiants 109, 112, 210, 229, 248; losses (July) 140; losses (Aug.) 278
Deichmann, Oberst Paul 183
Delight, HMS 135
Denmark: German invasion of 23, 27

Desford factory 359
Detling, RAF: bombing of 178, 262
Deutsche Lufthansa 48
Devitt, Squadron Leader Peter 69
Dewar, Squadron Leader John 196
Dishforth, RAF 189
Dixon, Sergeant Frederick 78
dominions: and Spitfire funds 159
Donahue, Pilot Officer Arthur 182
Donald, Flight Lieutenant Ian 109
Donaldson, Teddy 382
Dornier, Claude 48
Dornier Do17 18, 64, 70–1, 233, **383**, *383*; armaments 383; facts and figures 383; losses (July) 140; losses (Aug.) 279; weaknesses 383
Dornier Do18 seaplane 87, *123*
Dornier Do217 *233*
Douglas, Air Vice-Marshal Sholto 374
Dover: abandonment of as a destroyer base 129; attacks on 129, 131, 136; defence of 136
Dover barrage balloons 160, 179
Dover, RAF (radar station): bombing of 163, 185
Dover Straits 125, 129, 151
Dowding, Sir Hugh 9, 25, 32, **40–1**, *40*, *41*, 60, 61, 68, 78, 135, 155, 188, 195, 231, *231*, 276, 295, 374; disagreements with Leigh-Mallory, 194; letter to 'fighter boys', 40
dragon's teeth 108
Driffield, RAF: bombing of 190, 191
'dummy raids' 106
Dundas, Hugh 264
Dundas, Flight Lieutenant John 79, *178*, 180, 180
Dunkirk evacuation 7, 38–9, *38–9*, 42–6, *45*, *46*, 100, 102, 107
Dunkirk, RAF (radar station) (near Canterbury) 166
Dunlop 172
Duxford, RAF 268, *268*
Duxford Wing 339, 340, 341, 345, 350, 354

E-boats 126, 154
Eagle Day *see* Adlertag
Earp, Flight Sergeant Richard 28
Eastbourne: bombing of 333
Eastchurch, RAF: bombing of 171, 196, 248, 268, 282
Eden, Anthony 35
Egan, Sergeant Edward 350
Einsatzgruppen 120
Elizabeth, Queen 332, *333*
Ellis, John *41*
Elliott, Pilot Officer Robert 189–90
Elswood, Sergeant Gunner Ben 271
Empire Air Day (20 May) 78
Empire Day certificate (24 May) 28
'enemy aliens': internment and deportation of in Britain 30, **33**, *33*
enemy landings: activities to combat 108, 110–11
Eurich, Richard: *Flight over Portland* 119
evacuations 18, **21**; of children **21**, *21*
Evers, W.H. 385
Expansion Plan A 24
Experimental Group (*Erprobungs-*

gruppe) No.210 163, 180, 193, 197, 356, 358, 359, 381

factories: aircraft *see* aircraft factories; armament 52; shadow **177**, 359
Fairey Battles 177, *331*
Fallschirmjäger (German paratroopers) **110–11**, *110–11*
Farnborough: bombing of 200; Royal Aircraft establishment at 175, 254
Ferriss, Flying Officer Henry 77–8, 200
fifth columnists 110–11, 156
fighter 'aces' 79, 225, 372; *see also* individual pilots
fighter aircraft: versus bomber debate 25, 40; *see also* aircraft, RAF; individual aircraft types
Fighter Command 8, 9, 25, 274–5, 336; American citizens fighting for **182**; approaching a crisis 291, 295, 298; Churchill's visit to HQ 197; continental missions 374; decline of military significance after Battle of Britain 375; highest daily tally of sorties flown 267; impact of Germany's decision to target London on 315, 336–7; losses (July) **140**; losses (Aug.) **278**; losses during Dunkirk campaign 46; maps 73, 222; nationalities of **326**; operations room at Bentley Priory 68–9; Order of Battle (10 July) **72**; Order of Battle (1 Aug.) **152**; Order of Battle (1 Sept.) **280**; problems and challenges 230; reduction in number of sorties after start of the Blitz 336; remustering of strength 336–7; replenishing of squadrons 150; structure and operations 26, **68–9**; success in 'Battle of Britain Day' (15 Sept.) 346; total losses 373; *see also* Dowding
Fighter Command 10 Group 68, 196, 229; map 73; *see also* Brand
Fighter Command 11 Group 68, 107, 131, 136, 166, 196, 198, 203, 229, 231; map 73, 222; *see also* Park
Fighter Command 12 Group 68, 231, 244, 261, 308, 321; map 73; *see also* 'Big Wing' tactics; Leigh-Mallory; Bader
Fighter Command 13 Group 68, 181, 188; map 73; *see also* Saul
Fighter Command HQ (Bentley Priory) **68–9**, *69*, 76
Fighter Interception Unit 124
Filton aeronautical factory: bombing of 358, *359*
Finlay, Squadron Leader Don 284
Fink, Oberst Johannes 58, 171, 174, 303–4
Finucane, Brendan 'Paddy' **372**, *372*, 373
First World War 19, 24, 26, 63, 79
Firth of Forth 189
Fiske, Pilot Officer William 'Billy' 182
fitters **186–7**
FitzGibbon, Theodora 315
Fleming, Pilot Officer R.D.S. 30
Fliegerdivision XI 181
Fliegerkorps (air corps) 59; Order of Battle (18 Aug.) 212, 213
Fliegerkorps II 58, 181, 183
Fliegerkorps VII 58

Fliegerkorps VIII 128
Folkestone: bombing of 236
Fopp, Sergeant Desmond 284, 285
Forbes, Flight Lieutenant *314*, *315*
Ford naval air station: bombing of 216, 220
Foreness, RAF (radar station): bombing of 185, 196
Foss, Jonathon 89
Foxley-Norris, Christopher 41, 133
France 29; Allied Order of Battle (9 May) *29*; and Dunkirk evacuation 7, 38–9, 38–9, 42–6, *45*, *46*, 100, 102, 107; fall of and surrender to Germans 7, 50, 102; German invasion 30–2, *30–1*, 34; setting up of bases by RAF at outset of war 18; withdrawal of BEF and RAF from 34, 50
France, Kay 205
Franco, General Francisco 19
František, Josef 153, *153*
Fredericks, Emma 312
Free French pilots *142–3*
Freeborn, John 23, 241
French First Army 18, 32
French fleet: destruction of by Britain 103, *103*
French Ninth Army 34
Freya radar system 127, *127*, 154
fuel, high-octane **255**

Galland, General Adolf 125, **133**, *133*, 135, 241, 337
Gamblen, Flying Officer D.R. 131
Gamelin, General 32, 34
Gardner, Charles 91, 92
Gard'ner, Pilot Officer John 109, 112
gas masks, issuing of 20, *20*
Gassner, Alfred A. 386
Gauntlets, Gloster *see* Gloster Gauntlets
George VI, King 8, *254*, *333*
German air force *see* Luftwaffe
German aircraft 380–5 *see also* individual aircraft types
German Armed Forces Supreme Command (OKW) 56
German High Command 23
German invasion ports: bombing of 329–30, *331*, 349, 355
German navy (*Kriegsmarine*) 104
GHQ Line **108**
Gibson, John 184, 255
Gillan, Flight Officer James 162–3
Gladiators, Gloster 18, 27, 46, 210
Glasgow: attack on Rolls-Royce works 196
Gleave, Squadron Leader Tom 258, 261, 271
Gledhill, Flight Sergeant Geoffrey 162
Gleed, Ian 'Widge' 234
Glorious, HMS (carrier) 27; sinking of 46, 50
Gloster Gauntlets *66*
Gloster Gladiators 18, 27, 46, 210
Gneisenau (German battlecruiser) 46
Gnys, Wladyslaw 14
Goddard, Bombardier Douglas 108
Goebbels, Joseph 237, *237*
Goering, Hermann 36, *37*, 39, 48, 49, 95, 105, 112–13, 123, *133*, *145*, 275, 285, 288, *288*, 290;

and *Adlerangriff* 144, 147, 163, 171; aims in air war against Britain 225; biography **36–7**; decision to alter strategy to bomb London 298, 315; issuing of directive (15 Aug.) 180–3; reaction to Luftwaffe losses 225; reverts to targeting airfields and factories after failure on 15 Sept. 349, 355; special train of (*Asia*) 291
Goodman, Sergeant Geoffrey 110
Goodson, Pilot Officer James 264, 379
Goodwin lightship 179
Gosport, RAF: bombing of 201, 216
Gossage, Air Marshal Sir E. Leslie 137
Gracie, Flight Lieutenant Edward 'Jumbo' 90
Graf Spee (pocket battleship) 104
Green, Bill 255, 257
Greenwood, Arthur 52
Gregory, Hazel 205
Guernica: bombing of by German Condor Legion 19, *19*
Guildford: bombing of 58
guns: anti-aircraft *271*, 320; Browning machine-guns 172, *173*, 377
gunsights **254**, *254*
Günther, Siegfried and Walter 384
Gyro gunsight (GGS) 254

Hague, Arthur 154, 155
Halder, General 105, 123
Halifax, Lord 8, 123–4
Halton Park training school 89
Hamilton, Pilot Officer Arthur 112
Hampden bombers 237
Handley, Tommy 157
Hanson, Flying Officer David 284
'Hardest Day, The' (18 Aug.) 210–24
Harriman, Averell 103
Harvard aircraft *89*
Harvey, Ron 234
Harwich 129; raid on 135
Haviland, Pilot Officer John 182
Haw, Sergeant Charlton 265
Haw-Haw, Lord *see* Joyce, William
Hawker Henley 76
Hawker Hurricane *see* Hurricanes
Hawkinge, RAF 65, 131, *257*; bombing of 166, *184–5*, 196, 255, 278, 327
Heinkel, Ernst 48
Heinkel He59 seaplane 87, *87*
Heinkel He111 27, *59*, *263*, *301*, *302*, *339*, **384**, *384*; facts and figures 384; losses (July) 140; losses (Aug.) 279
Helmswell, RAF 168
Henderson, Keith: *A North-east Coast Aerodrome 181*
Herrmann, Hauptmann Hans-Joachim ('Hajo') 124–5
Hertz, Heinrich 127
Higgs, Flying Officer Tom 76
Hill, Captain F.W. 172
Hillary, Richard 199, 250, *253*, 272, 273, 281, 282, 283–4
Hispano-Suiza cannon 173
Hitler, Adolf 7–8, 10, 14, 23, 37, *49*, 57, 104, 145, 325, 368; and bombing of London 285, 289, 300, 331; Directive No.16 **95**, 96–7; Directive No.17 **144**, 146, 147; hoping for British surrender 113; 'The Last Appeal to Reason' speech (1940) 113, *116*, 117,

123, 147; and Munich 20; Operation Sea Lion and postponements of 95, 96–7, 100, 120, 122–3, 285, 330, 333, 350, 355, 368; in Paris, *57*, 100; and Soviet Union 144, 147
Hoffmann, Feldwebel Karl 167
Hollmann, Hans 127
Holmbury St Mary 58
Holmes, Sergeant Ray 340, 341
Home Chain stations *see* radar stations, Chain Home
Home Guard **35**, *35*, 52, 111, 310
Hood, Squadron Leader Hilary 284
Hopkins, Harry 103
Hornchurch, RAF 64, 126, 210, 229; bombing of 200, 223, 228, 271–3, 284
Hughes, Pat 305
Hull, Squadron Leader Caesar 304
Hülsmeyer, Christian 127
Hunter, Squadron Leader Philip 229
Hurricanes 8, 9, 22, *80*, *85*, 95, *104*, 122, *184–5*, *247*, *343*, 363, **377**, *377*, 378; aircraft factory losses 352; armaments for 172, 173, 377; facts and figures 377; inability to operate effectively at heights of 30,000 feet 363; losses (July) 140; losses (Aug.) 278; modifications 377; production of *362*; rugged construction of 88; use of high-octane fuel 255

Imperial Chemical Industries (Ardeer): bombing of 105
Inskip, Sir Thomas 9, 25
internment: of 'enemy aliens' 30, **33**, *33*
Ironside, General Sir Edmund 108, 110
Ironside, Flight Lieutenant Hugh 377
Isaac, Sergeant Lewis 151
Isle of Wight 64, 169; *see also* Ventnor, RAF (radar station)
Ismay, General Hastings 203, 206, 373
Italian air force 368
Italians: internment of in Britain 33

Jagdgeschwader (fighter wings) 58, 227; Order of Battle (18 Aug.) 212, 213
Jagdgeschwader 1 248
Jagdgeschwader 2 175
Jagdgeschwader 3 224, 254
Jagdgeschwader 5 176
Jagdgeschwader 26 58, 178, 179, 197, 210–11, 223, 254, 321
Jagdgeschwader 27 176, 221
Jagdgeschwader 51 109, 112–3, 131, 132, 193, 248, 254
Jagdgeschwader 52 163, 193, 254
Jagdgeschwader 53 58, 176, 236, 350
Jagdgeschwader 54 151, 193, 254
Jennings, Pilot Sergeant *186*
John Lewis department store (Oxford Street): bombing of 350, *354*
Johnstone, Captain Kenneth 108
Johnstone, Squadron Leader A.V.R. (Sandy) 295, 305
Jones, Wing Commander Ira 76
Jowitt, L. 86
Joyce, William (Lord Haw-Haw) 156–7, *156*
Junkers, Hugo 48, 383

Junkers Ju87 (Stuka) 27, 34, 59, 62, *155*, *167*, 221, 225, **382**, *382*; disadvantages 382; engine 382; facts and figures 382; losses (July) 140; losses (Aug.) 279; numbers deployed in July (1940) 90
Junkers Ju88 22, **385**, *385*; armaments 385; facts and figures 385; losses (July) 140; losses (Aug.) 279
Kampfgeschwader (battle wing) 59; Order of Battle (18 Aug.) 212, 213
Kampfgeschwader 1 262, 326, 333
Kampfgeschwader 2 171, 200, 202, 223, 239, 303–4
Kampfgeschwader 3 190, 193, 238, 239, 248, 279, 338
Kampfgeschwader 5 239
Kampfgeschwader 26 188, 196, 326–7
Kampfgeschwader 27 331
Kampfgeschwader 30 167, 190, 191, 358
Kampfgeschwader 51 166, 233
Kampfgeschwader 53 223, 248
Kampfgeschwader 54 175, 176, 233
Kampfgeschwader 55 358, 359, 364
Kampfgeschwader 76 215, 302, 338
Kampfgeschwader 77 354, 362
Kanalkampf (Channel Battle) 58, 95, 104, 123
Keitel, Generalfeldmarschall Wilhelm 283, 368
Kellett, Squadron Leader Ronald 303, 344
Kenley, RAF 64, 254, 258, 261; bombing of 197–8, 205, 216, 219, 224, 238, 261, 278
Kennedy, Flight Lieutenant John 88
Kennedy, US Ambassador Joseph 102, *102*, 103, 150, 331
Kennington, Eric: portrait of Richard Hillary *253*
Kent Battle of Britain Museum 257
Keogh, Vernon 182, *182*
Kesselring, Generalfeldmarschall Albert 29, 49, **115**, *115*, 123, 227, 285, 290, 291, 351, 359, 363, 365
Kieser, Egbert 105
Kilmartin, Flight Lieutenant John 'Killy' 304
King, Mackenzie 103
King, Vera 204
Kingcome, Flying Officer Brian 45, 77, *77*
Knight, Laura: portrait of Daphne Pearson *210*
Korda, Alexander 23
Kosciuszko, Tadeusz 153
Kratz, Oberleutnant Rudolf 191
Kreipe, General Werner 373
Kup, Edith 265

Lacey, Sergeant James 'Ginger' 117, **118**, *118*, 255, 263, 265, 331, 1214
Lambert, Peter 44
Lamberty, Oberleutnant 215–16
Land Girls *12–13*
Lane, Flight Lieutenant B.J.E. 'Sandy' *16*, *66*, *206*, *270*, *334*
Lawson, W.J. 'Farmer' 270
Leckrone, Pilot Officer Phillip 182
Leconfield, RAF 190
Lee, Raymond 68, 103, 324
Lee-on-Solent 201
Lehrgeschwader (teaching wing) 59

Lehrgeschwader 1 176, 178, 182, 196, 233
Lehrgeschwader 2 367
Leigh-Mallory, Air Vice-Marshal Trafford 190, **194**, *194*, 229, 231, *231*, 244, 374; *see also* 'Big Wing' tactics
Leighton-Porter, Christabel 218
Leng, Sergeant Maurice 265
Leopold, King 43
Lewis, Albert G. 'Zulu' *202*
Lewis, Cecil 199
Lindemann, Professor Frederick 111
Lion Has Wings, The 23
Liverpool: bombing of port 250, 253
Local Defence Volunteer force *see* Home Guard
logbooks, pilots' *16–17*, *66–7*, *164–5*, *175*, *286–7*, *334*
London: bombing of before Blitz 230, 232, 234; bombing of during First World War 19; decision for an all-out offensive against by Germany 285, 289, 298, 300; first bombing raid on (7 Sept. 1940) 300–13, *302*, *306–7*; protecting against air raids 20; *see also* Blitz
London County Council Rest Centre Service 370
London Transport: Spitfire fund 159
London Underground stations: used as shelters *312*, 318–19
London's docklands: bombing of *233*
Lörzer, General Bruno 181
losses in combat *see under* Luftwaffe and RAF
Low, David 28
Lowe, Ann 201
Luftflotte(n) (German air fleets) 59; map *51*; Order of Battle (18 Aug.) **212–13**
Luftflotte 1 114
Luftflotte 2 29, *51*, 52, 114, 212; map *51*; *see also* Kesselring
Luftflotte 3 29, *51*, 52, 115, 213; map *51*; *see also* Sperrle
Luftflotte 5 52, 56, 21; map *51*; *see also* Stümpf
Luftwaffe (German air force) 8, 10, 22, 24, 95, 375; and 'Black Thursday' (15 Aug.) 181–200; creation and history of **48–9**; establishment of bases 50, *51*, 52; lack of success in 'Battle of Britain Day' (15 Sept.) and change in tactics 346, 348; launching of last substantial daylight effort 368; losses (July) 140; losses (Aug.) 279; objectives 105; officers gazing across Channel *290–1*; Order of Battle (18 Aug.) 212–13; ranks of **275**; structure and formations 29, **59**; tactics 59, 88, 230, 298, 365; total losses 373; training of pilots 48–9; types and numbers of aircraft deployed in July **90**; *see also Luftflotte(n)*
Luftwaffe, individual units of *see* Experimental Group 210; *Fliegerkorps*; *Jagdgeschwader*; *Kampfgeschwader*; *Lehrgeschwader*; *Sturzkampfgeschwader*; *Zerstörergeschwader*
Luton: bombing of 262
Lympne, RAF: bombing of 166, 185, 278

McArthur, Flight Lieutenant J.H.G. 308, *359*
McGrath, Raymond: *Fitters Working on a Spitfire 187*
machine-guns: anti-aircraft 320; Browning 172, *173*, 377
McIndoe, Sir Archibald 353
Maclean, Flight Lieutenant Charles 247, 385
McNabb, Betty 215
Maginot Line 18
Malan, Adolph 'Sailor' 23, *23*, **130**, *130*, 131, 136, 171
Mallory, George 194
Mamedoff, Andrew 182, *182*
Mannock, Edward 'Mick' 79
Manston, RAF 74, 131; bombing of 168–9, 170, 180, 188, 203, 228, 229
maps: plotting of raids on 68
March of Time, The (newsreel) 11
Margate 151
Marsh, Sergeant Henry 161, 175–6
Marshall, Walter 313
Martin, Bert 310–11
Martini, General Wolfgang 163, 170
Martlesham Heath, RAF: raid on 131, 193, 227
Mason, Francis K. 301
mechanics, aircraft 186
Merlin engines 377
Mers-el-Kébir (Algeria) 103, *103*
Messerschmitt, Willy 48
Messerschmitt Me109 8, 26, 29, 62, 95, 135, *141*, 181, *214*, *258*–*9*, 355, *367*, 379, **380**, *380*; armaments 172; conversion of to carry 250kg bomb 365–6; design faults 380; engine 380; evasive measures against 259; facts and figures 380; instruction to British pilots to avoid tangling with 106; losses (July) 140; losses (Aug.) 279; numbers deployed in July (1940) 90; numbers produced in June and July (1940) 94; qualities 380; shooting down of first 22; used as fighter-bombers 129
Messerschmitt Me110 48, 59, 62, 88, 95, *98*–*9*, *121*, *175*, 182, 189, 225, **381**, *381*; armaments 381; disadvantages 381; facts and figures 381; losses (Aug.) 279; numbers deployed in July 90; shooting down of first 22–3, 381
'Messerschmitt Month' (Oct. 1940) 365–8
Middle Wallop, RAF 56, 79, 85, 88, 106, 117, 128, 176, 178, 305, 363, 364; advantages of 120; bombing of 180, 183
Milch, Erhard 48, 49
Miles M20 177
mine-laying sorties, German 124
Ministry of Home Security 156
Ministry of Information *134*; job of sustaining morale 157, *157*
Mitchell, Pilot Officer Gordon 81
Mitchell, Reginald 9, 60, 378, *379*
Mölders, Major Werner 131, **132**, *132*, 133
Möllenbrook, Heinz 202
morale, civilian 373; and Ministry of Information 157, *157*
Morfill, Peter 281
Morris, Pilot Officer Geoffrey 124
Mosley, Sir Oswald 33, *156*
Mould, Peter 'Boy' 18, *18*, 22
Mungo-Park, Flying Officer John 76–7

Munich Crisis (1938) 20, *320*
Mussolini, Benito 368, *368*

Nash, Paul: *Battle of Britain 138*–*9*; *The Raider on the Shore 74*–*5*
Natural History Museum: bombing of 323
Neil, Pilot Officer Thomas 347, *347*, 353
Netherlands, The 29, 30; capitulation of 32
New York Times 156
Newbould, Frank *10*
Nicolson, Flight Lieutenant James 201, 203, *203*
Nicolson, Harold 331, 351
night raids: during the Blitz 311, 318, 323, 324, 329, 331, 349, 350–1, 368; problems in intercepting 124
night-flying 323–4; and radar 122
Nockolds, Roy: convoy painting *82*
North, Pilot Officer Harold 239
North Weald, RAF 223, 238, 273; bombing of 244, 267–8, 284
Northolt, RAF 14, *58*, 85, 153, 227, 260, 293, 344
Norwegian campaign 27–8, *27*, 46, 50
Norwich: bombing of 147
Nuffield Group 177

Oberkommando der Wehrmacht (OKW) 56
O'Brian, Joe 305
Observer Corps *63*, *63*, 68, 70, 256, 355
Odiham, RAF 175
Operation Dynamo 110
Operation Sea Lion 95, 96–7, 100, 256, 368; build-up of German forces for 282–3, *283*; end of 355; Hitler's directive establishing 95, **96**–**7**, 105; plan for landings *97*; planning and preparations 120, 122, *310*, 330; postponements 10, 324–5, 333, 350
Operational Training Units (OTUs) 89, 207, 225
Operations Room: Bentley Priory 68–9
Orde, Cuthbert: drawing of Josef František *153*
Order of Battle: Allied (May 1940) *29*; Fighter Command (10 July) **72**, *152*, (1 Sept.) **280**; Luftwaffe (18 Aug.) **212**–**13**
Orley, Marian 204–5
Orwell, George 7–8, 52
Ostaszewski-Ostoja, Piotr 236
Over-Seas League 28

Page, Geoffrey 90–1
Palliser, Sergeant George 362
paratroopers, German: threat of and defence against 110–11, *110*–*11*
Park, Air Vice-Marshal Keith 106, **107**, *107*, 117, 131, 195, 200, 229, 231, 244, **294**, 315, 318, 325, *337*, *338*–*9*, 343, 346, 366, 374
Parrot, Peter 155
Parsons, Avis 220
Pas de Calais 64, 65, 76
Paszkiewicz, Flying Officer Ludwik 153, 260
Patton, Lieutenant J.M.S. 356
Peake, Felicity 262
Pearson, Corporal Daphne *210*
'Peewit' convoy 154–5, 158

Pembrey, RAF 76
Pétain, Marshal Philippe 50
Pevensey, RAF (radar station) 163, 166
Phoney War 14, 52
Pile, Sir Frederick 320, 324
pill-boxes 108, *150*
pilots, German: calculating how long fuel would last 223; captured **218**; highest-scoring 132; suffering from 'Channel Sickness' 135, 136
pilots, RAF 119, *128*; American 182; attempt to preserve 135, 225, 227; attitudes to death **199**; average life expectancy of 199; burning of **353**; as celebrities 373; class distinctions among, **274**; culture of fighter 'aces' 79, 372, 373; Czech 239, **246**; and death of comrades 88; deaths of in Battle of Britain 373; deaths of in rest of war 374; effects of high-altitude flying on 366; fear felt by **121**, 126, 264; feelings over killing **192**; feelings on using forward bases 120; hazards of night-flying 323–4; and 'Lacking Moral Fibre' **265**; loss of as threat to effectiveness of Fighter Command 88; mental strain suffered by and breakdowns 264–5; nationalities of **326**; numbers killed 88, 135, 199, 225; Polish 14, 153, 336; recruiting poster 89; relationship with groundcrew 187; scrambling of *70*–*1*, *142*–*3*, 252, *252*; tiredness and exhaustion of 269, 282, 298; top-scoring 117, 153; training of 88, **89**; vulnerability of inexperienced 236, 295, 298
Poland: invasion of by Hitler 14
Poling, RAF (radar station) 124, 166; bombing of 216, 220
Polish pilots 14, **153**, **260**, **293**, *314*, 336, **344**; see also squadrons, RAF: No.302; No.303
Portland naval base: attack on 62, 79, 161, 176
Portsmouth: bombing of 85, 169, 201, 230, 232
posters *235*; Air Ministry *357*; Civil Defence *217*; Ministry of Information *134*; propaganda *9*, *266*; RAF recruiting *89*
Prchal, Sergeant Edward 239
Priestley, J.B. 44, 151
Priller, Oberst Josef 223, 321
propaganda (British and German) *8*, *9*, *266*, *116*, **156**-**7**, *157*

Quayle, Elizabeth 41
Queen Victoria Hospital 353
Quill, Jeffrey 170, 378

radar, British 8, **60**–**1**, *63*, 78, 122; airborne **122**; 124; German countermeasures against 106; map *149*, weakening of network by raids 230
radar, German **127**, *127*, 154
radar stations, Chain Home 61, 68, 70, 122, 133; attacks on 163, 166, 169, 170, 182, 185, 201, 220, 333; map *149*
radio: broadcasts 91, 92, 156; as form of intelligence 327
Raeder, Grossadmiral Erich 104, *105*, 325

RAF (Royal Air Force) 8, 22; bombing raids on Germany 100; class distinctions **274**; number of personnel 25; origins of **24**–**5**; ranks of **275**; role in Dunkirk evacuation 42–3, 46; setting up of bases in France at outset of war 18; training schools 89; see also Fighter Command
RAF squadrons see squadrons, RAF
RAFVR see Royal Air Force Volunteer Reserve
Ramsay, Admiral Sir Bertram 110, 273
Ramsgate *289*
Raven, Pilot Officer A.L.B. 65
Ravenshill School (West Ham): bombing of 331
'Readiness': memo on states of *148*
Red Cross German aircraft: shooting down of *87*
Reilley, Pilot Officer Hugh 182
Reynaud, Paul 32
Reynell, Flight Lieutenant Richard 304–5
Rhodes-Moorhouse, Flying Officer William 95
Richardson, Squadron Leader William 109
Richey, Paul 31–2
riggers **186**–**7**
Roberts, Fred 186–7, *186*, 270
Robertson, Ben 311
Robinson, Flight Lieutenant Michael 292
Rochester: bombing of city 230
Rochester, RAF: bombing of 196
Rochford, RAF 85; bombing of 248, 267, 279
Roddis, Joe 186, 187
Roell, Werner 382
Rolls-Royce 177
Roosevelt, US President 102, 103, 356
Roper, Betty 303
Rosyth, Royal Navy base at 22
Rotte formation 59
Royal Air Force see RAF
Royal Air Force Volunteer Reserve (RAFVR) 25, **80**
Royal Aircraft Establishment (Farnborough) 175, 254
Royal Flying Corps 24
Royal Naval Air Service 24
Royal Navy 46, 52, 104, 129
Royal Observer Corps see Observer Corps
Royal Victoria and Surrey Commercial Docks 345
Rubensdörffer, Hauptmann Walter 163, 198
Russell, Bertrand 19
Rye, RAF (radar station): attacks on 163, 185
Ryneveld, Pierre van 195, *195*

St Eval, RAF 179, *183*; bombing of 227
St Katherine's Dock: bombing of 324
St Paul's Cathedral 329, *371*
Sample, Squadron Leader John 340
Saul, Air Vice-Marshal Richard **188**, *188*
Scharnhorst (German battle-cruiser) 46
Schmid, Major Josef 95
Schneider Trophy 378
Schöpfel, Major Gerhard 36–7, 214, 215

Schwarm formation 59
Scott, Flying Officer William 318
Sea Lion, Operation see Operation Sea Lion
Seabourne, Sergeant Eric 88, 90, 120, 174, 179
Sealand, RAF 180
searchlights 320, *320*
sector stations, RAF bombing of 227, 273, 283, 291; map 73
Sedan fortress (France) 32
Seelöwe see Operation Sea Lion
'shadow' factories **177**, 359
Sheerness 129
shelters 311–12, 324; Anderson 19, 20; and London Underground stations 312, 318–19
Shipman, Pilot Officer E.A. 189
Shirer, William L. 113, 117, 237
Siegfried Line 18
Signal magazine 8
Silvertown *306–7*, 311
Smith, Alan 241
Smith, Flight Lieutenant Roddick 171
Somerset House: bombing of 323
Southampton: bombing of 176, 180–1
Soviet Union 122, 144, 147, 370
Spanish Civil War 49, 132, 380, 383
Sperrle, Generalfeldmarschall Hugo 29, 49, **114**, *114*, 115, 227, 285, 365, 1123
Spitfire funds **159**, *159*
Spitfires 7, 8, 9, *26*, *34*, *42–3*, 95, *142–3*, 186, 272, 356, 366, **378–9**, *378–9*; aircraft factory losses *352*; armaments 172, 173, 379; campaign for communities to 'buy' their own 154; disadvantages 378; facts and figures 379; losses (July) 140; losses (Aug.) 278; production of 177, *352*; qualities 379; technical improvements 378; use of high-octane fuel 255
'Spot at Sight' chart *110–11*
squadrons, RAF: class distinctions **274–5**; formation attack patterns 236; reaching end of physical and mental reserves 236; rotation of 248, 273, 282, 318, 336–7; states of availability 69; structure 26; withdrawal from France 50
squadrons, RAF Fighter Command:
  No.1 18, *25*, 31, 34, 160, 193, 248, 276, 303; *377*
  No.1 (Royal Canadian Air Force) 238, 267, 325
  No.17 86, 163, 193, 233–4, 284, 285, 327
  No.19 *206*, 239, 268, **270**, *270*, 290, 308, 326, 354;
  No.32 34, 76, 117, 126, 197, 207, 224, 236
  No.41 126, 131, 189, 190, 282, *284*, 290–1, 304, 318, 343, 354, 355
  No.43 46, 64, 120, 158, 175, 196, 221, 239, 281, 304–5, 318
  No.46 273, 284, 318
  No.54 62, 85, 125, 126, 184, 188, 198, 200, 224, 228, 236, 248, 248–9, 252, 256, 276, 282
  No.56 23, 90–1, 126, 131, 178, 224, 239, 267–8, 273
  No.63 303
  No.64 105, 126, 151, 160

No.65 64, 125, 126, 178, 227, 248
No.66 70–1, 188, 282, 289, 290, 343
No.71 (American) 182
No.72 189–90, 273, 276, 279, 281, 323, 339, 343, 355, 356
No.73 18, 34, 190, 290, 327, 335, 343, 356
No.74 23, 130, 131, 136, 141, 160, 163, 171, 326
No.79 31, 65, 160, 190, 248, 267, 276, 278, 279, 290, 318
No.85 18, 110–11, 221, 238, 249–50, 254, 256, 258, 268–9, 276, 278, 282, *343*
No.87 18, 30, 196–7, 234, 236
No.92 76, 227, 318, 339, 355, 356
No.111 76–8, *85*, 136, 162, 163, 171, 174, 198, 200, 216, 239, 256, 268, 269, 281, 282, 290, 318
No.141 109, 112, 229
No.145 64, 154, 155, 158
No.151 91, 135, 151, 171, 229, 273
No.152 170, 176, 329
No.213 *66*, 196–7, 344
No.222 121, 253–4, 258, 261, 279, 281, 321, 325, 355
No.234 160, *183*, 186, 197, 216, 221, 305
No.238 88, 113, 117, 119, 120, 128, 161–2, 175, 179, 227, 325, 329, 363
No.242 (Canadian) 81, 240–1, 308, *319*, 321
No.249 201, 203, 273, 279, 283, 301, 303, 315, 347, 362
No.253 258, 261, 271, 289, 339
No.257 264, 267, 284, 290–1
No.263 27–8, 46
No.264 109, 229, 238, 248, 253
No.266 171, 200
No.302 (Polish) 153
No.303 (Polish) 153, *153*, **260**, *260*, 284, 290, 291, **293**, 303, *314*, *315*, 327, 343–4, **344**
No.310 (Czech) 239, **246**, 285, 321, 323
No.501 31, 78, 117, 118, 131, 184, 210, 214, 215, 224, 229, 255, 257, 263, 267, 282, 331, 339, 350
No.504 31, 340, 359
No.601 64, 85, 95, 128, 160, 162, 175–6, 176, 182, 196, 291, 374–5
No.603 248, 250, 281, 282, 283–4, 339, 343
No.605 190, 321
No.607 18, 318, 321, 344
No.609 78–9, 81, 87–8, 106, 128–9, 155, 160, 163, *164–5*, 169, *175*, 178, 180, 229–30, 305, 308, 339, 359, 362, 364, *378–9*
No.610 65, 75, 91, 106, 117, 125, 135, 163, 197, 228–9
No.611 *34*
No.615 18, 91, 117, 126, 216, 227
No.616 190, 236, 238
Staal, Helmut 302
Stahl, Unteroffizier Peter 322, 358
Stalin, Joseph 144
Stanford-Tuck, Bob 133
Staxton Wold, RAF (radar station) 190
Steborowski, Flying Officer Michal 161–2

Steinhilper, Ulrich 136
Steinke, Gioya 370
Stevenson, Pilot Officer Peter 160, 162
stop-lines 108
Stormy Down, RAF 76
Street, A.G. 218
Strelitz, Gladys 311
strong-points 108
Stukas see Junkers Ju87
Sturzkampfgeschwader (Stuka or dive-bomber wing) 59; Order of Battle (18 Aug.) 212, 213
Sturzkampfgeschwader 1 184, 196
Sturzkampfgeschwader 2 176, 178
Sturzkampfgeschwader 77 176, 216
Sunderland 160
Supermarine Spitfire see Spitfires
Supermarine works (Woolston) 356, 359, *360–1*, 378
Surrey Docks, bombing of 308–9
Swanage 362
Swansea, attack on 76

'tail-end-Charlie' 22
Tangmere, RAF 64, 69, 95, 106, 124, 128, 155, 162, 182, 220, 241, 247; bombing of 201, 207, 261
Taylor, Flying Officer Donald 105
Tedder, Lord 107
television broadcasts 156
Ten Group 56
Thameshaven: bombing of 291
Thompson, Joanna 185
Thompson, John 202
Thorney Island, RAF 216; bombing of 220
Thoroughgood, Laurence 'Rubber' 234, 236
Tiger Moths 89
Times , The 151, 319
Tizard, Henry 60
Tobin, Eugene 'Red' 180, 182, *182*
Townsend, Squadron Leader Peter 81, 84, *84*, 111, 192, 221, 249–50, 254–5, 256, 258, 259, 268, 269, 278
training schools 89
Trautloft, Hauptmann Hannes 109
Trefusis-Forbes, Katherine 204
Trenchard, Sir Hugh 24, *24*, 80, 89
trenches, digging of 20

U-boats 104
Udet, Ernst 49
United States 7, 10–11, **102–3**, 150, 182
Unwin, George 26, 199, *270*, 274, 345, 378, 383
Usworth, RAF 189
Uxbridge, RAF 203, 206, 216, 300, 337, 338, 366
Uxbridge, RAF Depot 89

Ventnor, RAF (radar station) 155, 160; bombing of 169, 201
Versailles, Treaty of (1919) 48, 'vic' formation *26*, *26*, 76, 258, *343*
Vickers Company 172, 378
Vigors, Pilot Officer Tim *41*, 121
Voigt, Werner 292
Von Brauchitsch, Hauptmann Berndt 178
Von Brauchitsch, Generalfeldmarschall Walther 105, 330
Von Richthofen, Manfred (the 'Red Baron') 132, 133
Von Richthofen, Wolfram 49

WAAF (Women's Auxiliary Air Force) 69, **204–5**, *204*, *210*, 262, *268*, 327

Wakeling, Sid 236, 245
Walch, Flight Lieutenant Stuart 161
Walker, Pilot Officer J.A. 'Johnny' 269
War Artists Advisory Committee 119
Warmwell, RAF 79, 81, 87, *87*, 120; bombing of 233–4
Waterloo station: bombing of 366
Watson-Watt, Sir Robert 60, 61, 122, 204
Waugh, Evelyn: *Put Out More Flags* 50
Webster, Flight Lieutenant John 131
Wedding, Ernest 384
Weitkus, Oberstleutnant Paul 303, 304
Welles, Sumner 102
West Beckham, RAF (radar station) 70
West Ham power station: bombing of 308
West Malling aerodrome: bombing of 197, 200
Westland factory (Yeovil) 364
Weston, Garfield 159
Wever, Walther 49
Wheeler, George 311
Whitfield, Sergeant Joseph 91
Wilkins, Arnold 60
Wilkins, George 313
Wilkinson, Norman: *Building Spitfires* 177
Wilkinson, Squadron Leader Rodney 200
Williams, Hazel 204
Williams, Max 241
Williams, Squadron Leader Cedric 233
Willisen, Hans-Karl von 127
Wimperis, W.E. 60
Women's Auxiliary Air Force see WAAF
Women's Royal Air Force (WRAF) 204
Women's Royal Naval Service (WRNS) 204
Woods-Scawen, Patrick 281–2
Woods-Scawen, Pilot Officer Tony 281–2
Woolston aircraft factory 356, 359, *360–1*
Woolwich Arsenal 308
Worthing *150*
WRAF 204
WRNS 204
Wren, HMS 129
Wright, Sergeant Stanley 264
Würzburg (German radar) 127
Wyllie, Sapper George 329

'Y-Service' **327**
Young, Flying Officer John 69

Zamoyski, Adam 153
Zeppelin airships 19
Zerstörergeschwader ('destroyer' wing) 59; Order of Battle (18 Aug.) 212, 213
Zerstörergeschwader 2 166, 175, 196, 233
Zerstörergeschwader 3 233
Zerstörergeschwader 26 171, 254, 358, 359
Zerstörergeschwader 53 166
Zerstörergeschwader 75 256
Zerstörergeschwader 76 188, 189, 254
Zonderlind, Hans 342

TABLES, MAPS AND SOURCES

TABLES

Fighter Command Order of Battle (10 July 1940)   p. 72
Luftwaffe aircraft deployed (July 1940)   p. 90
Fighter Command losses in July 1940   p. 140
Luftwaffe losses in July 1940   p. 140
Fighter Command Order of Battle (1 Aug. 1940)   p. 152
Luftwaffe Order of Battle (18 Aug. 1940)   pp. 212–13
Equivalent ranks of the RAF and Luftwaffe   p. 275
Fighter Command losses in August 1940   p. 278
Luftwaffe losses in Aug. 1940   p. 279
Fighter Command Order of Battle (1 September 1940)   p. 280
Nationalities of Fighter Command   p. 326
Civilian air raid casualties   p. 330
Aircraft wastage   p. 352
Air raids on Great Britain (tonnage of bombs)   p. 366
Aircraft facts and figures   pp. 377–85

MAPS

British and French Air Forces, Order of Battle (9 May 1940)   p. 29
German air fleets threatening Britain in summer 1940   p. 51
Fighter Command in summer 1940   p. 73
Chain Home radar network in summer 1940   p. 149
Air defences of Great Britain (Aug. 1940)   p. 222

SOURCES (for passages of quotation)
IWM = Imperial War Museum, London

Adams, Perry, *Hurricane Squadron: No. 87 Squadron at War 1939–1941,* 1988

Allen, H.R., *Battle For Britain,* 1973

Arnold, Gwen, *Radar Days,* 2000

Bailey, Jim, 'Defiant Survivor', *Battle of Britain Remembered,* Vol. 1, No. 1, 1999

Bamberger, Cyril, IWM Sound Archive Recording 27074

Barclay, George and Humphrey Wynn, *Fighter Pilot: A Self-portrait,* 1976

Batt, L.G., *Sgt Pilot 741474 RAFVR: A Flying Memoir 1938 1959,* privately published, 1990

Bennions, George, IWM Sound Archive Recording 10296

Bickers, Richard Townsend, *Battle of Britain,* 1990

Bird-Wilson, Harold, IWM Sound Archive Recording 10093

Bob, Hans-Ekkehard, IWM Sound Archive Recording 26965

Bowyer, Chaz, *Albert Ball VC,* 1994

Brand, Stanley, IWM Sound Archive Recording 27347

Brickhill, Paul, *Reach for the Sky: The Story of Douglas Bader DSO, DFC,* 1954

Brothers, Peter, interview with author

Brothers, Peter, IWM Sound Archive Recording 10218

Brown, Ronald, IWM Sound Archive Recording 12404

Calder, Angus, *The People's War,* 1969

Channel 4 history website, http://www.channel4.com/history/microsites/H/history/a-b/bader.html

Channon, Sir Henry, *'Chips': The Diaries of Sir Henry Channon,* 1996

Churchill, Winston, *The Second World War,* 6 vols, 1948–54

Ciano, Galleazzo, *The Ciano Diaries,* edited by Hugh Gibson, 1946

Clark, Percy, IWM Sound Archive Recording 20982

Collier, Richard, *Eagle Day,* 1966

Colville, John, *The Fringes of Power,* 1985

Coonts, Stephen, *War in the Air: True Accounts of the 20th Century's Most Dramatic Air Battles – By the Men Who Fought Them,* 2003

Crang, Jeremy A. '"Come into the Army, Maud": Women, Military Conscription, and the Markham Inquiry', *Defence Studies,* Vol. 8, Issue 3, 2008

Crook, D.M., *Spitfire Pilot,* 1942

Davy, Horace, IWM Sound Archive Recording 20324

Deere, Alan, *Nine Lives,* 1959

Devitt, George, IWM Sound Archive Recording 10667

Dundas, Hugh, *Flying Start,* 1988

Earp, Richard, IWM Sound Archive Recording 11772

Escott, Beryl E., *The WAAF: A History of the Women's Auxiliary Air Force in the Second World War,* 2003

Foxley-Norris, Christopher, interview with author

Foxley-Norris, Christopher, IWM Sound Archive Recording 10136

Franks, Norman, *Battle of Britain,* 1981

Freeborn, John, interview with author

Gelb, Norman, *Scramble: A Narrative History of the Battle of Britain,* 1986

Gilbert, Martin, *Finest Hour,* 1983

Gillies, Midge *Waiting For Hitler: Voices From Britain on the Brink of Invasion,* 2006

Goddard, Douglas IWM Sound Archive Recording 20982

Goodson, James, IWM Sound Archive Recording 11623

Holmes, Ray, IWM Sound Archive Recording 2807

Hough, Richard Alexander and Denis Richards, *The Battle of Britain,* 1989

Haw, Charlton, IWM Sound Archive Recording 12028

Ishoven, Armand van, *The Luftwaffe in the Battle of Britain,* 1980

Ismay, James, *The Memoirs of General the Lord Ismay,* 1960

James, T.C.G., *The Battle of Britain: Air Defence of Great Britain,* 2000

Johnstone, Kenneth, IWM Sound Archive Recording 9185

Johnstone, Sandy, *Enemy in the Sky: My 1940 Diary,* 1976

Jullian, Marcell, *The Battle of Britain, July–September 1940,* 1967

Kennedy, Irving, *Black Crosses Off My Wingtip,* 1994

Kershaw, Alex, *The Few: The American 'Knights of the Air' Who Risked Everything to Save Britain in the Summer of 1940,* 2007

Kieser, Egbert, *Hitler On The Doorstep – Operation 'Sea Lion': The German Plan to Invade Britain 1940,* translated by Helmut Bögler, 1997

King, Vera, IWM Sound Archive Recording 10221

Kingcome, Brian, IWM Sound Archive Recording 10152

Kingcome, Brian, *A Willingness to Die,* 1999

Kup, Edith, IWM Sound Archive Recording 13967

Lambert, Peter, unpublished memoir

Lee, (General) Raymond E., *The London Observer,* 1972

Leng, Maurice, IWM Sound Recording 12217

Leighton-Porter, Christabel, IWM Sound Archive Recording 11246

Lewis, Cecil, *Sagittarius Rising,* 1988

Longmate, Norman, *Island Fortress,* 1991

Lucas, Laddie, *Flying Colours: The Epic Story of Douglas Bader,* 1981

MacLean, Charles, IWM Sound Archive Recording 10788

Marshall, Walter, IWM Sound Archive Recording 23849

Mason, Francis K., *Battle over Britain,* 1990

Moss, Norman, *Nineteen Weeks: America, Britain, and the Fateful Summer of 1940,* 2003

Neil, Thomas, IWM Sound Archive Recording 26977

Nicolson, Harold, *Diaries and Letters,* Vol. 2, *1939–45,* 1967

Orley, Marian, IWM Sound Archive Recording 14764

Overy, Richard, 'The Few versus the Very Few', *BBC History Magazine,* June 2000

Page, Geoffrey, *Shot Down in Flames,* 1999

Parker, Matthew *The Battle of Britain, July–October 1940,* 2000

Pellet, George, IWM Sound Archive Recording 9185

Pile, (General) Sir Frederick, *Ack-Ack,* 1949

Price, Alfred, *The Hardest Day,* 1979 edition

Quayle, Elizabeth, IWM Sound Archive Recording 10609

Quill, Jeffrey, IWM Sound Archive Recording 10687

Ray, John, *The Battle of Britain: New Perspectives,* 1994

Richey, Paul, *Fighter Pilot: A Personal Record of the Campaign in France,* 1990 (first published 1941)

Roberts, Fred, IWM Sound Archive Recording 26973

Robertson, Ben, *I Saw England,* 1941

Roddis, Joe, IWM Sound Archive Recording 26966

Roell, Werner, IWM Sound Archive Recording 12563

Schöpfel, Gerhard, interview with author

Schöpfel, Gerhard, IWM Sound Archive Recording 14770

Shirer, William, *Berlin Diary,* 1941

Stahl, Peter, *Diving Eagle: A Ju88 Pilot's Diary,* translated by Alex Vanags-Baginskis, 1984

Steinke, Gioya, IWM Sound Archive Recording 18724

Terraine, John, *The Right of the Line,* 1985

Townsend, Peter, *Duel of Eagles,* 1970

Townsend, Peter, *Time and Chance,* 1978

Turner, John Frayn, *The Battle of Britain,* 1998

Turner, John Frayn, *The Bader Tapes* 1986

Unwin, George, IWM Sound Archive Recording 11544

Vigors, Tim, unpublished MS for *Life's Too Short to Cry,* 2006

Waite, Robert G.L., *The Pyschopathic God: Adolf Hitler,* 1977

Walker, Oliver, *Sailor Malan,* 1953

Wedding, Ernest, IWM Sound Archive Recording 26960

Wheatley, Ronald, *Operation Sea Lion,* 1958

Winged Words: Our Airmen Speak For Themselves, 1941

Wood, Derek and Dempster, *The Narrow Margin,* 1961

Wright, Stanley, IWM Sound Recording 11744

Young, John, IWM Sound Archive Recording 20468

Ziegler, Frank H., *The Story of 609 Squadron,* 1971

Ziegler, Philip, *London at War,* 1995

Compiling this book has been made easier by the wealth of material amassed over the years by historians of, and participants in, the Battle of Britain. I am particularly grateful to two of the leading historians in the field: Francis K. Mason, author of *Battle over Britain,* which provided the first comprehensive chronology of the summer of 1940, and Kenneth H. Wynn, whose *Men of the Battle of Britain* is the prime reference work on the airmen of Fighter Command. I would also like to record my deep thanks to Matthew Parker, himself a distinguished Battle of Britain historian, for his invaluable help with the research and writing, and I am grateful to Victoria Kingston, who researched images for the book. PATRICK BISHOP

PICTURE ACKNOWLEDGEMENTS

Imperial War Museum, London: front jacket (CH003056); 10–11 (PST0069), 15 (HU036171), (inset) 18 (C001592), 23 (CH012859), 25 (Q012063), 26 (COL000190), 34 (C000413), 36 (MH006041), (top) 40 (D001417), 41 (CH016283), 57 (HU003266), 59 (GER000053), 60 (CH015331), 60–61 (CH015174), 63 (LD003830), 68–9 (CH000740), 69 (C001869), 77 (CH003553), 80 (CH001638), 84 (CH000087), 86 (CH009455), 87 (HU075969), 89 (CH000606, PST3774), 94 (D011129), 96 (HU075533), 105(A014906), 107 (CM003513), 108 (H002185), 116 (Col.54), 118 (CH002793), 119 (LD000769), 120 (CH003962), 121 (C001703), 122 (CH002250), 127 (C005477), 130 (CH008119), 132–3 (HU076020), 133 (HU004128), 138–9 (LD001550), 150 (H001947), 152 (CH001533, LD000421), 156 top (PST14817), 168 (CH001300), 170 (CH001829), 177 (LD6014), 180 (CH002583), 181 (LD257), 182 (CH001442), 186 (CH001458), 187 (LD142), 188 (CH003193), 198 (HU075997), 203 (CH001700), 204 (PST2831), 206 (CH001461), 211 (LD626), 214 (HU002742), 219 (CH010090), 230 (CH001561), 231 (CH011054), 237 (HU076018), 245 (D007143), 246 (CH001299), 247 (HU69946), 249 (H003499), 251 (LD14), 252 (HU049253), 256 (CH000787), 258–9 (MH007433), 260 (CH001535), 263 (MH006547), 264 (CH017324), 266 (PST14971), 268 (CH001401), 270 (CH001366), 272 (HU069943), 274 (CH001355), 275 (HU075816), 277 (H003508), 283 (MH006657), 284 (CH001871), 288 (MH013382), 289 (H003514), 294 (CM005631), 299 (MH005321), 301 (HU075943) 302 (C005422), 305 (CH003826), 309 (PST13850), 310 (HU093074), 328 (H002628), 336–7 (H004219), 343 (CH001503), 347 (CH002750), 359 (CH001823), 366 (H005603), 372 (CH003757), back jacket (planes; MH006547 repeated).
Getty Images: endpapers, 2–3, 4–5, 12–13, (left) 21, 24 (x2), (bottom) 28, 30–1, 33, 35, 37, 38–39, (bottom) 40, 42–3, 46, 49, 70–1, 85, 102, 103, 104, 123, 128, 140, 145, 156, (left) 159, 161, 172, 175, 184–5,194, 195, 202, 208–9, 218, 220, 226, 233, 240–1, 254, 257, 269, 273, 279, 312, 316–317, 319, 320, 324, 331, 332, 333, 340, 342, 348, 352, 353, 354, 360–1, 367, 368, 369, 371, 374–5, 378.
Mary Evans Picture Library: (right) 7, 19, 20, 27, 54–55, 78, 92–3, 98–99, 101,141, 167, 292.
The Bridgeman Art Library: 8 (Private Collection), 74–5 (Art Gallery and Museum, Kelvingrove / Culture and Sport Glasgow (Museums)).
The National Archives, Kew: 9 (TNA INF3/87), 16–17 (TNA AIR4/58 Pt1), (right) 21 (TNA INF13/171), (map) 28–9 (TNA AIR41/22), 58 (TNA AIR4/21 Pt1), 66 (TNA AIR4/58 cover), 67 (TNA AIR4/21 Pt1), 82–3 (TNA INF3/1516), 110–11 (TNA INF13/215(16)), 134 (TNA INF13/301(10)), 148 (TNA AIR16/356), 157 (bottom, TNA EXT1/119(13)), 164–5 (TNA AIR4/21 Pt1), 176 (TNA AIR4/21 Pt1), 217 (TNA INF2/94), 222 (TNA AIR41/16), 235 (TNA EXT1/116), 286–7 (TNA AIR4/21 Pt1), 314 (TNA AIR50/117), 334 (TNA AIR4/58), back jacket (poster; EXT1/119(13) repeated).
The Australian War Memorial: (background) 18 (SUK14579), 183 (PO1171_003), 241 (SUK14727).
Justin Hunt: 28 (top)
akg images: 45, 48, 62, 132, 155, 290–1.
Camera Press London: 53 Photograph by Yousuf Karsh
Alamy: 64–5.
Wikipedia: 79.
AP/PA: 92, 129, 192, 339, 377.
RAF Museum, Hendon: 112, 137, 172, 173, 242–3 (x 2), 357.
Corbis: 114–15, 142–3, 278, 296–7 (repeated 322), 330, 350, 365.
London Transport Museum: (right) 159.
The Lordprice Collection / Heritage-Images / Imagestate: 224, 392.
National Portrait Gallery, London: 253.
Newham Archives and Local Studies Library collection: 306–7.

Endpapers
(front) 'Geordie', a fighter squadron's canine mascot, sits in front of a line of Supermarine Spitfires at RAF Duxford before the outbreak of war, May 1939. The aircraft were about to take part in an aerial display.
(back) Fighter pilots returning from a sortie rest in front of a Hawker Hurricane, at an airfield 'somewhere in England', in the months following the Battle of Britain.

Quercus Publishing Plc
21 Bloomsbury Square
London
WC1A 2NS

First published in 2009

Copyright © Patrick Bishop

The moral right of Patrick Bishop to be identified as the author of this work has been asserted in accordance with the Copyright, Design and Patents Act, 1988.

All rights reserved. No part of this publication may be reproduced, stored in a retrieval system, or transmitted in any form or by any means, electronic, mechanical, photocopying, recording, or otherwise, without the prior permission in writing of the copyright owner and publisher.

The picture credits constitute an extension to this copyright notice.

Every effort has been made to contact copyright holders. However, the publishers will be glad to rectify in future editions any inadvertent omissions brought to their attention.

Quercus Publishing Plc hereby exclude all liability to the extent permitted by law for any errors or omissions in this book and for any loss, damage or expense (whether direct or indirect) suffered by a third party relying on any information contained in this book.

A catalogue record of this book is available from the British Library

Cloth case edition:
ISBN 13: 978 1 84724 984 5

Printed and bound in Spain

10 9 8 7 6 5 4 3 2 1

Managing editor Mark Hawkins-Dady
Designer Justin Hunt
Publishing Director Richard Milbank
Art Director Nick Clark
Picture researcher Victoria Kingston
Cartographer William Donohoe
Illustrator Richard J. Caruana
Proofreader Fintan Power
Indexer Patricia Hymans